The Psychology of Leadership

New Perspectives and Research

LEA'S ORGANIZATION AND MANAGEMENT SERIES

Series Editors

Arthur P. Brief
Tulane University

James P. Walsh
University of Michigan

Associate Series Editors

P. Christopher Early
London Business School

Sara L. Rynes
University of Iowa

Ashforth • *Role Transitions in Organizational Life: An Identity-Based Perspective*

Bartunek • *Organizational and Educational Change: The Life and Role of a Change Agent Group*

Beach (Ed.) • *Image Theory: Theoretical and Empirical Foundations*

Brett/Drasgow (Eds.) • *The Psychology of Work: Theoretically Based Empirical Research*

Darley/Messick/Tyler (Eds.) • *Social Influences on Ethical Behavior in Organizations*

Denison (Ed.) • *Managing Organizational Change in Transition Economies*

Earley/Gibson • *Multinational Work Teams: A New Perspective*

Garud/Karnoe • *Path Dependence and Creation*

Jacoby • *Employing Bureaucracy: Managers, Unions, and the Transformation of Work in the 20th Century, Revised Edition*

Kossek/Lambert (Eds.) • *Work and Life Integration: Organizational, Cultural, and Individual Perspectives*

Lant/Shapira (Eds.) • *Organizational Cognition: Computation and Interpretation*

Lord/Brown • *Leadership Processes and Follower Self-Identity*

Margolis/Walsh • *People and Profits? The Search Between a Company's Social and Financial Performance*

Messick/Kramer (Eds.) • *The Psychology of Leadership: New Perspectives and Research*

Pearce • *Organization and Management in the Embrace of the Government*

Peterson/Mannix (Eds.) • *Leading and Managing People in the Dynamic Organization*

Riggio/Murphy/Pirozzolo (Eds.) • *Multiple Intelligences and Leadership*

Schneider/Smith (Eds.) • *Personality and Organizations*

Thompson/Levine/Messick (Eds.) • *Shared Cognition in Organizations: The Management of Knowledge*

The Psychology of Leadership

New Perspectives and Research

Edited by

David M. Messick
Northwestern University

Roderick M. Kramer
Stanford University

LEA
LAWRENCE ERLBAUM ASSOCIATES, PUBLISHERS
2005   Mahwah, New Jersey   London

Lawrence Erlbaum Associates, Inc., Publishers
10 Industrial Avenue
Mahwah, New Jersey 07430

Cover design by Kathryn Houghtaling Lacey

Library of Congress Cataloging-in-Publication Data
The psychology of leadership : new perspectives and research /
edited by David M. Messick, Roderick M. Kramer.
    p.   cm.
Includes bibliographical references and index.
ISBN 0–8058–4094-X (cloth)—ISBN 0–8058–4095–8 (paper)
1. Leadership—Psychological aspects—Congresses. I. Messick,
David M. II. Kramer, Roderick Moreland, 1950–
BF637.L4P79 2004
158'.4—dc22   2004047154

Books published by Lawrence Erlbaum Associates are printed on acid-free paper, and their bindings are chosen for strength and durability.

Printed in the United States of America
10 9 8 7 6 5 4 3 2 1

We would like to dedicate this book, which has taken more than a reasonable number of years to complete, to many supportive organizations and people. The conference that formed the basis of the book was supported financially by the Ford Motor Company Center for Global Citizenship at the Kellogg School of Management. The Center's Assistant, Andrew Marfia, was immensely helpful in all stages of the project, from the conference to the creation of the indices. We are immensely grateful to him for his dedication and hard work. Kramer was supported by a Stanford Business School Trust Faculty Fellowship and by the William R. Kimball family. Both editors were encouraged by their respective deans, Robert Joss from Stanford, and Donald Jacobs and Dipak Jain from the Kellogg School. We could not have undertaken this project without their support. Anne Duffy of Lawrence Erlbaum Associates has been more than patient with the project, and the series editors, Jim Walsh and Art Brief, have been equally supportive and understanding. Finally, we were supported by our wives and families, Judith Messick, Catherine and Matthew Kramer, and Maureen McNichols.

Contents

Series Foreword

Arthur P. Brief
Tulane University

James P. Walsh
University of Michigan

When "leadership" enters the conversation, the regrettable response of too many organizational scholars is a yawn. While many sense that the study of leadershp is stale, we all know that leadership is central to understanding how organizations function. Dave Messick and Rod Kramer have gathered a set of essays that remind us that the study of leadership should still occupy a central place in our field. There are no yawns here. This is a lively and exciting book. We hope it wakes you up to the research potential in this area. Enjoy.

Contributors

Scott T. Allison
Department of Psychology
University of Richmond

Kristin J. Behfar
Northwestern University

Michelle C. Bligh
School of Behavioral and
  Organizational Sciences
Claremont Graduate University

Hannah R. Bowles
Kennedy School of Government
Harvard University

Arthur P. Brief
A. B. Freeman School of Business
Tulane University

Suzanne Chan
A. B. Freeman School of Business
Tulane University

Dafna Eylon
Robins School of Business
University of Richmond

Adam D. Galinsky
Kellogg School of Management
Northwestern University

Marshall Ganz
Harvard University

Dana Gavrieli
Graduate School of Business
Stanford University

George R. Goethals
Williams College

Deborah H Gruenfeld
Graduate School of Business
Stanford University

J. Richard Hackman
Department of Psychology
Harvard University

Michael A. Hogg
University of Queensland

Dacher J. Keltner
University of California Berkeley

Roderick M. Kramer
Graduate School of Business
Stanford University

Joe C. Magee
Graduate School of Business
Stanford University

Kathleen L. McGinn
Graduate School of Business
    Administration
Harvard University

James R. Meindl
School of Management
State University of New York
    at Buffalo

David M. Messick
Kellogg School of Management
Northwestern University

Randall S. Peterson
London Business School
University of London

Tom R. Tyler
Department of Psychology
New York University

1

Introduction: New Approaches to the Psychology of Leadership

David M. Messick
Northwestern University

Roderick M. Kramer
Stanford University

Most of the chapters in this volume were presented as papers at a small research conference held in 2001 at the Kellogg School of Management of Northwestern University in Evanston, Illinois. The purpose of this conference was to explore new ideas about the psychology of leadership, an important and long-enduring research topic within the field of social psychology. It was the opinion of the editors of this book and the conveners of the conference that the social psychological study of leadership had launched off into several new, interesting, and important directions. It was also our belief that interest in the topic, within both social and organizational psychology as well as within the business community, had grown rapidly. It was an ideal time, therefore, to ask some of the world's leading scholars to come together to describe their thinking and research. This book is the result of those efforts. The contributions span traditional social psychological areas as well as organizational theory. They examine leadership as a psychological process and leadership as afforded by organizational constraints and opportunities. Our goal has not been to focus the chapters on a single approach to the study and conceptualization of leadership but rather to display the diversity of issues that surround the topic.

Leadership scholars have identified a host of approaches to the study of leadership. What are the personal characteristics of leaders? What is the nature of the relation between leaders and followers? Why do we perceive some people to be better leaders than others? What are the circumstances that evoke leadership qualities in people? Can leadership be taught? And so on. The contributions to this book examine these important questions and fall into three rather coherent categories. Part I concerns conceptions of leadership. How has leadership been defined? What are the social and psychological processes that constitute leadership? There are four chapters that fall within this category.

Part II includes contributions dealing with factors that influence the effectiveness of leadership. Some conditions make leadership relatively unimportant, whereas others make good leadership essential. Some modes of relating to other people enhance the effectiveness of leaders, whereas others reduce the influence of leaders. This part of the book contains five chapters.

Part III examines a less popular but essentially important topic in leadership scholarship, namely the effects of being in a position of leadership on the leader himself or herself. If we were to observe that leaders have some qualities in common, it could either be that people with these qualities ascend to positions of leadership, or that the position of power or influence creates these qualities in whomever accepts the role. The arrow of causality could point in either or both directions.

In chapter 2, Michelle Bligh and James Meindl examine the thousands of books that are available on the topic of leadership. They ask if there are some "natural" categories into which these titles fall. By coding these legions of books by their characteristics, and using a "natural learning" process for classification, they find that seven distinct categories of leadership books emerge. These categories range from books about leading change in organizations to books about leadership and religion. This vast range of books not only signals the breadth of interests in the topic of leadership, it also sets the stage nicely for the variety of approaches to leadership that are offered in this book.

One of those approaches, and a rather modern one, is described by Michael Hogg in the chapter 3. Hogg sees leadership as a relational concept, as does Messick in chapter 4. However, Hogg's emphasis is on the fact that the leadership relationship often occurs in a group that has assumed qualities and characteristics. Hogg's theory notes that many groups can be thought of as having a "prototypical" member, someone who most embodies the qualities of the group. This member will be perceived to be more influential than others, will be liked more than others, and, partly as a result, will be seen has having better leadership qualities than the other members. This person will also have an edge in maintaining the perception of leader over time. One interesting implication of this theory, an implication that derives from the social identity theory of group psychology, is that a person need not actually be more influential than others to be seen as a leader. If one is prototypical, one may be better liked and seen as more central than another, and be believed to be influential and charismatic. This perception may then become a self-fulfilling prophecy; such a person may actually derive more influence because of these perceptions. Hogg guides the reader through some of the clever research literature that supports these hypotheses.

Messick's relational theory is of a different sort; it asks why people voluntarily become leaders and/or followers. Coming from more of an interdependence perspective, Messick asks what the benefits are that are afforded to both parts of this relationship. His theory identifies five dimensions along which such benefits may be exchanged. Like Hogg's theory, this is a relational theory, but it is one in which social identity plays only a modest role. Instead, it highlights the important psychological benefits followers gain from the relationship. In particular, Messick argues that followers are often given vision, protection, and achievement by leaders. These are among the task effectiveness dimensions that have been discussed by past theorists. They are also given social inclusion and respect, qualities that are subsumed by the traditional role of social-emotional leadership. Leaders in return, get focus, loyalty, and commitment, respectively, from their followers. They also get self-sacrifice and pride in the social domain. The proposal by Messick is that the exchange is not a contractual quid pro quo but rather an exchange that results from mundane social psychological processes. From this view, leadership and followership are social roles that emerge from everyday ordinary psychological activities.

The final chapter in Part I of the book is Goethals' reevaluation of Freud's theory of leadership from the perspective of modern social psychological theory. Although Freud has been largely dismissed by modern psychologists, Goethals notes that aspects of his theory strike a modern chord. He seems to predate the concept of charismatic leadership in some of his descriptions, for instance. Moreover, his analysis seems to highlight the extent to which the leader exemplifies prototypical traits of the followers, as emphasized by social identity theorists like Hogg. Leaders influence followers through the stories that they tell, according to Freud, presaging the approach to leadership taken by Howard Gardner in his book, *Leading Minds*. Leaders' ideas, the ideas that can motivate and influence people, are communicated by stories that delimit and expand the leaders' vision, that communicate the "message" to the people who are the followers. Finally, Goethals notes the "illusion of equal love," the perception that all are the same in the eyes of the leader. This point is made again by Tyler in a later chapter, although Tyler would argue that the equal and respectful treatment of members of a group or organization should not be a mere "illusion," it should be genuine to the extent possible. Goethals thus suggests that Freud presaged the idea of charismatic leadership, highlighted the role of storytelling as a form of communication, emphasized the common social identity of leaders and their followers, and he glimpsed the importance of what we now refer to as procedural justice in leadership.

The second part of this book deals with the conditions under which leadership is more or less effective. What are the dimensions of effective leadership? What do leaders attempt to promote among team members? Are there better or worse ways of achieving these ends? Part II begins with a chapter by Richard Hackman that calls into question the standard research approach of many social psychologists and leadership researchers. Hackman questions the assumption that excellent team performance is the product of excellent leadership, an assumption he refers to as the "leader attribution error." In chapter 6, Hackman reviews evidence that suggests that leaders may provide the conditions under which teams may excel or fail, but that these conditions should not be confused with "causes" in the traditional social science sense of the word. Hackman then outlines four conditions that tend to increase the chances that groups will function well. These conditions include creating real (as opposed to bogus) teams, giving the teams compelling directions in which to work, giving them an enabling design (a structure that does not handicap them from the outset), and providing expert coaching to help with the rough patches. Hackman not only spells out and illustrates these points, he also discusses the timing of the conditions. Perhaps his most original contribution is in noting that some types of teams are so constrained that the quality of leadership is immaterial to their performance. What difference does it make how well a plane's flight crew works together if the plane is being flown on automatic pilot?

Chapter 7, by Peterson and Behfar, adopts the framework of self-regulation to group functioning. These authors identify three conditions for successful group performance to balance the often-conflicting demands of getting the problem right while maintaining group cohesion, maintaining both group identity as well as recognition for the individuals involved, and keeping the right mix of willingness to change and stability. These three conditions are a sense of group self-awareness, having clear standards and goals, and developing the willingness and the ability to make changes. Peterson and Jackson make the intriguing proposal that leadership may derive from a person's ability to help groups maintain these three functions. Leaders, in other words, function as regulatory mechanisms that aid groups in understanding themselves, in maintaining their goals and their knowledge of where they are with regard to the achievement of these goals (a feature highlighted in chapter 6 by Hackman), and in providing the encouragement for and resources to enable change within the group. This chapter not only overlaps nicely with the preceding and succeeding chapters, it also provides a conceptual framework that allows the authors to generate novel hypotheses about the functions of effective leadership.

Tyler (chapter 8) offers a theory of *process based leadership,* which builds directly from his previous research on the social psychology of procedural justice. At the heart of this important chapter is the core idea that procedural fairness, more than positive outcomes, is the power that motivates people to cooperate in groups, to refrain from disruptive behaviors, and to work for a common collective good. To the extent that this characterization is true, it has important implications for leadership because it suggests that it may be more important for leaders to be fair and just in the processes they adopt than it is for them to provide rich rewards and successes for their members. This is precisely the picture that Tyler paints in his chapter. Summarizing research from several prior studies, he marshals evidence that people are more sensitive to the fairness of procedures than to the favorability of their outcomes in determining their commitment to organizations and in their willingness to follow rules and abide by group principles. In places, the story that Tyler tells echoes the theory of Hogg in highlighting social identity; in places it resembles Peterson and Jackson's thoughts about self-regulation and the mechanisms that maintain it. But Tyler probes into the sources of people's concerns with fair process and concludes that the major source of this concern has to do with the ability to construct and nurture a positive image of oneself. Pride and positive self-regard seem to be the drivers of the system, and leaders who understand the importance of this psychological need are likely to excel as leaders.

One cannot be an effective leader unless one is in a position to exercise leadership. This observation leads to the puzzling question raised by

Bowles and McGinn, as to why it is, when the bulk of the research evidence says that women are at least as good at being leaders as men, that women hold proportionally fewer leadership roles in organizations than men. These authors review four possible explanations of why women are relatively scarce in leadership positions, and point out that what seems to be at stake is the ability and willingness of women to claim, through negotiation and influence, leadership roles which they would be perfectly able to execute if only they occupied them. Bowles and McGinn note that research on gender in negotiation has uncovered gender differences that would tend to handicap women in their pursuit of these leadership positions.

The final chapter in Part II poses the interesting question of how it can be that the underdog, David, occasionally slays the favorite, Goliath. What is the role of leadership that can allow organizational upsets, when the presumably weaker team wins? Ganz suggests that the key concept to grasp in these cases is that of *strategic capacity*. Strategic capacity is the ability of an organization to fashion a novel solution to an emerging crisis. It requires creativity and resources. Ganz proposes that the leadership teams add to strategic capacity to the extent that they enhance the motivation, relevant skills, and the heuristic problem-solving capabilities of their members. They can do this, he argues, by making sure that the leadership team is heterogeneous, that it contains members who are at the same time central to and peripheral to other groups, and that it has a diverse set of (relevant) abilities. Moreover, the organizational structure that fosters strategic capacity will entail open deliberations, access to a variety of types or resources, and an accountability system that makes the leaders answerable to the other members. These leadership features can maximize the chance that when an opportunity arises, a group with the proper strategic capacity can spring to the front and succeed where other less prepared but apparently powerful groups, like Goliath, will fail. Ganz notes the relationship between his ideas and the development of entrepreneurial enterprises.

The final part of this book deals with the consequences of leadership. As we noted earlier, studies of leadership have asked many questions. What are the qualities of leaders? What are their styles? How are they seen? The remaining chapters ask, "What are the consequences of being in a position of leadership?" The three chapters look at this question with three different foci in mind. In chapter 11, Kramer and Gavrieli focus on the tendencies of leaders, especially but not exclusively, political leaders to develop and nourish the perception that they are the targets of conspiracies organized by their political enemies. These authors point out that leaders are often scrutinized because of the power and authority that reside in their offices. This scrutiny may easily be interpreted as a malicious interest that belies an underlying desire to unseat leaders and to replace them. The fact that such conspiracies often exist in organizations makes such a suspicion potentially realistic.

While Kramer and Gavrieli argue convincingly that a kind of paranoia may often accompany leadership roles, Magee, Gruenfeld, Keltner, and Galinsky argue that having a position of leadership often means having power over other people and that this power may have psychological consequences on the leaders. Specifically, they review research that supports their hypothesis that power tends to make people action prone—leaders tend to act. This tendency may be fine when action is called for, but it may interfere if caution and patience are called for. Moreover, they present data that suggest that this tendency toward action is, partly at least, a result of *disinhibition,* the weakening of normal inhibitory mechanisms. Thus leaders may also display more sexual forwardness than others and they may be less able to resist temptation. Finally, evidence is presented that suggests that powerful persons tend to objectify others, that is to treat them as objects and to ignore others' internal states, like emotions, values, preferences, and the like. Through these mechanisms, if leading is the exercise of power, then that power tends to corrupt.

Finally, chapter 13 asks about the reputations and perceptions of leaders when they are dead as opposed to alive. Allison and Eylon present research on the effects of a leader's legacy and reputation as a function of whether the leader is believed to have died. They present evidence of a "death positivity bias," the tendency to think more highly of a person if that person is believed to be dead than if the same person is believed to be alive, and then show that although this bias is prevalent it is not universal. Leaders whose lives were characterized by immoral acts were found to be more negatively judged if they were dead (despite the fact that incompetent people were judged more positively, indicating that it is not merely an extremization of the judgment). It is an important discovery that judgments of competence and morality seem to follow different patterns with regard to death, a fact of some importance in our evaluations of contemporary leaders of failed organizations.

The book concludes with Chan and Brief's wise and thoughtful overview of the implications of these chapters for the question of when leadership matters and when it does not. Their review of the ideas in this book challenge the common assumption in books about leadership that leadership is everything. They note that some of the chapters imply that, in some circumstances, leadership is rather unimportant. But they were foiled in hoping to be able to claim that leadership never matters, and it is this question of "when" that becomes pivotal for them.

All in all, the chapters of this volume display part of a broad spectrum of novel and important approaches to the study of the psychology of leadership. We hope that they are equally useful to those who are or would be leaders and to those who study the topic. As the recent failures of leadership in corporations, governments, and churches have served to remind us, it is too important a topic to be ignored by psychologists.

I

Conceptions of Leadership

2

The Cultural Ecology of Leadership: An Analysis of Popular Leadership Books

Michelle C. Bligh
Claremont Graduate University

James R. Meindl
State University of New York at Buffalo

Today's world has far too few real leaders. Now there's a statement we can all get behind. Having said that, could we please endorse the following statement with equal fervor? One thing the world doesn't need is another book purporting to tell us how we can all become good leaders.

—John Huey, 1994

Leadership is indisputably one of the most discussed, studied, and written-about topics in our society. A keyword search in the *Expanded Academic Index* for occurrences of the word "leadership" in a title or abstract reveals over 1,200 citations in the year 2000 alone. A subject search of "leadership" on *Amazon.com* returns more than 6,300 books on the subject, and over 1,400 hardcover books with leadership in the title are offered (Krohe, 2000). From *Jesus CEO* to *1001 Ways to Take Initiative at Work,* fortunes are made (or not!) and fads are launched by many of these titles. But what wisdoms and lessons are truly to be gleaned from this popular genre of leadership writings? What techniques and approaches are most frequently utilized to deliver these so-called truisms? What can these leadership books tell us about how our society views the construct of leadership? And perhaps most importantly, how does this vast array of cultural knowledge about leadership and leadership processes affect leader–follower interactions? To answer these questions, we embarked on a qualitative and quantitative study of popular leadership books in order to understand this unique and fascinating genre.

THE SOCIAL CONSTRUCTION
OF LEADERSHIP

We adopt a social constructionist view (Berger & Luckmann, 1966; Gergen, 1999), which argues that our understandings and implicit theories about organizations are likely to be strongly influenced by our interactions with the social agents who are most readily able to influence the availability, salience, or perceived importance of the information we receive (Salancik & Pfeffer, 1978). Leadership concepts thus represent particularly prominent features of these socially constructed realities (see Calder, 1977; Chen & Meindl, 1991; Salancik & Pfeffer, 1978; Meindl, 1990; Meindl, Ehrlich, & Dukerich, 1985).

In this chapter, we explore popular conceptions of leadership with the explicit recognition that these conceptualizations are embedded within the culture that surrounds them. Social psychological approaches to leadership often highlight the relational aspects of leadership, focusing on that which transpires between leader and follower. These relational aspects include power and mutual influence, reciprocal exchanges, identity and categorization processes, causal attribution, arousal and affect, and the like. Less attention, however, has been paid to the general cultural milieu within which leaders and followers play out their relationships with one another. In this chapter, we explore the social construction of leadership in the context of widely accepted approaches and conceptualizations of leadership as they are reflected in popular leadership books. These books provide a window on our beliefs as a society about leadership: what constitutes leadership, what makes it successful, and what assumptions we make about the effects of leadership.

We embark on an analysis of popular leadership books from an ecological perspective, emphasizing the societal, cultural, and environmental factors that shape our discourse about leadership. The content of popular leadership books represents a highly accessible and voraciously consumed collection of beliefs, ideas, and perspectives about leadership that contextualize and inform the leadership process. Popular leadership books thus reflect the societal and cultural factors that shape the process of leadership, providing an ambience that orients both leaders and followers and conditions their actions and reactions to each other.

This research is also influenced by the romance of leadership perspective developed by Meindl et al. (1985). Their examination of the leadership literature and empirical studies revealed that leaders and leadership issues often become the favored explanations for various events in and around organizations. In addition, subsequent research has demonstrated that people value performance results more highly when those results are attributed to leadership, and that a halo effect exists for leadership attributes. In other words, if an individual is perceived to be an effective leader, his or her personal shortcomings and/or poor organizational performance may be overlooked (Meindl & Ehrlich, 1987).

This so-called "romance of leadership" is strongly reflected in the constructions of leadership that are regularly and widely produced for our consumption in the popular press (e.g., Klapp, 1964; Goode, 1978). Whether in the form of portraits or images of great leadership figures (e.g., Boorstin, 1961), or portrayed as the never-before-revealed secrets of leadership effectiveness, these images reflect our appetite as a society for leadership products. Such leadership images not only appeal to our cultural fascination with the power of leadership, but also serve to fixate us on the personas and characteristics of leaders themselves (Meindl, 1990).

In the current study, we sought to address the following two questions: (a) What issues, perspectives, and characteristics are the primary focus of popular leadership books today, and (b) how do these themes and principles contextualize and influence leadership processes, specifically how leaders and followers interact? In sum, the current study seeks to explore what constitutes leadership in the popular press, what underlying principles (if any) can help us to make sense of this body of literature, and what assumptions about the nature of leadership and its effects are reflected in this genre. In addition, we suggest that the plethora of literature that is produced on leadership provides an environment for how leadership is interpreted and evaluated in today's society.

THE LEADERSHIP CRAZE

According to Debra Hunter, senior VP and publisher at Jossey-Bass, her editors continually worry that the word *leadership* may be getting worn out. Hunter concedes, "We've asked ourselves, 'Should we get a different word?' But readers are really hungry for anything with the word leadership in the title" (Krohe, 2000, p. 18). Although a large proportion of current leadership titles do end up on the clearance table (some probably deservedly so), the market for leadership books remains strong in a society that is eager to snatch up the latest leadership techniques and secrets. According to Krohe (2000):

> By now the fad is well along on a predictable cycle, one we know from a hundred other how-to crazes. Interest is ignited by the promise of a miracle cure. Then come the variations on the theme, some of which are elaborations of the original idea (*Results-Based Leadership*), while others a mere reworking (or simply a repackaging) of earlier works. Then comes the hybridizing with other hot topics (*Real Power: Business Lessons from the Tao Te Ching*) and the mining of secondary markets (*Business Leader Profiles for Students*). Last come skeptical rejoinders aimed at readers disillusioned or unpersuaded by the first batch of books. (p. 19)

So why do we continue to support this seemingly predictable cycle, particularly amidst criticisms that that all business books today are the same, or for that matter, are often not even written by the management gurus themselves? Why do leadership books continue to sell despite reviews that assure us we are unlikely to make it through the first chapter before our eyes glaze over (e.g., O'Toole, 2000)?

One answer may be found in a concept that is deeply rooted in our cultural psyche: the American Dream. Many Americans subscribe to the idea that anyone in our society can "make it to the top"; all one needs is desire, education, and a willingness to make sacrifices. As Krohe (2000) judiciously puts it, "the readers who assume that they can be leaders, and that they can do it by reading a book, show a belief in equality of opportunity that is dizzily optimistic or, perhaps more accurately, optimistically dizzy" (p. 23). Optimism aside, this genre of leadership books in part reflects our belief in the reality of the American Dream, and suggests that in turning to the plethora of leadership books that fill the shelves, many readers are buying a piece of this seductive promise of psychological and economic fulfillment.

Efforts to understand this genre of leadership writings have ranged from cynical to comical. Huey's (1994) somewhat scathing review of popular leadership books begins with *The Leader Within: An Empowering Path of Self-Discovery.* Writes Huey, "This volume contains a sentence that, to me, perfectly captures the passion of most business-book prose: 'When I became president of the breakfast division in 1971, I had to go out and educate myself over matters such as investment banking.' Can you bear not knowing what comes next?" (p. 239). On a more humorous note, Goodman's (1995) review of the top 10 leadership books attempts to classify the books based first on overall management style, then on how well-regarded by the experts the books are, and finally by which of the "old masters" the book draws upon. After all of these fail, Goodman turns to classifying the books based on readability and good taste, but comically concludes that none of the books fall into these categories. Finally, Goodman comes to a realization: the best solution, he concludes, is to rate the books based on one simple criterion—page count. Although by turns cynical and facetious, these reviews highlight the difficulties inherent in systematically understanding this widely disparate genre.

METHODOLOGY

Sampling Issues

The first step in pursuing the preceding research questions was to identify a suitable sample of leadership books. This proved to be a much more challenging undertaking than we had anticipated, and our study of popular conceptions of leadership quickly digressed into a crash course in library science. To our dismay, we discovered that a database that categorizes books into subject headings (such as leadership), as well as provides a synopsis or summary of those books, simply does not exist for all books. While journal articles provide the reader with an abstract and/or key words in order to summarize the key points and findings of the article, online and print databases provide no such synopses for books.

Several print publications summarize academic-oriented books for libraries, but these publications are extremely limited in the books they include. In addition, we discovered publications that list books (i.e., in the area of business) that are recommended for libraries to include in their collections. These publications did not, however, provide any summaries of the books listed, nor were they broken down into subject headings within the area of business. We were thus faced with the daunting task of developing our own criteria for what books should be classified under the area of leadership, as well as the equally challenging task of reading hundreds of books. In addition, since our research questions focus more specifically on how leadership is constructed in the popular literature, we did not want to limit our sample solely to those books recommended for a library collection.

To further complicate matters, we discovered that different databases use different classification systems for their books. In other words, a book that may be classified under the subject heading of "leadership" in one database may not necessarily be classified under that same subject heading in another database. While the Library of Congress provides a standard list of subject headings for libraries, many online and print databases use their own in-house librarians to classify books under subject headings. In addition, some databases follow the Library of Congress headings only loosely, while others do not utilize the Library of Congress system at all.

So how does a search for books with the subject heading of "leadership" result in a neat list of titles corresponding to that category? After consulting with representatives from several database companies as to *how* their librarians make these classification decisions, we were told that an effort is made to use headings that are both as broad *and* as specific as possible. In other words, an attempt is made to accommodate people who are not exactly sure what they are looking for (and so may enter "leadership") as well as those who are looking for a very specific cross-section of books (and so may enter a more narrow topic such as "union leadership"). Books are given a minimum of three subject headings, with no limit as to how many subject headings are given to each book.

A final complication in the selection of our sample was to determine which leadership books are "popular." Our research questions focused specifically on *popular* leadership books because we wanted to incorporate some measure of which of those approaches or constructions are more widely consumed, and thus assumedly more influential. This necessitated obtaining some measure of success for a given leadership book. We decided book sales would be the most appropriate proxy measure for how widely read a book is (although we certainly recognize that some books may be purchased with good intentions, only to end up as shelf decorations; as venture consultant Eileen Shapiro (2000) eloquently put it, "You know what people do with leadership books? They put them on their shelves. They're office décor"; cited in Krohe, 2000, p. 23).

We soon learned, however, that publishers' protection of sales information rivals the secrecy of international espionage. After being firmly rejected by several large publishers despite our expressed intentions to use the information solely for research purposes, we turned to the *New York Times* bestsellers list. Again, however, we were faced with the problem of separating leadership books from business books in general, as well as the additional problem of only being able to focus on the handful of most popular books at a given point in time. This would have modified our study significantly: rather than studying popular conceptions of leadership, we would have been limited to studying the hyper-popular fads of leadership (an interesting study in itself, but not our main focus).

A Multi-Method Approach

Faced with all of this complexity, we decided to utilize a variety of methods to ensure that we were capturing both the diversity of leadership books on the market as well as a variety of perspectives about the books themselves. Although we considered manually reading, classifying, and summarizing popular leadership books ourselves, we hoped to identify a sampling methodology that would more accurately reflect how these books are interpreted and consumed by society as well. Therefore, we decided to take the approach that many consumers do when deciding which leadership book to purchase: we turned to *Amazon.com* and Barnes and Noble (*bn.com*). Each of these sites includes a wide variety of information on a given book, which between the two sites might include any or all of the following sources of information: (a) the publisher's promotional information; (b) a brief synopsis of the book; (c) the table of contents; (d) the full text of one or more chapters; (e) text from the dust jacket and/or back cover of the book; (f) the author's brief biography; (g) reviews from other authors or recognized authorities in the field; (h) customer reviews; (i) third-party reviews from publications such as *Booklist;* (j) statements from the author; and (k) sales rank information. In addition, these sites provide a color picture of the cover, which we suspect may also influence potential buyers, providing salient marketing cues as to the promising contents of the book. Overall, these sites provide a rich source of data about a given book from a wide variety of different sources.

In addition to providing different sources of information in many situations, the choice to utilize both Amazon and Barnes and Noble was made to more accurately reflect overall book sales as well. Although *Amazon.com* has emerged as one of the preeminent vendors of online books (of course, without top-secret information, we do not know how preeminent precisely), it still accounts for a relatively small proportion of overall book sales nationwide. For this reason, we decided to incorporate

BarnesandNoble.com as well, whose sales information incorporates online as well as bookstore sales. Through utilizing both sources of information, we reasoned that we would be capturing a significant proportion of the leadership books that are sold both online and in bookstores.

Overall, two separate coders reviewed the top 200 books from both *Amazon.com* and *BarnesandNoble.com*, giving us a potential sample of 400 books. To partially mitigate the possibility that the information presented on *Amazon.com* and *BarnesandNoble.com* is positively biased to enhance book sales, we decided to search for third-party book reviews through an online database called *ABI-Inform*. (It should be noted, however, that *BarnesandNoble.com* specifically provides the following disclaimer to publishers: "We don't remove reviews because they are 'negative.' But if your author wants to provide a rebuttal or send along some additional reviews we may not have seen, we will be happy to upload them directly preceding the 'negative' review.") *ABI-Inform* was chosen because it is a full-text, comprehensive collection of a wide variety of business publications, and it allowed us to limit our search to include only book reviews. Thus, each title selected for the sample was checked to see if it had been reviewed in one of the over 1,000 worldwide business periodicals included in the *ABI-Inform Global Database*, in addition to the 1,800 periodicals and newspapers included in the PA Research II Database. Popular press publications such as *The New York Times, USA TODAY, Wall Street Journal, Barron's, Time,* and *Newsweek* were therefore included in our sample. However, to our surprise, only 136 of the 257 books (or 53%) in our final sample had not been reviewed in any of these publications, although in some cases third-party reviews were included on *Amazon.com* and *BarnesandNoble.com*. All in all, we read a total of 354 reviews of the books in our final sample through *ABI-Inform*, an average of 3.09 reviews per book (with a range of zero to 42 reviews).

In order to overcome the problem of what constitutes a popular book, we decided to utilize the sales ranking information from *Amazon.com* and *BarnesandNoble.com*. Although precise sales figures are not provided for a particular book, each book receives a sales ranking in terms of how many copies it has sold relative to all of the other books available through these two sites. According to official company information, this bestseller list is much like the *New York Times* bestsellers list, except instead of listing just the top 50 or so titles, it lists more than 2 million. The lower the number, the higher the sales for that particular title. Therefore, by limiting our search to books with a subject heading of leadership and sorting them by sales ranking, we were able to obtain an approximation of which leadership books were selling better relative to other leadership books. Where books were listed in the top 200 on both sites, the average sales ranking from the two sites was calculated.

According to official information the companies provide regarding these rankings, the top 10,000 best sellers are updated each hour to reflect sales over the preceding 24 hours. The next 100,000 are updated daily. The rest of the list is updated monthly, based on several different (undisclosed) factors. Therefore, the sales ranking data fluctuated slightly throughout the 2-month period in which the books were analyzed. This did not concern us, however, as we were interested more in a general indication of which leadership books were currently being sold (and thus presumably read) than in which leadership book was currently among the top 10 best-selling leadership books versus the top 50. The top-selling book in our sample was ranked 52 in overall book sales, and the lowest-selling book in our sample was ranked 1,279,663 in overall book sales, with an average sales ranking of 39,438. It is important to keep in mind that these figures are in relation to all of the books sold, of which leadership books are only a small proportion. Thus, these sales ranking data reflect the relative popularity of leadership books in relation to one another, and are not a reflection of actual sales. We were able to obtain this information for all but eight of the books in our sample.

Development of the Classification Scheme

In order to uncover prevalent themes in the sample, the two coders worked together to develop a classification scheme that would capture the primary characteristics of the book being reviewed. We first attempted to separate the books based on abstract, theoretically derived categories. We started with general areas, such as author characteristics and major leadership theories, as a loose framework. The guiding question that we asked ourselves in the development of the categories was this: "If someone wanted to read one of these books, could they get a good feel for what the book is about simply by reading the list of descriptors the book falls into?" Thus, we hoped our coding would have a good deal of face validity, and it would be easy for others to see why we coded the book as we did. Secondarily, in the interest of parsimony, we asked ourselves: "What are the minimum number of descriptors we need to include in the study to capture the main themes of the books in our sample?"

We then followed an iterative approach, classifying a random sample of books together in detail until we were satisfied that the coding scheme was adequate, and to assure agreement on category assignment. When we were not in full agreement, we maintained broader, more abstract options so as not to narrow the focus prematurely. We then used the full set of new categories to reclassify a different sample of books, creating more distinct subcategories within those that contained the largest amount of data. We subsequently discussed the new categories, and evaluated our previous classifications again. We did not limit ourselves to checking only one descriptor within each category, since the preceding goals were sometimes best achieved by checking more than one descriptor in one category but no descriptor in other categories.

The classification scheme we developed, along with the frequencies for each category, is presented in Table 2.1. After reading all of the available information on a particular book, the book was given either a 1 or a 0 for each of the classification categories. Again, we did not limit ourselves to just one attribute per category for each book; in some cases, it was appropriate to make several classifications in a given category (see Table 2.1). The first broad category concerns the characteristics and background of the author or authors of the book. For example, if the author's biography listed him or her as a professor, a 1 would be placed in the "Academic Author" column. Where authors had more than one characteristic, multiple columns in this section were modified. For example, a book with several authors who collaborated on a single book might have a 1 placed in academic, consultant, and business. The author was considered a writer or reporter if that was his or her sole occupation, and the business classification was reserved for authors who were in the business industry writing about their own or others' experiences.

The second broad category that emerged from our classification process considered the primary setting of the book. For example, *Elizabeth I, CEO: Strategic Lessons From the Leader Who Built an Empire* would be classified as "Historical" because the book primarily concerns a distinct historical period of time. On the other hand, *Peak Performance: Business Lessons From the World's Top Sports Organizations* would receive a 1 in the "Sports Setting" column because the book takes place in the world of sports.

The "Primary Approach" category represents the tactic, approach, or technique that the author or authors use to make their points or get their ideas across in the book. If the book utilized an allegory, fable, or fictional story, such as *Fish! A Remarkable Way to Boost Morale and Improve Results,* or if it primarily utilized a fictional character to illustrate important points, it would receive the appropriate classification. The "Trait/

TABLE 2.1

**Descriptive Statistics for Key
Variables (*n* = 257 Books)**

	Mean	Std. Dev.
Author Background		
Writer/Reporter	0.06	0.24
Historian	0.05	0.21
Military	0.04	0.20
Consultant	0.36	0.48
Business	0.20	0.40
Academic	0.28	0.45
Religious Leader	0.05	0.21
Political	0.03	0.18
Sports	0.02	0.14
Target		
Personal Development	0.40	0.49
Developing Others	0.16	0.37
Organizational Change	0.32	0.46
Academic	0.09	0.29
Setting		
Business	0.66	0.48
Education	0.06	0.23
Religious	0.09	0.29
Political	0.12	0.33
Historical	0.12	0.32
Military	0.07	0.25
Sports	0.03	0.18
Primary Approach		
Fictional Story	0.07	0.25
Fictional Character	0.02	0.14
Trait/Competency	0.33	0.47
Books with Numbered Suggestions	7.09	0.59
Metaphors/Anecdotes/Cases/Interviews	0.28	0.45
Research based	0.18	0.39
Collection or Edited Volume	0.09	0.29
Voice		
Expert	0.37	0.48
"Evangelical"	0.13	0.33
Personal Account/Autobiography	0.09	0.29
Third-Person Account/Biography	0.18	0.38
Philosophical	0.29	0.45
Self-Actualization	0.11	0.31

Competency" category includes books that focus on a specific set of skills or characteristics, with the explicit idea that by following the book's guidelines, the reader can improve his or her behavior appropriately. "Books with Numbered Suggestions" includes books such as *1001 Ways to Energize Employees,* which offer a specifically ordered and numbered set of guidelines, steps, suggestions, or tenets of leadership. The number of suggestions given by a single book in our sample ranged from 1 to 1,001.

Another classification in the "Primary Approach" category encompasses books that incorporated metaphors, anecdotes, specific cases, or interviews to illustrate topical areas. Books in this category may analyze a specific set of companies, interview top executives, or use anecdotes or metaphors derived from the authors' experiences. "Research based" books utilized a scientifically based study with evidence from multiple executives, companies, or industries, and the primary purpose of the book was to share the results and findings from the authors' research. Finally, the last classification in this category, "Collection or Edited Volume," incorporates books that utilize a collection of chapters and ideas from a variety of authors to address a common theme, such as *Schools That Learn: A Fifth Discipline Fieldbook for Educators, Parents, and Everyone Who Cares About Education.*

The last primary category in our classification scheme is "Voice." This aspect of the book concerns the primary tone or approach the author takes in order to convince the reader of his or her credibility, the contribution the book makes, or more generally, why the reader should choose to read this leadership book over any other. The "Expert" classification was given to books that claimed to make a contribution to leadership based on their experiences and expertise. "Evangelical" books, on the other hand, try to aggressively convince the reader that he or she will profit in an intrinsically satisfying or motivational manner through reading a particular book. While some books given this classification were religious in nature, others, such as *Don't Fire Them, Fire Them Up: Motivate Yourself and Your Team* conveyed an almost evangelical fervor about leadership that was strongly motivational but not religious in nature. "Personal Account/ Autobiography" and "Third Person Account/Biography" classifications were given to books that fit these standard terms, while the "Philosophical" classification encompasses books that focus on morality, ethics, or integrity in leadership, or advocates a new philosophy for leadership such as *Simplicity: The New Competitive Advantage in a World of More, Better, Faster.* Finally, the "Self-Actualization" category includes books that explicitly prescribe passion and/or excitement for leaders to make work an adventure. Books in this category, such as *Leadership and Self-Deception: Getting Out of the Box,* explicitly prescribe a leadership style or approach that will lead to self-fulfillment, personal growth, and allow the reader to realize his or her dreams.

Of the 400 books in the original sample, 110 books appeared on both lists and were used to calculate interrater reliability. The interrater reliability coefficient for the sample was obtained by first calculating the differences in classification attributes and then calculating the percentage of different classifications relative to the total (i.e., if one rater judged the book's voice to be "expert" and the other rater judged the book's voice to be "philosophical," and all other classifications were the same, that book would have an agreement factor of 94%). Averaging this coefficient over the 110 books rated by both coders, the final coefficient of interrater reliability proved to be acceptable at .86 (Fan & Chen, 2000).

Six of the books in our initial sample did not appear to have anything to do with leadership, and 21 books were deleted from the sample because we failed to find sufficient information from any of our sources to adequately classify the book. Some books, for example, were not reviewed by any third-party sources and did not have enough information from the publisher, author, "experts," or customers to give us confidence in an appropriate classification. Finally, six books were deleted from the sample because the two raters made significantly different classifications. This left us with a total sample size of 257 different books on leadership (see Appendix 2.A for a list of the titles included in our sample).

Neural Networks

In order to understand the broader patterns or clusters of types of books in our sample, we utilized a relatively new area of information processing technology known as neural networking. Although this technology has only recently entered the mainstream, research on neural networking dates back to the 1940s (Zhu & Chen, 2000). The underlying concept is that, much like the human brain, computing systems are able to learn from experience how to distinguish between similar objects and recognize patterns. Neural networks have been employed for a wide variety of research problems, including understanding market structuring (Reutterer & Natter, 2000), forecasting electrical power usage (Cottrell, Girard, & Rousset, 1998), identifying individuals' cognitive styles and learning strategies (Ford, 2000), predicting automobile injury claims fraud (Brockett, Xia, & Derrig, 1998) and detecting associations between text documents

(Roussinov & Chen, 1998). Although neural networks have been utilized for a wide variety of applications, their application to the social sciences is relatively new and holds a great deal of promise, particularly since they are particularly well suited to capturing nonlinear relationships among variables (Somers, 2001).

Our research questions led us to neural networking for a number of reasons. Unlike more conventional statistical methods, neural networks do not require assumptions about the form or distribution of the data to analyze it. Given the discovery orientation of our study and our desire to let patterns emerge from the data rather than imposing classifications a priori, neural networking is an ideal technique. While traditional statistical analyses require one to assume a certain form to the data and test its validity until the correct form is found, neural networks require no such assumptions. In addition, neural networks are more tolerant of imperfect or incomplete data than other methodologies.

Finally, neural networks have been demonstrated to perform better than traditional statistical methods when the form of the data is unknown, nonlinear, or complex, yet there are strong underlying relationships in the data. For example, Reutterer and Natter's (2000) comparative study of two neural network approaches versus multi-dimensional scaling (MDS) found that neural network approaches showed both higher robustness and a higher stability of partitioning results in determining brand preferences. Roussinov and Chen's (1998) study compared how closely clusters produced by a computer neural networks correspond with clusters created by human experts, and concluded that both techniques work equally well in detecting associations. Soylu, Ozdemirel, and Kayaligil (2000) similarly concluded that artificial neural network algorithms such as the one utilized in this study obtain promising results both in terms of solution quality and computation time (see Lin, Chen, & Nunamaker, 2000, for a detailed comparison of statistical versus neural approaches to cluster analyses).

The Kohonen Self-Organizing Map

This study utilized an unsupervised neural network known as the Kohonen Self-Organizing Map (SOM), which is appropriate for research questions in which the correct answers are unknown. The Kohonen SOM is an unsupervised learning technique for summarizing high-dimensional data so that similar inputs are mapped closely to one another (Kohonen, 1990, 1995). Several studies have adapted the Kohonen SOM approach specifically for textual analysis and classification (see Lin et al., 2000; Ritter & Kohonen, 1989). When applied to textual data, the Kohonen SOM has been shown to be able to group together related concepts in a data collection and to present major topics within the collection with larger regions (Lin et al., 2000). Previous research has strongly suggested the SOM algorithm as an ideal candidate for classifying textual documents (Chen, Schuffels, & Orwig, 1996).

Neural Connection, a software system for neural computing compatible with *SPSS,* was employed for our analysis. The Kohonen tool in this software package allows the user to reduce the multi-dimensionality of a data set into a one- or two-dimensional array of artificial nodes. Pattern recognition is attained by summing the input variables, assigning weights to them, and then using a statistical function or algorithm to approximate the value of the outcome variable. Unlike other statistical methods, such as linear regression, neural networks require many passes or training runs to minimize the error between the predicted and outcome values. Each time the input data is run through the Kohonen Network, the weights are adjusted, and the prediction of the network is improved. This process is referred to as "learning" (Somers, 2001).

Due to the relatively small size of the data set, a number of defaults in the Kohonen settings were changed. The specifics of the Kohonen SOM analysis were therefore determined as follows: The initial weights in the Kohonen layer were set by taking random samples from within the input data set to eliminate any systematic bias. The neighborhood size, or area around a "winning" node that is modified along with that node, was allowed to decay by one tenth of one percent per training iteration. The advantage of allowing neighborhood decay is that as the training proceeds, areas of the Kohonen layer become more sharply defined with regard to specific example types. The multiple Kohonen layer module was enabled, as creating more than one Kohonen layer is particularly useful for classification problems (SPSS, 2001). The learning rate was defaulted at .6, and the training of the Kohonen network was stopped at 20 epochs. This indicates that every book in the data set was passed through the Kohonen layer a total of 20 times. Finally, due to the small size of the data set and the assumption that there were a few basic clusters in the data, the initial size of the Kohonen layer was kept small. If data from a particular cluster needed to be analyzed for further sub-clusters, this could be done after the initial training of the network. Therefore, the size of the Kohonen Layer side field was initially set to five nodes.

Generalizability. As in other statistical methods, generalizability is an important issue in neural networks. Following Bishop (1995) and Somers (2001), data was randomly partitioned into two samples: a training sample and a test sample. According to Somers (2001), "in a process similar to cross-validation (e.g., use of a hold-out sample), model parameters (weights and functions) are generated using a training sample and then the generalizability of these results is assessed with a test sample (which serves as the hold-out sample)" (p. 54). Twenty percent of the total sample was utilized for the test data, producing a final data allocation of 206 books for training and 51 books for testing.

RESULTS

The initial Kohonen SOM analysis resulted in twenty-five nodes. The Kohonen Network Viewer (see Fig. 2.1) was examined to give us an indication of the relative proximity of each node to its neighbors, in order to determine how the nodes should be spatially divided into clusters. The nodes plot represents each artificial node as a square, which is colored according to how close it is to its neighboring neurons. Light colored neurons indicate close proximity to their neighbors; dark colors indicate greater distance from neighboring nodes. In addition to examining the Network Viewer, the numerical centers for each of the 25 nodes were examined to determine the primary book classifications that typified each node. Nodes that shared at least one of the three primary characteristics

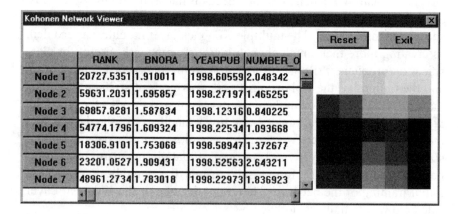

FIG. 2.1. Kohonen network output.

TABLE 2.2

Map of Node Clusters, Primary Characteristics,
and Book Title Samples

Cluster	Primary Characteristics	Sample Book Title
Cluster 1 Leading change	Organizational change Collection/edited volume Expert voice	Organization 2000: The Essential Guide for Companies and Teams in the New Economy
Cluster 2 Leading scientifically	Academic author Trait/competency approach Business setting	Radical Innovation: How Mature Companies Can Outsmart Upstarts
Cluster 3 Learning from leadership in context	Subcluster characteristics Political setting	Eyewitness to Power: The Essence of Leadership, Nixon to Clinton
Cluster Characteristics Biography Autobiography	Historical setting	The Prince
	Educational setting	Fundamental Concepts of Educational Leadership and Management
	Military setting	Leadership Secrets of Attila the Hun
	Sports setting	Everyone's a Coach: Five Business Secrets for High-Performance Coaching
Cluster 4 Leading through imagination	Fictional story Fictional characters "Evangelical voice"	The Servant: A Simple Story About the True Essence of Leadership
Cluster 5 Insider accounts	Business author Autobiography Expert voice	Get Better or Get Beaten: 31 Leadership Secrets from GE's Jack Welch
Cluster 6 Consultants on leadership	Consultant author Business setting Numbered suggestions	The Leader of the Future: New Visions, Strategies, and Practices for the Next Era
Cluster 7 Leading through religion	Religious leader "Evangelical voice" Religious setting	Spiritual Leadership: Principles of Excellence for Every Believer

with their immediate neighbors were grouped into clusters. These analyses indicate the presence of seven distinctive clusters: five major clusters and two minor clusters ranging in size from 17 to 74 books. The seven clusters, along with their primary characteristics and a sample book title from each cluster, are listed in Table 2.2. A detailed explanation of each of the clusters follows.

Cluster 1: Leading Change

Perhaps not surprising in today's fast-paced global economy, the second largest cluster of leadership books ($n = 69$, or 27% of the sample) consists of books that deal with various aspects of the change process. Leadership is interpreted as the ability to enact and sustain lasting change, and the books in this cluster serve as "how-to" guides on how the change process can best be managed. Authors in this cluster are primarily academics or self-proclaimed experts who claim to have the key to understanding the mechanics of changing organizations on the path to success. These books provide both the "nuts and bolts" of various organizational change initiatives, as well as a list of traits and/or competencies that a leader must have before he or she can institute lasting change.

Many of the books in this cluster are collections or edited volumes that seek to educate the reader about the nuances of leading change in various business settings. These books are often a collaborative effort between consultants, leading business people, and academics, who are touted as experts or gurus in their fields. In addition, this group of books frequently utilizes case studies of successful businesses and/or interviews with successful leaders in order to illustrate how change was achieved. The result is sometimes theme-based and coherent, and at other times appears to be a hodgepodge of seemingly disjointed topic areas. Nevertheless, the books in this group claim that the expertise within their pages will help leaders to strategically cope with the future and the changes it may bring.

Cluster 2: Leading Scientifically

This smaller cluster of books ($n = 26$, or 10%) takes a scientific or research-based approach to the field of leadership. Books in this cluster are primarily written by academics or consultants who have undertaken various forms of research endeavors, and wish to share the results of their labors. These books, as a result, are much more dense than books in the other clusters in our sample, and many are written primarily for an academic audience. They deal with a wide variety of specific topical areas, including the organizational change theme which makes up the first cluster of books. This accounts for the close proximity of these two clusters in the Kohonen network. However, this cluster of books is differentiated by its philosophical approach to leadership that either explicitly or implicitly treats leadership as something that can be studied, understood, and subsequently taught.

Cluster 3: Learning From Leadership
Outside Organizational Contexts

This cluster of books represents the largest in our sample ($n = 74$, or 29%). Its large size and clear differentiation of primary characteristics indicate the presence of five smaller subclusters. This cluster of books is predominantly written by people who claim to have either witnessed great leadership firsthand, or those people who claim to have been great leaders themselves and are willing to share their experiences. What is unique about this group of books is that the context is explicitly *not* managerial. In other words, this cluster claims to have discovered the secrets of leadership outside of traditional organizational settings. These books therefore consist largely of biographies and autobiographies broken into five smaller clusters, corresponding to different contextual areas or realms of leadership (military, political, historical, educational, and sports-related). The authors' backgrounds in each of these subclusters corresponds to the settings they write about. Thus, this group of popular leadership books consists of historians writing about leadership throughout history, and politicians or political insiders writing about political leadership. In addition, books such as Thomas Paine's *Common Sense* and Machiavelli's *The Prince,* which advocated a particular philosophy of leadership that has influenced readers over the centuries, are included in this cluster as well.

This group of leadership books is heavily characterized by the competency approach, selling the idea that great leadership consists of having "the right stuff," which fortunately the reader can learn through the experiences of the leader and his or her leadership actions described in these books. This cluster of books may thus be most accurately characterized as contextually based and experientially oriented: these authors have either "done it" or "seen it firsthand" and as a result, they have gleaned lessons about the requirements of good leadership to pass on to their readers. Inherent in this approach is the assumption that there are certain universal laws, rules, or secrets of leadership that are relevant regardless of the field you are in (which seems to fly directly in the face of more contingency-based approaches to leadership). However, it is worth noting that the emphasis is heavily placed on the *competencies* of leadership rather than the traits; *The Leadership Lessons of Robert E. Lee* discusses the *Tips, Tactics, and Strategies for Leaders and Managers* we can glean from Lee's experiences, not the message that Robert E. Lee was born with certain traits that may be difficult or even impossible for the rest of us to attain.

Cluster 4: Leading Through Imagination

This minor cluster in our sample consists of just 14 books, or 5% of the total sample. It is, however, quite distant from its neighbors in the network due to its distinctive characteristics. All of the books in this cluster utilize fictional stories and characters to address the concept of leadership. In addition, these books are characterized by an approach to leadership that emphasizes how leadership that develops both the self and others can be a self-actualizing and immensely satisfying endeavor. Readers are taken on a fictional journey that reveals the rewards of realizing one's potential as a leader. These stories and parables act primarily as motivational models for how the reader may develop his or her own leadership skills, and have the feeling of a fairy tale or parable applied to the business world. This cluster of books thus utilizes stories to illustrate how the reader can achieve happiness and fulfillment through leadership development. There is a strong underlying message of empowerment that is almost evangelical in its fervor. Through bringing out the best leader in oneself and in others, the individual will achieve not only happiness, but an intrinsic gratification that comes from seeing others realize their potential.

Cluster 5: Insider Accounts

The fifth cluster in our sample of books ($n = 28$, or 11%) is primarily authored by current or former executives or organizational insiders from successful, well-recognized companies. The tone of these books is simple and direct: the author has run a successful organization, staged a major turnaround, and/or managed others for decades, and is willing to sell his or her experience to the reader. The books in this cluster are strongly managerial in focus, primarily written in the first person, and present a "behind the scenes" personal account of leadership. The underlying message is that by reading one person's tale of success, the reader can glean hints or tactics that can be applied to his or her own leadership skills and career prospects.

Cluster 6: Consulting on Leadership

This cluster ($n = 30$, or 12%) consists of books written by professional consultants, who claim that their years of working with companies qualifies them to divulge the secrets of how to lead change. This group of books emphasizes visionary leadership, "leading the revolution," and a plethora of other catchy phrases that are argued to capture the essence of leadership. These books frequently offer numbered suggestions for the reader to follow in order to build the skills of others, and offer a more commonsensical, practical, guide-oriented approach to leadership than many of the other popular books on the market. In addition, books in this cluster are filled with tips, lists, checklists, worksheets, and exercises for how to help others be better team members, how to coach effectively, and tips and tactics for helping others hone their leadership skills, to name just a few. Often, the books in this cluster read like mini-courses in leadership, or cookbooks for how to mix the right ingredients and skills to create a good leader.

Cluster 7: Leading through Religion

The last cluster of books in our sample ($n = 17$, or 7%) is made up of books that approach leadership through the lens of religious beliefs. These books frequently draw on religious lessons and allegories to guide readers toward the development of their leadership skills, which is seen as a key component of individual self-fulfillment. The books in this cluster are evangelical in their quest to incorporate spirituality as a guide toward the reader's personal development, and they view leadership as either partially or completely guided by higher forces.

CONCLUSION

The preceding analyses point out a number of different characteristics of popular leadership books today. At the beginning of this chapter, we asked two primary questions: (a) What issues, perspectives, and characteristics are the primary focus of popular leadership books today, and (b) how do these themes and principles contextualize and influence leadership processes, specifically how leaders and followers interact? We now turn toward the conclusions we can draw from our analysis of how leadership is portrayed in books today.

The Romance Continues

Our analysis of nearly 300 popular leadership books confirmed one of our initial suspicions: at times we were amazed by the seemingly infinite diversity of perspectives and approaches in our sample, whereas at other times we had the impression we were reviewing the same book 50 times with different titles. It is clear from our study that there is a massive amount of information, knowledge, and wisdom being produced about leadership. In addition, these leadership products are readily available, highly accessible, and voraciously consumed. In the end, this study has given us a thorough taste of what is currently "out there" in terms of popular leadership books, and represents a cultural body of conventional thought and philosophy regarding the concept of leadership that contextualizes the occurrences of leadership that are the usual foci of studies in this area. We argue that the seven major clusters of books we uncovered in this study represent an initial attempt to map the general "leadership ambience" that conditions and orients leader–follower interactions. We now turn to the themes that constitute the ecology of leadership, what they reveal about the concept of leadership in today's society, and how these clusters continue to reflect a romance with the concept of leadership and its capabilities.

The clusters unearthed by the Kohonen network analysis suggest that our appetite for leadership products is satisfied in distinctive ways. On one hand, we continue to be fascinated with the seemingly inexhaustible power and influence leaders have to enact change, both in organizational structures and in people themselves. The large "Leading Change" cluster that emerged in our analysis indicates that it is an extremely prosperous area of the leadership literature. This cluster of books takes a nearly limitless approach to change, seemingly without exception. Simply by reading a book, readers are persuaded that they will be able to *Break the Code of Change, Manage the Dream,* or become *A Force for Change.* Spurred by technological changes, globalization, and demographic changes in the workforce, this group of books reflects a seemingly never-ending belief in the capacity of leadership to effect change on nearly anything and everything.

The ever-quickening pace of change in the modern world has also led to increased uncertainty. This uncertainty, in turn, makes it much easier to "identify [the ever-widening] gaps in the guru market" (Levy, 2000, p. 22).

> Nothing boosts book sales like a little panic among the managerial classes. People have always sought out oracles in uncertain times, and for business-people the times are very uncertain indeed. A lot of people want to learn how to be leaders because being a follower is not much of a career option anymore. The problem is not just that the traditional corporate hierarchy is being flattened. Management's fundamental assumptions are being undone. The locus of decision-making, indeed of policy formulation, is becoming diffused throughout the typical organization. (Krohe, 2000, p. 21)

These changes are leaving today's leaders scrambling to manage an ever-increasing uncertainty, increasing our appetites for management gurus and experts who can provide easy answers (represented in the "Consultants on Leadership" and "Insider Accounts" clusters). Jackson's (1999) rhetorical critique of Stephen Covey and the effectiveness movement demonstrates how gurus' work resonates with the material, existential, and spiritual needs of individuals within our society that are peculiar to the late modern age. While this is by no means a new phenomenon (see "Memorable Gurus and Cutting-Edge Theories" [Anonymous, 1999] for a decade-by-decade flashback of some memorable management gurus and leading principles), this study suggests that the demand for gurus and experts to lead us through uncertain times is not likely to abate any time soon.

Our appetite for leadership is also somewhat sated by our seeming confidence in the wisdom and tools that the experts claim to have gleaned from their vast experiences. While the clusters we titled "Leading Scientifically" and "Learning From Leadership in Context" vary tremendously in terms of subject area, readability, and the credentials of the author or leader depicted, they strongly suggest that we are still enamored with the idea that there are certain universal leadership competencies that lead to success, whether one is a martial arts coach, Attila the Hun, or the pope himself. The wisdom, skills, and lessons that an individual learns as a leader are illustrated by emissaries all around us, and these books sell the notion that these universal truisms can be learned and subsequently utilized by everyone. In essence, this is a very democratic, egalitarian, and somewhat romanticized image of leadership: we can all be leaders, given the right knowledge and skills (although this may eventually leave us without any followers!).

Finally, the clusters titled "Leading Through Imagination" and "Leading Through Religion" suggest that our society's thirst for books that promise happiness and self-fulfillment is not easily satiated. Embedded in a capitalistic, consumer-driven society, it is not surprising that many of us are compelled to buy the latest leadership book. We may even pick it up along with the latest exercise fad, wrinkle cream, or cleaning product, all of which come with underlying promises. Of course we want to be a little healthier, a little younger, our lives a little easier. Why not be a better leader too? Why not help develop those around us to be better leaders too? Krohe (2000) sums it up: "What the self-help book is really selling is hope; most leadership books are doomed to frustrate hope, because they purport to do something no book can do" (p. 18).

Overall, the results of this study suggest that themes of change, expert and guru appeal, self-actualization and fulfillment constitute the ecology of leadership. Leaders who are seen as affecting change, possessing great experience and knowledge, and providing their followers with the opportunity to reach their unique potentials fit our cultural stereotypes of what a great leader should be. Leadership skills are identifiable and accessible to all, regardless of social standing, formal training, or experience. What is interesting about this ubiquitous and consistent message from popular leadership books is that it implies that every leader is able to easily attain these standards, simply by spending a few hours with a leadership book. Faced with real-life leaders who do not seem to bring about great changes, possess the right knowledge or skills in every situation, or have enough time or energy to ensure that their followers are able to realize their potential as employees and as people, it is not difficult to see how this leadership ecology can negatively affect leader–follower relations.

Although the sheer number, popularity, and demand for leadership books hints strongly that we are as obsessed with leadership as ever, our study of leadership books makes clear that our fascination with the personas of celebrity leaders and their experiences continues. We are continually compelled by the idea that these leaders have created tremendous outcomes through the force of their amazing personalities, and we line up in droves to get a glimpse of this magic. Yet the authors of these books are not only selling a front-row seat to the fame and glory that surround these popular leaders; they are selling the implication that by buying and reading these books, we can become one of these heroes. In other words, "the celebrity leader is precisely the person so many leadership-book readers seem to wish to be" (Krohe, 2000, p. 20).

This leaves the reader with a tremendous paradox. On the one hand, according to James O'Toole (1999) in *Leadership A to Z: A Guide for the Appropriately Ambitious,* every sane person knows that not everyone can be an Abe Lincoln, a Jack Welch, or a Margaret Thatcher. In fact, O'Toole concludes that "leadership talent and ability are as widely dispersed as the ability to play the piano or hit a curve ball" (p. 6). Yet the books in Cluster 3 all sell the idea that these personalities' talents and abilities can be distilled into a neat list of tips, tools, and techniques. Perhaps this is the answer to why as a society we continue to consume the latest bestseller; we are not so much buying the secrets of being a great leader as we are buying the myth that anyone can be one. Most of us would agree that *Elizabeth I, CEO: Strategic Lessons From the Leader Who Built an Empire* sounds much more promising than *You Are Not Elizabeth I and You Never*

Will Be. According to guru experts (ironic as this term may be), "leadership comes down to the fact that with all of the posturing and promises, no guru, regardless of his or her mettle or meddling, can make you an instant leader. Leaders aren't born—at least not full-blown. Neither are they made like instant coffee. Instead, they are slow brewed" (Boyett & Boyett, cited in Pospisil, 1998, p. 71).

Although this continued fascination with leaders and their influence is perhaps not surprising when the larger changes in the business environment are taken into consideration, this fact does not mitigate the danger. According to Krohe (2000):

> It's no coincidence that the leadership-book fad has bloomed as we begin what may come to be called the post-management era. Frustrated with the quotidian miseries of managing, firms first resorted to structural changes such as reengineering as a miracle cure. That failed; it made for leaner firms but not redirected or re-energized ones. The new way to make management unnecessary is to substitute for it the charismatic influence of The Leader. (p. 21)

Combined with subsequent research, this study suggests that we need to use a great deal of caution in overemphasizing this charismatic influence. Truly great leadership is not likely to be as easily attained as this cultural ecology might lead us to believe. Although it may not be a bestseller, perhaps what we really need in the post-management era is a more realistic portrayal of the skills people at all levels of organizations can be taught to utilize effectively, as well as a realistic portrayal of the work it takes to get there and the limitations and constraints that each and every leader must face. But then again, are we really sure we need another leadership book?

Whatever one's opinions about this genre of books and the value of what is produced and consumed, it seems inevitable that more books about leadership will continue to be written and read. We argue, however, that the books themselves are less important than what they represent and reveal. In our view, what transpires between leaders and followers occurs against this backdrop of conventional—and in some cases more avant-guard—thoughts, wisdom, and philosophies regarding leadership that are constantly produced, consumed, and embedded. In other words, we see this genre of books as providing a general leadership ambience within which leaders and followers interact and respond to one another. Between their covers lies a cacophony of multiple voices, and a veritable alphabet soup of different perspectives. Thus, popular leadership books are a reflection of the production and consumption of these culturally ambient aspects of leadership, a mirror image of how we as a society define and interpret leadership itself. Through our analysis of these popular books, we provide a first, somewhat crude mapping of the topography and texture of these ambient aspects of leadership. It is our hope, however, that further research will continue to extensively map and explicitly consider the eco-logical backdrop that contextualizes modern leadership in all of its forms.

ACKNOWLEDGMENT

Special thanks to Courtney Walsh for her assistance in completing this project.

REFERENCES

Anonymous. (1999). Memorable gurus and cutting-edge theories. *Association Management, 51*(10): 22–23.

Berger, P. L., & Luckmann, T. (1966). *The social construction of reality.* Garden City, NY: Doubleday.

Bishop, C. (1995). *Neural networks for pattern recognition.* Oxford: Oxford University Press.

Boorstin, D. J. (1961). *The image.* New York: Atheneum.

Brockett, P. L., Xia, X., & Derrig, R. A. (1998). Using Kohonen's self-organizing feature map to uncover automobile bodily injury claims fraud. Journal of Risk and Insurance, 65(2), 245–274.

Calder, B. J. (1977). An attribution theory of leadership. In B. M. Staw & G. R. Salancik (Eds.), *New directions in organizational behavior* (pp. 179–204). Chicago: St. Clair.

Chen, C., & Meindl, J. R. (1991). The construction of leadership images in the popular press: the case of Donald Burr and People Express. *Administrative Science Quarterly, 36*(4), 521–552.

Chen, H., Schuffels, C., & Orwig, R. (1996). Internet categorization and search: A self-organiz-ing approach. *Journal of Visual Communications and Image Representation, 7*(1), 88–102.

Cottrell, M., Girard, B., & Rousset, P. (1998). Forecasting of curves using a Kohonen Classifica-tion. *Journal of Forecasting, 17*(5): 429–439.

Fan, X., & Chen, H. (2000). Published studies of interrater reliability often overestimate reli-ability: Computing the correct coefficient. *Educational and Psychological Measurement, 60*(4), 523–542.

Ford, N. (2000). Cognitive Styles and virtual environments. *Journal of the American Society for Information Science, 51*(6), 543–557.

Gergen, K. J. (1999). *An invitation to social construction.* Thousand Oaks, CA: Sage Publica-tions.

Goode, W. J. (1978). *The celebration of heroes.* Berkeley, CA: University of California Press.

Goodman, H. (1995). Shelf help. *The Journal of Business Strategy, 16*(1): 54–64.

Huey, J. (1994). Take me to your leadership books. *Fortune, 130*(2), 239–241.

Jackson, B. G. (1999). The goose that laid the golden egg? A rhetorical critique of Stephen Covey and the effectiveness movement. *The Journal of Management Studies, 36*(3): 353–377.

Klapp, O. E. (1964). *Symbolic leaders.* Chicago: Aldine.

Kohonen, T. (1990). The self-organizing map. *Proceedings of the IEEE, 78*(9), 1464–1480.

Kohonen, T. (1995). *Self organizing maps*. Berlin: Springer-Verlag.

Krohe, J. (2000). Leadership books: Why do we buy them? *Across the Board, 37*(1), 28–34.

Levy, M. (2000). On the guru circuit. *Director, 53*(10), 22–25.

Lin, C., Chen, H., & Nunamaker, J. F. (2000). Verifying the proximity and size hypothesis for self-organizing maps. *Journal of Management Information Systems, 16*(3), 57–70.

Meindl, J. R. (1990). On leadership: An alternative to the conventional wisdom. In B. M. Staw & L. L. Cummings (Eds.), *Research in Organizational Behavior, 12,* 159–203. Greenwich, CT: JAI Press.

Meindl, J. R., & Ehrlich, S. B. (1987). The romance of leadership and the evaluation of organizational performance. *Academy of Management Journal, 30,* 91–110.

Meindl, J. R., Ehrlich, S. B., & Dukerich, J. M. (1985). The romance of leadership. *Administrative Science Quarterly, 30,* 78–102.

O'Toole, J. (1999). *Leadership A to Z: A guide for the appropriately ambitious*. San Francisco: Jossey-Bass.

O'Toole, J. (2000) Yet another leadership book? *Across the Board, 37*(1), 22.

Pospisil, V. (1998). Practical guide to gurudom. *Industry Week, 247*(14), 71.

Reutterer, T., & Natter, M. (2000). Segmentation-based competitive analysis with MULTI-CULS and topology representing networks. *Computers and Operations Research, 27*(11), 1227–1247.

Ritter, H., & Kohonen, T. (1989). Self-organizing semantic maps. *Biological Cybernetics, 61,* 241–254.

Roussinov, D., & Chen, H. (1998, Spring). A scalable self-organizing map algorithm for textual classification: A neural network approach to thesaurus generation. *Communication Cognition and Artificial Intelligence*.

Salancik, G. R., & Pfeffer, J. (1978). A social information processing approach to attitudes and task design. *Administrative Science Quarterly, 23,* 224–253.

Somers, M. J. (2001). Thinking differently: Assessing nonlinearities in the relationship between work attitudes and job performance using a Bayesian neural network. *Journal of Occupational and Organizational Psychology, 74,* 47–61.

Soylu, M., Ozdemirel, N. E., & Kayaligil, S. (2000). Self-organizing neural network approach for the single AGV routing problem. *European Journal of Operational Research, 121*(1), 124–137.

SPSS for Windows, Release 9.0. (2001). SPSS, Inc. Chicago, IL.

Zhu, B., & Chen, H. (2000). Validating a geographical image retrieval system. *Journal of the American Society for Information Science, 51*(7), 625–634.

APPENDIX 2.A:
COMPLETE LISTING OF BOOK TITLES

Leadership From The Inside Out: Becoming a Leader for Life
A Work of Heart: Understanding How God Shapes Spiritual Leaders
American Rhapsody
Brand Leadership
Breaking the Code of Change
Cigars, Whiskey & Winning: Leadership Lessons From General Ulysses S. Grant
Clicks and Mortar

Co-Leaders: The Power of Great Partnerships
Coaching for Leadership: How the World's Greatest Coaches Help Leaders Learn
Common Knowledge: How Companies Thrive by Sharing What They Know
Corps Business: The 30 Management Principles of the U.S. Marines
Digital Transformation: The Essentials of e-Business Leadership
Elizabeth I, CEO: Strategic Lessons From the Leader Who Built an Empire
Executive Coaching With Backbone and Heart: A Systems Approach to Engaging Leaders With Their Challenges
Executive Instinct: Managing the Human Animal in the Information Age
Eyewitness to Power: The Essence of Leadership—Nixon to Clinton
Failing Forward: Turning Mistakes Into Stepping Stones for Success
Fish! A Remarkable Way to Boost Morale and Improve Results
Funky Business: Talent Makes Capital Dance
Leadership: What Every Manager Needs to Know
Going to the Top: A Road Map for Success From America's Leading Women Executives
Harnessing Complexity: Organizational Implications of a Scientific Frontier
How Hitler Could Have Won World War II: The 10 Fatal Errors That Led to Nazi Defeat
Lead to Succeed: 10 Traits of Great Leadership in Business and Life
Leadership and Self-Deception: Getting out of the Box
Leadership Secrets of the Rogue Warrior
Leadership Wisdom From the Monk Who Sold His Ferrari: The 8 Rituals of Visionary Leaders
Leadership Wisdom
Leadership: A Treasury of Great Quotations for Those Who Aspire to Lead
Leading at the Edge: Leadership Lessons From the the Extraordinary Saga of Shackleton's Antarctic Expedition
Leading the Revolution
Learning Journeys: Top Management Experts Share Hard-Earned Lessons on Becoming Great Mentors and Leaders
Lightning in a Bottle: Proven Lessons for Leading Change
Lives of Moral Leadership
Managing the Dream: Reflections on Leadership and Change
Maxwell 3-in-1: The Winning Attitude, Developing the Leaders Around You, Becoming a Person of Influence
More Than a Motorcycle: The Leadership Journey at Harley-Davidson
Obsessions of an Extraordinary Executive: The Four Disciplines at the Heart of Making Any Organization World Class
The Strategy Focused Organization
Peak Performance: Business Lessons From the World's Top Sports Organizations

*Peterman Rides Again: Adventures Continue with the Real "J. Peterman"
Through Life & the Catalog Business*
POTUS Speaks: Finding the Words That Defined the Clinton Presidency
Power Plays: Shakespeare's Lessons in Leadership and Management
Radical Innovation: How Mature Companies Can Outsmart Upstarts
*Rites of Passage at $100,000 to $1 Million+: Your Insider's Lifetime Guide to
Executive Job-Changing and Faster Career Progress in the 21st Century*
*Schools That Learn: A Fifth Discipline Fieldbook for Educators, Parents, and
Everyone Who Cares About Education*
Secrets of Power Negotiating
Sellout: The Inside Story of President Clinton's Impeachment
Simplicity: The New Competitive Advantage in a World of More, Better, Faster
*Stop Whining, and Start Winning: Recharging People, Reigniting Passion, and
Pumping up Profits*
Terms of Engagement: Changing the Way We Change Organizations
*The 12 Simple Secrets of Microsoft Management: How to Think and Act Like a
Microsoft Manager and Take Your Company to the Top*
*The 21 Most Powerful Minutes in a Leader's Day: Revitalize Your Spirit and
Empower Your Leadership*
The 7 Habits of Highly Effective People
The Arc of Ambition: Defining the Leadership Journey
*The Board Book: Making Your Corporate Board a Strategic Force in Your
Company's Success*
The Breach: Inside the Impeachment and Trial of William Jefferson Clinton
The Case Against Hillary Clinton
*The Code of the Executive: Forty-Seven Ancient Samurai Principles Essential
for Twenty-First Century Leadership Success*
The Entrepreneurial Mindset
The Monk and the Riddle: The Education of a Silicon Valley Entrepreneur
*The Next Pope: A Behind-The-Scenes Look at How the Successor to John Paul
II Will Be Elected and Where He Will Lead the Catholic Church*
The Presidential Difference: Leadership Style from Roosevelt to Clinton
The Reader's Companion to the American Presidency
The Real Work of Leaders: A Report From the Front Lines of Management
*The Shadow Negotiation: How Women Can Master the Hidden Agendas That
Determine Bargaining Success*
*The Strategy-Focused Organization: How Balanced Scorecard Companies
Thrive in the New Business Environment*
Papal Sin: Structures of Deceit
The Wave 4 Way to Building Your Downline
Theremin: Ether Music and Espionage (Music in American Life)
*True Professionalism: The Courage to Care About Your People, Your Clients,
and Your Career*

What Would Machiavelli Do?
Working With Emotional Intelligence
1001 Ways to Take Initiative at Work
Accountability: Getting a Grip on Results
AquaChurch: Essential Leadership Arts for Piloting Your Church in Today's Fluid Culture
Becoming a Woman of Influence: Making a Lasting Impact on Others
Blown to Bits: How the New Economics of Information Transforms Strategy
Bringing out the Best in People: How to Apply the Astonishing Power of Positive Reinforcement
Cultural Proficiency: A Manual for School Leaders
Day of Deceit: The Truth About FDR and Pearl Harbor
Dialogue and the Art of Thinking Together: A Pioneering Approach to Communicating in Business and in Life
Don't Step in the Leadership
Encouraging the Heart: A Leader's Guide to Rewarding and Recognizing Others
Essential Managers: How To Delegate
Flawed Advice and the Management Trap: How Managers Can Know When They're Getting Good Advice and When They're Not
Getting It Done: How to Lead When You're Not in Charge
High Velocity Leadership: The Mars Pathfinder Approach to Faster, Better, Cheaper
How to Be a Star at Work: 9 Breakthrough Strategies You Need to Succeed
John P. Kotter on What Leaders Really Do: A Harvard Business Review Book
Leader to Leader: Enduring Insights on Leadership from the Drucker Foundation's Award Winning Journal
Leadership and the New Science Revised: Discovering Order in a Chaotic World
Leadership by the Book: Tools to Transform Your Workplace
Leadership by the Book
Leadership for Dummies
Leadership From the Inside Out: Becoming a Leader for Life
Leadership Lessons of Robert E. Lee: Tips, Tactics, and Strategies for Leaders and Managers
Leading Beyond the Walls
Leading With Integrity: Competence With Christian Character (The Pastor's Soul)
Lean Transformation: How to Change Your Business Into a Lean Enterprise
Learning the 21 Irrefutable Laws of Leadership (Study Guide)
Learning to Lead
Lessons from the Top: The Search for America's Best Business Leaders
Managing People Is Like Herding Cats

Mission Possible: Becoming a World-Class Organization While There's Still Time

Nothing's Impossible: Leadership Lessons From Inside and Outside the Classroom

Patton on Leadership: Strategic Lessons for Corporate Warfare

Political Savvy: Systematic Approaches to Leadership Behind the Scenes

Results-Based Leadership

Rethinking the Future: Rethinking Business, Principles, Competition, Control and Complexity, Leadership, Markets, and the World

Right From The Start: Taking Charge in a New Leadership Role

Robert E. Lee on Leadership: Executive Lessons in Character, Courage, and Vision

Say It With Presentations: How to Design and Deliver Successful Business Presentations

Self-Help Stuff That Works

Succeeding Generations: Realizing the Dream of Families in Business

The 21 Indispensable Qualities of a Leader: Becoming the Person Others Will Want to Follow

The American President

The Ascent of a Leader: How Ordinary Relationships Develop Extraordinary Character and Influence

The GE Way Fieldbook: Jack Welch's Battle Plan for Corporate Revolution

The Gifted Boss: How to Find, Create and Keep Great Employees

The Heart of a Leader

The Leadership Moment: Nine True Stories of Triumph and Disaster and Their Lessons for Us All

The Military 100: A Ranking of the Most Influential Military Leaders of All Time

Topgrading: How Leading Companies Win by Hiring, Coaching and Keeping the Best People

Winning With Integrity: Getting What You're Worth Without Selling Your Soul

Age of Unreason

Basic Principles of Policy Governance

Becoming a Woman of Influence: Making a Lasting Impact on Others

Empowerment Takes More Than a Minute

Executive EQ: Emotional Intelligence in Leadership and Organizations

Harvard Business Review on Change

Harvard Business Review on Leadership

The Tao of Leadership: Lao Tzu's Tao Te Ching Adapted for a New Age

Joining Forces: Making One Plus One Equal Three in Mergers, Acquisitions, and Alliances

Julie's Wolf Pack

Organization 2000: The Essential Guide for Companies and Teams in the New Economy

Organization 2000: Achieving Success With Ease in the New World of Work
Organizing Genius: The Secrets of Creative Collaboration
Outlearning the Wolves: Surviving and Thriving in a Learning Organization
God's Politicians
Rules & Tools for Leaders
Rules and Tools for Leaders: A Down-to-Earth Guide to Effective Managing
Semper Fi: Business Leadership the Marine Corps Way
Jack Welch and the G.E. Way: Management Insights and Leadership Secrets of the Legendary CEO
Synchronicity: The Inner Path of Leadership
The 21 Irrefutable Laws of Leadership: Follow Them and People Will Follow You
The Big Book of Team Building Games: Trust-Building Activities, Team Spirit Exercises, and Other Fun Things to Do
The Complete Idiot's Guide to Business Management
The Courage to Teach: A Guide for Reflection and Renewal
The Five Temptations of a CEO: A Leadership Fable
The Leader's Handbook: Making Things Happen, Getting Things Done
The Nature of Leadership
The Rogue Warrior's Strategy for Success: A Commando's Principles of Winning
The Servant: A Simple Story About the True Essence of Leadership
The Stuff of Heroes: The Eight Universal Laws of Leadership
Virtual Leadership: Secrets from the Round Table for the Multi-Site Manager
Winning Everyday
Zapp!: The Lightning of Empowerment: How to Improve Quality, Productivity, and Employee Satisfaction
1001 Ways to Energize Employees
A Higher Standard of Leadership: Lessons From the Life of Gandhi
A Peacock in the Land of Penguins: A Tale of Diversity and Discovery
Biblical Eldership: Restoring Eldership to Rightful Place in Church
Board Self-Assessment
Boards That Make a Difference: A New Design for Leadership in Nonprofit and Public Organizations
Co-opetition: 1. A Revolutionary Mindset That Redefines Competition and Cooperation; 2. The Game Theory Strategy That's Changing the Game of Business
Common Sense
Get Better or Get Beaten!: 31 Leadership Secrets from GE's Jack Welch
It's Just a Thought . . . but It Could Change Your Life: Life's Little Lessons on Leadership
Riding the Tiger: Addressing the Many Ways Information Management Affects You in Your Organization

Leaders: The Strategies for Taking Charge/The 4 Keys to Effective Leadership
Leadership 101: Inspirational Quotes and Insights for Leaders
Learning to Lead: A Workbook on Becoming a Leader
Managing by Values
Net Gain: Expanding Markets Through Virtual Communities
The New American Democracy
Nixon's Ten Commandments of Statecraft: His Guiding Principles of Leadership and Negotiation
Organizational Culture and Leadership
Putting Emotional Intelligence To Work: Successful Leadership Is More Than IQ
Real Change Leaders: How You Can Create Growth and High Performance at Your Company
Shaping School Culture: The Heart of Leadership
Reinventing Your Board: A Step-By-Step Guide to Implementing Policy Governance
The Articulate Executive: Learn to Look, Act, and Sound Like a Leader
The Complete Idiot's Guide to Leadership
The Corporate Mystic: A Guidebook for Visionaries With Their Feet on the Ground
The Handbook of Strategic Public Relations & Integrated Communications
The Leader of the Future: New Visions, Strategies, and Practices for the Next Era (The Drucker Foundation Future Series)
The Leadership Engine: How Winning Companies Build Leaders at Every Level
The New Economics: For Industry, Government, Education
The Power Principle: Influence with Honor
Credibility: How Leaders Gain and Lose It, Why People Demand It
Deep Change: Discovering the Leader Within
Desarrolle El Líder Que Está En Usted (Be All You Can Be)
Everyone's a Coach: Five Business Secrets for High-Performance Coaching
Jack Welch Speaks: Wisdom from the World's Greatest Business Leader
Jesus CEO: Using Ancient Wisdom for Visionary Leadership
Leader as Coach: Strategies for Coaching & Developing Others
Leading Change
Leading Minds: An Anatomy of Leadership
Lincoln
Never Give In: The Extrordinary Character of Winston Churchill
The Future of Leadership: Riding the Corporate Rapids Into the 21st Century
The Leadership Challenge: How to Keep Getting Extraordinary Things Done in Organizations
101 Stupid Things Trainers Do to Sabotage Success
Beyond Entrepreneurship: Turning Your Business Into an Enduring Great Company

Certain Trumpets: The Nature of Leadership
Developing the Leaders Around You
Don't Fire Them, Fire Them Up: Motivate Yourself and Your Team
Fundamental Concepts of Educational Leadership and Management
Give and Take: The Complete Guide to Negotiating Strategies and Tactics
Improving Performance: How to Manage the White Space on the Organiza-
*   tional Chart*
Leading Out Loud: The Authentic Speaker, the Credible Leader
Leading With Soul: An Uncommon Journey of Spirit
Masterful Coaching: Extraordinary Results by Impacting People and the Way
*   They Think and Work Together*
Mining Group Gold: How to Cash in on the Collaborative Brain Power of a
*   Group*
On-The-Level: Performance Communication That Works
Smart Moves for People in Charge: 130 Checklists to Help You Be a Better
*   Leader*
The Art of War for Executives
The Female Advantage: Women's Ways of Leadership
The Last Word on Power: Reinvention for Executives Who Want to Change
*   Their World*
The Leader's Guide: 15 Essential Skills
The Leader in You: How to Win Friends, Influence People, and Succeed in a
*   Changing World*
Enlightened Leadership: Getting to the Heart of Change
Flight of the Buffalo: Soaring to Excellence, Learning to Let Employees Lead
Leadership Without Easy Answers
On Becoming a Leader
Spiritual Leadership: Principles of Excellence for Every Believer (Commitment
*   to Spiritual Growth)*
The Ecology of Commerce: A Declaration of Sustainability
The Fifth Discipline: The Art and Practice of the Learning Organization
The Fifth Discipline Fieldbook: Strategies and Tools for Building a Learning
*   Organization*
Developing the Leader Within You
Getting Things Done When You Are Not in Charge
In the Name of Jesus: Reflections on Christian Leadership
Leadership Jazz: The Art of Conducting Business Through Leadership, Follow-
*   ership, Teamwork, Voice, Touch*
Lincoln on Leadership: Executive Strategies for Tough Times
Negotiating Rationally
The Effective Executive
The Team Building Tool Kit: Tips, Tactics, and Rules for Effective Workplace
*   Teams*

Thinking Strategically: The Competitive Edge in Business, Politics, and Everyday Life
10 Steps to Empowerment: A Common-Sense Guide to Managing People
Principle-Centered Leadership
Principle-Centered Leadership: Strategies for Personal and Professional Effectiveness
Successful Team Building
The Prince (Everyman's Library)
Leadership Secrets of Attila the Hun
A Force for Change: How Leadership Differs from Management
Leadership Is an Art
New Kind of Leader
Leaders on Leadership
The Making of a Leader
Leadership and the One Minute Manager: Increasing Effectiveness Through Situational Leadership
Reframing Organizations: Artistry, Choice, and Leadership
Servant Leadership: A Journey into the Nature of Legitimate Power and Greatness
Life Is Tremendous
How to Think Like a CEO: The 22 Vital Traits You Need to Be the Person at the Top
The Inner Work of Leaders: Leadership as a Habit of Mind
The Leadership Challenge Planner: An Action Guide to Achieving Your Personal Best

APPENDIX 2.B:
KOHONEN NETWORK NODE CENTERS

	Cluster 1				
	Node 1	Node 2	Node 3	Node 4	Node 5
Rank	−0.161	0.174	0.261	0.132	−0.182
Src	0.136	−0.109	−0.232	−0.208	−0.044
Year	−0.016	−0.196	−0.276	−0.221	−0.025
ABI	0.055	−0.114	−0.295	−0.222	−0.141
AbI Read	0.056	−0.127	−0.306	−0.245	−0.148
Gender	0.084	0.023	0.054	−0.128	−0.184
Writer/Reporter	−0.260	−0.170	−0.146	−0.120	−0.157
Historian	−0.226	−0.226	−0.226	−0.226	−0.226
Military	−0.214	−0.214	−0.214	−0.214	−0.214
Consultant	0.408	0.507	0.459	0.289	0.125

	Cluster 1 (continued)				
	Node 1	Node 2	Node 3	Node 4	Node 5
Business	0.423	0.370	0.225	−0.055	−0.263
Academic	0.952	0.657	0.011	−0.132	−0.093
Relig. Leader	−0.226	−0.226	−0.226	−0.226	−0.226
Political	−0.188	−0.188	−0.188	−0.188	−0.188
Sports	−0.141	−0.141	−0.141	−0.141	−0.141
Personal Development	−0.442	−0.553	−0.403	0.394	−0.431
Developing Others	−0.186	−0.043	0.084	0.155	0.138
Organizational Change	1.014	1.126	1.067	0.630	1.024
Academic	0.951	0.396	−0.251	−0.269	−0.233
Business	0.483	0.554	0.674	0.620	0.621
Education	0.241	0.021	−0.249	−0.249	−0.248
Religious	−0.319	−0.319	−0.319	−0.319	−0.319
Political	−0.274	−0.315	−0.372	−0.372	−0.372
Historical	−0.363	−0.320	−0.304	−0.327	−0.363
Military	−0.270	−0.270	−0.270	−0.270	−0.270
Sports	−0.188	−0.188	−0.188	−0.188	−0.187
Collection/Edited Volume	1.171	0.515	0.698	0.533	1.030
Fictional Story	−0.270	−0.270	−0.270	−0.270	−0.270
Fictional Character	−0.141	−0.141	−0.141	−0.141	−0.141
Metaphors/Anecdotes	0.499	0.447	0.336	0.150	0.023
Research based	0.337	0.180	0.051	0.095	0.181
Expert	1.240	0.710	0.545	0.430	0.380
"Evangelical"	−0.230	0.056	0.162	−0.079	−0.380
Autobiography	−0.032	−0.140	−0.188	−0.319	−0.319
Biography	−0.400	−0.397	−0.372	−0.360	−0.352
Philosophical	0.011	−0.008	−0.099	−0.207	−0.333
Self Actualization	−0.069	−0.145	−0.286	−0.185	−0.138
Trait/Competency	−0.450	−0.398	−0.245	0.433	0.998
Num Sugg	−0.093	0.130	0.245	0.143	−0.036

	Cluster 2				
	Node 6	Node 7	Node 8	Node 9	Node 10
Rank	−0.140	0.082	0.131	0.037	−0.161
Src	0.135	−0.009	−0.053	−0.054	0.036
Year	−0.059	−0.219	−0.228	−0.212	−0.033
ABI	0.227	−0.006	−0.237	−0.180	−0.115
AbI Read	0.237	0.010	−0.191	−0.156	−0.092
Gender	0.093	0.019	0.048	−0.035	−0.050
Writer/Reporter	−0.260	−0.142	−0.110	−0.077	−0.109
Historian	−0.226	−0.226	−0.226	−0.226	−0.226
Military	−0.214	−0.214	−0.214	0.098	0.330
Consultant	0.360	0.392	0.363	0.167	0.015
Business	0.267	0.228	0.198	0.109	0.070
Academic	0.442	0.585	−0.001	−0.151	−0.166
Relig. Leader	−0.226	−0.226	−0.226	−0.226	−0.226

	Cluster 2 (continued)				
	Node 6	*Node 7*	*Node 8*	*Node 9*	*Node 10*
Political	−0.188	−0.188	−0.188	−0.188	−0.188
Sports	−0.141	−0.141	−0.141	0.179	0.410
Personal Development	−0.386	−0.382	−0.237	0.319	0.514
Developing Others	−0.221	0.117	0.337	0.271	0.117
Organizational Change	0.792	0.359	0.273	0.116	−0.352
Academic	0.947	0.595	0.759	0.320	0.790
Business	0.885	0.464	0.571	0.498	0.527
Education	0.596	0.273	−0.125	−0.116	−0.156
Religious	−0.040	−0.042	−0.150	−0.211	−0.319
Political	0.045	−0.156	−0.372	−0.372	−0.372
Historical	0.104	−0.099	−0.295	−0.318	−0.318
Military	−0.094	−0.184	−0.233	−0.047	0.114
Sports	−0.188	−0.188	−0.188	0.216	0.314
Collection/Edited Volume	0.885	0.276	−0.181	−0.229	−0.161
Fictional Story	−0.270	0.382	0.236	0.274	−0.270
Fictional Character	−0.141	0.209	0.315	0.148	−0.141
Metaphors/Anecdotes	0.629	0.405	0.189	0.055	−0.007
Research based	0.340	0.113	−0.045	0.022	0.111
Expert	0.624	0.356	0.210	0.179	0.263
"Evangelical"	−0.263	−0.070	0.004	−0.141	−0.322
Autobiography	−0.091	−0.147	−0.084	0.064	0.266
Biography	−0.201	−0.281	−0.351	−0.316	−0.286
Philosophical	0.148	0.246	0.207	0.050	−0.182
Self Actualization	−0.083	−0.023	−0.099	−0.079	−0.143
Trait/Competency	0.894	0.780	0.577	0.420	0.925
Num Sugg	−0.087	0.066	0.139	0.063	−0.046

	Cluster 3						
	Node 11	*Node 12*	*Node 13*	*Node 14*	*Node 15*	*Node 16*	*Node 17*
Rank	−0.119	−0.158	−0.210	−0.175	−0.140	0.123	0.026
Src	0.094	0.155	0.301	0.250	0.270	−0.030	0.083
Year	−0.121	−0.180	−0.073	−0.070	0.072	0.041	−0.092
ABI	0.562	0.504	−0.139	−0.131	−0.063	1.063	0.342
AbI Read	0.940	0.448	0.008	−0.040	0.008	0.956	0.271
Gender	−0.216	−0.143	0.060	0.621	0.299	−0.285	0.024
Writer/Reporter	1.102	0.844	0.962	0.557	0.621	0.446	0.587
Historian	0.790	0.286	−0.226	−0.226	−0.226	1.126	0.337
Military	−0.027	−0.122	−0.214	0.469	1.228	0.096	−0.021
Consultant	−0.284	−0.135	−0.018	−0.173	−0.333	−0.561	−0.487
Business	−0.231	−0.156	0.084	0.402	0.877	−0.344	−0.332
Academic	0.753	0.332	−0.150	−0.269	−0.391	0.010	−0.236
Relig. Leader	−0.226	−0.226	−0.226	−0.226	−0.226	−0.226	−0.226
Political	−0.188	−0.188	−0.188	−0.188	−0.188	0.963	0.350
Sports	−0.141	−0.141	−0.141	0.555	1.299	−0.141	−0.141

Cluster 3 (continued)

	Node 11	Node 12	Node 13	Node 14	Node 15	Node 16	Node 17
Personal Development	−0.277	−0.074	0.093	0.155	0.202	−0.430	−0.306
Developing Others	−0.346	0.214	0.772	0.511	0.159	−0.437	−0.124
Organizational Change	−0.014	−0.075	−0.034	−0.112	−0.141	−0.428	−0.445
Academic	0.877	0.305	−0.319	−0.319	−0.319	0.374	−0.023
Business	−0.445	−0.063	0.314	0.248	0.124	−0.977	−0.691
Education	0.939	0.774	0.864	0.240	0.136	0.156	0.124
Religious	0.248	0.214	0.027	−0.079	−0.313	0.119	0.026
Political	1.284	0.503	−0.372	−0.372	−0.372	1.966	0.669
Historical	1.671	0.982	−0.236	−0.301	−0.223	1.850	0.629
Military	0.611	0.192	−0.108	0.206	0.725	0.818	0.223
Sports	−0.188	−0.188	−0.188	0.717	1.706	−0.188	−0.188
Collection/Edited Volume	−0.051	−0.194	−0.229	−0.239	−0.165	−0.197	−0.270
Fictional Story	−0.270	0.773	1.490	0.947	−0.263	−0.270	0.450
Fictional Character	−0.141	0.483	0.821	0.520	−0.141	−0.141	0.247
Metaphors/Anecdotes	0.474	0.110	−0.312	−0.230	−0.102	−0.085	−0.226
Research based	0.403	0.193	−0.146	−0.060	−0.098	0.100	−0.064
Expert	−0.154	−0.344	−0.460	−0.329	−0.074	−0.633	-0.647
"Evangelical"	−0.162	−0.265	−0.303	−0.243	−0.118	−0.008	−0.205
Autobiography	0.987	0.652	0.665	0.716	1.568	−0.220	−0.224
Biography	1.287	0.967	0.854	−0.128	−0.016	1.650	0.565
Philosophical	0.213	0.609	0.821	0.610	0.131	−0.158	0.035
Self Actualization	0.017	0.134	0.171	0.020	−0.179	−0.254	−0.088
Trait/Competency	−0.230	−0.242	−0.209	0.152	0.556	−0.036	−0.323
Num Sugg	−0.080	−0.087	−0.095	−0.085	−0.071	−0.078	−0.064

Cluster 4

	Node 18	Node 19	Node 20
Rank	−0.018	−0.095	−0.094
Src	0.172	0.151	0.121
Year	−0.109	−0.086	0.029
ABI	−0.265	−0.274	−0.286
AbI Read	−0.271	−0.266	−0.294
Gender	0.158	0.168	0.038
Writer/Reporter	0.176	0.017	−0.040
Historian	−0.226	−0.173	−0.103
Military	−0.124	0.233	0.617
Consultant	−0.421	−0.205	0.051
Business	−0.248	−0.017	0.308
Academic	−0.438	−0.450	−0.491
Relig. Leader	−0.226	0.325	1.030
Political	−0.076	−0.188	−0.188
Sports	−0.141	0.254	0.693
Personal Development	−0.226	0.027	0.332
Developing Others	0.076	0.134	0.136

	Cluster 4 (Continued)		
	Node 18	Node 19	Node 20
Organizational Change	−0.457	−0.462	−0.459
Academic	−0.319	−0.319	−0.319
Business	−0.459	−0.294	−0.124
Education	0.067	0.056	0.004
Religious	0.117	0.365	0.795
Political	−0.310	−0.372	−0.372
Historical	−0.229	−0.331	−0.287
Military	−0.047	0.003	0.309
Sports	−0.188	0.319	0.894
Collection/Edited Volume	−0.271	−0.237	−0.149
Fictional Story	0.704	0.458	0.977
Fictional Character	0.382	0.359	0.652
Metaphors/Anecdotes	−0.330	−0.319	−0.276
Research based	−0.221	−0.237	−0.317
Expert	−0.613	−0.436	−0.197
"Evangelical"	0.381	0.355	0.768
Autobiography	−0.031	0.266	0.265
Biography	−0.128	−0.230	−0.141
Philosophical	0.142	0.253	0.313
Self Actualization	0.096	0.253	0.508
Trait/Competency	−0.515	−0.259	0.055
Num Sugg	−0.060	−0.062	−0.074

	Cluster 5	
	Node 21	Node 22
Rank	0.213	0.123
Src	−0.115	0.007
Year	0.102	−0.018
ABI	0.981	0.313
AbI Read	0.889	0.219
Gender	−0.413	0.047
Writer/Reporter	0.703	0.394
Historian	1.332	0.502
Military	0.158	0.058
Consultant	−0.749	−0.707
Business	−0.311	−0.411
Academic	−0.284	−0.465
Relig. Leader	−0.226	−0.226
Political	1.362	0.613
Sports	−0.141	−0.141
Personal Development	−0.520	−0.507
Developing Others	−0.437	−0.383
Organizational Change	−0.441	−0.556
Academic	0.224	−0.057
Business	1.510	1.082

	Cluster 5 (Continued)	
	Node 21	Node 22
Education	−0.249	−0.166
Religious	−0.200	−0.264
Political	1.014	0.788
Historical	0.859	0.562
Military	0.739	0.255
Sports	−0.188	−0.188
Collection/Edited Volume	−0.190	−0.260
Fictional Story	−0.270	−0.270
Fictional Character	−0.141	−0.141
Metaphors/Anecdotes	−0.393	−0.413
Research based	−0.009	−0.094
Expert	1.421	0.825
"Evangelical"	0.067	−0.149
Autobiography	1.825	0.723
Biography	1.332	0.265
Philosophical	−0.381	−0.344
Self Actualization	−0.250	−0.236
Trait/Competency	0.004	−0.368
Num Sugg	−0.083	−0.057

	Cluster 6
	Node 23
Rank	0.064
Src	0.076
Year	−0.119
ABI	−0.329
AbI Read	−0.409
Gender	0.282
Writer/Reporter	0.257
Historian	−0.226
Military	−0.078
Consultant	0.632
Business	−0.449
Academic	−0.618
Relig. Leader	−0.226
Political	−0.029
Sports	−0.141
Personal Development	−0.455
Developing Others	−0.289
Organizational Change	−0.633
Academic	−0.319
Business	0.830
Education	−0.045
Religious	0.045

	Cluster 6 (Cont.)
	Node 23
Political	−0.283
Historical	−0.224
Military	−0.008
Sports	−0.188
Collection/Edited Volume	−0.319
Fictional Story	−0.269
Fictional Character	−0.141
Metaphors/Anecdotes	−0.393
Research based	−0.215
Expert	−0.606
"Evangelical"	−0.098
Autobiography	−0.177
Biography	−0.073
Philosophical	−0.298
Self Actualization	−0.052
Trait/Competency	−0.607
Num Sugg	0.641

	Cluster 7	
	Node 24	*Node 25*
Rank	−0.048	−0.086
Src	0.079	0.035
Year	−0.051	0.039
ABI	−0.395	−0.462
AbI Read	−0.460	−0.550
Gender	0.236	−0.070
Writer/Reporter	0.011	−0.073
Historian	−0.133	−0.005
Military	−0.106	−0.214
Consultant	−0.253	0.290
Business	−0.340	−0.151
Academic	−0.618	−0.611
Relig. Leader	0.736	2.072
Political	−0.188	−0.188
Sports	−0.141	−0.141
Personal Development	−0.080	0.476
Developing Others	−0.079	0.227
Organizational Change	−0.679	−0.679
Academic	−0.319	−0.319
Business	−0.638	−0.267
Education	−0.066	−0.079
Religious	0.617	1.694
Political	−0.372	−0.372

	Cluster 7 (Continued)	
	Node 24	Node 25
Historical	−0.363	−0.363
Military	−0.270	−0.270
Sports	−0.188	−0.187
Collection/Edited Volume	−0.247	−0.148
Fictional Story	−0.193	−0.070
Fictional Character	−0.141	−0.141
Metaphors/Anecdotes	−0.429	−0.423
Research based	−0.316	−0.476
Expert	−0.500	−0.374
"Evangelical"	0.467	1.513
Autobiography	−0.027	0.294
Biography	−0.239	−0.104
Philosophical	0.010	0.420
Self Actualization	0.334	1.053
Trait/Competency	−0.521	−0.297
Num Sugg	−0.052	−0.081

3

Social Identity
and Leadership

Michael A. Hogg
University of Queensland

Leadership is a relational term—it identifies a relationship in which some people are able to persuade others to adopt new values, attitudes and goals, and to exert effort on behalf of those values, attitudes and goals. The relationship is almost always configured by and played out within the parameters of a group—a small group like a team, a medium-sized group like an organization, or a large group like a nation. The values, attitudes and goals that leaders inspire others to adopt and to follow are ones that define and serve the group—and thus leaders are able to transform individual action into group action. This kind of characterization of leadership, which is certainly not uncommon (e.g., Chemers, 2001), places a premium on the role of group membership and group life in the analysis of leadership. My goal in this chapter is to describe just such an analysis of leadership—a new analysis based on the social identity approach in social psychology (see Hogg, 2001a; Hogg & van Knippenberg, 2003).

A BRIEF COMMENTARY
ON LEADERSHIP RESEARCH IN SOCIAL
AND ORGANIZATIONAL PSYCHOLOGY

The Rise and Fall of Leadership
in Social Psychology

Leadership is about dealing with people, usually within a group, and about changing people's behaviors and attitudes to conform to the leader's vision for the group. Not surprisingly, the study of leadership has long been a core research focus for social psychology, particularly during the boom years of small group dynamics (e.g., Cartwright & Zander, 1968; Shaw, 1981), and has been a component of some of social psychology's classic research programs (e.g., Bales, 1950; Hollander, 1958; Lippitt & White, 1943; Sherif, 1966; Stogdill, 1974). This tradition of leadership research culminated in Fiedler's (1965, 1971) contingency theory, which purports that the leadership effectiveness of a particular behavioral style is contingent on the favorability of the situation to that behavioral style.

During the 1970s and 1980s, however, there was a new emphasis in social psychology on attribution processes, and then social cognition (e.g., Devine, Hamilton, & Ostrom, 1994; Fiske & Taylor, 1991). These developments were associated with a well-documented decline in interest in groups (e.g., Steiner, 1974, 1986) that carried across to the study of leadership. The last edition of the *Handbook of Social Psychology* had a chapter dedicated to leadership (Hollander, 1985), whereas the current edition (Gilbert, Fiske, & Lindzey, 1998) does not. The study of small group processes and of leadership shifted to neighboring disciplines, most notably organizational psychology (Levine & Moreland, 1990, 1995; McGrath, 1997; Sanna & Parks, 1997; Tindale & Anderson, 1998).

The Rise and Rise of Leadership
in Organizational Psychology

The study of leadership has a natural home in organizational psychology. Businesses can thrive or perish largely due to the quality of organizational leadership. Not surprisingly, organizational psychology places the study of leadership very high on its agenda (e.g., Bass, 1990a; Yukl, 2002). It is a booming research field that generates an enormous amount of literature spanning the complete range from weighty research tomes to fast moving self-help books. In recent years organizational psychologists have paid particular attention to transformational leadership and the role of charisma. Charismatic leaders are able to motivate followers to work for collective goals that transcend self-interest and transform organizations (Bass, 1990b; Bass & Avolio, 1993; see Mowday & Sutton, 1993, for critical comment). This focus on "charisma" is particularly evident in "new leadership" research (e.g., Bass, 1985, 1990b, 1998; Bryman, 1992; Burns, 1978; Conger & Kanungo, 1987, 1988), which proposes that effective leaders should be proactive, change-oriented, innovative, motivating and inspiring, and have a vision or mission with which they infuse the group. They should also be interested in others, and be able to create commitment to the group, and extract extra effort from and empower members of the group.

Social Psychology Rediscovers Leadership

Over the past 20 years, social psychology has, with the help of social cognition, become more sophisticated in its methods and theories (Devine et al., 1994), and, with the help of the social identity approach, has begun once again to focus on group processes, intergroup phenomena and the collective self (Abrams & Hogg, 1998; Moreland, Hogg, & Hains, 1994; Sedikides & Brewer, 2001). There has been a revived focus on leadership (e.g., Chemers, 2001; Lord, Brown, & Harvey, 2001; van Knippenberg & Hogg, 2002), an integration of social cognition and social identity approaches within social psychology (Abrams & Hogg, 1999), and a closer relationship between social identity research and organizational psychology (e.g., Haslam, 2000; Haslam, van Knippenberg, Platow, & Ellemers, 2003; Hogg & Terry, 2000, 2001; van Knippenberg & Hogg, 2001).

The recent social psychological focus on leadership has raised some concerns about contemporary organizational psychology leadership research. Although most research now acknowledges that leadership is a relational property within groups (i.e., leaders exist because of followers, and followers exist because of leaders), the idea that leadership may emerge through the operation of ordinary social-cognitive processes associated with psychologically belonging to a group, has not really been elaborated.

Instead, the most recent organizational psychology emphasis is mainly on (a) individual cognitive processes that categorize individuals as leaders—the social orientation between individuals is not considered, and thus group processes are not incorporated, or (b) whether individuals have the charismatic properties necessary to meet the transformational objectives of leadership—leadership is a matter of situationally attractive individual characteristics rather than group processes. Both these perspectives have attracted criticism for neglecting the effects of larger social systems within which the individual is embedded (e.g., Hall & Lord, 1995; Lord et al., 2001; Pawar & Eastman, 1997; also see Chemers, 2001; Haslam & Platow, 2001). Lord et al. (2001) explain that leadership cannot be properly understood in terms of a leader's actions or in terms of abstract perceptual categories of types of leader. They advocate a paradigm shift in how we understand leadership. Haslam and Platow (2001) echo this concern, and warn against any explanation of leadership that rests too heavily, or at all, on invariant properties of individuals and their personalities.

The aim of this chapter is to offer a social identity analysis of leadership, as a group membership-based perspective on leadership. This perspective has attracted growing interest, and produced a number of conceptual and empirical publications (e.g., de Cremer, 2002; Duck & Fielding, 1999; Fielding & Hogg, 1997; Foddy & Hogg, 1999; Hains, Hogg, & Duck, 1997; Haslam et al., 1998; Haslam & Platow, 2001; Hogg, 1996, 2001a, 2001b, 2001c; Hogg, Hains, & Mason, 1998; Hogg & Martin, 2003; Hogg & Reid, 2001; Hogg & van Knippenberg, 2003; Platow, Hoar, Reid, Harley, & Morrison, 1997; Platow, Reid, & Andrews, 1998; Reicher, Drury, Hopkins, & Stott, in press; Reicher & Hopkins, 1996; Van Vugt & de Cremer, 1999).

SOCIAL IDENTITY

The social identity perspective (e.g., Hogg & Abrams, 1988; Tajfel & Turner, 1986; Turner, Hogg, Oakes, Reicher, & Wetherell, 1987) has become increasingly central to social psychology, and has recently been summarized in detail elsewhere (e.g., Abrams & Hogg, 2001; Hogg, 2001d, 2003). I provide only a brief overview of key features here.

From the social identity perspective, a group exists psychologically when people share a self-conception in terms of the defining features of a self-inclusive social category. More specifically, this representation of the group is a prototype—a fuzzy set of features that captures ingroup similarities and intergroup differences regarding beliefs, attitudes, behaviors and feelings. Prototypes are configured according to the principle of metacontrast, to maximize the ratio of intergroup differences to intragroup differences.

A key insight of the social identity approach is that the basis of perception, attitudes, feelings, behavior, and self-conception is contextually fluid. Self-conception can vary from being entirely based on idiosyncratic per-

sonal attributes and the unique properties of a specific interpersonal relationship, to being entirely based on a shared representation of "us" defined
in terms of an ingroup prototype. In the latter case, the situation represents
a group situation and perceptions, attitudes, feelings and behavior acquire
the familiar characteristics of inter- and intragroup behaviors—conformity, normative behavior, solidarity, stereotyping, ethnocentrism, intergroup discrimination, ingroup favoritism, and so forth. Put another way,
the more that an aggregate of people is a salient basis for self-definition as
a group member, then the more strongly is self-definition, perception, cognition, affect, and behavior based on prototypicality. When group membership is the salient basis of self-conception people, including self, are
represented and treated in terms of the relevant in- or outgroup defining
prototype. Self-categorization depersonalizes self in terms of the ingroup
prototype (producing self-stereotyping, conformity, normative behavior,
social attraction, social identification, and so forth), and it depersonalizes
perception of others so that they are seen as more or less exact matches
to the relevant prototype. Prototypicality is the yardstick of life in salient
groups.

Because groups define self, the social value or status of a group becomes
the social value or status of self. Intergroup relations become, therefore, a
struggle for evaluatively positive distinctiveness for one's own group relative to other groups. This, in turn, is underpinned by a self-enhancement
motive and a striving for positive self-esteem. The strategies that groups
and their members adopt to manage positive distinctiveness and self-
enhancement is influenced by people's beliefs about the nature of relations between groups—beliefs about the legitimacy and stability of status
relations, about the permeability of intergroup boundaries, and about the
possibility of an alternative social order.

SOCIAL IDENTITY THEORY
OF LEADERSHIP

The effect of social identity processes on leadership is quite straightforward. As group membership becomes increasingly salient, leadership perceptions, evaluations and effectiveness become increasing based on how
group-prototypical the leader is perceived to be (e.g., Hogg, 2001a, 2001b,
2001c; Hogg & van Knippenberg, 2003).

Where group membership is situationally or enduringly salient, people
self-categorize in terms of the ingroup prototype and become deperson-

alized—they conform to the ingroup prototype and exhibit normative behavior. In a highly salient group the prototype is likely to be relatively consensual, and thus the group as a whole appears to be influenced by a single prototype which prescribes a single norm or goal. Social identity research on conformity and social influence shows that self-categorization produces conformity to an ingroup prototype that may capture the central tendency of the group or may be polarized away from a relevant outgroup (for reviews, see Abrams & Hogg, 1990; Turner, 1991; Turner & Oakes, 1989).

Prototypicality and Influence

Within any salient group there is a prototypicality gradient, with some members being more prototypical than others. Because depersonalization is based on prototypicality, group members are very sensitive to prototypicality. Prototypicality is the basis of perception and evaluation of self and other members, and thus people notice and respond to subtle differences in how prototypical fellow members are—they are very aware not only of the prototype, but also of who is most prototypical (e.g., Haslam, Oakes, McGarty, Turner, & Onorato, 1995; Hogg, 1993).

Within a salient group, then, people who are perceived to occupy the most prototypical position are perceived to best embody the behaviors to which other, less prototypical, members are conforming. There is a perception of differential influence within the group, with the most prototypical member appearing to exercise influence over less prototypical members. This "appearance" probably arises due to the human tendency to personify and give human agency to abstract forces—perhaps a manifestation of the fundamental attribution error (Ross, 1977) or correspondence bias (e.g., Gilbert & Malone, 1995). In new groups, this is only an "appearance" because the most prototypical person does not actively exercise influence; it is the prototype, which he or she happens to embody, that influences behavior. In established groups the appearance is reinforced by actual influence.

Where the social context is in flux, the prototype will likewise be in flux. As the prototype changes so will the person who appears to be most prototypical and thus most influential. Under conditions of enduring contextual stability the same individual may occupy the most prototypical position over a long period, and so appear to have enduring influence over the group. In new groups this person will be perceived to occupy an embryonic leadership role; although leadership has not been exercised. There is nascent role differentiation into "leader" and "followers."

So far, social identity processes ensure that as group membership becomes more salient, and members identify more strongly with the group, prototypicality becomes an increasingly influential basis for leadership perceptions. However, it is important to keep this in perspective—prototypicality is not the only basis of leadership. People also rely on general and more task-specific schemas of leadership behaviors (what Lord and his colleagues call *leader categories* or *leader schemas*—e.g., Lord, Foti, & DeVader, 1984). However, the importance of these schemas is either unaffected by self-categorization, or it diminishes as group prototypicality becomes more important. In either case, leadership schemas should become less influential *relative* to group prototypicality as group membership becomes psychologically more salient.

Social Attraction

Social categorization affects not only perceptions, but also feelings, about other people. Social identification transforms the basis of liking for others from idiosyncratic preference and personal relationship history (personal attraction) to prototypicality (social attraction)—ingroup members are liked more than outgroup members and more prototypical ingroupers are liked more than less prototypical ingroupers. Where there is a relatively consensual ingroup prototype, social categorization renders more prototypical members socially popular—there is consensual and unilateral liking for more prototypical members. This depersonalized social attraction hypothesis (Hogg, 1992, 1993) is supported by a series of laboratory and field studies (e.g., Hogg, Cooper-Shaw, & Holzworth, 1993; Hogg & Hains, 1996, 1998; Hogg & Hardie, 1991; Hogg, Hardie, & Reynolds, 1995).

From the point of view of leadership, the person occupying the most prototypical position may thus acquire, in new groups, or possess, in established groups, the ability to actively influence because he or she is socially attractive and thus able to secure compliance with suggestions and recommendations he or she makes. If you like someone you are more likely to agree with them, and comply with requests and suggestions (e.g., Berscheid & Reis, 1998). In this way, the most prototypical person can actively exercise leadership by having his or her ideas accepted more readily and more widely than ideas suggested by others. This empowers the leader, and publicly confirms his or her ability to influence. Consensual depersonalized liking, particularly over time, confirms differential popularity and public endorsement of the leader. It imbues the leader with prestige and status, and begins to reify the nascent intragroup status differential between leader(s) and followers. It allows someone who is "merely" prototypical, a passive focus for influence, to take the initiative and become an active and innovative agent of influence.

Social attraction may also be strengthened by the behavior of highly prototypical members. More prototypical members tend to identify more strongly, and thus display more pronounced group behaviors; they will be more normative, show greater ingroup loyalty and ethnocentrism, and generally behave in a more group serving manner. These behaviors further confirm prototypicality and thus enhance social attraction. A leader who acts as "one of us," by showing ingroup favoritism and intragroup fairness, is not only more socially attractive, but is also endowed with legitimacy (Tyler, 1997; Tyler & Lind, 1992; see Platow et al., 1998).

Attribution and Information Processing

Prototypicality and social attraction work alongside attribution and information processing to translate perceived influence into active leadership. Attribution processes operate within groups to make sense of others' behavior. As elsewhere, attributions for others' behavior are prone to the fundamental attribution error (Ross, 1977) or correspondence bias (Gilbert & Jones, 1986; also see Gilbert & Malone, 1995; Trope & Liberman, 1993); a tendency to attribute behavior to underlying dispositions that reflect invariant properties, or essences, of the individual's personality. This effect is more pronounced for individuals who are perceptually distinctive (e.g., figural against a background) or cognitively salient (e.g., Taylor & Fiske, 1978).

We have seen that when group membership is salient, people are sensitive to prototypicality and attend to subtle differences in prototypicality of fellow members. Highly prototypical members are most informative about what is prototypical of group membership (see Turner, 1991), and so in a group context they attract the most attention. They are subjectively important and are distinctive or figural against the background of other, less informative members. Research in social cognition shows that people who are subjectively important and distinctive are seen to be disproportionately influential and have their behavior dispositionally attributed (e.g., Erber & Fiske, 1984; Taylor & Fiske, 1975). We have also seen how highly prototypical members may appear to have influence due to their relative prototypicality, and may actively exercise influence and gain compliance as a consequence of consensual social attraction. Together, the leadership nature of this behavior and the relative prominence of prototypical members is likely to encourage an internal attribution to intrinsic leadership ability, or charisma.

In groups, then, the behavior of highly prototypical members is likely to be attributed, particularly in stable groups over time, to the person's personality rather than the prototypicality of the position occupied. The consequence is a tendency to construct a charismatic leadership personality for that person that, to some extent, separates that person from the rest of the group and reinforces the perception of status-based structural differentiation within the group into leader(s) and followers. This may make the leader stand out more starkly against the background of less prototypical followers, as well as draw attention to a potential power imbalance; thus further fueling the attributional effect.

It should be noted that this analysis views charisma as a product of social-cognitive processes operating under conditions of self-categorization, and not as an invariant personality attribute that determines leadership effectiveness. In this respect our analysis is consistent with Haslam and Platow's (2001) critical appraisal of the role of charisma in contemporary transformational leadership theories.

There is some empirical support for the idea that followers tend to focus on the leader and make dispositional attributions for that person's behavior. Fiske (1993; Fiske & Dépret, 1996) shows how followers pay close attention to leaders, and seek dispositional information about leaders because detailed individualized knowledge helps redress the perceived power imbalance between leader and followers. Conger and Kanungo (1987, 1988) describe how followers attributionally construct a charismatic leadership personality for organizational leaders who have a "vision" that involves substantial change to the group. Meindl, Ehrlich, and Dukerich (1985) showed that simplified dispositional attributions for leadership were more evident for distinctive leadership behaviors, and under crisis conditions.

Maintaining Leadership

Thus far we have seen how prototype-based depersonalization fairly automatically imbues the most prototypical member of a group with many attributes of leadership—for example, status, charisma, popular support, and the ability to influence. These attributes also allow the leader to actively maintain his or her leadership position. The longer an individual remains in a leadership position the more they will be socially "liked," the more consensual will social attraction be, and the more entrenched will be the fundamental attribution effect.

Social contextual changes impact prototypicality. Thus, over time and across contexts, the leader may decline in prototypicality while other members become more prototypical; opening the door, particularly under high salience conditions, to a redistribution of influence within the group. An established leader is well placed in terms of resources to combat this by redefining the prototype in a self-serving manner to prototypically marginalize contenders and prototypically centralize self. This can be done by accentuating the existing ingroup prototype, by pillorying ingroup deviants, or by demonizing an appropriate outgroup. Generally all three tactics are used, and the very act of engaging in these tactics is often viewed as further evidence of effective leadership (e.g., Reicher et al., in press; Reicher & Hopkins, 1996).

Leadership endurance also benefits from consensual prototypicality, because of the latter's effect on social attraction. In groups with less consensual prototypes, there is less consensus of perceptions of and feelings for the leader and thus the leader may have less power and may occupy a less stable position. It is in the leader's interest to maintain a clearly defined and consensual prototype. Simple and more clearly focused prototypes are less open to ambiguity and alternative interpretations and are thus better suited to consensuality. One way to do this is to construct and then foment rejection of ingroup deviates—a process that clarifies the prototype that the leader best represents (see Marques, Abrams, Páez, & Hogg, 2001). Another strategy is to polarize or extremitize the ingroup relative to a specific "wicked" outgroup. These processes are most likely to operate in extremist groups with all-powerful leaders (e.g., Hogg, 2001b; Hogg & Reid, 2001).

EMPIRICAL SUPPORT

The core idea of the social identity analysis of leadership is that as groups become more salient, leadership processes become more strongly influenced by perceptions of prototypicality that work in conjunction with social attraction and attribution processes.

Direct tests have focused on the key prediction that as a group becomes more salient emergent leadership processes and leadership effectiveness perceptions become less dependent on leader schema congruence and more dependent on group prototypicality. There is solid support for this idea from laboratory experiments (e.g., Duck & Fielding, 1999; Hains, Hogg, & Duck, 1997; Hogg, Hains, & Mason, 1998) and a naturalistic field study of "outward bound" groups (Fielding & Hogg, 1997). There is also indirect support from a range of studies of leadership that are in the social identity tradition (de Cremer, 2002; Foddy & Hogg, 1999; Haslam et al., 1998; Haslam & Platow, 2001; Hogg & Martin, 2003; Platow et al., 1997; Platow et al., 1998; Reicher et al., in press; Reicher & Hopkins, 1996; Van Vugt & de Cremer, 1999). There is also support for the idea that prototype-based depersonalized social attraction may facilitate leadership. There is some direct evidence from the study by Fielding and Hogg (1997), whereas in other studies social attraction is a component of the leadership evaluation measure (e.g., Hains et al., 1997; Hogg et al., 1998). The role of attribution and information processing remains to be fully investigated.

To illustrate social identity research on the role of prototypicality in leadership, let me describe two experiments—a minimal group study by Hains et al. (1997), and a gender study by Hogg et al. (2001).

Hains, Hogg, and Duck (1997)

Hains, Hogg, and Duck (1997) conducted a laboratory study of emergent leadership perceptions and evaluations in ad hoc and relatively minimal groups. Three independent variables (group salience, group prototypicality, and leader schema congruence) were manipulated in a $2 \times 2 \times 2$ design. Under conditions of high or low group salience, student participants ($N = 184$) anticipated joining a small discussion group formed on the basis of attitude congruence. They were informed that a randomly appointed group leader was group prototypical or nonprototypical (group prototypicality) in terms of the attitude dimension, and had a behavioral style (on the basis of a pretest) that was congruent or incongruent with a very general schema of effective leadership (leader schema congruence). Dependent measures were taken ostensibly in anticipation of the upcoming discussion. In addition to checks on each of the three manipulations, we also measured group identification (11-item scale, $\alpha = .87$) and perceived leader effectiveness (10-item scale, $\alpha = .88$).

As predicted, when group membership was salient, people identified more strongly with the group and endorsed the prototypical leader as being much more effective than the nonprototypical leader; low salience participants did not differentiate between prototypical and nonprototypical leaders (Fig. 3.1). Although leader schema congruent leaders were perceived

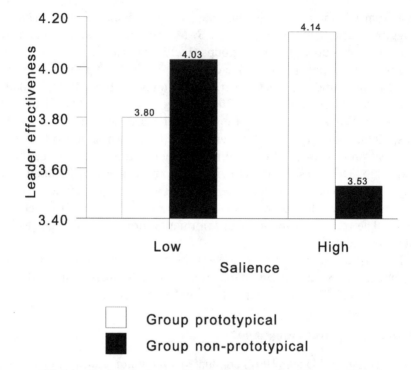

FIG. 3.1.   Leader effectiveness (1–9 scale, 10 items, $\alpha = .88$) as a function of group salience, and group prototypicality of the leader ($p < .001$). From "Self-Categorization and Leadership: Effects of Group Prototypicality and Leader Stereotypicality," by S. C. Hains, M. A. Hogg, and J. M. Duck, 1997, *Personality and Social Psychology Bulletin, 23,* p. 1095. Copyright © 1997 by Sage Publications, Inc. Reprinted by permission of Sage Publications.

overall to be more effective than schema incongruent leaders, we found that this effect disappeared for high salience participants on one leadership effectiveness item measuring the extent to which the leader was anticipated to exhibit leadership behavior (Fig. 3.2).

Although social attraction for the leader was not explicitly tested, the 10-item leadership effectiveness scale contained an item measuring liking for the leader; thus leadership effectiveness was associated with liking.

Hogg, Fielding, Johnston, Masser, Russell, and Svensson (2001)

Hogg et al. (2001) employed a similar paradigm in which student participants anticipated joining a group to discuss university resource alloca-

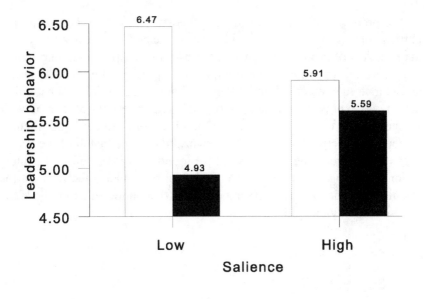

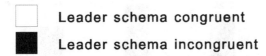

FIG. 3.2. Leader behavior (1–9 scale, 1 item) as a function of group salience, and leader schema congruence of the leader ($p < .01$). From "Self-Categorization and Leadership: Effects of Group Prototypicality and Leader Stereotypicality," by S. C. Hains, M. A. Hogg, and J. M. Duck, 1997, *Personality and Social Psychology Bulletin, 23*, p. 1095. Copyright © 1997 by Sage Publications, Inc. Reprinted by permission of Sage Publications.

tions for undergraduate classes. Group salience was manipulated and participants were informed that their group had an agentic/instrumental (i.e., male stereotypical) or a communal/expressive (i.e., female stereotypical) norm for how the discussion was to be conducted. Participants were also told that a leader had been randomly appointed—they discovered that the leader was either male or female. The three manipulated variables were thus: 2 (group salience) × 2 (group norm) × 2 (sex of leader). There was a fourth variable formed by median split of participants into those with traditional and those with progressive sex role orientations—according to Glick and Fiske's (1996) ambivalent sexism inventory. Aside from manipulation checks, the key dependent variables included a four-item measure of group effectiveness ($\alpha = .84$) and a 12-item measure of leader effectiveness ($\alpha = .91$).

The prediction from social identity theory was that among traditional participants, group salience would increase the perceived effectiveness of male leaders of groups with an agentic/instrumental (i.e., male) norm and female leaders of groups with a communal/expressive (i.e., female) norm, and reduce the perceived effectiveness of male leaders of groups with a communal/expressive (female) norm and female leaders of groups with an agentic/instrumental (male) norm. In other words, under high salience, leadership effectiveness depends more heavily on the match of the leader to the group prototype. This is what we found—Fig. 3.3 shows the interaction of salience by norm by sex of leader on leader effectiveness, for traditional participants only. Hogg et al. (2001) conducted a modified replication which yielded the same finding.

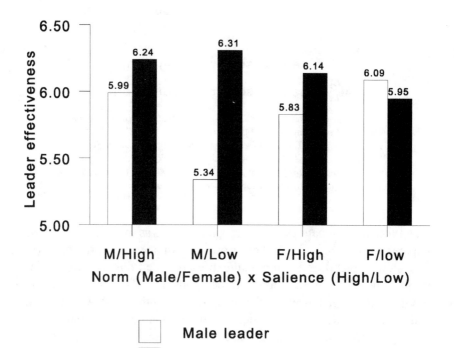

FIG. 3.3.   Hogg et al. (2001): Leader effectiveness (1–9 scale, 12 items, $\alpha =$ .91) as a function of group salience (High/Low), group norm (Male/Female), and sex of leader (Male/Female), for participants with traditional sex-role attitudes ($p = .05$).

CONCEPTUAL EXTENSIONS

The social identity analysis of leadership has a number of conceptual extensions and applications. I will describe four here.

The Glass Ceiling

One application, which framed the Hogg et al. (2001) study just described, is to the glass ceiling effect that has been reported in many organizations. Highly cohesive groups that are very salient may consolidate organizational prototypes that reflect dominant rather than minority cultural attributes and thus exclude minorities from top leadership positions. Research suggests that in Western societies, demographic minorities (e.g., people of color, ethnic minorities, women) can find it difficult to attain top leadership positions in organizations—there is a "glass ceiling" (e.g., Eagly, Karau, & Makhijani, 1995). If organizational prototypes (e.g., of speech, dress, attitudes, interaction styles) are societally cast so that minorities do not match them well, then minorities are unlikely to be endorsed as leaders under conditions where organizational prototypicality is more important than leadership stereotypicality; that is, when organizational identification and cohesion are very high. This might arise under conditions of uncertainty when, for example, organizations are under threat from competitors, a take-over is looming, or there is an economic crisis; situations where leaders, rather than managers, may be badly needed. Thus, minorities may find it difficult to attain top leadership positions in organizations because they do not fit culturally prescribed organizational prototypes, and thus are not endorsed under conditions where real leadership may be needed.

The Hogg et al. (2001) study, described previously, provided some support for this analysis. As salience increased, group members' leadership evaluations of males and females became increasingly grounded in the extent to which the stereotypical properties of males or females (agentic/instrumental vs. communal/expressive) matched the local norms of the group (agentic/instrumental vs. communal/expressive). For example, where the group's norm was agentic/instrumental, females became less effective and males more effective as salience increased.

Mergers and Acquisitions

Another application is to organizational mergers and acquisitions. Mergers and acquisitions have a disappointingly low success rate—pre-merger loyalties can hinder smooth operation of the post-merger organization (e.g., Cartwright & Cooper, 1992). Recent social psychological research offers an analysis in terms of social categorization processes, intergroup relations, and social identity theory (e.g., Terry & Callan, 1998; Terry, Carey, & Callan, 2001; van Knippenberg & van Leeuwen, 2001). From a leadership perspective, merged organizations pose a particular problem, which is actually part of a broader leadership issue—to which pre-merger organization (or subgroup) does the leader belong (e.g., Duck & Fielding, 1999)?

From the social identity analysis presented here we would expect that pre-merger organizational (subgroup) membership of the leader would be absolutely critical if pre-merger affiliations were highly charged—conditions that are likely to prevail given the assimilationist goal of mergers (see Hogg & Hornsey, in press; Hornsey & Hogg, 2000). Organizational members would be focused on pre-merger (subgroup) organizational prototypes, and would thus endorse a leader who was "one of us" (ingroup prototypical) and spurn a leader who was "one of them" (decidedly not ingroup prototypical). More specifically, leadership effectiveness in merged organizations would, among other things, depend on the relative levels of pre- and post-organizational identification, and the level of ingroup or outgroup prototypicality of the leader.

Leader–Member Relations

A third extension of the social identity analysis is to the nature of relations that exist between leaders and followers in a group, and the leadership effectiveness of those relations. Leader–member exchange theory (e.g., Graen & Uhl-Bien, 1995) argues that effective leaders need to develop high-quality personalized relationships with followers—relationships that recognize followers' individual qualities and contributions to the group.

The social identity perspective offers the novel analysis that although these personalized leader–member relations may be effective in many groups, they may be less effective in groups that are highly salient and with which people identify very strongly (Hogg & Martin, 2003; Hogg et al., in press; Hogg, Martin, & Weeden, 2004). The logic underlying this analysis is that personalized relations in a high-salience group may run counter to the collective spirit of such groups because it is seen to identify favorites, separate members who feel joined through common identity, and so forth. Members may actually prefer to be treated alike by the leader. Depersonalized leader–member relations may appear more in the spirit of enhanced collective self-conception, and may promote enhanced feelings of trust and legitimacy for an apparently group-focused egalitarian leader (e.g., Tyler & Lind, 1992).

Hogg, Martin, and Weeden report two studies (a laboratory experiment and a field study of organizations) that provide some preliminary support for this analysis (also see Hogg et al., in press). As group salience increased and members identified more strongly, depersonalized leader–member relations were an increasingly positively valued basis for effective leadership. However, these data suggest a slight qualification to the depersonalized leader–member relations hypothesis. In highly salient groups, followers certainly prefer depersonalized relations; but, because they are focused on prototypicality they actually prefer *circumscribed depersonalization*. That is, depersonalized leader–member relations that recognize that some followers are more prototypical than others—relations that favor more prototypical members over more marginal members (e.g., Marques et al., 2001). This idea has yet to be tested empirically.

Leadership and Power

The social identity analysis of leadership generates some ideas about the relationship between leadership and power, which builds in a consideration of leadership as an intergroup relationship within a group (Hogg, 2001b; Hogg & Reid, 2001). Scholars generally distinguish leadership from power. Leadership involves getting followers to believe in and pursue your vision for the group, whereas power involves getting people to do what you tell them, even if they do not subscribe to your vision for the group. In the language of social influence (e.g., Turner, 1991), leadership produces internalized cognitive change, whereas power produces surface compliance.

From this distinction, it is quite clear that prototypical leaders exercise leadership, not power. After all, high levels of social identification, coupled with the leader's prototypical position, ensure that the influence process associated with such leadership is referent informational influence (e.g., Hogg & Turner, 1987; Turner, 1982) underpinned by self-categorization and prototype-based depersonalization on the part of followers. Leaders define group norms that followers internalize as highly identified group members. Under these circumstances leaders would find it very difficult to coerce or harm followers. In a very real sense there exists an empathic bond between leader and followers, which is based on common ingroup identity and the extent to which the group is internalized as part of the self (e.g., Tropp & Wright, 2001; Wright, Aron, & Tropp, 2002; also see Smith, Coates, & Walling, 1999; Smith & Henry, 1996). Coercion and harm directed at followers is akin to coercion and harm directed at self.

However, a paradox arises. Occupying a highly prototypical position, particularly in an enduring and stable high entitativity group with a focused and consensual prototype, makes one gradually appear enduringly influential, consensually socially attractive, and essentially charismatic. There is a gradual perceptual separation of the leader from the rest of the group, through structural role differentiation grounded in social attraction and attribution processes—the leader is gradually perceived as "other" rather than "one of us." The person who embodied the essence of the group by being most prototypical has now become effectively an outgroup member within the group. An embryonic intergroup relationship begins to emerge between leader (along with his/her inner clique) and followers.

This intergroup relationship is grounded in a status differential that is perceived to be relatively consensual, stable, and legitimate—a potent mix that has potential for a competitive intergroup relationship between leader(s) and followers, in which the leader has most of the power. Although the seeds of autocracy are sown, they may not germinate. Intergroup boundaries may be considered permeable, and the relationship may still be construed as a mutually beneficial role relationship in the service of superordinate, non-zero-sum goals—everyone is on the same team, working for the same goals, but making different contributions to the greater good of the group. The leader may not be "one of us," but he or she is certainly working with us, and for us.

However, there are circumstances that may make potential power-based intergroup behavior a reality. A relatively inevitable consequence of role differentiation is that the leader gradually realizes that he or she is effectively treated by followers as an outgroup member—a positive high-status deviant, but nonetheless a deviant who cannot readily share in the life of the group. The leader may at this point try to veer away from the abyss by engaging in behaviors aimed at confirming his or her ingroup prototypicality. If this is unsuccessful, a sense of rejection by, and distance and isolation from, the group may arise (possibly also a recognition of reduced influence among followers). This may "embitter" the leader and, since the empathic bond just mentioned is severed, allows the leader to gain compliance through the exercise of power over others. This may involve coercive behavior, because the interests of the leader and the group have diverged— the leader is effectively exercising his or her will over others. The influence process is one that involves coercion rather than attitude change.

This effect is stronger in hierarchical extremist groups where the leader–follower role and power differentiation is more tangible, stark, and impermeable—the potential for coercion is much accentuated in these types of groups. The effect will also be stronger in groups where there is a leadership clique rather than a single leader, because a typical intergroup relationship has effectively emerged and thus the relationship between leader(s) and followers is an intergroup relationship where one group (the leader[s]) has disproportionate legitimate power over the other group (the followers). Such a relationship will be competitive and potentially exploitative—far removed from prototype-based leadership.

Leaders generally react negatively to perceived threats to their leadership position. Where a leader is prototypically influential and no intergroup differentiation has yet emerged, threats to leadership largely come from prototype slippage—social contextual factors may reconfigure the group prototype and thus reduce the leader's prototypicality. We described previously how leaders then strive to redefine the prototype to better fit themselves—they can accentuate the existing ingroup prototype, pillory ingroup deviants, or demonize an appropriate outgroup. These tactics generally do not involve coercion. However, where an intergroup differentiation is clearly evident, threats to leadership are automatically perceived in intergroup terms as collective challenge/revolt on the part of the followers. This makes salient the latent intergroup orientation between leader(s) and followers, and engenders competitive intergroup relations between leader(s) and followers—competitive relations in which one group has consensually legitimate and overwhelming power over the other. Under these circumstances leadership becomes coercion, based on the relatively limitless exercise of coercive power over others. The dynamic is similar to the way in which a power elite "reacts" to a perceived challenge to its privileged position (e.g., Wright, 1997), but because it occurs within the power-legitimizing framework of a common group membership the "reaction" is potentially all the more extreme.

Let us recap on the argument. There is a series of steps that may transform prototype-based leadership into power-based leadership. Highly prototypical leaders of salient groups, particularly newly emerged leaders, provide leadership through influence—they do not need to exercise power over followers, and indeed may not actually be able to behave in this way. Enduring tenure renders leaders more influential and facilitates normative innovation—leaders still do not need to exercise power over followers because they now have the capacity to ensure that they remain prototypical and thus influential. Further tenure differentiates the leader(s) from the followers. It creates an intergroup differentiation based on widening, reified and consensually legitimized role and power differences—the potential to use power is now very real. The conditions that translate the potential into reality are ones that make salient the latent power-based intergroup relationship between leaders and followers—for example, a sense of threat to one's leadership position, a feeling of remoteness and alienation from the group, or a sense of becoming less influential in the life of the group.

The exercise of leadership through coercion rests on the psychological reality (based on self-categorization and social identity processes) of a sharp role, status, and power discontinuity between leaders(s) and followers that reconfigures cooperative intragroup role relations as competitive intergroup relations. Such intergroup relations within a group provide ideal conditions for unilaterally exploitative intergroup behavior. This is because the overarching common group identity and the diachronic process of leadership emergence legitimize the status quo—there exists what social identity theory refers to as a social change belief structure without cognitive alternatives (Tajfel & Turner, 1986; also see Hogg & Abrams, 1988). Because power and leadership are attractive to some people, this belief system can be coupled with a belief in intergroup permeability that encourages followers to try to gain admittance to the leadership clique—this, of course, marshals support for the leader(s) and prevents the followers from forming a united front in opposition to the leader.

The transformation of prototype-based leadership into power-based leadership is not inevitable. Leadership through influence is psychologically and materially less costly all around—it may be much better for the group. However, the challenge is that it is the group, not the leader, that has to take the initiative in arranging conditions that limit power, and yet the group is relatively powerless in the face of a leader who is wielding power in oppressive ways. Nevertheless, anything that inhibits the attribution of charisma and the process of structural differentiation, and which re-grounds leadership in prototypicality will inhibit the exercise of power. This may include quite contrasting conditions—on the one hand, reduced group cohesion, reduced prototype consensuality, and increased diversity, and on the other hand any external group threat that refocuses attention on common group identity. Although the natural course of intergroup relations may create these conditions, powerful leaders can protect themselves to some extent against them. The processes may be complicated. For example, if a group becomes less cohesive, more diverse, and less consensual about its prototype, it is less likely that followers will agree on and endorse the same person as the leader. The leader's power base is fragmented, and numerous new "contenders" emerge. Although this limits the leader's ability to exercise power, it is a threatening state of affairs, particularly for a leader who has been accustomed to exercising power— powerful incumbent leaders are likely to "react" in draconian ways.

External threat can make the group so cohesive and consensual that leader and group become re-fused and the empathic bond re-established— the leader no longer needs, or indeed is able, to exercise power, partic- ularly in destructive ways. External threat may also focus the group on promotively interdependent goals, with the consequence that followers do not grant status to leaders unless leaders earn such status through an appro- priate perceived contribution to group goal achievement (e.g., Ridgeway, 2001; Ridgeway & Diekema, 1989). Leaders who exercise power in order to mis-appropriate a share of rewards will face a resistant coalition of followers. Coercion becomes a less effective or viable form of leader- ship—leaders need to reposition themselves to act as prototypical group members who, through being prototypical, contribute more to the group's goals than do less prototypical followers.

SUMMARY AND CONCLUSIONS

After many years in the wilderness, leadership has once again become a topic of interest for social psychologists. This new interest has largely been spurred by conceptual advances in social cognition and social identity, and by growing synergies between social cognition, social identity, and organizational psychology. Scholars have become concerned that current leadership theories are inadequately grounded in an analysis of the role of group membership. The social identity theory of leadership described in this chapter goes some way towards addressing this concern.

The key point of the social identity analysis is that because leadership is a group process, leadership effectiveness becomes increasingly based on the group prototypicality of the leader, as group membership becomes psychologically more salient. In other words, in salient groups in which people feel a strong sense of belonging, effective leaders are group mem- bers who are perceived to have a good fit to the prototypical properties of the group. Under these circumstances there is a tendency for consensual depersonalized attraction for the leader, and also for the construction of a charismatic leadership personality for the leader, to occur. Together these processes allow the leader to be innovative, and influential in motivating followers to exert effort on behalf of group goals rather than individual goals.

There is reasonably good direct empirical support for the hypothesized role of prototypicality in leadership (I briefly described some studies), and some support for the role of social attraction. Further research is required to explore the attribution dynamic that constructs charisma, and to explore the limits of charisma in leadership.

I finished the chapter by describing some extensions and applications. In particular, how the theory can help explain the glass ceiling effect, leadership processes in merged organizations, and the leadership effectiveness of different leader–member relations. I spent more time describing a social identity analysis of the relationship between leadership and power. This extension, which sticks closely to a social identity perspective, views group leadership as a complex interplay of prototypicality processes and intergroup processes operating between and within groups.

REFERENCES

Abrams, D., & Hogg, M. A. (1990). Social identification, self-categorization and social influence. *European Review of Social Psychology, 1,* 195–228.

Abrams, D., & Hogg, M. A. (1998). Prospects for research in group processes and intergroup relations. *Group Processes and Intergroup Relations, 1,* 7–20.

Abrams, D., & Hogg, M. A. (Eds.). (1999). *Social identity and social cognition.* Oxford, UK: Blackwell.

Abrams, D., & Hogg, M. A. (2001). Collective identity: Group membership and self-conception. In M. A. Hogg & R. S. Tindale (Eds.), *Blackwell handbook of social psychology: Group processes* (pp. 425–460). Oxford, UK: Blackwell.

Bales, R. F. (1950). *Interaction process analysis: A method for the study of small groups.* Reading, MA: Addison-Wesley.

Bass, B. M. (1985). *Leadership and performance beyond expectations.* New York: Free Press.

Bass, B. M. (1990a). *Bass and Stogdill's handbook of leadership: Theory, research and managerial applications.* New York: The Free Press.

Bass, B. M. (1990b). From transactional to transformational leadership: Learning to share the vision. *Organizational Dynamics, 18,* 19–31.

Bass, B. M. (1998). *Transformational leadership: Industrial, military, and educational impact.* Mahwah, NJ: Lawrence Erlbaum Associates.

Bass, B. M., & Avolio, B. J. (1993). Transformational leadership: A response to critiques. In M. M. Chemers, & R. A. Ayman (Eds.), *Leadership theory and research: Perspectives and directions* (pp. 49–80). London: Academic Press.

Berscheid, E., & Reis, H. T. (1998). Attraction and close relationships. In D. T. Gilbert, S. T. Fiske, & G. Lindzey (Eds.), *The handbook of social psychology* (4th ed., Vol. 2, pp. 193–281). New York: McGraw-Hill.

Bryman, A. (1992). *Charisma and leadership in organizations.* London: Sage.

Burns, J. M. (1978). *Leadership.* New York: Harper & Row.

Cartwright, D., & Zander, A. (Eds.) (1968). *Group dynamics: Research and theory* (3rd ed.). London: Tavistock.

Cartwright, S., & Cooper, C. L. (1992). The impact of mergers and acquisitions on people at work: Existing research and issues. *British Journal of Management, 1,* 65–76.

Chemers, M. M. (2001). Leadership effectiveness: An integrative review. In M. A. Hogg & R. S. Tindale (Eds.), *Blackwell handbook of social psychology: Group processes* (pp. 376–399). Oxford, UK: Blackwell.

Conger, J. A., & Kanungo, R. N. (1987). Towards a behavioral theory of charismatic leadership in organizational settings. *Academy of Management Review, 12,* 637–647.

Conger, J. A., & Kanungo, R. N. (1988). Behavioral dimensions of charismatic leadership. In J. A. Conger & R. N. Kanungo (Eds.), *Charismatic leadership: The elusive factor on organizational effectiveness.* San Francisco, CA: Jossey-Bass.

de Cremer, D. (2002). Charismatic leadership and cooperation in social dilemmas: A matter of transforming motives? *Journal of Applied Social Psychology, 32,* 997–1016.

Devine, P. G., Hamilton, D. L., & Ostrom, T. M. (Eds.). (1994). *Social cognition: Impact on social psychology.* San Diego, CA: Academic Press.

Duck, J. M., & Fielding, K. S. (1999). Leaders and sub-groups: One of us or one of them? *Group Processes and Intergroup Relations, 2,* 203–230.

Eagly, A. H., Karau, S. J., & Makhijani, M. G. (1995). Gender and the effectiveness of leaders: A meta-analysis. *Psychological Bulletin, 117,* 125–145.

Erber, R., & Fiske, S. T. (1984). Outcome dependency and attention to inconsistent information. *Journal of Personality and Social Psychology, 47,* 709–726.

Fiedler, F. E. (1965). A contingency model of leadership effectiveness. In L. Berkowitz (Ed.), *Advances in experimental social psychology* (Vol.1, pp. 149–190) New York: Academic Press.

Fiedler, F. E. (1971). *Leadership.* Morristown, NJ: General Learning Press.

Fielding, K. S., & Hogg, M. A. (1997). Social identity, self-categorization, and leadership: A field study of small interactive groups. *Group Dynamics: Theory, Research, and Practice, 1,* 39–51.

Fiske, S. T. (1993). Controlling other people: The impact of power on stereotyping. *American Psychologist, 48,* 621–628.

Fiske, S. T., & Dépret, E. (1996). Control, interdependence and power: Understanding social cognition in its social context. *European Review of Social Psychology, 7,* 31–61.

Fiske, S. T., & Taylor, S. E. (1991). *Social cognition* (2nd ed.). New York: McGraw-Hill.

Foddy, M., & Hogg M. A. (1999). Impact of leaders on resource consumption in social dilemmas: The intergroup context. In M. Foddy, M. Smithson, S. Schneider, & M. A. Hogg (Eds.), *Resolving social dilemmas: Dynamic, structural, and intergroup aspects* (pp. 309–330). Philadelphia, PA: Psychology Press.

Gilbert, D. T., Fiske, S. T., & Lindzey, G. (Eds.). (1998). *The handbook of social psychology* (4th ed.). New York: McGraw-Hill.

Gilbert, D. T., & Jones, E. E. (1986). Perceiver-induced constraint: Interpretations of self-generated reality. *Journal of Personality and Social Psychology, 50,* 269–280.

Gilbert, D. T., & Malone, P. S. (1995). The correspondence bias. *Psychological Bulletin, 117,* 21–38.

Glick, P., & Fiske, S. T. (1996). The Ambivalent Sexism Inventory: Differentiating hostile and benevolent sexism. *Journal of Personality and Social Psychology, 70,* 491–512.

Graen, G. B., & Uhl-Bien, M. (1995). Relationship-based approach to leadership: Development of leader-member exchange (LMX) theory of leadership over 25 years: Applying a multi-level multi-domain approach. *Leadership Quarterly, 6,* 219–247.

Hains, S. C., Hogg, M. A., & Duck, J. M. (1997). Self-categorization and leadership: Effects of group prototypicality and leader stereotypicality. *Personality and Social Psychology Bulletin, 23,* 1087–1100.

Hall, R. J., & Lord, R. G. (1995). Multi-level information processing explanations of followers' leadership perceptions. *Leadership Quarterly, 6,* 265–287.

Haslam, S. A. (2000). *Psychology in organisations: The social identity approach.* London: Sage.

Haslam, S. A., McGarty, C., Brown, P. M., Eggins, R. A., Morrison, B. E., & Reynolds, K. J. (1998). Inspecting the emperor's clothes: Evidence that random selection of leaders can enhance group performance. *Group Dynamics: Theory, Research, and Practice, 2,* 168–184.

Haslam, S. A., Oakes, P. J., McGarty, C., Turner, J. C., & Onorato, S. (1995). Contextual changes in the prototypicality of extreme and moderate outgroup members. *European Journal of Social Psychology, 25,* 509–530.

Haslam, S. A., & Platow, M. J. (2001). Your wish is our command: The role of shared social identity in translating a leader's vision into followers' action. In M. A. Hogg & D. J. Terry (Eds.), *Social identity processes in organizational contexts* (pp. 213–228). Philadelphia, PA: Psychology Press.

Haslam, S. A., van Knippenberg, D., Platow, M., & Ellemers, N. (Eds.). (2003). *Social identity at work: Developing theory for organizational practice.* New York: Psychology Press.

Hogg, M. A. (1992). *The social psychology of group cohesiveness: From attraction to social identity.* New York: New York University Press.

Hogg, M. A. (1993). Group cohesiveness: A critical review and some new directions. *European Review of Social Psychology, 4,* 85–111.

Hogg, M. A. (1996). Intragroup processes, group structure and social identity. In W. P. Robinson (Ed.), *Social groups and identities: Developing the legacy of Henri Tajfel* (pp. 65–93). Oxford, UK: Butterworth-Heinemann.

Hogg, M. A. (2001a). A social identity theory of leadership. *Personality and Social Psychology Review, 5,* 184–200.

Hogg, M. A. (2001b). From prototypicality to power: A social identity analysis of leadership. In S. R. Thye, E. J. Lawler, M. W. Macy, & H. A. Walker (Eds.), *Advances in group processes* (Vol. 18, pp. 1–30). Oxford, UK: Elsevier.

Hogg, M. A. (2001c). Social identification, group prototypicality, and emergent leadership. In M. A. Hogg & D. J. Terry (Eds.), *Social identity processes in organizational contexts* (pp. 197–212). Philadelphia, PA: Psychology Press.

Hogg, M. A. (2001d). Social categorization, depersonalization, and group behavior. In M. A. Hogg & R. S. Tindale (Eds.), *Blackwell handbook of social psychology: Group processes* (pp. 56–85). Oxford, UK: Blackwell.

Hogg, M. A. (2003). Social identity. In M. R. Leary & J. P. Tangney (Eds.), *Handbook of self and identity* (pp. 462–479). New York: Guilford.

Hogg, M. A., & Abrams, D. (1988). *Social identifications: A social psychology of intergroup relations and group processes.* London: Routledge.

Hogg, M. A., Cooper-Shaw, L., & Holzworth, D. W. (1993). Group prototypicality and depersonalized attraction in small interactive groups. *Personality and Social Psychology Bulletin, 19,* 452–465.

Hogg, M. A., Fielding, K. S., Johnston, D., Masser, B., Russell, E., & Svensson, A. (2001). *On glass ceilings and demographic disadvantage: Social identity and leadership in small groups.* Unpublished manuscript, University of Queensland, Centre for Research on Group Processes.

Hogg, M. A., & Hains, S. C. (1996). Intergroup relations and group solidarity: Effects of group identification and social beliefs on depersonalized attraction. *Journal of Personality and Social Psychology, 70,* 295–309.

Hogg, M. A., & Hains, S. C. (1998). Friendship and group identification: A new look at the role of cohesiveness in groupthink. *European Journal of Social Psychology, 28,* 323–341.

Hogg, M. A., Hains, S. C., & Mason, I. (1998). Identification and leadership in small groups: Salience, frame of reference, and leader stereotypicality effects on leader evaluations. *Journal of Personality and Social Psychology, 75,* 1248–1263.

Hogg, M. A., & Hardie, E. A. (1991). Social attraction, personal attraction and self-categorization: A field study. *Personality and Social Psychology Bulletin, 17,* 175–180.

Hogg, M. A., Hardie, E. A., & Reynolds, K. (1995). Prototypical similarity, self-categorization, and depersonalized attraction: A perspective on group cohesiveness. *European Journal of Social Psychology, 25,* 159–177.

Hogg, M. A., & Hornsey, M. J. (in press). Self-concept threat and differentiation within groups. In R. J. Crisp & M. Hewstone (Eds.), *Multiple social categorization: Processes, models, and applications.* New York: Psychology Press.

Hogg, M. A., & Martin, R. (2003). Social identity analysis of leader-member relations: Reconciling self-categorization and leader-member exchange theories of leadership. In S. A. Haslam, D. van Knippenberg, M. Platow, & N. Ellemers (Eds.), *Social identity at work: Developing theory for organizational practice* (pp. 139–156). New York: Psychology Press.

Hogg, M. A., Martin, R., Epitropaki, O., Mankad, A. Svensson, A., & Weeden, K. (in press). Effective leadership in salient groups: Revisiting leader-member exchange theory from the perspective of the social identity theory of leadership. *Personality and Social Psychology Bulletin.*

Hogg, M. A., Martin, R., & Weeden, K. (2004). Leader-member relations and social identity. In D. van Knippenberg & M. A. Hogg (Eds.), *Leadership and power: Identity processes in groups and organizations* (pp. 18–33). London: Sage.

Hogg, M. A., & Reid, S. A. (2001). Social identity, leadership, and power. In A. Y. Lee-Chai & J. A. Bargh (Eds.), *The use and abuse of power: Multiple perspectives on the causes of corruption* (pp. 159–180). Philadelphia, PA: Psychology Press.

Hogg, M. A., & Terry, D. J. (2000). Social identity and self-categorization processes in organizational contexts. *Academy of Management Review, 25,* 121–140.

Hogg, M. A., & Terry, D. J. (Eds.). (2001). *Social identity processes in organizational contexts.* Philadelphia, PA: Psychology Press.

Hogg, M. A., & Turner, J. C. (1987). Social identity and conformity: A theory of referent informational influence. In W. Doise & S. Moscovici (Eds.), *Current issues in European social psychology* (Vol. 2, pp. 139–182). Cambridge, UK: Cambridge University Press.

Hogg, M. A., & van Knippenberg, D. (2003). Social identity and leadership processes in groups. In M. P. Zanna (Ed.), *Advances in experimental social psychology* (Vol. 35, pp. 1–52). San Diego, CA: Academic Press.

Hollander, E. P. (1958). Conformity, status, and idiosyncrasy credit. *Psychological Review, 65,* 117–127.

Hollander, E. P. (1985). Leadership and power. In G. Lindzey & E. Aronson (Eds.), *The handbook of social psychology* (3rd ed.., Vol. 2, pp. 485–537). New York: Random House.

Hornsey, M. J., & Hogg, M. A. (2000). Assimilation and diversity: An integrative model of subgroup relations. *Personality and Social Psychology Review, 4,* 143–156.

Levine, J. M., & Moreland, R. L. (1990). Progress in small group research. *Annual Review of Psychology, 41,* 585–634.

Levine, J. M., & Moreland, R. L. (1995). Group processes. In A. Tesser (Ed.), *Advanced social psychology* (pp. 419–465). New York: McGraw-Hill.

Lippitt, R., & White, R. (1943). The "social climate" of children's groups. In R. G. Barker, J. Kounin, & H. Wright (Eds.), *Child behavior and development* (pp. 485–508). New York: McGraw-Hill.

Lord, R. G., Brown, D. J., & Harvey, J. L. (2001). System constraints on leadership perceptions, behavior and influence: An example of connectionist level processes. In M. A. Hogg & R. S. Tindale (Eds.), *Blackwell handbook of social psychology: Group processes* (pp. 283–310). Oxford, UK: Blackwell.

Lord, R. G., Foti, R. J., & DeVader, C. L. (1984). A test of leadership categorization theory: Internal structure, information processing, and leadership perceptions. *Organizational Behavior and Human Performance, 34,* 343–378.

Marques, J. M., Abrams, D., Páez, D., & Hogg, M. A. (2001). Social categorization, social identification, and rejection of deviant group members. In M. A. Hogg & R. S. Tindale, (Eds.), *Blackwell handbook of social psychology: Group processes* (pp. 400–424). Oxford, UK: Blackwell.

McGrath, J. E. (1997). Small group research, that once and future field: An interpretation of the past with an eye to the future. *Group Dynamics: Theory, Research, and Practice, 1,* 7–27.

Meindl, J. R., Ehrlich, S. B., & Dukerich, J. M. (1985). The romance of leadership. *Administrative Science Quarterly, 30,* 78–102.

Moreland, R. L., Hogg, M. A., & Hains, S. C. (1994). Back to the future: Social psychological research on groups. *Journal of Experimental Social Psychology, 30,* 527–555.

Mowday, R. T., & Sutton, R. I. (1993). Organizational behavior: Linking individuals and groups to organizational contexts. *Annual Review of Psychology, 44,* 195–229.

Pawar, B. S., & Eastman, K. (1997). The nature and implications of contextual influences on transformational leadership. *Academy of Management Review, 22,* 80–109.

Platow, M. J., Hoar, S., Reid, S. A., Harley, K., & Morrison, D. (1997). Endorsement of distributively fair and unfair leaders in interpersonal and intergroup situations. *European Journal of Social Psychology, 27,* 465–494.

Platow, M. J., Reid, S. A., & Andrew, S. (1998). Leadership endorsement: The role of distributive and procedural behavior in interpersonal and intergroup contexts. *Group Processes and Intergroup Relations, 1,* 35–47.

Reicher, S. D., Drury, J., Hopkins, N., & Stott, C. (in press). A model of crowd prototypes and crowd leaders. In C. Barker (Ed.), *Leadership and social movements.* Manchester, UK: Manchester University Press.

Reicher, S. D., & Hopkins, N. (1996). Self-category constructions in political rhetoric: An analysis of Thatcher's and Kinnock's speeches concerning the British miners' strike (1984–5). *European Journal of Social Psychology, 26,* 353–371.

Ridgeway, C. L. (2001). Social status and group structure. In M. A. Hogg & R. S. Tindale (Eds.), *Blackwell handbook of social psychology: Group processes* (pp. 352–375). Oxford, UK: Blackwell.

Ridgeway, C. L., & Diekema, D. (1989). Dominance and collective hierarchy formation in male and female task groups. *American Sociological Review, 54,* 79–93.

Ross, L. (1977). The intuitive psychologist and his shortcomings. In L. Berkowitz (Ed.), *Advances in experimental social psychology* (Vol. 10, pp. 174–220). New York: Academic Press.

Sanna, L. J., & Parks, C. D. (1997). Group research trends in social and organizational psychology: Whatever happened to intragroup research? *Psychological Science, 8,* 261–267.

Sedikides, C., & Brewer, M. B. (Eds.). (2001). *Individual self, relational self, collective self* (pp. 123–143). Philadelphia, PA: Psychology Press.

Shaw, M. E. (1981). *Group dynamics: The psychology of small group behavior* (2nd ed.). New York: McGraw-Hill.

Sherif, M. (1966). *In common predicament: Social psychology of intergroup conflict and cooperation.* Boston, MA: Houghton-Mifflin

Smith, E. R., Coats, S., & Walling, D. (1999). Overlapping mental representations of self, ingroup, and partner: Further response time evidence and a connectionist model. *Personality and Social Psychology Bulletin, 25,* 873–882.

Smith, E., & Henry, S. (1996). An in-group becomes part of the self: Response time evaluation. *Personality and Social Psychology Bulletin, 22,* 635–642.

Steiner, I. D. (1974). Whatever happened to the group in social psychology? *Journal of Experimental Social Psychology, 10,* 94–108.

Steiner, I. D. (1986). Paradigms and groups. *Advances in Experimental Social Psychology, 19,* 251–289.

Stogdill, R. (1974). *Handbook of leadership.* New York: Free Press.

Tajfel, H., & Turner, J. C. (1986). The social identity theory of intergroup behavior. In S. Worchel & W. Austin (Eds.), *Psychology of intergroup relations* (pp. 7–24). Chicago: Nelson-Hall.

Taylor, S. E., & Fiske, S. T. (1975). Point-of-view and perceptions of causality. *Journal of Personality and Social Psychology, 32,* 439–445.

Taylor, S. E., & Fiske, S. T. (1978). Salience, attention, and attribution: Top of the head phenomena. In L. Berkowitz (Ed.), *Advances in experimental social psychology* (Vol. 11, pp. 249–288). New York: Academic Press.

Terry, D. J., & Callan, V. J. (1998). In-group bias in response to an organizational merger. *Group Dynamics, 2,* 67–81.

Terry, D. J., Carey, C. J., & Callan, V. J. (2001). Employee adjustment to an organizational merger: An intergroup perspective. *Personality and Social Psychology Bulletin, 27,* 267–280.

Tindale, R. S., & Anderson, E. M. (1998). Small group research and applied social psychology: An introduction. In R. S. Tindale, L. Heath, J. Edwards, E. J. Posavac, F. B. Bryant, Y. Suarez-Balcazar, E. Henderson-King, & J. Myer (Eds.), *Social psychological applications to social issues: Theory and research on small groups* (Vol. 4, pp. 1–8). New York: Plenum Press.

Trope, Y., & Liberman, A. (1993). The use of trait conceptions to identify other people's behavior and to draw inferences about their personalities. *Personality and Social Psychology Bulletin, 19,* 553–562.

Tropp, L. R., & Wright, S. C. (2001). Ingroup identification as inclusion of ingroup in the self. *Personality and Social Psychology Bulletin, 27,* 585–600.

Turner, J. C. (1982). Towards a cognitive redefinition of the social group. In H. Tajfel (Ed.), *Social identity and intergroup relations* (pp. 15–40). Cambridge, UK: Cambridge University Press.

Turner, J. C. (1991). *Social influence.* Buckingham, UK: Open University Press.

Turner, J. C., Hogg, M. A., Oakes, P. J., Reicher, S. D., & Wetherell, M. S. (1987). *Rediscovering the social group: A self-categorization theory.* Oxford, UK: Blackwell.

Turner, J. C., & Oakes, P. J. (1989). Self-categorization and social influence. In P. B. Paulus (Ed.), *The psychology of group influence* (2nd ed., pp. 233–275). Hillsdale, NJ: Lawrence Erlbaum Associates.

Tyler, T. R. (1997). The psychology of legitimacy: A relational perspective on voluntary deference to authorities. *Personality and Social Psychology Review, 1,* 323–345.

Tyler, T. R., & Lind, E. A. (1992). A relational model of authority in groups. In M. P. Zanna (Ed.), *Advances in experimental social psychology* (Vol. 25, pp. 115–191). New York: Academic Press.

van Knippenberg, D., & Hogg, M. A. (Eds.) (2001). *Social identity processes in organizations. (Special issue of Group Processes and Intergroup Relations, 4).* London: Sage.

van Knippenberg, D., & Hogg, M. A. (Eds.). (2004). *Leadership and power: Identity processes in groups and organizations.* London: Sage.

van Knippenberg, D., & van Leeuwen, E. (2001). Organizational identity after a merger. Sense of continuity as the key to post-merger identification. In M. A. Hogg & D. J. Terry (Eds.), *Social identity processes in organizational contexts* (pp. 265–282). Philadelphia, PA: Psychology Press.

Van Vugt, M., & de Cremer, D. (1999). Leadership in social dilemmas: The effects of group identification on collective actions to provide public goods. *Journal of Personality and Social Psychology, 76,* 587–599.

Wright, S. C. (1997). Ambiguity, social influence, and collective action: Generating collective protest in response to tokenism. *Personality and Social Psychology Bulletin, 23,* 1277–1290.

Wright, S. C., Aron, A., & Tropp, L. R. (2002). Including others (and groups) in the self: Self-expansion and intergroup relations. In J. P. Forgas & K. D. Williams (Eds.), *The social self: Cognitive, interpersonal, and intergroup perspectives* (pp. 343–363). New York: Psychology Press.

Yukl, G. (2002). *Leadership in organizations* (5th ed.). Upper Saddle River, NJ: Prentice-Hall.

4

On the Psychological Exchange Between Leaders and Followers

David M. Messick
Northwestern University

There are an almost infinite number of ways to study or think about the phenomenon of leadership. Some deal with the traits or personal qualities of leaders (in contrast to those of nonleaders), some deal with the skill sets of leaders, and other approaches examine the situations that elicit leadership. Approaches that focus on personal traits tend also to engage the question of how leaders are selected; approaches that focus on skills, on the other hand, tend to highlight the training of leaders; and those that feature the situational determinants of leadership focus on the specific tasks that leaders must master in order to lead. Some theories highlight leadership as the ability to execute tasks, to have the expertise to solve problems, while other theories focus on leadership as a set of interpersonal skills—the ability to influence people rather than work environments. And other theories ask not what constitutes leadership, but what are the characteristics that cause people to attribute leadership qualities to other people. Why do we *think* that some people are good leaders while others are not?

The ideas that I describe focus on leadership as the relationship between leaders and their followers. In this sense my ideas fall within the area of leadership theory that is called *leader–follower exchange*. But the ideas that I describe deal less with concrete behavioral exchanges between leaders and followers and more with the dimensions along which leaders and their followers provide support and gratifications for each other. The basic question this approach poses is why do people follow or allow themselves to be led? And why do people lead when leading is often costly, risky, or dangerous? The answer I offer to these questions is that there is a type of equilibrium that is established between leaders and followers that reflects incentives that both have to maintain their relationship. By focusing on the nature of this relationship, I also mean to imply that leadership and followership are roles that people can adopt when the conditions are auspicious. In contrast to theories that focus on individual traits, my approach implies that a person can be in a leadership position in one relationship (with her subordinates, for instance) and in a followership position in another (with her superior, for instance). In the outline that follows I sketch the major dimensions that I think maintain this psychological exchange between leaders and followers.

The heart of this idea is that followers follow because they get something from being followers. In other words, leaders provide some value that benefits followers. Followers respond in ways that benefit the leader. Thus, leaders and followers become linked in a mutually beneficial relationship through the exchange of benefits. I think that this exchange has at least five dimensions. These dimensions will vary in importance from situation to situation, and from person to person. I do not claim that they are all of equal importance or that any one of them is crucial in any particular situation. Let me begin by outlining the nature of the benefits that leaders give followers, and then I will discuss the reciprocal benefits that leaders get in return.

VISION AND DIRECTION

Leaders provide vision and direction to their followers. They provide answers to the questions, "Where are we going? What are our objectives? What are we trying to achieve?" In some cases these objectives are modest and concrete, but in others the vision is quite grand. Some authors (Collins & Porras, 1994) have described the vision as a *BHAG*, a "big, hairy, audacious, goal." It is a vision that says we are here to do more than meet our numbers or to pass the next inspection. We are here, in this group or organization, for a far grander purpose. So the vision not only provides a sense of direction, it can also provide "meaning," or an answer to the question, "Why are we here?"

Sometimes the vision is concrete, limited, and proximal. In military contexts, understanding the objective of a mission, to take a hill or to defend a passage, may be necessary to ensure that everyone will know what needs to be done by whom if the leader of the unit is disabled. In organizational contexts, leaders may make not only the broad goals clear to the members, but also the means of implementing the goals. The implementation is usually described in broad strokes rather than great detail. Room needs to be left to allow followers flexibility in implementation.

PROTECTION AND SECURITY

A second benefit that a leader can provide is security and protection for followers. This is an important function in military contexts and also in corporate and political domains. In extreme cases leaders can place themselves in harm's way to protect followers. Less extreme versions of this type of behavior can be seen when executives put their own careers in jeopardy to argue against laying off subordinates, or when political leaders take risks to protect the interests of their constituencies. In hostile environments, be they military or economic, leaders place their personal well-being at risk to shield their followers.

An interesting illustration of this principle occurs in the film *Bridge on the River Kwai* when Alec Guiness's character, British officer Colonel Nicholson, refuses to allow his men to take orders from the Japanese prison camp commander, Commander Saito. Nicholson first risks being shot in front of his men, and then endures days in a confined, sun-baked cage called the "oven," to protect his men and to defend his authority. His bravery was not lost on his captors, nor on his men.

Another element of protection is the design of a crew that has the skills and ability to complete a task, even if misfortune befalls it. A good illustration of attention to this detail is Roald Amundsen's selection of the men to go on his polar expedition in 1911. In his race to the South Pole, having the ability to navigate was critical. There had been controversy about priority in reaching the North Pole because of possible errors made by Perry in calculating precisely where he was. Amundsen, the indefatigable learner, understood that success meant having unimpugnable navigational readings. As a result, at least four of the five men he took with him to the Pole were experienced navigators. This meant that every reading could be independently taken by several different people, enhancing the group's certainty about their location.

ACHIEVEMENT AND EFFECTIVENESS

Through the completion of group or organizational tasks, leaders allow their followers to achieve goals that would be difficult or impossible to achieve by one person alone or by a group without the leader. The need to be effective is one of the frequently overlooked human motives. There are many goals that can only be attained through group or collective effort— economic prosperity by corporations, pleasant and livable neighborhoods by communities, or military victories by battalions, to name but a few. Leaders coordinate and orchestrate to make success real. Success leads to a sense of power and competence in followers, competence to achieve things that one alone could never accomplish.

There are many dimensions to this important aspect of leadership. One of the first that must be recognized is that leaders must be able to convince followers that difficult goals are achievable. This means not only that a plausible plan for goal achievement has to be outlined, but also that the leader must communicate his or her conviction that the plan is workable. This may be the single greatest achievement of Sir Ernest Shackleton in his doomed voyage on the *Endurance*. It is difficult to imagine the gloom that must have settled over the 28 crew members of the *Endurance* when the ship, lodged in the ice floes off the coast of Antarctica, was crushed. The men were thousands of miles from help, in a completely unknown location, and equipped with minimal gear for survival. When the ship was destroyed, Shackleton told his men that it was time to go home since their original goal of crossing Antarctica was now impossible. The problem was how to convince them that this was a realistic vision, something that they could actually achieve. Despite the bleak prospects for survival, Shackleton maintained the belief that they would come out of the ordeal intact. Indeed, Shackleton wrote, "Tonight the temperature had dropped to −16 degrees Fahr., and most of the men are cold and uncomfortable. After the tents had been pitched I mustered all hands and explained the position to them briefly and, I hope, clearly. I have told them the distance to the Barrier and the distance to Paulet Island, and have stated that I propose to try to march with equipment across the ice in the direction of Paulet Island. I thanked the men for the steadiness and good *morale* they have shown in these trying circumstances, and told them I had no doubt that, provided they continued to work their utmost and to trust me, we will all reach safety in the end" (Shackleton, 1999, p. 84). The men trusted his ability to plan, his physical strength and tenacity, and his dedication to keeping them alive. They knew that he could change tactics quickly if circumstances required it (as indeed they did when the march to Paulet Island proved impossible). Shackleton wrote, "The task was to secure the safety of the party, and to that I must bend my energies and mental power and apply every bit of knowledge that experience of the Antarctic had given me. The task was likely to be long and strenuous, and an ordered mind and a clear program were essential if we were to come through without a loss of life. A man must shape himself to a new mark directly the old one goes to ground" (1999, p. 85). He must have a plan but be willing to change it. Shackleton himself remained optimistic. For months he fostered the assurance that they would eventually prevail and return home. It is one of the truly astounding feats of leadership in this or any century that Shackleton convinced his men that they could achieve the impossible. He convinced them because he himself believed it. And in the end they did achieve the impossible. Shackleton did not lose a single man.

An important ingredient in instilling the will to achieve in followers is optimism. This is a feature that has been noted by many scholars who have written about leadership. Perkins (2000), for instance, in writing about Shackleton's adventure, notes how Shackleton not only instilled optimism in himself but also how he fostered a spirit of optimism in his men. The optimism not only maintained the belief that they could eventually survive and return home, but it also improved the mood of the men and made their lives more pleasant and bearable, thereby increasing the chances of success.

INCLUSION AND BELONGINGNESS

Humans are one of the most social species known. We have long periods of infant dependency during which we would die without care and protection. We, as a species, are programmed to provide this protection. Were we not, we would not have survived. To put it somewhat differently, those in our ancestral prehistory who did not tend their children did not leave the offspring of which we are all the descendents. We have powerful needs to be members of groups and to enjoy human contact. Leaders include followers as valued members of groups and organizations, be they groups, families, nations, corporations, or universities. Our sociality is a fact that is often overlooked by leaders.

I think it is important to recall that among the early settlers in North America, one of the most severe forms of punishment for people who violated the norms of the community was ostracism, the practice of treating people as if they did not exist. Modern versions of this practice are called "shunning"or being given the silent treatment. Allowing people to be a member of a group is to permit them to share vicarious pleasures of others' successes. We all experience a satisfaction when the strangers who represent *our* team are victorious over the strangers who are *their* team. Who *we* and *they* are can change from situation to situation. Today it may be *my* university against *theirs*. Tomorrow it could be *my* Olympic team against *theirs*. And the following day it could be *my* neighborhood against *theirs*. But the underlying psychology remains the same. People want to belong, and good leaders provide inclusion.

PRIDE AND SELF-RESPECT

The final benefit that leaders afford their followers is a sense of pride and self-respect. This benefit derives partly from the other dimensions that I have already described; from acheivement, from belonging to a valued group, or from knowing what one is working toward. However, I think there is an independent contribution that comes from being treated like a valuable person, from being respected and entrusted to undertake challenging jobs. Leaders can make their followers feel respected as individuals, and trusted as group members who can cause a team or organization to succeed or fail. In other words, good leaders make the followers feel important as individuals, and they make them feel important because good leaders make the followers important. What I am talking about is not deception, it is about empowerment and it is about empowerment at an individual level.

I can illustrate this point with a couple of examples. First, in their book about Shackleton's leadership style, Morrell and Capparell (2001) highlight the following characteristics. Shackleton allowed his men to put their individual stamp on the immediate surroundings (when he decided that the dogs should live in shelters off the *Endurance* he allowed the men to create "dogloos" for their dogs and some created quite elaborate frozen steeples on these structures; p. 114); he made sure everyone had meaningful work to do; he gave individual feedback in terms of praise or corrections; and he treated each of his men as a human being, not just a worker. This, of course, meant that he had to know his men individually and to know them well.

A second illustration comes from Abrashoff's (2001) description of how he changed the climate of the U.S.S. *Benfold* when he took command of the destroyer. As he tells the story, the situation on the *Benfold* was disastrous: low morale, high turnover, and poor performance. One of the extraordinary steps that Abrashoff took was to interview each sailor on the ship personally and ask each why he or she had joined the Navy, where they had come from, what they liked about their work, and what they did not like about it. Furthermore, he made his crew feel important because he made them important. "I vowed to treat every encounter with every person on the ship as the most important thing in my world at that moment" (p. 138). Abrashoff recognizes that treating people with respect not only changes followers, it also changes the leader. "Getting to know someone as an individual prevents you from zoning out when they're talking. It forces you to listen. You can't ignore or shut down people you know and respect" (p. 139).

It seems obvious that followers gain a great deal from their leaders. They get direction, security, empowerment, inclusion, and pride. But what do leaders get in return from followers? One of the keys to understanding the flip side of this exchange is to grasp the fact that leaders' goals are group goals. The leader wants to achieve something that only the team, group, or organization can achieve. The person in the leadership role may have personal ambitions, to be sure, but that person understands that personal success is attained via the success of the organization or group or team.

My hypothesis is that in each of the dimensions on which leaders provide benefits for followers, followers reciprocate by providing benefits to the leader and advancing the leader toward his or her goal. I do not think of this exchange as a *quid pro quo* in which people sit down and legalistically work out the terms of an agreement about who gets how much of what. I see the exchange as emerging from natural social psychological processes in a more or less uncalculated, spontaneous, and unpremeditated fashion. The psychological exchange is the *result* of someone taking on leadership responsibilities, but it is not the *goal* of such a step. With this said, I will outline what I think leaders get from followers.

FOCUS AND SELF-DIRECTION

For the vision and direction that is provided by leaders, in exchange they get followers who know where to go, what they are there for, and the ability to govern themselves without external monitoring and surveillance.

Part of what happens here is that people (followers) internalize the goals of the leader and become able to pursue these goals on their own. Often this also entails the internalization of the culture of an organization, the values and norms that characterize a group or organization's beliefs about itself. This alignment of individual and leaders' (groups or organizations) goals is a huge benefit for the groups being represented by leaders.

In military operations, this dimension of the exchange is of crucial importance. What happens to a unit if the leader is injured or killed? If the members of the unit were totally dependent on the leader for orders and instructions, the unit would falter or halt when the leader disappears. So what is essential is that everyone knows what the mission is and what the lines of succession are. If the leader fails, who is next in the chain of command? If everyone knows their job, they can execute it without the supervision of the leader. In this way, good leadership seems to make itself unnecessary.

Abrashoff (2001) offers a vivid illustration of this point. During a technical inspection on the *Benfold,* the ship was to leave the dock. This is a high-risk event. Lots of things can happen, and most of them are bad (like running into another ship or a dock). Because of the risk, the commander is typically on the bridge guiding the the ship safely out of harbor. Abrashoff describes a crucial inspection when he stayed below with a senior inspector while his most junior officer moved the ship to sea. His conviction was that if he had done his job properly, his crew could safely get the ship away and he could deal with the inspector. Although he describes himself as "a nervous wreck" during this operation, his understanding of leadership was profound. He knew (hoped) that his crew could take the ship out without him.

GRATITUDE AND LOYALTY

One of the most fundamental axioms of social behavior has been called the norm of reciprocity—you scratch my back and I'll scratch yours. When a leader provides protection and security to followers, the followers generally know it and feel themselves to be under an obligation to reciprocate. The form of this reciprocation is through gratitude and loyalty. The obligation, I repeat, is not a legalistic obligation. It is experienced as a moral or personal obligation to the protector. Gratitude we may experience towards favors of all sorts; it is a special type of gratitude we feel toward those who have shielded us from harm. We owe those people loyalty.

The importance of reciprocity, for humans as well as other species, has been appreciated by social scientists for decades. Trivers (1971) made it a central pillar of a theory of cooperation. The basic idea is that people (organisms) who are willing to provide (costly) aid to others who would be willing to aid them, will do better, on average, than people (organisms) who decline such aid. One important cue to another's willingness to provide aid is if that person has provided aid in the past. The provision of protection is a type of aid that places the protector in the category of "people for whom reciprocal aid is merited." When the protector is a leader, the reciprocation is loyalty.

The phenomenon of reciprocity is a basic part of human social nature. However, it has different layers that are important in understanding leadership. Let me illustrate with an incident that occurred in 2001 while I was leaving Victoria Falls in Zimbabwe to fly back to Johannesburg, South Africa. I was with a group of MBA students who had been told and reminded that there was a departure tax of US$20 required to leave Zimbabwe. Only foreign currency was acceptable to pay this exit tax. All the students had the money ready. However, as I was passing through customs, when we had to display the receipt for the tax, a couple (of strangers) in the line in front of me were quite agitated and engaged in an emotional confrontation with the customs officer. One of the tourists turned to me and explained that they had no foreign cash, only the Zimbabwe dollars that the cash machine dispensed, and that credit cards were not acceptable for the exit tax. They could see no way to leave the country and make their flight, which was the same one on which we were booked. Then one of the distraught tourists asked, "Would you loan us $40 until we get to Johannesburg when we can repay you?" Knowing that my risk was at most $40, I gave them the money and said I expected to see them when we arrived in Johannesburg airport. They thanked me sincerely, paid the customs agent, and went to the bar to use their Zimbabwe dollars.

We left Zimbabwe and arrived in Johannesburg an hour or so later. I was involved with some of the students retrieving our luggage when the gentleman from the customs incident came up to me with the money. "You are the fellow who loaned us the departure money in Vic Falls aren't you?" he asked. I acknowledged that I was and he gave me the $40 back. "You saved us from an ugly situation," he said, "and we are deeply grateful. Furthermore, if I am ever in the position to help another in this kind of situation I will surely do it." I believe that he will do it. This type of reciprocity is called "generalized reciprocity" which refers to the fact that the "downstream" beneficiary may not be the same person as the upstream initiator.

COMMITMENT AND EFFORT

When leaders allow their followers to achieve important goals, their followers come to believe that hard work and effort can bring about positive effects. The levels of commitment and effort become enhanced because people feel that the work pays off. Nothing dampens effort like the belief that effort is futile and doomed to failure. By providing group members with the sense that they can achieve difficult goals and succeed in challenging endeavors, leaders motivate followers to work hard, to put in the hours, and to make the commitment to accomplish goals because the followers believe that success will be the result of their efforts.

The power of common goals to bond people together was recognized years ago by the celebrated social psychologist Muzafer Sherif. He created an environment in which the boys in a summer camp were divided into two "tribes" that competed and fought with each other over the course of a week or more. Rivalry and competitiveness between the groups grew as they competed on a number of tasks, and the hostility eventually reached a level where the staff became concerned for the physical safety of the boys. The question was how to reduce the level of animosity to try to re-join the tribes as members of one team. After a number of futile and self-defeating tactics were tried, the staff created a series of problems that could only be solved through the cooperation of both groups. For instance, one morning the boys were being taken to church on a common bus, and the bus experienced (an engineered) breakdown. The only way the boys could get to church was to collectively pull the bus up a hill. Neither of the groups could accomplish this alone. A rope was wrapped around the axle of bus and each group took one end of the rope and pulled the bus to the top of the hill. Together they achieved something that they could not have done as individuals or as single groups. (The ironic touch about this story is that the rope that was used to accomplish the joint task is the same one that was used in a tug-of-war to intensify the rivalry earlier in the experience.)

COOPERATION AND SACRIFICE

One of the most reliable findings from innumerable studies of group membership is that when people are made to feel part of a group, they behave differently towards other members of the group (in-group persons) and people who are not members (out-group persons). The basic finding is that people are willing to make sacrifices to help in-group members that they will not make for out-group persons. Moreover, it is well known that groups will be more effective to the extent that the members of groups are willing to put aside personal agendas in order to help one another and to achieve a common goal. Making followers members of a group or organization induces them to trade off their personal interests for the interests of other members of the group or organization (but not necessarily for outsiders).

People take vicarious pleasure in the achievements of fellow group members. One year I was living in eastern Holland during the winter Olympics and I could watch the games either on Dutch or on German television. Switching channels between them was like watching two totally different events. The Dutch channels gave detailed coverage of the skating events in which the Dutch excelled. Everyone knew the names and backgrounds of the Dutch skaters. On the German channels, there was extensive coverage of cross-country skiing, a sport at which the Germans excelled. It was rare to see skating on German television. Why should countries broadcast the sports at which their athletes excelled? It is obviously because citizens identify with their national representatives, not with the best athletes in the games. In this case, nationality is the in-group, and people's awareness of their citizenship is enhanced during the games.

RESPECT AND OBEDIENCE

What leaders reap from imparting pride and self-respect to their followers is respect, in return, and obedience to rules and norms of the organization or group. There is ample research that indicates that people obey laws and other rules not because they fear the consequences of disobedience, but more because they see that the laws and rules are just and legitimate and that they pertain to everyone, including themselves. A necessary condition for this acceptance seems to be that the follower must believe himself to be a valued member of the group, that is to say, one who is treated with dignity and respect (by leaders). In return, the leader and the group are treated with respect, and the follower willingly obeys the rules and does his or her duty.

Perhaps the best research on this topic has been conducted by Tyler (1990), whose investigation contrasted an instrumental versus a procedural justice explanation of why people obey the law. The former assumes that people obey laws because they fear the consequences of not doing so. The instrumental view implicitly assumes that people are governed by expected utility calculations, that they calculate the likelihood of being caught transgressing and they obey the law when it is more profitable psychically than transgressing. Studies that show that violations decrease with increases in either the likelihood of detection or the severity of punishment tend to support this view. Such a theory has trouble explaining the decrease in transgressions that accompanies an increase in the perceived legitimacy of the laws. As Tyler points out, obedience as a result of legitimacy is more effective than obedience as a result of deterrence. Deterrence requires surveillance and the possibility that transgressions will be detected and punished. Surveillance and punishment are costly to establish and maintain. Obedience that results from legitimacy, on the other hand, does not require surveillance. It is internalized. It is also cheaper.

These are the basic elements of what I have called the psychological exchange between leaders and followers. The exchange is not an economic or legalistic exchange in the sense that there is an explicit contract between leaders and followers. There may well be an implicit contract, an informal understanding about the duties and obligations of people in the different roles (Rousseau, 1995). Leaders, for instance, may feel betrayed if followers do not work sufficiently hard or if they violate the rules that should have been internalized. Followers may feel that leaders have violated the implicit contract if leaders fail to act on behalf of the group and instead act to promote their own personal interests. Leaders may feel that followers are not living up to their side of the arrangement if they fail to show the appropriate signs of belonging, in their dress, for instance, or comportment toward other group members. And followers may feel that leaders are violating the implicit agreement if the leader is rude, insulting, or demeaning to a follower. So to say that there is no explicit contract is not to say that there are no expectations as to the appropriate roles for leaders and followers. A leader, in contrast to an individual, is expected to have the best interest of the group or organization in mind and to operate so as to promote this interest. This is the requirement of *benevolence.* The leader is also expected to display the quality of *objectivity,* to put aside personal friendships, preferences, and biases in making decisions and allocating resources. The equilibrium or exchange between leaders and followers comes about in my view as the result of the natural social psychological processes that are involved when groups of people organize themselves to solve common problems.

Obviously, the five dimensions are not equally important in all circumstances. When external dangers are salient, protection and security and the resulting loyalty may be the primary dimensions of the relationship. When deadlines become salient, achievement and commitment may become the major issues in the relationship. There are times when cooperation and mutual aid become paramount, and there are other times when the major chore for the leader is to provide the direction, goals, and vision that is needed for the followers to be effective. In this regard, it also seems reasonable that some people will have a different portfolio of talents to offer as leaders and that some people may be inspirational in providing vision while others may provide inclusion and self-respect. In this regard, our analysis agrees with the widely held view that different types of groups or different types of tasks may require different types of leaders (Steiner, 1972). It is also consistent with the distinction made early on in the social psychological literature that it is possible to differentiate "task specialists" from "socio-emotional specialists" (Thibaut & Kelley, 1959). Task functions, from the current perspective, include vision, protection, and achievement, whereas the so-called socio-emotional functions are those of inclusion and pride.

I need to also make it clear that the dimensions I have described are interrelated. I have somewhat artificially separated them out into five categories. In the real world, it is hard to separate pride from group membership because people are usually proud of the groups to which they belong. It is hard to tease apart effort and obedience when a job needs to be done by a deadline. And all of the dimensions can contribute to pride and self-respect. We like ourselves when we know what to do, when we can do our part, *and* when we are part of the ingroup. It is possible to write about the five dimensions of exchange, but in any real work environment, these dimensions will be hopelessly intertwined.

There is yet an additional point that I would like to mention about the dimensions that I have proposed. Once when I was discussing these ideas publicly, a colleague[1] asked if I intended the dimensions to be related to the hierarchy of needs proposed by Abraham Maslow (see Maslow, 1943, for example). I answered that I had no such intention and that it had been decades since I had read anything by Maslow. Needless to say, shortly after the conversation I went back to Maslow and was interested to see that there seemed to be a relationship between his ideas and the ones I had proposed. Specifically, Maslow proposed that people have a hierarchy of needs. The hierarchy begins with *physiological* needs including hunger, thirst, and protection from extremes of cold and heat. If these needs are relatively well satisfied, a new set of needs emerge, collectively referred to

---

[1] My colleague, Professor Walter Scott, was the astute listener.

as *safety* needs that include needs for order, regularity, protection against danger, law, structure, and predictability. These safety needs, according to Maslow, are powerful needs whose satisfaction is critical for effective performance and personal development. Following the safety needs, Maslow proposes that *social or affection-based* needs emerge. These include the needs to be loved, to have friends, to avoid ostracism and social rejection, and to maintain positive social relationships. Maslow suggests that much of human unhappiness stems from the failure to satisfy these needs. The next category of needs in Maslow's scheme are what he calls *esteem* needs. These needs are of two types. First there are concerns of competence, achievement, effectiveness, and independence. These seem to deal with one's ability to be influential in effecting the physical and social world and to not be vulnerable to undue influence from it. The second component of the esteem category reflects the need for respect, admiration, and attention from others. This component is more a matter of reflective appraisal, having one's qualities seen and admired in a social mirror, than one of having objective standards by means of which to assess one's abilities. Finally, there is the need of *self-actualization,* the keystone of Maslow's theory. Although the notion of a need for self-actualization is somewhat vague and elusive, Maslow seems to take it to mean that people have a need to fulfill their capabilities, to become what their potential permits, to "be all they can be," in the words of an advertising slogan for the U. S. Army. He also suggests that this need differs in one essential way from the more basic needs, and that is that the need for self-actualization becomes stronger as it becomes satisfied, not weaker, like other needs. As other needs become satisfied, they fade in importance as determinants of behavior; as self-actualization needs become satisfied, they gain in importance as determinants of behavior.

There clearly seems to be a relationship between the five dimensions of leadership that I have identified and the hierarchy of needs that Maslow wrote about. My dimension of protection and security seems closely related to Maslow's physiological and safety needs. When I write about inclusion and belonging, I am very close to the issues Maslow includes with social and loving needs. Maslow's esteem needs include my category of achievement and effectiveness and points as well to the need to have one's abilities acknowledged socially. Finally, my category of pride and self-respect overlaps with Maslow's idea of self-actualization and social esteem.

There are several interesting implications of the correspondence between my hypothesis of the dimensions of leader–follower exchange and Maslow's theory. First, there is the suggestion that some dimensions of the exchange will emerge in importance only if there is a satisfactory exchange on prior dimensions. An implication is, for instance, that in a context in which followers are fearful of their lives and safety, leaders will not be effective in appealing to the group good (inclusion) or to self-respect (esteem). The hierarchical structure suggests that it will be difficult in an organization threatened with layoffs (safety needs activated) to induce employees to take pride in the organization's work or to feel good about its reputation. The general implication of Maslow's notion is that needs at lower levels must be more or less satisfied for needs at higher levels to become activated. Thus, to the extent that Maslow's hierarchy is valid and to the extent that the dimensions of leadership that I have sketched here are linked to Maslow's needs, clear implications about effective leader behavior should follow. A challenge will be to develop the measurement instruments that will allow these hypotheses to be tested.

A second implication of the correspondence between Maslow's ideas and the leader–follower exchange that I have outlined is that the ethical context of leading and following would seem to change as a function of the major dimension or need category involved. It seems obvious that a person's unethical behavior is less blameworthy if the behavior is intended to satisfy basic physiological needs (finding food or saving a life) than if it is for achievement or recognition (to complete a project or gain fame). There is a corollary hypothesis that a leader's transgression that is intended to satisfy physiological or safety needs will be seen as less serious than a similar behavior that is intended to satisfy needs like esteem or reputation maintenance. We further propose that the exchange creates expectations between leaders and their followers, not generalized expectations for any observer. Leaders should behave toward their followers in a way that may be very different from the way they would behave to non-followers.

Finally, I want to note that the integrity of the leader is essential to this exchange. The reciprocity works when the leader is seen as sincere and motivated by benevolence, by the interests of the group. If the leader is seen as self-interested, as I have said before, his or her actions will appear false, hypocritical, and manipulative. Our species is very sensitive to sham altruism. Sham leadership, the pursuit of personal gain by mimicking leadership and concern for others, will not be successful in the long run. In the long run, sham leaders will not reap benefits from followers but will elicit the contempt and derision of followers.

5

The Psychodynamics of Leadership: Freud's Insights and Their Vicissitudes

George R. Goethals
Williams College

This chapter discusses Sigmund Freud's (1921) theory of leadership, and several modern theories that deal with issues raised earlier by Freud. I am not a Freudian, but have found Freud's treatment of leadership unusually original and provocative and still highly relevant to understanding leadership. His theory is visionary given his intellectual time and place. He cut a trail, but no one really followed until the trail had grown over. Looking back, we can see that he was there first in regard to many important leadership issues. Most important perhaps, Freud deals in fascinating ways with the affective relations between leaders and followers. While dubious in many respects, his ideas shine the light on highly important issues, and, as will become clear, Freud took on issues that other important theorists pursued after Freud's writing.

The chapter first outlines some of Freud's key ideas and then shows how many of them have been pursued by later scholars. None of these later scholars explicitly references Freud's work. But perhaps using Freud's leadership theory as a basis for juxtaposing them will enable readers to appreciate the important connections between theories not generally combined.

I first discuss Freud's theory of leadership as articulated in *Group Psychology and the Analysis of the Ego* (1921). Then I discuss his concepts of a "thirst for obedience" and the group's attraction to a leader who possesses "a strong and imposing will" in relation to current theories of charismatic leaders. Next I discuss Freud's ideas about leaders having to possess "the typical qualities" of a group "in a particularly marked and pure form" and to "give an impression of greater force" in relation to modern theories discussing leader schemas and leader prototypicality. Fourth, I consider Freud's emphasis on a leader's ideas or faith in relation to Howard Gardner's (1995) theory emphasizing the stories leaders tell, particularly stories about identity. Finally, I compare Freud's (1921) hypothesis that "the members of a group stand in need of the illusion that they are equally and justly loved by their leader" (p. 123) to Tyler and Lind's (1992) relational model of procedural justice and its emphasis on the importance of fair treatment. I conclude by discussing aspects of Freudian theory that have not been pursued by modern scholars and aspects of leadership that are addressed by entirely different traditions. My goal is to suggest the utility of an integrated, psychoanalytically based approach to leadership combined with recent, seemingly remote, theory and research.

FREUD'S GROUP PSYCHOLOGY

In 1921 Sigmund Freud published a remarkable book called *Group Psychology and the Analysis of the Ego*. In it Freud explores the problem of group behavior, beginning with Gustave LeBon's treatment of crowd or mob behavior. In his 1895 classic *The Crowd,* LeBon considered groups in panic situations, hostile crowds, crowds at political rallies and entertainment events, and people caught up in cultural trends or fads. LeBon argued that in groups people became unthinking, emotional, and often hostile. Their raw, irrational side comes to the fore, and their cultivated, intellectual side disappears. LeBon argued that an important mechanism in producing these effects was suggestibility, and that leaders take advantage of this suggestibility.

LeBon was a French physician who feared the unruly mob behavior that often marked French political and social life following the 1789 revolution. He was aware of and fascinated with the dark side of human motivation and behavior. Freud was fascinated not only with LeBon's ideas about groups and leadership, but more generally with his concept of a primitive unconscious that lay beneath people's more civilized personas.

Freud took LeBon's notion of suggestibility much further. He quotes LeBon's account of the way a person in a crowd is like an individual in the hands of a hypnotist: "having entirely lost his conscious personality, he obeys all suggestions of the operator who has deprived him of it, and commits acts in utter contradiction with his character and habit (LeBon, 1895/1965, quoted in Freud, 1921, Standard Edition, Volume XVIII, p. 75). For Freud, the key question was what gave someone in the group, a leader, this kind of power. LeBon provided part of the answer. He argued that individuals in groups have "a thirst for obedience" such that "they place themselves instinctively under the authority of a chief" (Freud, p. 81). Somewhere in the human soul lies an instinct to submit and to obey. This instinct or need results in group submission to "anyone who appoints himself its master" (Freud, p. 81).

In short, two elements produce blind obedience in groups. First, there is an instinct to submit to authority. Second, there is an individual who has the qualities that allow him or her to assume the position of master or authority. The "needs of a group carry it half-way to meet the leader, yet he too must fit in with it in his personal qualities" (Freud, p. 81). Later, I consider the nature of the group's needs or "thirst for obedience." For the moment, we can ask what qualities a leader must have to become the group's master? People want leadership and they want it in a particular form. What is that form? LeBon described a mysterious "prestige" or domination that attaches to leaders and to their ideas. Prestige is granted to leaders who have typical characteristics of group members "in particularly marked and clear form" who "give an impression of greater force" and who "possess a strong and imposing will" (Freud, p. 81, 129). Once individuals are accorded this prestige, "it has the effect of making everyone obey them as though by the operation of some magnetic magic" (Freud, p. 81). Individuals who represent the group's members in an ideal and strong way gain prestige, and prestige commands obedience.

The ideas of leaders also acquire prestige. If a leader holds a strong faith, if he is a "fanatical believer" in a set of ideas, he can "awaken the group's faith" (Freud, p. 81). To do so the leader must express his ideas using "the truly magical power of words." Ideas expressed powerfully with words can completely capture a group and control its behavior. The words in Thomas Jefferson's first draft of a declaration of independence in 1776 crystallized the thoughts and feelings of the Continental Congress, and propelled them to take action that would have been unthinkable just a few months earlier. Freud argued that the leader's words "must paint in the most forcible colors, he must exaggerate, and he must repeat the same thing again and again" (Freud, p. 78). Freud's idea was echoed in hauntingly similar terms by Ronald Reagan during his campaigns for president of the United States. Reagan talked about expressing basic principles of the Republican Party in bold colors, and avoiding pastels. Reagan also believed in the key principle of repetition. He would often begin his arguments with the preface "As I've said many times . . ." (Morris, 1999). And in his 1980 debate with Jimmy Carter he repeated a phrase accusing Carter of repetition, saying "There you go again . . ." when he wanted to characterize one of Carter's statements as an attack. LeBon and Freud, along with Reagan, recognized the power of repetition to move an audience.

The crux of these ideas is that forceful and impressive individuals who can express clear ideas in vivid form can master or dominate a group. Furthermore, their mastery is complete. Like a hypnotist, they can suggest almost anything. But Freud wanted to understand in much more depth why leaders could exercise such power. What in the human psyche could a leader touch to gain such mastery?

Freud wrote that the leader reawakens unconscious archaic images of the powerful male who ruled despotically over primitive human societies. Taking up Darwin's notion of a "primal horde," Freud argued that the father or chief was a strong and independent figure who imposed his beliefs and his will on all other members of the group. He was unbound from normal social constraints. His will and wishes must be satisfied. He was totally narcissistic, giving very little love to others. The leader was the only person in the primal horde whose sexual desires were completely unrestrained. On the contrary, they were satisfied "without any need for delay or accumulation," and he was sexually jealous and intolerant of other men's sexuality.

This jealousy and intolerance was dangerous to other male members of the group. They had to curb their sexual appetites out of fear of the king or chieftan. But there was more than fear that engendered obedience to the leader. Followers had the illusion that the leader loved each of them equally. Consequently, they loved him in return. The illusion of equal love helped bind members of the horde together in their common allegiance to the primal father. The result was almost complete obedience.

Freud argued that while social dynamics have evolved far beyond those of the primal horde, people retain "an archaic heritage" which is sometimes reawakened in the present. When that archaic heritage is awakened individuals experience again, as their ancestors had, "the idea of a para-mount and dangerous personality . . . to whom one's will has to be surren-dered." There are two important instances where these ideas and attitudes toward authority do actually resurface. One is in the state of hypnosis. Hypnotists take the place of the parents and command people, or at least some people, as parents could. They literally have the power of sugges-tion, where they can command the subject's total attention and, within bounds, the subject's will and action. The other person with this kind of power is the leader in a group. The strong leader "is still the dreaded pri-mal father" and the group still has "an extreme passion for authority" and a "thirst for obedience" acquired from experience with the primal father (Freud, 1921, p. 127).

Freud also wrote at length about the precise nature of the affective or emotional relationship between leaders and followers. In the cases of both the Oedipal conflict and the primal horde, the fear that boys or young men feel toward their fathers is replaced by identification. In both cases the identification "is ambivalent from the very first; it can turn into an expression of tenderness as easily into a wish for someone's removal." (1921, p. 105). The tender side of identification combines with another dynamic in the relation between the leader and follower—the affectionate feelings that accompany sexually based sensual love. These affectionate feelings produce toward the loved object "a certain amount of freedom from criticism" such that the loved one's "characteristics are valued more highly than those of people who are not loved," and judgment of that per-son is clouded by "*idealization*" (p. 112). Both identification and idealiza-tion lead the follower to seek to satisfy the loved one in any way that is asked: "Everything that the object does and asks for is right and blame-less" (p. 113).

These intense feelings for an imposing figure are the basis of power for many leaders. Examples are not hard to find. Consider soldiers' reac-tion to George Washington in the early days of the American Revolu-tion. Washington was an imposing physical presence. He was six feet two inches tall, well-muscled, athletic and commanding. Importantly, for the time, he was an excellent horseman. The Marquis de Lafayette wrote of "his graceful bearing on horseback, . . . calculated to inspire the highest degree of enthusiasm." And later, "I thought then as now that I had never beheld so superb a man" (Brookhiser, 1996, p. 52). A body builder looked at a portrait of Washington after the battle of Trenton in 1776. It shows "a pair of well-developed thighs"; she remarked, "Nice quads" (Brookhiser, 1996, p. 52).

Not only was Washington impressive looking, he was striking, and somewhat intimidating, in the way he comported himself. First, he was graceful and dignified. Washington's body "organized the space around it, as a dancer's arms or legs seem to stretch beyond the tips of the fingers or toes" (Brookhiser, 1996, p. 52). He was, in fact, an enthusiastic dancer himself. When he was a member of the Continental Congress he struck one delegate as "sober, steady, and calm" (Flexner, 1965, p. 343). Size, strength, grace, and bearing were qualities vividly perceived by others.

Freud indicated that the primal leader was perceived as "dangerous" as well as "paramount." Was Washington perceived as dangerous? It is clear that he had a tremendous temper, and was capable of demonstrating a volatile mixture of anger and irritation. Thomas Jefferson wrote that Washington's "temper was naturally irritable" and that when "it broke its bonds, he was most tremendous in his wrath" (Brookhiser, 1996, p. 57). People did not trifle with George Washington. He valued and imposed discipline. He combined a strong streak of high, sometimes barely controlled anger with his poise and affability. In sum, Washington had tremendous presence. It reflected a smooth-working, well-coordinated combination of physical bearing and interpersonal action. The grace and poise combined with the "wrath" made him both "dangerous" and "paramount" and commanded the respect of even the most substantial men under his command.

Before comparing Freud's views of leadership with important current theories, let us review the four major elements of Freud's thinking on which we have touched thus far. First, human beings are prepared to respond with a combination of fear, envy, love and, ultimately, obedience, to powerful figures who reawaken images of a dominant and dangerous primal horde leader. Second, an important part of what makes a person such a potential leader is his or her "possession of a strong and imposing will" and embodiment of ideal group standards "in a particularly clearly marked and pure form." Third, an additional component in enabling a potential leader to produce these highly charged emotional responses is his or her expression of faith in ideas: "He must himself be held in fascination by a strong faith (in an idea) in order to awaken the group's faith" (p. 81). Furthermore, this faith must be expressed using "the magical power of words." Fourth and finally, critical to keeping followers in an obedient stance is their illusion "of there being a head . . . who loves all the individuals in the group with an equal love" (p. 94).

We now proceed to see how these ideas resonate with current work on the psychology of leadership.

EMOTIONAL RESPONSES TO LEADERS:
THE ROLE OF CHARISMA

Freud's idea that people form highly emotionally charged psychological attachments to leaders which form the basis for unquestioned obedience is well-represented in several theories of transformational and charismatic leadership. Two highly relevant versions are Bass's theory of transformational leadership (Bass, 1997; Bass & Avolio, 1993) and House and Shamir's (1993) theory of charismatic and visionary leadership. While these theories are similar in many ways, particularly in their focus on charisma, Bass' theory highlights the behavior of leaders, whereas House and Shamir give more attention to the experience and emotional responses of followers.

In Bass' theory, charisma, also called "idealized influence," is marked by the leader's display of conviction, an emphasis on values and trust, setting high standards and challenging goals, and inspiring emulation and identification. Followers want to be like these leaders and attain the goals set forth by the leader. Leaders who combine these qualities with "inspirational motivation" (the ability to articulate a vision for the group's future) "intellectual stimulation" (questioning old ways and stimulating the exploration of new ones), and "individualized consideration" (dealing with each person's "needs, abilities, and aspirations"; Bass, 1997, p. 133) are thought of as transformational leaders. Perhaps the key element in these ideas is that charismatic or transformational leaders inspire identification with themselves as persons and with their ideas and goals. Furthermore, people who follow these leaders experience "pride, loyalty, confidence and alignment around a shared purpose" (1997, p. 133). This formulation is highly reminiscent of Freud's emphasis on identification and the appeal of a leader's ideas. Bass does not deal with the dynamic basis for responding to this kind of leader with this kind of emotional response, but his description fits Freud's ideas closely. One final point of similarity between Bass' findings about leaders who show charisma and Freud's analysis of group dynamics: Freud argued that there are strong libidinal ties between followers in the group because of their common ego-ideal, the leader. Bass' reference to "alignment around a shared purpose" resonates with Freud's formulation. House and Shamir discuss charisma in very similar terms. They cite three behaviors of charismatic leaders: (a) articulation of an ideological vision; (b) modeling the values implied by the vision through personal example, including risk-taking and self-sacrificing behaviors, and careful image building; and (c) empowering followers by expressing both high performance expectations and high confidence in the followers' ability to meet those expectations. In other words, charismatic leaders lead both by word and by example, and they make followers believe that they are capable of great things. Like Freud, there is an emphasis on both the personal qualities and the ideas of the leader.

There are also several concepts related to Freud's idea of the group's strong identification with the leader and establishing the leader as their ego ideal. House and Shamir argue that charismatic leadership leads followers to have a higher sense of collective identity and a sense of greater consistency between their identity and behavior on behalf of the leader and the group. From acting consistently with the ideals of the group, as expressed by the leader, there is a gain in self-esteem. Positive self-esteem, a powerful reward, derives from a clear identity and a behavioral commitment to the values and goals associated with that identity. People believe in the leader's vision, and their sense of self comes from working with other group members toward actualizing it. The result is an increased sense of "meaningfulness."

Although neither Bass nor House and Shamir include in their theory any element that parallels Freud's idea of a "thirst for obedience" or for a strong chief, that idea does seem better understood in light of the psychological rewards of self-esteem, meaning, and common purpose that charismatic leadership can provide.

Two examples of charismatic leadership illustrating the ideas of Bass and House and Shamir are Adolf Hitler and Martin Luther King. Both were figures whom followers could emulate, whose vision was articulated dramatically, who crafted an image that would appeal to followers, who raised their followers' sense of collective identity and collective efficacy, and who persuaded their followers that self-esteem and meaning would come from a commitment to their vision. Many leadership theorists, such as James MacGregor Burns (1978) and Ronald Heifetz (1994), have explicitly rejected Hitler as an example of a leader. Burns feels that transformational leaders only include those who raise followers to a higher level of motivation and morality. Heifetz defines leaders as those who help groups do adaptive work, work that solves real group problems, not leaders who take their groups to death and destruction. Without evaluating these claims, we can note the similarities between Hitler and King in producing the emotional and behavioral reactions in their followers that are well described by Freud, Bass, and House and Shamir.

THE PERSONAL QUALITIES OF LEADERS
AND THE EXPECTATIONS OF FOLLOWERS

Freud argued that "the needs of the group carry it half-way to meet the leader, yet he too must fit in with it in his personal qualities" (1921, p. 81). The personal qualities of the leader must meet or fit certain leader expectations. Several modern psychologists have talked about schemas that people have for leaders, either quite general schemas about leaders or schemas about leader attributes and behavior in specific situations (Eden & Leviatan, 1975; Emrich, 1999; Hollander & Julian, 1969; Kenney, Blascovich, & Shaver, 1994). One of the most useful of these approaches is Simonton's (1987) discussion of perceptions of U.S. presidents and his suggestion that they must have qualities related to the basic dimensions of meaning identified by Osgood, Suci, and Tannenbaum (1957). Specifically, successful presidents must be perceived as strong, active, and good. "The presidential role is also perceived to demand that its occupant display drive, forcefulness, firmness, determination, courage and decisiveness (strength); initiative, persuasiveness, enthusiasm, extroversion, and mental and physical alertness (activity); and a sincere interest in people, diplomacy and consideration, and good moral judgment (goodness)" (Merenda, 1964: summarized in Simonton, 1987, p. 238). The emphasis on strength echoed by these authors echoes Freud's insistence that the leader "must possess a strong and imposing will" (p. 81) and "give an impression of greater force." Followers need a "strong chief" (p. 129).

The qualities of strength, activity, and goodness likely apply to many kinds of leaders other than U.S. presidents. For example, the boxer Muhammad Ali has emerged during the past 40 years as a recognized cultural icon, not only because of his athletic prowess but because of his role in fighting for the tangible interests and self-respect of African Americans, and for religious and racial understanding and tolerance. Ali possesses nearly all of the qualities of strength, activity, and goodness specified by Simonton. Interestingly, Ali was "an acquired taste" for White Americans. Reviled by many for his religious and political beliefs in the 1960s, more recently his presence was used to stir interest in the 1996 Olympic Games in Atlanta and his image was used to sell Wheaties breakfast cereal in 1999. He appeared in information technology ads in 2004. What accounts for this change? Partly, Ali undeniably possessed qualities of strength and activity. But for many in the majority culture, he was associated with threat, evil, and badness rather than goodness. However, as dominant

American values about race and religion changed as a result of the many social upheavals of the 1960s, Ali and what he stood for came to be perceived as more "good." This change did not happen by accident. Many people, including Ali, contributed to it. Ali's strong and active, and consistent, articulation and embodiment of his political, social, and religious beliefs was one element in changing those dominant American values.

A current perspective on leadership grounded in social identity theory (Hogg, 2001) also emphasizes the important match between a leader's personal qualities on the one hand and group expectations on the other in suggesting that individuals become leaders in groups to the extent that they match ingroup prototypes, defined as "context specific, multidimensional fuzzy sets of attributes that define and prescribe attitudes, feelings, and behaviors that characterize one group and distinguish it from other groups" (Hogg, 2001, p. 187). Highly prototypical individuals are likely to emerge as leaders. It is striking how similar this formulation is to Freud's suggestion that leaders "need often only possess the typical qualities of the individuals concerned in a particularly clearly marked and pure form . . ." (p. 129).

In sum, recent theory and research support the idea that people have schemas or expectations of leaders. It seems that in some ways they can be quite general ideas, such as images of strength, activity, or goodness, but that they may also be quite specific to particular groups.

THE IDEAS OF LEADERS: THE IMPORTANT ROLE OF STORIES

One of the most interesting of Freud's ideas, borrowed heavily from LeBon, is that leaders match the needs and expectations of the group through their ideas as well as their personal qualities. He wrote that the leader "must himself be held in fascination by a strong faith (in an idea) in order to awaken the group's faith" (1921, p. 81). He noted that LeBon ascribes to both leaders and their ideas "a mysterious and irresistible power" or domination. He even asked whether ideas can take the place of a leader.

The importance of ideas is underlined in the work of Bass and House and Shamir that I have already noted. Both emphasize the articulation of a vision. Bass notes that leaders provide symbols and emotional appeals to make clear the group's goals. House and Shamir list the articulation of an ideological vision as the first and foremost defining quality of charismatic leadership. The importance of ideas is probably best represented in Howard Gardner's (1995) book *Leading Minds*. Gardner describes his account of leadership as a cognitive approach. Its central concept is that of the story. Stories present a *"dynamic"* perspective to followers, "a drama that unfolds over time, in which they—leaders and followers—are the principal characters or heroes" (p. 14). Gardner argues that leaders achieve their influence through the stories they *relate* or *embody*. He uses the term "relate" rather than "tell" because leaders can relate stories without using words, as in works of art. But typically leaders tell stories. Also, they embody them in their behavior. They act in ways that are consistent with the stories they tell.

Gardner's idea of embodying stories is similar to House and Shamir's point that charismatic leaders engage in image building and model the values implied in the vision they articulate through personal example. A significant part of leadership for them is crafting an image such that one can be perceived as appropriately embodying the story they tell or relate. One of Gardner's most interesting examples is Pope John XXIII, leader of the Roman Catholic church from 1958–1963. His writing advocated an open, tolerant church that would work well with other religious leaders, that would welcome into its orbit people of varied sorts from various religions. In Pope John's view, this ecumenical stance rediscovered the basic principles of Christianity. His message or story was supported by John's behavior. He was modest, kind, open and accepting of different views and different groups. Gardner notes that his philosophy was highly inclusive, and his entire being embodied the trait of inclusiveness and its correlated attributes.

The stories that leaders tell are fundamentally about identity. They are about the leaders themselves and their groups. Leaders tell "stories—in so many words—about themselves and their groups, about where they were coming from and where they were headed, about what was to be feared, struggled against, and dreamed about" (p. 14). He argues that it is *"stories of identity*—narratives that help individuals think about and feel who they are, where they come from, and where they are headed—that constitute the single most important weapon in the leader's literary arsenal" (p. 43). In the last speech he gave before he was assassinated in Memphis, Tennessee, Martin Luther King, Jr. told his audience that he wanted to do God's will, that he had been to the mountain top and seen the promised land: "I may not get there with you, but I want you to know tonight that we as a people will get to the promised land. . . . I'm not worried about anything, I'm not fearing any man. Mine eyes have seen the glory of the coming of the Lord" (ABC News, 1999). King's powerful rhetoric said something about both himself and the future of his group. His group would fare well no matter what happened to him. His fate was one thing, the fate of Black people was another. African Americans would prevail, with or without him.

Abraham Lincoln provides another example of a leader using stories, in this case political stories. Lincoln made perhaps his greatest speech on the occasion of his second inaugural to try to point the people, and political leaders, of the United States in the direction he sought for the nation at the end of the Civil War. Lincoln wanted peace and reconciliation. He wanted the war to be forgotten. He argued that the "scourge" of the Civil War was divine retribution for the offence of slavery and that if God willed it "every drop of blood drawn with the lash shall be paid by another drawn with the sword." He thus told a story about the conflict's spiritual significance. More importantly, Lincoln pointed the way to the future, toward national reconciliation. "With malice toward none; with charity for all; with firmness in the right as God gives us to see the right, let us strive to finish the work we are in; to bind up the nation's wounds; to care for him who shall have borne the battle, and for his widow, and his orphan—to do all which may achieve and cherish a just and lasting peace, among ourselves, and with all nations." These words (which are inscribed on the Lincoln memorial in Washington, D.C.) provided Lincoln's followers with a story about where the group was headed, and what it needed to do.

Among Gardner's other points, two stand out as particularly important. First, stories can be inclusive or exclusive. For example, they can paint a picture of a large and varied group that is open and inclusive. Lincoln's rhetoric—"with malice toward none; with charity for all"—is striking in its inclusiveness. Similarly, Pope John XXIII related and embodied an inclusive story. On the other hand, leaders can paint a vastly different picture of conflict between groups. Hitler's exclusive rhetoric about the destruction of Jews in Europe stands as an example. Second, a leader's stories exist in a context of "counterstories" which compete with the stories of other individuals vying for leadership of the same group or overlapping groups. Not everyone shared King's optimistic vision of the fate of African Americans. After the Civil War, not everyone shared Lincoln's generous and conciliatory attitude toward the south. In both cases their vision and their story had to compete with counterstories told by others.

THE ILLUSION OF EQUAL LOVE

A final element in Freud's theory of leadership is the powerful idea that followers in groups feel that they are held in equal regard, that they are equally loved, by the leader. "The members of a group stand in need of the illusion that they are equally and justly loved by their leader" (1921, p. 123). The perception of similarity, commonality, and equality is important. It binds followers together. Not only are there strong libidinal ties between the leader and his followers, but because the followers have a common ego ideal, the leader, there are also strong libidinal ties among them: "The essence of a group formation consists in . . . libidinal ties among members of the group" (p. 103). In addition to the common ego ideal, the followers, like the young males in the primal horde, share in their terror of, and love for, the angry chief. In the primal horde "all of the sons knew that they were equally *persecuted* by the primal father, and *feared* him equally. . . . The indestructible strength of the family as a natural group formation rests upon the fact that this necessary presupposition of the father's equal love can have a real application in the family" (p. 125).

Freud cites two kinds of organized groups where the illusion of equal love is critical in obtaining compliance with the leader's authority, the Christian church and the military. "However different the two may be in other respects, the same illusion holds good of there being a head—in the Catholic Church Christ, and in an army its Commander-in-Chief—who loves all the individuals in group with an equal love. Everything depends upon this illusion" (p. 94). Freud further argues that in the military, and many other kinds of organized groups as well, the illusion of equal love is important not only with respect to the overall commander, but within every level of command. "Every captain is, as it were, the Commander-in-Chief and father of his company, and so is every non-commissioned officer of his section" (p. 94).

Freud's idea that equal treatment is critical to compliance with a leader is central in work on procedural justice by Tyler and his colleagues (Tyler & Lind, 1992). Voluntary compliance with the directives of authority depend very much on the authority treating members of the group fairly, specifically with procedural as opposed to distributive justice. Distributive justice refers to whether rewards in the group are divided in an even or equitable way. Procedural justice refers to whether the process of deciding who gets what is carried out fairly. Do people have a chance to make themselves heard? Does the authority seem to be unbiased? Extensive research shows that it is more important that the decision be made fairly, in terms of procedure, than that it be made favorably, in terms of the distribution of benefits. People will go along with decisions that are made fairly, even if the actual decision seems flawed.

Why is procedural justice so important? Tyler and Lind argue that if people have a chance to express themselves to authority they will feel that they have standing in the group. Their group membership is not in question. Also, if decisions are made using fair procedures in the present, there is a better chance that they will be made fairly in the future. When a leader grants a follower standing by listening, he or she shows that the group member is taken seriously and is well regarded by the person who symbolizes and speaks for the group. They are treated with respect by someone who matters. "Above all, the leader must be concerned with the appearance of fairness, with convincing followers that he or she is willing to consider their point of view, and that he or she will be even-handed and nondiscriminatory in decision-making" (p. 161). When this happens, with the result that the individual feels credibly validated by the most prominent group member, he or she is much more likely to follow the leader. "The belief that the authority views one as a full member of the society, trust in the authority's ethicality and benevolence, and belief in the authority's neutrality—these appear to be the crucial factors that lead to voluntary compliance with the directives of authority" (p. 163).

In his book *The Path Between the Seas,* David McCullough (1977) provides a compelling example of the important consequences of a leader fostering the belief that he treats people fairly. In 1907 Col. George W. Goethals was named the third American chief engineer on the construction of the Panama Canal. The two previous to him had abruptly quit. Goethals' immediate predecessor, John Stevens, was enormously popular with the work force. Goethals was drawn from the military (Theodore Roosevelt appointed an army man as the third chief engineer, because he couldn't quit) and was more stiff and formal in his manner than Stevens. Initially he was not liked. He won over the labor force with a highly unusual way of dealing with worker's problems. Every Sunday morning starting at sunup he would meet with any member of the force about any complaint or problem. People were seen on a first-come-first-served basis without regard to rank, race, or nationality. Goethals resolved matters instantaneously or pledged to get to the bottom of them expeditiously. The results were impressive. McCullough writes, "The new approach was in fact wholly unorthodox by the standards of the day. In labor relations Goethals was way in advance of his time, and nothing that he did had so discernable an effect on the morale of the workers or their regard for him" (p. 538). Joseph Bucklin Bishop served as secretary to the commission that Goethals headed, and also, by the way, as Theodore Roosevelt's personal informant on conditions at the Isthmus of Panama. He wrote that as a result of Goethals' approach, workers "were treated like human beings, not like brutes, and they responded by giving the best service within their power" (McCullough, 1977, p. 538).

The idea that such considered treatment of followers is important ties nicely to Bass' (1997) formulation of transformational leadership. Besides charisma and inspirational motivation, Bass has evidence for the importance of "intellectual stimulation" and "individualized consideration." Individualized consideration by a leader includes listening attentively and considering individual needs. The concept has some overlap with that of procedural justice. They both involve demonstrating to followers that they are important and are taken seriously as individual members of the group. Both produce high regard for the leader, and deep engagement in group goals by the follower.

CONCLUSIONS

Sigmund Freud's (1921) *Group Psychology and the Analysis of the Ego* offers a fascinating and surprisingly broad account of leadership. It includes the ideas that groups have an instinctive need for leadership, and that individuals whose personal qualities are strong and prototypical, and whose ideas are compelling, are likely to succeed as leaders. It argues that followers have strong emotional attachments to leaders, even though these attachments may contain some ambivalence. It holds that fair treatment by leaders is key to producing obedience. Many of these ideas are echoed, and treated in great depth, by modern theories of leadership. Certainly, there are ideas of Freud's that have not been pursued. For example, even though modern theories have talked about the powerful psychological rewards of following charismatic leaders, or of gaining identity through leaders' stories, the idea of a thirst for obedience or of an instinct to follow leaders does not have currency. Also, there are clearly important ideas in the leadership literature that have no roots in Freudian theory. For example, exchange or transactional theories of leadership, and important concepts such as Hollander's (1993) idea of "idiosyncrasy credit," or Fiedler's (1993) idea of contingent success, bear little or no relation to Freud's work. On the whole, however, the range of important leadership phenomena that Freud treated in an integrated theory is impressive.

REFERENCES

ABC News. (1999). *The century: America's time* [video]. New York: Author.

Bass, B. M. (1997). Does the transactional-transformational leadership paradigm transcend organizational and national boundaries? *American Psychologist, 52,* 130–139.

Bass, B. M., & Avolio, B. J. (1993). Transformational leadership: A response to critiques. In M. M. Chemers & R. Ayman (Eds.), *Leadership theory and research* (pp. 49–80). San Diego: Academic Press.

Brookhiser, R. (1996). A man on horseback. *Atlantic Monthly, 227* (January), 50–64.

Burns, J. M. (1978). *Leadership.* New York: Harper & Row

Eden, D., & Leviatan, U. (1975). Implicit leadership theory as a determinant of the factor structure underlying supervisory behavior scales. *Journal of Applied Psychology, 60,* 736–741.

Emrich, C. G. (1999). Contexts effects in leadership perception. *Personality and Social Psychology Bulletin, 25,* 991–1006.

Fiedler, F. E. (1993). The leadership situation and the black box in contingency theories. In M. M. Chemers & R. Ayman (Eds.), *Leadership theory and research* (pp. 1–28). Boston: Academic Press.

Flexner, J. T. (1965) *George Washington: The forge of experience.* Boston: Little, Brown.

Freud, S. (1921). Group psychology and the analysis of the ego. In J. Strachey (Ed.), *The standard edition of the complete works of Sigmund Freud: Vol. 28. Beyond the pleasure principle, Group psychology and other works* (pp. 65–143). London: Hogarth Press.

Gardner, H. (1995). *Leading minds: An anatomy of leadership.* New York: Basic Books.

Heifetz, R. A. (1994). *Leadership without easy answers.* Cambridge, MA: Harvard University Press.

Hogg, M. A. (2001). A social identity theory of leadership. *Personality and Social Psychology review, 5,* 184–200.

Hollander, E. P. (1993). Legitimacy, power, and influence: A perspective on relational features of leadership. In M. M. Chemers & R. Ayman (Eds.), *Leadership theory and research* (pp. 29–48). San Diego: Academic Press.

Hollander, E. P., & Julian, J. W. (1969). Contemporary trends in the analysis of leadership processes. *Psychological Bulletin, 71,* 387–391.

House, R. J., & Shamir, B. (1993). Toward the integration of transformational, charismatic, and visionary theories. In M. M. Chemers & R. Ayman (Eds.), *Leadership theory and research* (pp. 81–107). San Diego: Academic Press.

Kenney, R. A., Blascovich, J., & Shaver, P. R. (1994). Implicit leadership theories: Prototypes for new leaders. *Basic and Applied Social Psychology, 15,* 409–437.

LeBon, G. (1969). *The crowd.* New York: Ballantine. (Original work published 1895)

McCullough, D. (1977). *The path between the seas: The creation of the Panama Canal, 1870–1914.* New York: Simon and Schuster.

Merenda, P. F. (1964). Perception of the role of the president. *Perceptual and Motor Skills, 19,* 863–866.

Morris, E. (1999). *Dutch: A memoir of Ronald Reagan.* New York: Random House.

Osgood, C. E., Suci, G. J., & Tannenbaum, P. H. (1957). *The measurement of meaning.* Urbana: University of Illinois Press.

Simonton, D. K. (1987) *Why presidents succeed: A political psychology of leadership.* New Haven: Yale University Press.

Tyler, T. R., & Lind, E. A. (1992). A relational model of authority in groups. *Advances in Experimental Social Psychology, 25,* 115–191.

II

Effectiveness of Leadership

6

Rethinking Team Leadership *or* Team Leaders Are Not Music Directors

J. Richard Hackman
Harvard University

Let us begin with a thought experiment. Think for a moment about one of the finest groups you have ever seen—one that accomplished its work superbly, that got better and better as a performing unit over time, and whose members came away from the group experience wiser and more skilled than they were before. Next, think about a different group, one that failed to achieve its purposes, that deteriorated in performance capability over time, and whose members found the group experience far more frustrating than fulfilling.

Now comes the question. In your opinion, what one factor is most responsible for the difference between these two groups? If you are like most people I've asked to perform this little thought experiment, the first explanation to come to mind may have been the quality of the leadership of the two groups. Indeed, "great leader" is almost always a central feature of the image we conjure up when we think about a great team. An operating room team successfully executes a demanding surgical procedure. The lead surgeon emerges from the operating room to receive the gratitude of the patient's family. An aircraft encounters serious problems in flight, but the crew finds a way to solve them and lands safely. The passengers applaud the captain. An industrial team sets a new plant production record. The team leader receives an award and subsequently is promoted.

Our tendency to assign to the leader credit or blame for successes or failures that actually are *team* outcomes is so strong and pervasive that I'm tempted to call it the "leader attribution error." It occurs for unfavorable as well as favorable outcomes—the standard remedy for an athletic team that experiences a string of losses, for example, is to replace the coach. Moreover, it is not just outside observers or bosses who overattribute responsibility for outcomes to leaders. Team members themselves, the people who actually generated the collective product, also are vulnerable. Organizational psychologist Richard Corn asked members of a diverse set of teams, ranging from community health groups to a mutual fund company to military units, to identify the "root cause" of their team performance. For teams that were performing well, over 60% of their initial explanations of why the team performed as it did had to do with someone's personality or behavior—and that someone frequently was the team leader. For teams that were performing poorly, 40% of the initial attributions were about personality or behavior (Corn, 2000).

Even *inaction* by a leader is often viewed as causing what transpires in a team. For example, leaders of self-analytic groups whose purpose is to help members learn from analysis of their own group experiences typically remain silent for the first few moments to ensure that all behaviors that occur are spontaneously generated by—and therefore owned by—group members themselves. The leader attribution error is so strong that the leader's silence itself often is viewed by members as the main cause of the rocky start that such groups invariably experience. Indeed, organizational psychologist Jim Meindl (1990) finds that the leader attribution error is muted only when there is significant ambiguity about whether a team's performance was a success or a failure.

The leader attribution error is understandable because people generally attribute responsibility more to things they can see (and the leader and his or her behavior usually are quite salient) than to things that operate in the background (and structural and contextual features that may powerfully shape team performance often go unnoticed). Even so, the error would be little more than a modestly interesting research tidbit, something worth perhaps a journal article or two, except for what it has spawned: a veritable industry of training programs intended to help leaders learn and execute those behaviors and leadership styles that are thought by those who design the programs to facilitate team performance.

"To fix the team, train the leader" could be the slogan of more than one successful enterprise in the management training industry. Everything I know about team leadership courses (and I've participated in them both as a student and as a teacher) suggests that, when well executed, attendees absolutely love them. Moreover, participants report—not just at the end of the course, but weeks or months later—that the courses have been enormously helpful to them. The problem is that research evidence that would document the benefits for team performance claimed by the offerers of such courses and attested to by participants is hard to find. I suspect, perhaps too pessimistically, that the evidence is hard to find because it does not exist.

In the pages that follow, I offer an alternative way of construing team leadership, one that is more in accord with research evidence about the factors that shape team behavior and performance. To begin, let us inspect in some detail a setting where leader-focused thinking is especially pervasive and deeply rooted.

LEADERSHIP IN PROFESSIONAL
SYMPHONY ORCHESTRAS

Nowhere is the leader attribution error more obvious than in the professional symphony orchestra. The images are vivid and compelling. The hushed anticipation of the conductor's arrival on stage once the orchestra has settled on the stage and tuned. The conductor's movement on the podium, as he or she (mostly he) plays the orchestra as if it were his very own cello. And the moment of fulfillment, as the final chords reverberate in the hall and the conductor, exhausted but beaming, turns to accept the ovation of the audience (although sometimes, after receiving their fill, conductors do signal to individual players or sections that they also may stand and share recognition for the performance).

Who could resist this imagery? Certainly not audiences and critics, who are quick to characterize an orchestral performance as the accomplishment (or, when things do not go well, as the failure) of the conductor. Even players, the ones who actually performed the music, are vulnerable. A member of a major U.S. symphony orchestra, describing to me an extraordinary performance by his orchestra, reported that the conductor had "pulled out of us a performance I didn't know we had in us." A player in a different orchestra, explaining an unsatisfactory concert, complained that the conductor "just couldn't get us to play beyond the notes on the page."

Those who sit in concert hall seats rarely wave their arms as if they themselves are on the podium, although sometimes they are tempted (or at least I am). It is exciting to imagine oneself up there, bringing into beautiful harmony the contributions of a diverse set of highly talented individuals, each playing her or his own instrument in a way that enriches the glorious sound of the ensemble. So it is no wonder that those conductors who offer management seminars in which they explicitly draw a parallel between conductors and organizational leaders find their students both receptive and appreciative. The metaphor is compelling, and it works beautifully as a pedagogical device.

Here, for example, is an excerpt from a marketing letter I received, inviting me to attend a management seminar offered by Dr. Stephen Covey, of *The Seven Habits of Highly Effective People* fame:

> Imagine synergy as the blending of individual talents within an orchestra to produce a unified sound that far exceeds the capability of each musician. A great conductor can show each musician how to look within and find even more potential. Dr. Covey has often used the example of the conductor who said, "I always speak to the highest and best inside a person. I see in them something that is beyond what they themselves see." Like conductors, leaders who understand synergy will help their teams achieve similar dramatic improvements. . . .

And here is what management guru Peter Drucker had to say in a 1988 *Harvard Business Review* article, in which he proposed symphony orchestras as a model for other kinds of organizations in the information age:

> The typical large business 20 years hence will have fewer than half the levels of management of its counterpart today, and no more than a third of the managers. In its structure, and in its management problems and concerns, it will bear little resemblance to the typical manufacturing company, circa 1950, which our textbooks still consider the norm. Instead, it is far more likely to resemble organizations that neither the practicing manager nor the management scholar pays much attention to today: the hospital, the university, the symphony orchestra. . . . (p. 45)

> A large symphony orchestra is . . . instructive, since for some works there may be a few hundred musicians on stage playing together. According to organization theory, then, there should be several group vice president conductors and perhaps a half-dozen division VP conductors. But that's not how it works. There is only the conductor-CEO—and every one of the musicians plays directly to that person without an intermediary. And each is a high-grade specialist, indeed an artist. . . ." (p. 48)

Leaving aside Drucker's misapprehension about their being a few hundred musicians on the concert stage (even a big Mahler symphony does not require *that* many players), the model he proposes is in many ways both attractive and sensible. But it overlooks one important feature of professional symphony orchestras: they are, in their artistic work, autocracies. The music director has almost total control of repertoire and artistic interpretations, and orchestra musicians, each of whom is indeed a high level professional, do precisely what they are told. It is not just the leader attribution error at work here. Music directors really are fully in charge of what happens on stage during rehearsals and concerts. It is altogether appropriate, therefore, that the conductor is the one who accepts the applause from the audience, takes the first bows, and is reviled by critics for poor orchestral performances.

But is this the model of team leadership we seek? It has some significant benefits, to be sure. For one thing, it is highly efficient. One person is in charge, and precious rehearsal time need not be spent debating what is to be played or how best to play it. By contrast, members of the Orpheus Chamber Orchestra, a superb 26-person orchestra that rehearses and performs without a conductor, spend perhaps three times as many hours in rehearsal for each concert hour as does a conductor-led orchestra (Lehman & Hackman, 2002). The Orpheus musicians would not have it any other way: they believe they get an extra 10% of quality by spending that additional time in rehearsal and, besides, the Orpheus musicians explicitly chose to rehearse and perform orchestral music in chamber music style. But efficient Orpheus is not.

A second benefit of conductor-centric orchestral leadership—and it is a significant benefit indeed—is that symphony orchestras provide settings for the expression of the musical genius of those extraordinary individuals who lead the best of them. The world is much enriched by the musical insight and artistry of the finest symphony orchestra conductors, and to bar them from the concert hall podium would be akin to locking up Yo-Yo Ma's cello.

The conductor-centric model of ensemble leadership also is in significant respects wasteful and costly, as Jutta Allmendinger, Erin Lehman, and I learned in our four-nation study of some 76 professional symphony orchestras a few years ago (for a summary of findings, see Allmendinger, Hackman, & Lehman, 1996). The level of musical talent in most symphony orchestras is nothing short of awesome. When a major orchestra has an opening for a section violin player, for example, the audition committee may receive as many as 200 applications from highly talented violinists. The applicant who wins the position is, understandably, overjoyed to have been selected as one of the relatively small number of talented musicians who will have the opportunity to be paid a living wage for performing some of the finest music ever composed.

But it does not take long, one violinist told me, for the joy of winning the audition to give way to the reality of orchestral life. As a section player, the violinist soon realized that she would be sitting with essentially the same people, playing essentially the same repertoire, possibly for the rest of her career. The playing would always be in unison with the 19 other second violins, and always under the direct and close supervision of a conductor. No musician would speak aloud during rehearsals except to ask for clarification of a conductor's instructions, and offering an interpretive idea of her own about a piece being prepared was completely out of the question. This was not the kind of musical life she had imagined for herself, not even after she had accepted the fact that a career as a concertizing soloist was not within her reach.

In a decade of research on professional symphony and chamber orchestras, I have encountered many players like that violinist, people who are struggling to stay fully alive musically while accommodating the demands and routines of life as a section player. One told me, "I have to be very careful to make sure that my job, which is playing in this orchestra, does not get too much in the way of my career, which is making music." Another musician, who had just retired from a major symphony orchestra, put it this way in an interview with my colleague Josephine Pichanick: "The younger people, when I first came, who are now in their 40s? I guess they sort of . . . 'mellow' is not the right word. They break down, they're broken down by the system. To the outsider, it may look like a glamorous job, but it's not. It's a factory job with a little bit of art thrown in" (Pichanick & Rohrer, 2002).

Our quantitative data affirm these gloomy reports, but also offer one hopeful sign. Over the last decade, we have administered surveys to a wide variety of groups and organizations. Three questions were included in all the surveys. First, how high is *internal work motivation?* Are people self-motivated to perform well, or do they rely on rewards or punishments administered by others, such as bosses? On the survey, people are asked how much they agree with statements such as these: "I feel good when I learn that I have performed well on this job," and "I feel awful when I do poorly in my work." People who agree with such statements are internally motivated. Second, how high is *general satisfaction?* To what extent do people agree with statements such as, "Generally speaking, I am very satisfied with this job." And third, how high is satisfaction with *growth opportunities?* Respondents are asked how happy they are with "the amount of personal growth and development I get in this job."

Players' responses to the first question, about internal motivation, provide the sign of hope. On this measure, symphony orchestra musicians push the top of the scale—their average score, across all orchestras and countries, is 6.2 out of a possible 7. No group or organization we have studied has scored higher. Orchestra players are, indeed, fueled by their own pride and professionalism.

The news is less good for the other two questions. For general satisfaction, orchestra players rank seventh among the 13 groups we have studied and, as is seen below, they rank ninth on the measure of satisfaction with growth opportunities:

1. Professional string quartet (highest, average score of 6.2).
2. Mental health treatment teams.
3. Beer sales and delivery teams.
4. Industrial production teams.
5. Economic analysts in the federal government.
6. Airline cockpit crews.
7. Airline flight attendants.
8. Federal prison guards.
9. *Symphony orchestra musicians* (average score of 4.9).
10. Operating room nurses.
11. Semiconductor fabrication teams.
12. Professional hockey team.
13. Amateur theater company (lowest, average score of 4.1).

Clearly, much talent and many musical ideas and possibilities are left on the rehearsal stage in the persons of the orchestra members. Their work life is not fulfilling, nor are their contributions harvested, at anywhere near the level they could be. The same is true, I venture, in many other leader-centric groups and organizations. The leader-centric model may be a fundamentally flawed way of thinking about the leadership of teams.

THINKING DIFFERENTLY
ABOUT TEAM LEADERSHIP

The symphony orchestra model is perhaps extreme in some ways, but it is consistent with the way many scholars and practitioners think about leadership—namely, that leader behaviors affect group processes, which in turn shape performance outcomes:

LEADER BEHAVIOR ➜ GROUP PROCESS ➜ PERFORMANCE OUTCOMES

This is a conventional input-process-output model, in which causality flows linearly from left to right, step by step. Yet, surprisingly, research on task-performing teams has failed to support the standard model (for a review, see Hackman, 1987). Indeed, there is evidence that, at least in some circumstances, causality flows in the opposite direction:

LEADER BEHAVIOR ⬅ GROUP PROCESS ⬅ PERFORMANCE OUTCOMES

In this unconventional alternative, how well a group is performing is viewed as one of the major influences on group interaction processes. Groups that are failing encounter more than their share of conflicts and other process problems, whereas groups that are performing well find the going significantly smoother. Moreover, the style of team leaders turns out to be significantly shaped by the behaviors of those who are led: If team members are behaving cooperatively and competently, leaders tend to operate more participatively and democratically, but if members are uncooperative or seemingly incompetent, leaders tilt toward a more uni-lateral, directive style (Farris & Lim, 1969; Lowin & Craig, 1968; Sims & Manz, 1984).

At the very least, causality runs in both directions—from leader to group, as in the conventional model, but also from group to leader, as in the unconventional alternative. Regardless of the direction of causal flow, however, both the conventional and the unconventional models posit lin-ear, cause–effect relationships. Our research suggests that a robust and useful understanding of group leadership may require more than merely changing the direction of the causal arrows. Specifically, it may be neces-sary to focus less on the *causes* of group behavior and performance and instead address the structural and contextual *conditions* within which groups form and develop over time. That possibility is explored next.

CONDITIONS RATHER THAN CAUSES

To think about the conditions within which groups chart their own courses is very different from conventional scholarly models (in which the attempt is to link external causes tightly to group effects) as well as from action strategies that derive from those models (in which practitioners attempt to manage team processes more-or-less continuously in real time). The basic idea is that certain conditions get established, sometimes deliberately and other times by happenstance, and groups unfold in their own idiosyncratic ways within them. Group behavior and performance is powerfully shaped by these conditions, but often without members even being aware of the ways in which (or the extent to which) they are being influenced by them.

As I have argued elsewhere, the difference between creating favorable conditions and actively managing causal factors in real time is evident in the two different strategies that can be used by a pilot in landing an aircraft (Hackman, 2002). One strategy is to actively fly the airplane down, continuously adjusting heading, sink rate, and airspeed with the objective of arriving at the runway threshold just above stall speed, ready to flare the aircraft and touch down smoothly. The alternative strategy is to get the aircraft stabilized on approach while still far from the field, making small corrections as needed to heading, power, or aircraft configuration to keep the plane "in the groove." It is well known among pilots that the safer strategy is the second one; indeed, when a pilot finds that he or she is in the first situation the prudent action is to go around and try the approach again.

To be stabilized on approach is to have the basic conditions established such that the natural course of events leads to the desired outcome—in this case, a good landing. The same considerations apply to the design and leadership of social systems, including work teams in organizations. Rather than trying to pinpoint and directly manipulate specific "causes" of group performance outcomes (the parallel of trying to "fly the airplane down"), scholars and practitioners would seek to identify the small number of conditions that, when present, increase the likelihood that a group will naturally evolve into an ever more competent performing unit (the parallel of getting stabilized on approach and then managing the landing by making adjustments at the margins).

To think about conditions rather than causes is to think differently about teams. And, as will be seen next, that simple change in how one construes the way team behavior is shaped has significant implications, both for practitioners who create and lead work teams and for social scientists who study them.

WHAT CONDITIONS?

The conditions that most powerfully set the stage for great group performances are few in number, and are explored in detail in my book *Leading*

Teams (Hackman, 2002). Those conditions are akin to Russian dolls, in that each one has within it subconditions that, in turn, spawn additional subconditions. The is no limit to the amount of learning a leader can do about the conditions that increase the likelihood (but, to reiterate, do not guarantee) excellent team performance.

Here, I briefly review four imperatives of those conditions for the behavior of those who would provide leadership to teams. First is to create a *real team* rather than a team in name only, and to make sure that the team has reasonable stability over time. Second is to provide the team with a *compelling direction* for its work. Third is to make sure that the team has an *enabling design,* one that encourages competent teamwork and provides ready access to the resources and contextual supports members need to carry out their collective work. And fourth is to make available to the team *expert coaching* that can help members take good advantage of their favorable performance circumstances.

Real Team

Managers sometimes attempt to capture the benefits of teamwork by simply declaring that some set of people (often everyone who reports to the same supervisor) is now a team and that members should henceforth behave accordingly. Real teams cannot be created that way. Instead, explicit action must be taken to establish and affirm the team's boundaries, to define the task for which members are collectively responsible, and to give the team ample authority to manage both their own team processes and their relations with external entities such as clients and co-workers.

Creating and launching real teams is not something that can be accomplished casually, as is illustrated by research on airline cockpit crews. It is team functioning, rather than mechanical problems or the technical proficiency of individual pilots, that is at the root of most airline accidents (Helmreich & Foushee, 1993). Moreover, crews are especially vulnerable when they are just starting out, as was found in a recent study by the National Transportation Safety Board (NTSB). Analysts discovered that 73% of the accidents in the NTSB database occurred on the crew's first day of flying together, and 44% of those accidents happened on the crew's very first flight (National Transportation Safety Board, 1994, pp. 40–41). Other research has shown that experienced crews, even when fatigued, perform significantly better than do rested crews whose members have not worked together (Foushee, Lauber, Baetge, & Acomb, 1986).

This body of research has a clear policy implication. Crews should be trained together and then remain intact long enough for members to develop themselves into the best performing unit that they are able to become. Moreover, on any given trip they would fly the same aircraft and work with the same cabin crew. And the leader of the crew, the captain, would conduct a team-oriented briefing before each trip to reduce as much as possible the crew's exposure to the liabilities of newness (Ginnett, 1993).

Yet in most airlines crew members are trained as individuals and crew composition constantly changes because of the long-standing practice, enforced by labor contracts, of assigning pilots to trips, positions, and aircraft as individuals—usually on the basis of a seniority bidding system (Hackman, 1993). In one airline my colleagues and I studied, for example, a normal day's flying could involve two or even three changes of aircraft and as many different cabin crews, and even one or two changes in the cockpit crew's own composition during its 1- or 2-day life span.

Why have airline managements, pilot unions, and federal regulators, all of whom are deeply committed to improving the safety of flight, not jumped to implement policies and practices based on the research findings just summarized? For one thing, to schedule crews as intact units whose members stay together for a significant period of time would be very costly—millions of dollars a year, according to one airline analyst. Moreover, airline managers, like most of the rest of us, are disinclined to believe research findings about the benefits of team stability. Everyone knows that if a team stays together too long members will become too comfortable with one another, lax in enforcing standard procedures such as checklists, and too ready to forgive teammates' mistakes and lapses. Yes, teams may become better at working together as they move through the early phases of their lives. But that learning happens quickly, then plateaus, and then, at some point, overfamiliarity sets in and dominates members' subsequent interaction. It is better, therefore, to have a constant flow-through of new members to keep teams on their collective toes.

Everyone knows such things—but they are not true. Members of competently designed teams do learn fairly rapidly how to work together, as claimed. But, except for one special type of team, I have not been able to find a shred of evidence to support the view that there comes a point at which the learning stops and the positive trend reverses, when compositionally stable teams function decreasingly well the longer members stay together. (The exception is research and development teams. Organizational researcher Ralph Katz, 1982, found that the productivity of such teams peaked when members had worked together for about 3 years, and then began to decline. It appears that research is a type of teamwork for which a moderate flow-through of new members really does help, probably because the new arrivals bring with them fresh ideas and perspectives to which the team might not otherwise be exposed.) The very best teams get better and better indefinitely, like a great marriage that is stronger on the couple's 50th anniversary than it was on their first, or like the Guarneri String Quartet whose members have continuously improved their music-making over more than three decades of playing together.

Compelling Direction

The "direction" of a group is the specification of its overall purposes. Our research suggests that a good direction for a team has three features: it is, simultaneously, challenging, clear, and consequential.

Challenging.   The performance target set for a team must be neither too demanding nor too easy. Too great a stretch, and people do not even bother to try; too small a stretch, and they do not *need* to try. Research by Atkinson (1958) and others has shown that individual motivation is greatest when a performer has about a 50–50 chance of succeeding on a task; I see no reason to doubt that the same is true for work teams.

Also critical in energizing a work team is whether those who specify its direction focus mainly on the end states to be achieved or on the procedures the team must use in carrying out its work. Leaders who create work teams should be insistent and unapologetic about exercising their authority to specify end states, but equally insistent about not specifying the details of the means by which the team pursues those ends. That state of affairs, shown in the upper right quadrant of Fig. 6.1, fosters energetic, task-focused work (in the jargon of the day, team "empowerment"). Specifying both ends and means (the lower right quadrant) mitigates the challenge to team members and, at the same time, under-uses the full complement of team members' resources; as was shown earlier, professional symphony orchestras exemplify this cell. Specifying neither (the upper left quadrant) invites anarchy rather than focused, purposive team work. And specifying means but not ends (the lower left quadrant) clearly is the worst of all possible cases.

Clear.   A work team's purposes must be clear as well as challenging. A clear direction orients the team toward its objective and is invaluable to members as they weigh alternative strategies for proceeding with

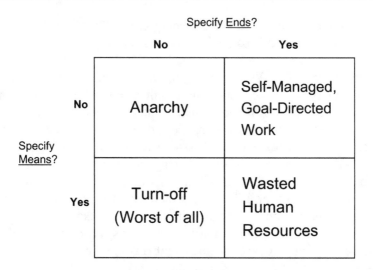

FIG. 6.1.   Setting direction about means versus ends.

the work. As a metaphor, consider a mountain-climbing team that has encountered a fork in the trail. Absent a clear and shared understanding of which peak is the team's objective, members may waste considerable time and fall into unnecessary conflict as members debate which way to go. The same is true for work teams. There are numerous choices to be made in the course of work on almost any task, and decision making about such matters is almost always facilitated by a clear and concrete statement of direction. To have a purpose of "serving customers" or "creating value for the firm," for example, is to have no real purpose at all, and to implicitly invite team members to spend excessive time wandering about trying to figure out what they are really supposed to do.

There is a twist, however, in that statements of direction sometimes can be *too* clear. When a team's purposes are spelled out explicitly and completely, there is little room for members to add their own shades of meaning to those purposes, to make sense of them in their own, idiosyncratic ways. Such sense-making processes are an essential part of coming to experience "ownership" of a piece of work, and an overly explicit statement of direction can preempt those processes. Moreover, if a team's direction is clear, specific, *and* of great consequence for team members (for example, if their jobs or a significant bonus hangs in the balance), then there is a real risk that the team will be tempted to engage in inappropriate behaviors such as fudging numbers to ensure their success, or that they will focus too intently on the measures used to gauge their success at the expense of the real purposes of their work (Kerr, 1975). Good direction for a work team is clear, it is palpable—and it is incomplete.

Consequential.   When a piece of work has clear consequences for team members or for the well-being of other people, members are more likely to engage the full range of their talents in executing the work than they are when group purposes are viewed as being of little real consequence. When its work is highly consequential, a team is unlikely to fall victim to the "free rider" problem in using member talents (that is, people not contributing what they know, or what they know how to do, to the team's work). Moreover, the chances increase that the team will weight members' contributions in accord with their actual expertise rather than use some task-irrelevant criterion such as status, gender, or equality of workload in deciding how to deploy member talents. When it is the championship game, the team cannot afford to let everybody play—even if that means that less talented or experienced members have to remain on the bench.

Leaders sometimes use rhetorical devices to try to make a team's direction seem more consequential than it really is (this is akin to the oft-cited motivational ploy of trying to convince brick carriers that they actually are building a cathedral). If such devices work at all, their effect is temporary because it becomes clear soon enough that what one really is doing, day after day, is carrying bricks. It is impossible to generate a statement of direction that engages the full range and depth of members' talents for work that is essentially trivial.

In sum, good direction for work teams is challenging (which *energizes* members), it is clear (which *orients* them to their main purposes) and it is consequential (which *engages* the full range of their talents). Direction has priority because so much else depends on it—how the team is structured and supported, and the character of leaders' hands-on coaching.

Enabling Design

Traditionally designed organizations often are plagued by constraining structures and contextual features that have been built up over the years to monitor and control employee behavior. When teams are used to perform work, structure often is viewed, by leaders and team members alike, as an unnecessary bureaucratic impediment to group functioning. Thus, just as some leaders mistakenly attempt to empower a team by relinquishing to members full authority to set the team's direction, so do some attempt to cut through bureaucratic obstacles to team functioning by dismantling all the structures they can. The assumption, apparently, is that removing structures will release the pent-up power of groups and make it possible for members to work together creatively and effectively.

Leaders who hold this view often wind up providing teams with less structure and fewer contextual supports than they actually need. Tasks are defined only in vague, general terms. Lots of people may be involved in the work, but the actual membership of the team is unclear. Norms of conduct are kept deliberately fuzzy. Contextual features, such as the reward system, the information system, and educational supports are kept as they traditionally have been. In the words of one manager I spoke with, "the team will work out the details." If anything, the opposite is true: Groups with appropriate structures and team-friendly contexts tend to develop healthy internal processes, whereas groups with insufficient or inappropriate structures tend to be plagued with process problems.

Among the most common design problems my colleagues and I have encountered in our research are flaws in how teams are composed. For one thing, teams often are far more homogeneous than they should be, because the managers who set up the teams assume that members who are similar to one another will work together more harmoniously and, therefore, more effectively. It is true that people who are similar tend to get along with one another, but it is not true that smoothly functioning teams perform especially well. In fact, diverse groups that experience a measure of conflict about the best way to proceed with the work often generate products that are more creative than those whose members agree from the beginning about how they should operate (see, for example, McLeod, Lobel, & Cox, 1996, or Watson, Kumar, & Michaelsen, 1993).

Excessive size also is a common and pernicious problem in team design. It takes four people to play a string quartet, two crewmembers to fly a Boeing 737 aircraft, and twelve persons to form a full-sized jury. Not a person more nor a person less will do, so those who compose such groups can focus on matters other than the size of the performing unit. More commonly, however, leaders who create work teams in organizations have considerable discretion about team size. Although they sometimes form teams that are too small to accomplish their work well, the far more common and dangerous mistake is overstaffing them.

The larger a group, the more process problems members encounter in carrying out their collective work—social loafing, the misweighting of members' contributions, and so on. Worse, the vulnerability of a group to such difficulties increases sharply as size increases. As is seen in Fig. 6.2,

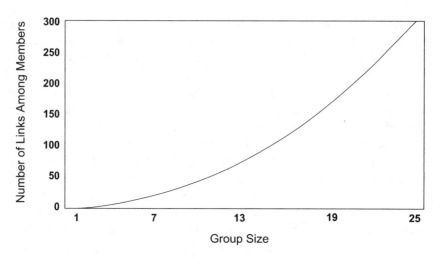

FIG. 6.2.   Group size and the number of links among members.

it appears that process problems track not the simple number of members, but the number of *links* among members (the number of links is given by the formula $[n * (n - 1) / 2]$, where n is group size).

So what is the best group size? It depends on the size of the task, of course, but I do have a rule of thumb that I relentlessly enforce for student project groups in my Harvard courses: A team cannot have more than six members. Even a six-person team has 15 pairs among members, but a seven-person team has 21, and the difference in how well groups of the two sizes operate is noticeable.

If the evidence is so strong that small team size is better, why do we see so many large teams struggling along in organizations? Certainly the faulty assumption that "more is better" for team effectiveness is part of the reason. But the main driver may have less to do with team performance than with emotional issues, such as using large numbers of people to share responsibility and spread accountability, and political considerations, such as ensuring that all relevant stakeholders are represented in the group so they will accept its product. For these reasons, individuals from various constituencies may be appointed to a team one by one, or even two by two, creating a large and politically correct team—but a team that can find itself incapable of generating an outcome that meets even minimum standards of acceptability, let alone one that shows signs of originality.

But what if one really does want one's board of directors (or top management team, or some other team whose work requires many members) to be an effective performing unit? One possible model is provided by the

Orpheus Chamber Orchestra, the conductorless ensemble briefly described earlier. Although all 26 players (or even more) are needed to perform many works in the chamber orchestra repertoire, a 26-person team is far too large to operate as collegially as does a string quartet. With everyone chiming in with thoughts and ideas, rehearsal could become a cacophony. So orchestra members came up with the idea of the "core," a small group consisting of the principal players for the piece being rehearsed. The core meets prior to the first full-orchestra rehearsal to work out the basic frame for the piece being prepared. Then, when the rest of the orchestra joins in, these individuals have special responsibility for helping other members of their sections understand and implement the ideas the core has roughed out. Any musician still can offer up new musical ideas for consideration by the ensemble, of course, but the starting point is the interpretive direction the core has set.

With size, as with all other aspects of team design, there always is a choice. But it takes the courage of informed conviction, plus a good measure of willingness to innovate and experiment, for leaders to find ways to exercise that choice that can simultaneously both harvest the diverse contributions of team members *and* foster efficient collective action.

Expert Coaching

It is not always easy for a team to take advantage of positive performance conditions, particularly if members have relatively little (or relatively negative) experience in teamwork. A leader can do much to promote team effectiveness by helping team members learn how to work interdependently. The role of the help provider is not, of course, to dictate to group members the one best way to proceed with their collaborative work. It is, instead, to help members learn how to minimize the process losses that invariably occur in groups (Steiner, 1972), and to consider how they might work together to generate synergistic process gains.

Such coaching can be provided at any point in the course of a team's work, but there are three times in a team's life when members are likely to be especially open to particular coaching interventions: (a) at the beginning, when a group is just starting its work, it is especially open to interventions that focus on the *effort* members will apply to their work; (b) at the midpoint, when the group has completed about half its work (or half the allotted time has elapsed), it is especially open to interventions that help members reflect on and refine their *performance strategies;* and (c) at the end, when the work is finished, the team is ready to entertain interventions aimed at helping members *learn from their experiences* (for details, see Hackman & Wageman, in press).

GETTING THE ORDER RIGHT

A *New Yorker* cartoon some years ago, as I recall it, depicted a bleary-eyed man sitting on the side of his bed, looking at a sign he had posted on the bedroom wall. The sign read: "First slacks, *then* shoes." Direction and design are the slacks. Coaching is the shoes. Unfortunately, coaches sometimes are called upon by their organizations to do the shoes first, to try to salvage a team that operates in a performance situation that is fundamentally flawed. Even expert coaching can make little constructive difference in such circumstances—and may even do more harm than good by distracting members' attention from more fundamental aspects of their design or context that they ought be addressing.

For example, consider a team working on a mechanized assembly line where inputs are machine paced, assembly procedures are completely programmed, and performance operations are simple and predictable. How could a coach help that team? Not by encouraging members to work harder or more efficiently, because the amount of work processed is under control of the engineers who pace the line, not the team. Not by helping them develop more task-appropriate performance strategies, because the way the work is to be done is completely pre-specified. And not by helping them develop or better use members' knowledge and skill, because the required operations are so easy that an increase in team talent would merely mean that an even smaller proportion of the team's total pool of talent would be used. In this situation, team performance processes are so severely constrained and controlled that the team has almost no leverage to improve them. For the same reason, there is little that even a great coach can do in working with the team to better its performance. Through no fault of the members, the team is essentially uncoachable.

Even when a performance situation is not as team-unfriendly as the one just described, the quality of a team's design strongly conditions the impact of leaders' coaching interventions, as was documented by organizational psychologist Ruth Wageman in a study of self-managing field service teams (Wageman, 2001). For each team studied, Wageman obtained independent assessments of the team's design, the coaching behaviors of its leader, the team's level of self-management, and its objective performance. She predicted that a team's design features would make a larger difference in both level of team self-management and in team performance outcomes than would the leader's coaching behaviors, and she was right. Design was four times as powerful as coaching in affecting a team's level of self-management, and almost 40 times as powerful in affecting team performance. Clearly, design features do have causal priority over leader coaching in shaping team performance processes and outcomes.

Perhaps the most fascinating finding of the Wageman study turned up when she compared the effects on team self-management of "good" coaching (such as helping a team develop a task-appropriate performance strategy) with those of "bad" coaching (such as identifying a team's problems and telling members exactly what they should do to fix them). Good coaching significantly helped well-designed teams exploit their favorable circumstances but made almost no difference for poorly designed teams. Bad coaching, on the other hand, significantly compromised poorly designed teams' ability to manage themselves, worsening an already difficult situation, but did not much affect teams that had an enabling team structure and a supportive organizational context.

We seem to have here yet another instance in which the rich get richer (well-designed teams are helped most by good coaching), and the poor get poorer (teams with flawed designs are hurt most by bad coaching). Great coaching can be enormously valuable to a team in exploiting the potential of a sound performance situation but cannot reverse the impact of poor direction or a flawed team structure. The key to effective team leadership, then, is first to ensure that the team's basic performance conditions *are* sound and then to help team members take the greatest possible advantage of their favorable circumstances.

LEADING TEAMS WELL

The main work of team leaders is to do whatever needs to be done to get the handful of conditions that foster team effectiveness in place—and to keep them there. Is the work team a *real* team, or just a collection of individuals who go by that name? Does it have a compelling direction? Does the team's structure and context enable rather than impede competent teamwork? And does the team have available ample and expert coaching to help members get over rough spots and take advantage of emerging opportunities?

Some of these conditions are best created before the team even meets for the first time, others when it is launched, others around the midpoint of its work, and still others when a significant piece of work has been completed. Serendipity and history play important roles in determining when the enabling conditions can be created or strengthened, how that might best be accomplished, and how hard it will be to do so. Sometimes most of the conditions will already be in place when a team is formed, and fine-tuning them will not pose much of a leadership challenge; other times, such as in an established organization that has been tuned over the years to support and control *individual* work, it can take enormous effort and ingenuity to establish even the basic conditions required for competent teamwork.

SHARING LEADERSHIP

There is no one best strategy or style for accomplishing team leadership, nor any one person who is solely responsible for providing it. Instead, team leadership involves inventing and competently executing whatever actions are most likely to create and sustain the enabling conditions. Anyone who helps do that, including both external managers and team members who hold no formal leadership role, is exercising team leadership. What is important is that the key leadership *functions* get fulfilled, not who fulfills them and certainly not how they go about doing it (Hackman & Walton, 1986).

The richer the set of leadership skills held by team members and organizational managers, the greater the number of options available for getting the enabling conditions in place. It is like the difference between driving and taking the train. When driving, there are always alternative routes to the destination if one road is blocked. A train, however, has but one set of tracks. If there is an obstruction on the tracks, the train cannot proceed until it is removed. Relying on any single person to provide all of a team's leadership is the equivalent of taking the train. By contrast, having multiple individuals with diverse skills pitching in to help create and sustain the enabling conditions provides more maneuvering room. If one strategy for moving forward is blocked, perhaps by a recalcitrant manager or by technological constraints that would be enormously expensive to change, there are other strategies that also could work.

The more members who contribute to the real work of leadership (that is, helping to create, fine tune, and exploit the benefits of the enabling conditions) the better. The Orpheus Chamber Orchestra again illustrates. Although that orchestra has no conductor on the podium, it has much more *leadership* than do orchestras known for their famous music directors. Every member has the right—and the responsibility—to do whatever he or she can to help the ensemble achieve the highest possible level of excellence. During rehearsals, for example, it is not uncommon to see a member quietly depart the stage and take an audience seat to listen to the orchestra's sound for a few moments. At the next pause in the rehearsal, that person reports on what he or she heard, perhaps suggesting some changes to improve the balance among the sections. Other members may spontaneously offer suggestions about tempo, or how best to manage the transition of a melodic line from one section to another, or even how the composer meant a solo passage to be interpreted.

Even so, shared leadership in Orpheus is far from a one-person-one-vote democracy. For each piece of music the orchestra performs, one violinist is selected by his or her peers to serve as concertmaster. That person manages the rehearsal process for that piece—beginning each rehearsal, fielding suggestions from members about interpretive matters, deciding when spirited disagreements among members must be set aside to get on with the rehearsal, and taking the lead in figuring out how to handle transitions in the music that in a traditional orchestra would be signaled by a conductor's baton.

Orpheus learned early in its life that is a good idea to have one person identified as the individual who will facilitate communication and coordination for a particular piece of work, and the same principle holds for teams that do other kinds of work. Who the designated leader is for a given piece of work can be selected by members themselves and can change from time to time, just as is done at Orpheus. But for virtually all task-performing teams making sure things do not fall between the cracks and that information finds its way to the people who need it are activities usually handled most efficiently by a single individual who has an overview of the entire work process.

CHOOSING AND TRAINING LEADERS

If it is a good idea to identify someone as team leader, how should that person be picked and trained? At Orpheus, members are very choosy about who gets to have a special "say" in the preparation of each piece. Players are not treated as equals, because in fact they are *not* equals: Each member brings special talents and interests to the ensemble, and also has some areas of relative disinterest and lesser strength. The orchestra's willingness to acknowledge, to respect, and to exploit the individual differences among members in the interest of collective excellence is one of its greatest strengths as a self-managing team.

Those who are selected by their peers for special leadership responsibilities at Orpheus are a highly diverse lot—some are quiet, others are exuberant; some are easygoing, others seem to be a tightly wrapped bundle of nerves; some jump at the chance to exercise leadership, others have to be coaxed into it. There is no discernible template that distinguishes those who are most often turned to for leadership from those who are less often asked to take the lead. What one observes at Orpheus is affirmed by the chastening findings from researchers' decades-long search for the personal traits of effective leaders. It was clear as long ago as the 1950s that researchers were unlikely to identify any set of universal traits that would reliably distinguish effective from ineffective leaders (for an early review, see Mann, 1959; for a more contemporary assessment, see Hogan, Curphy, & Hogan, 1994).

Neither hope nor the leader attribution error dies easily, however, and the commonsense belief that a leader's personal traits somehow determine his or her effectiveness in leading teams continues to guide both research and practice. The power of such thinking is perhaps best exemplified by the readiness of many to accept the claim that a leader's "emotional intelligence" is the key determinant of his or her effectiveness. The irony is that many of the skills that are grouped under the emotional intelligence label are not only helpful for leaders to have but also trainable. But use of the word *intelligence* as part of the label implies that whatever it is that emotionally intelligent leaders possess is at least an enduring personal attribute and perhaps even innate. It is bad enough that analytic intelligence, the kind of thing often referred to as "IQ," is so widely viewed as wired in at birth; it is even more troublesome that trainable leadership and interpersonal skills sometimes are labeled in a way to suggest that they are as well.

My own research points to four personal qualities that distinguish excellent team leaders from those for whom team leadership is a struggle. First, effective leaders *know* some things—they are aware of the conditions that most powerfully shape team effectiveness. Such knowledge, briefly summarized in these pages, can be taught. If a team leader does not already know what it takes to foster team effectiveness, he or she can readily learn it. Second, effective leaders know how to *do* some things—they have skill both in extracting from the complexity of performance situations those themes that are consequential for team performance and in taking actions to narrow the gap between a team's present reality and what could and should be. These skills also can be taught, but not by reading books, listening to lectures, or doing case analyses. Skill training requires the provision of positive models, coupled with repeated practice and feedback, which is a far more time-consuming (and expensive) training activity than merely transferring content knowledge from an instructor to a trainee.

The third attribute is of a different kind: Effective team leaders have sufficient *emotional maturity* to deal competently with the demands of the leadership role. Leading a team is an emotionally challenging undertaking, especially in dealing with anxieties—both one's own and those of others. Leaders who are emotionally mature are willing and able to move toward anxiety-arousing states of affairs in the interest of learning about them rather than moving away to get anxieties reduced as quickly as possible. Finally, team leaders need a good measure of *personal courage.* Leadership involves moving a system from where it is now to some other, better place. That means that the leader must operate at the margins of what members presently like and want rather than at the center of the collective consensus. To help a team address and modify dysfunctional group dynamics, for example, often requires challenging existing group norms and disrupting established routines, which can elicit anger and resistance from group members. Leaders who behave courageously are more likely than their more timid colleagues to make significant and constructive differences in their teams and organizations—but they often wind up paying a substantial personal toll in the bargain.

The four qualities just discussed are differentially amenable to training—and in the order listed. It is relatively straightforward to help team leaders expand what they know about the conditions that foster team effectiveness. It is more challenging, but with sufficient time and effort entirely feasible, to help them hone their skills in diagnosis and execution. To foster team leaders' emotional maturity is harder still, and is perhaps better viewed as a developmental task for one's life than as something that can be taught. Courage may be the most trait-like of the four attributes. Although there indisputably are differences in courage across individuals, it is beyond me to imagine how one might help leaders become more willing than they already are to take courageous actions with their teams, peers, and bosses to increase the chances that their teams will excel.

These four personal attributes may seem strange to those who are accustomed to thinking of leadership qualities mainly in terms of personality or behavioral style, and I offer my views in speculative spirit. But it is nonetheless true that the superb team leaders I have observed over the years have most, if not all, of these very qualities. It may be worthwhile to give new thought to old questions about how team leaders might be selected and trained on attributes such as the four just discussed.

HOW LEADERS MAKE MAGIC

Michelle Walter, former executive director of the Richmond Symphony, tells of that orchestra's performance of Beethoven's fifth symphony for an audience of local youngsters and their parents, many of whom were making their first foray into the concert hall. Although neither Michelle nor the musicians could explain afterwards why it happened, the orchestra that day gave a transcendental performance of a symphony that is surely one of the most-played pieces in the repertoire. As the final chords echoed and faded, complete silence held for 4 or 5 seconds, a sure sign that something special had just happened. Then the hall, filled with people who knew not the first thing about classical music, simply erupted.

The Richmond orchestra, that day, had a magical moment. We all have experienced such moments, times when a team somehow comes together in a way that produces an extraordinary outcome—a great performance, a brilliant insight, an amazing come-from-behind win. It would be wonderful if leaders could create magic at will, if they could somehow engineer it, but they cannot.

There are two certain ways leaders can ensure that team magic does *not* occur, however, both of which are seen far too often in work organizations. One way to go wrong, to stay with music for another moment, is to act like a maestro on the podium, body and limbs in constant motion in an effort to pull greatness from an orchestra. Team leaders in maestro tradition would prefer to do the work all by themselves, without having to engender and coordinate the efforts of others. But since that is not possible, they do the next best thing and personally manage every aspect of the work process, keeping a close eye on all that is transpiring and issuing to team members an unending stream of instructions and corrections. Magic is not commonly observed in teams whose leaders act like maestros.

The other way leaders can get it wrong is to do nothing much at all, on the assumption that the magic of teamwork comes automatically and therefore the best thing to do is to stay out of the way. A guest conductor who was rehearsing a symphony orchestra for an upcoming "pops" concert took exactly this strategy. "You people know this music better than I do," he said, "so just go ahead and play it. I'll wave my arms around a lot at the concert to please the audience, but don't pay much attention to what I'm doing." I am not making this up. It was the purest, most beautiful example of leader abdication I have had the pleasure to observe.

So what *should* a leader do to increase the likelihood that a team will have a magical moment every now and then? Split the difference between the maestro and the abdicator, being half controlling or being controlling half the time? Of course not. What is required, as I have argued throughout this chapter, is a different way of thinking about the leadership of teams. A leader cannot make a team be great, but a leader can create conditions that increase the chances that moments of greatness will occur—and, moreover, can provide a little boost or nudge now and then to help members take the fullest possible advantage of those favorable conditions.

This model, too, is sometimes seen on the podium in concert halls. Some years ago, I had the opportunity to watch Russian conductor Yuri Temirkanov conduct a major U.S. orchestra in a performance of a Mahler symphony—the kind of piece that can invite the grandest arm-waving, body-swaying pyrotechnics. But not from Temirkanov. He cued the musicians to begin, and then his hands went to his sides. The orchestra played, and he *listened.* When some adjustment or assistance was needed, he provided it—signaling players with his eyes or body, or guiding a transition with his arms and hands. But that was about the extent of it. He had prepared the orchestra well during rehearsals, and all the right conditions were in place. Now, at the performance, when it counted the most, he was managing at the margin. And the orchestra responded by creating a little magic for itself and its audience.

CONCLUSION

The approach to team leadership summarized in these pages is more complex than any list of "principles of good management" or "one-minute" prescriptions. Yet it also is simpler (there are just a few key conditions) and more flexible (create and sustain those conditions any way you can) than either contingency models of leadership or those that require fundamental reprogramming of leaders' personal models of intervention. This way of thinking differs from common sense notions about leadership, in which influence is viewed as flowing dominantly from the person identified as "leader" to the team rather than in all directions—upwards to bosses and laterally to peers as well as downwards from formal leaders to regular members. It differs as well from leadership theories that focus mainly on identifying the personal characteristics of effective leaders, or that specify the best leadership styles, or that lay out in detail all the major contingencies that researchers have documented among traits, styles, and situational properties.

Throughout this chapter, my aspiration has been to generate a way of thinking about team leadership that can be useful to *both* scholars and practitioners. That is a challenge, because scholars and organizational actors construe influences on work team performance differently. We scholars want to know specifically what causes a team's level of performance. To find out, we take the performance situation apart piece by piece—we carefully think through what might be the ingredients that are most critical for team effectiveness, and then we collect data to test our ideas empirically. We do whatever we have to do to pin down the *true* causal agent. Organizational actors, on the other hand, are not much interested in teasing out the relative influence of various possible causes of performance. Instead, they are prepared to draw upon all resources at their disposal to overdetermine outcomes in the direction they prefer. They welcome rather than shun both the confounding of variables and redundant causation (which are sure signs in scientific work that one has not thought carefully enough about one's phenomena).

Although the preferences of scientists and practitioners do differ, they are not mutually exclusive. I believe it is entirely feasible to generate models of social system phenomena that are, at the same time, conceptually sound, capable of guiding constructive action, *and* amenable to empirical assessment and correction. The model of team performance summarized in these pages was generated in that spirit. Rather than specify the main causes of group performance (or provide a long list of all possible causes) I have proposed a small set of conditions which, when present, increase the chances—but by no means guarantee—that a group will develop into an effective performing unit.

The challenge for social scientists is to take more seriously than we have heretofore the implications of thinking about social systems in terms of conditions rather than causes. Moreover, we need to find ways of studying the evolution of social systems that do not destroy or caricature systemic phenomena in order to make them amenable to study using conventional cause–effect conceptual models and research methodologies.

The challenge for practitioners is to make sure that team leaders are carefully selected and competently trained, to be sure. But even fine leaders can make little constructive difference if they have little latitude to act—for example, if all team performance processes are dictated by technology or pre-specified operating procedures. It is the difference between a jazz musician and a section player in a symphony orchestra: The former has lots of room to improvise, whereas the latter must follow exactly a detailed score, and do so under the direct and constant supervision of a conductor. Team leaders should be more like jazz musicians.

Both scholars and practitioners compromise their own espoused objectives when they hold constant conditions that may be among the most substantial influences on their phenomena of interest. Yet we regularly do this: researchers do it to achieve experimental control, and practitioners do it to preserve established organizational structures, systems, and authority hierarchies. Until both scholars and practitioners accept the risks of breaking out of our traditional ways of construing and leading social systems, we will remain vulnerable to the leader attribution error—and we will continue to mistakenly assume that the best leaders are those who stand on whatever podium they can command and, through their personal efforts in real time, extract greatness from their teams.

ACKNOWLEDGMENTS

An earlier version of this chapter was presented at a conference on leadership sponsored by the Kennedy School of Government's Center for Public Leadership on March 15, 2002. Parts of the chapter are adapted from *Leading Teams: Setting the Stage for Great Performances* by J. R. Hackman, 2002, Boston, MA: Harvard Business School Press.

REFERENCES

Allmendinger, J., Hackman, J. R., & Lehman, E. V. (1996). Life and work in symphony orchestras. *The Musical Quarterly, 80,* 194–219.

Atkinson, J. W. (1958). Motivational determinants of risk-taking behavior. In J. W. Atkinson (Ed.), *Motives in fantasy, action, and society* (pp. 322–339). Princeton: Van Nostrand.

Corn, R. (2000). *Why poor teams get poorer: The influence of team effectiveness and design quality on the quality of group diagnostic processes.* Unpublished doctoral dissertation, Harvard University.

Drucker, P. F. (1988, January-February). The coming of the new organization. *Harvard Business Review,* 45–53.

Farris, G. F., & Lim, F. G., Jr. (1969). Effects of performance on leadership, cohesiveness, influence, satisfaction, and subsequent performance. *Journal of Applied Psychology, 53,* 490–497.

Foushee, H. C., Lauber, J. K., Baetge, M. M., & Acomb, D. B. (1986). *Crew factors in flight operations: III. The operational significance of exposure to short-haul air transport opera-*

tions (Technical Memorandum No. 88342). Moffett Field, CA: NASA Ames Research Center.

Ginnett, R. C. (1993). Crews as groups: Their formation and their leadership. In E. L. Wiener, B. G. Kanki, & R. L. Helmreich (Eds.), *Cockpit resource management* (pp. 71–98). Orlando, FL: Academic Press.

Hackman, J. R. (1987). The design of work teams. In J. Lorsch (Ed.), *Handbook of organizational behavior* (pp. 315–342). Englewood Cliffs, NJ: Prentice-Hall.

Hackman, J. R. (1993). Teams, leaders, and organizations: New directions for crew-oriented flight training. In E. L. Wiener, B. G. Kanki, & R. L. Helmreich (Eds.), *Cockpit resource management* (pp. 47–69). Orlando, FL: Academic Press.

Hackman, J. R. (2002). *Leading teams: Setting the stage for great performances.* Boston: Harvard Business School Press.

Hackman, J. R., & Wageman, R. (in press). A theory of team coaching. *Academy of Management Review.*

Hackman, J. R., & Walton, R. E. (1986). Leading groups in organizations. In P. S. Goodman (Ed.), *Designing effective work groups* (pp. 72–119). San Francisco: Jossey-Bass.

Helmreich, R. L., & Foushee, H. C. (1993). Why crew resource management? Empirical and theoretical bases of human factors training in aviation. In E. L. Wiener, B. G. Kanki, & R. L. Helmreich (Eds.), *Cockpit resource management* (pp. 3–45). Orlando, FL: Academic Press.

Hogan, R., Curphy, G. J., & Hogan, J. (1994). What we know about leadership. *American Psychologist, 49,* 493–504.

Katz, R. (1982). The effects of group longevity on project communication and performance. *Administrative Science Quarterly, 27,* 81–104.

Kerr, S. (1975). On the folly of rewarding A while hoping for B. *Academy of Management Journal, 18,* 769–783.

Lehman, E. V., & Hackman, J. R. (2002). *Nobody on the podium: Lessons for leaders from the Orpheus Chamber Orchestra* (Case No. 1644.9). Cambridge, MA: Case Services, Kennedy School of Government, Harvard University.

Lowin, B., & Craig, J. R. (1968). The influence of level of performance on managerial style: An experimental object-lesson in the ambiguity of correlational data. *Organizational Behavior and Human Performance, 3,* 440–458.

Mann, R. D. (1959). A review of the relationships between personality and performance in small groups. *Psychological Bulletin, 56,* 241–270.

McLeod, P. L., Lobel, S. A., & Cox, T. H. (1996). Ethnic diversity and creativity in small groups. *Small Group Research, 27,* 248–264.

Meindl, J. R. (1990). On leadership: An alternative to the conventional wisdom. *Research in Organizational Behavior, 12,* 159–203.

National Transportation Safety Board. (1994). *A review of flightcrew-involved major accidents of U.S. air carriers, 1978 through 1990.* Washington, DC: Author.

Pichanick, J. S., & Rohrer, L. H. (2002). Rewards and sacrifices in elite and non-elite organizations: Participation in valued activities and job satisfaction in two symphony orchestras. In A. Sagie & M. Stasiak (Eds.), *Work values and behavior in an era of transformation* (pp. 347–353). Poland: Academy of Humanities and Economics.

Sims, H. P., & Manz, C. C. (1984). Observing leader verbal behavior: Toward reciprocal determinism in leadership theory. *Journal of Applied Psychology, 69,* 222–232.

Steiner, I. D. (1972). *Group process and productivity.* New York: Academic Press.

Wageman, R. (2001). How leaders foster self-managing team effectiveness: Design choices versus hands-on coaching. *Organization Science, 12,* 559–577.

Watson, W. E., Kumar, K., & Michaelsen, L. K. (1993). Cultural diversity's impact on interaction process and performance: Comparing homogeneous and diverse task groups. *Academy of Management Journal, 36,* 590–602.

7

Leadership
as Group Regulation

Randall S. Peterson
London Business School

Kristin J. Behfar
Northwestern University

Groups often fail to successfully regulate all of the competing tensions they experience. Past research suggests, for example, that groups often misregulate these tensions by focusing on one force to the exclusion of others (e.g., focusing exclusively on consensus leads to groupthink). Relatively little research attention has been paid, however, to how groups manage the natural tensions in their lives, such as the trade-offs between efficiency and effectiveness, task and relationship, etc.—with virtually no attention at all focused on any potential role for leaders in helping groups balance these tensions. This chapter addresses this gap in the literature by proposing that effective groups have leaders who play a critical role in the regulation of these tensions. We use self-regulation theory to derive hypotheses about what makes leaders effective, including, (a) promoting self-awareness among group members, (b) setting clear standards and goals for the group, and (c) motivating group members to reduce the discrepancy between the goals and the current performance of the group. We end the chapter by developing a number of novel hypotheses that derive from this theoretical perspective.

It is natural and inevitable that work groups experience tensions in coordinating the interaction of their members (e.g., Arrow, McGrath, & Berdahl, 2000; Guzzo & Shea, 1992; Smith & Berg, 1987). One of the classic trade-offs in group life, for example, is the tension between task and relationship focus (e.g., Blake & Mouton, 1964; Guetzkow & Gyr, 1954). Does the group prefer harmonious relations or the absolute highest quality decisions? How any group handles this type of trade-off has profound implications for the relative success or failure of that group. If a group strongly prefers harmonious relations, for example, this is likely to reduce the chances of group members challenging one another intellectually due to the risk of offending those who are challenged. The overly cooperative atmosphere in the group may not allow minority dissent to be voiced, discouraging the group from thinking creatively or divergently (cf. Nemeth, 1986). Thus, a strong relationship focus increases the likelihood that the group will not rigorously process all task information available to it. Irving Janis' (1982) groupthink phenomenon is a classic example of regulating for relationships to the exclusion of quality of the task at hand. In his book *Victims of Groupthink,* Janis (1982) argued that extreme pressures for unanimity can build in a cohesive group that confronts serious threat (high stress) and lacks norms of deliberative decision making. These pressures cause decision makers to censor any misgivings they may have, ignore outside information, and overestimate the group's chances of success. Groupthink is a failure to appropriately regulate group tensions—a recipe for poor quality decisions and an open invitation to disaster.

The tension between task and relationship focus is one of many trade-offs that groups face continually. Other tensions inherent in group life include the trade-offs between efficiency and effectiveness (e.g., how much time to spend on a problem), the mix of cooperation and competition among members (e.g., working together or independently), group versus individual identity (e.g., a single common goal or multiple compatible goals), how open or closed the group should be to the outside world (e.g., the amount of external information used in decision making), and how much to emphasize change versus stability. Although relatively little research attention has been paid to how groups manage these tensions (for exceptions see Altman, Vinsel, & Brown, 1981; Smith & Berg, 1987), virtually no energy has been focused on the role of leaders in helping the group to balance these tensions. This chapter addresses this gap in the literature by proposing that effective leadership is about helping a group maintain an appropriate balance across these various tensions. We use self-regulation theory, also known as control theory, as the basis of our analysis, arguing that regulation of group tensions is analogous to how individuals self-regulate the natural tensions in their lives—and is essential to successful group performance and decision making.

UNDERSTANDING GROUPS
AS SELF-REGULATING SYSTEMS

While the self-regulation perspective is most commonly applied to individual behavior, we also propose it here as a useful framework for explaining the relationship between naturally occurring group tensions, group performance, and the role of leadership in groups. Here we present it as a mid-range theory that recognizes groups as adaptive and self-organizing systems (Carver & Scheier, 1982; Vancouver, 2000). We argue that groups operate in a system of tensions that effects their performance—including the interaction and processes within their boundaries as well as feedback and events beyond their boundaries within the larger organization (Arrow et al., 2000; Karoly, 1993; McGrath, 1991). As applied to groups, the self-regulation perspective recognizes that groups are able to adapt and reorganize work practices in response to multiple system tensions by maintaining awareness of the trade-offs they make around these tensions. This process includes, (a) receiving task or goal assignments from the external organization, (b) interacting internally to coordinate their resources to best accomplish these assigned tasks or goals, and (c) using external feedback during the course of task completion to adapt work practices and reduce any discrepancy between their goal progress and the desired goal (Carver & Scheier, 2000).

This cycle of receiving feedback to assess current goal achievement and then modifying behavior accordingly is analogous to the psychological process of self-regulation in individuals. Here we call it *group regulation*. The word "group" is added to the word "regulation" because it assumes that the ability to adapt and re-organize comes from within the group system itself, rather than from any external source (cf. Vancouver, 1996). Group regulation means that the ability to adapt and respond to external feedback comes from refocusing internal activity. In other words, responding to external feedback requires an awareness of how internal tensions are focusing (or biasing) group activity, of any discrepancy between current group progress toward the desired goal and external expectations, and of any changes to group activity necessary to accomplish that goal. Figure 7.1 shows this process. The main difference between individual

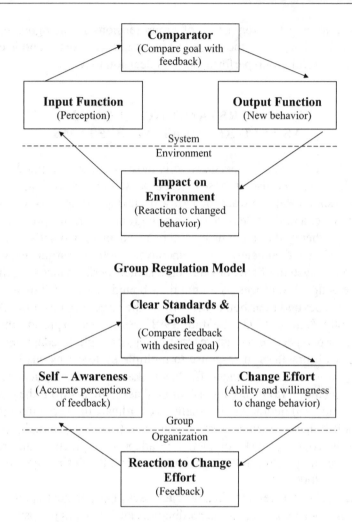

FIG. 7.1.   Self-regulation model (derived from Carver & Scheier, 1982).

self-regulation and group self-regulation is that group regulation is more complex, as it requires balancing competing motives and interests of multiple individuals. This becomes especially difficult if groups are juggling multiple goals simultaneously, if goals change or become muddied in response to external pressures, or if resources available to achieve those goals increase or decrease—all circumstances that aggravate naturally occurring and competing group tensions.

The literature on individual self-regulation suggests three necessary conditions for successful group regulation (i.e., explaining superior group performance). Failure to uphold these three conditions constitutes a self-regulation failure where groups, (a) fall off of their "balance beam" of competing tensions, (b) experience declining performance, and (c) need team leader intervention.

The first condition is self-awareness. This is probably the most difficult condition of the regulation process for groups to satisfy because problems often remain concealed to group members, as over-regulating to one side of a tension can produce symptoms that are not easily linkable to their original source (Moreland & Levine, 1992). For example, an initial conflict about a task-related issue might spiral into a personality or relationship conflict (see Simons & Peterson, 2000; Wall & Callister, 1995). If the group then reacts by focusing on relationship issues, they will miss the more fundamental problem of underlying differences that caused the original task conflict (e.g., differences in values and approaches to the problem at hand). These tendencies, identified by Argyris (1985) as defensive routines, are often self-reinforcing, but are not necessarily self-correcting. This makes them difficult to be aware of and change if they persist over time because they become part of the operating norms of the group. These routines enable groups to avoid painful conflict, but can significantly limit the group's awareness of its actions and flexibility to adapt to changing circumstances. As a result, groups often become self-aware only through the benefit of hindsight after a decision-making failure. While hindsight may help those who follow, these failures can be very costly to the group that commits them.

The second necessary condition for regulation success is clear standards and goals. Teams are designed and created by organizations in order to meet specific goals or accomplish particular tasks. Clear goals are necessary because feedback on clear goals (as opposed to ambiguous goals) gives more precise direction to groups on how well they are making progress in achieving their assigned objective (Ilgen, Fisher, & Taylor, 1979). When feedback is clear and concise, it also gives groups more information on how successful they are at balancing their group tensions. For example, if the group has missed an important interim deadline, that is critical information suggesting that they are overemphasizing effectiveness at the expense of efficiency. Goal clarity is especially important for success in situations where natural competing group tensions are likely to increase—such as with complex or difficult goals, when the group is working toward multiple goals simultaneously, or in an environment of scarce resources (Austin & Vancouver, 1996; Locke, Shaw, Saari, & Latham, 1981).

The third necessary condition for regulation success is the ability and willingness to make changes. This requires not only that the group be aware of the need for change (i.e., the two other necessary conditions), but also that it have the necessary resources to make the change (e.g., cognitive, affective, financial, etc.). Group members may understand that something *should* be changed, but may not believe it *can* be changed because they lack the necessary resources or do not want to confront painful conflict (Smith & Berg, 1987). In order for a change effort to be initiated, the group must also agree, (a) that there are alternative solutions, (b) that the change is an important one to make, and (c) how to coordinate existing resources (Moreland & Levine, 1992; Steiner, 1972; Zander, 1968).

These three necessary conditions for group regulation success are interdependent and cumulative. Goals and feedback cannot stand alone—they must give a reference point to each other in order to increase awareness and generate willingness to correct a goal shortfall or discrepancy (Arrow et al., 2000; Campion & Lord, 1982; Locke et al., 1981). If done successfully, the ability to recognize problems or goal discrepancies is motivating to a team in and of itself (Campion & Lord, 1982). If the group feels it can attain a goal and is aware of the any current discrepancies it has from that goal, group members will be more willing to try to achieve the goal. This kind of awareness also gives individual group members an indication of whether or not delaying immediate gratification of their own motives or needs as an investment in the group's future will be beneficial (Baumeister, 1998). Such beliefs about the likelihood of group success are also known as *collective efficacy* (Bandura, 1986; Whyte, 1998), which has been linked with a positive impact on performance (e.g., Lindsley, Brass, & Thomas, 1995). Groups that experience success and high performance tend to attribute that success to their own ability (Zander, 1968) and continue to be motivated by such challenges (Locke et al., 1981). While collective efficacy is generally positive, it must be balanced with healthy self-awareness. If groups develop a self-serving bias they may become less aware of negative feedback or might escalate their commitment to bad decisions (Riess, Rosenfeld, Melbury, & Tedeschi, 1981; Staw & Ross, 1987; Whyte & Peterson, 2001).

While successful self-regulation can produce positive performance spirals, unsuccessful self-regulation generally produces negative performance spirals by leading groups to over-regulate to one side of group tensions (i.e., creating ineffective process routines; cf. Lindsley et al., 1995). For example, if a group experiences repeated failures at correcting problems, regulation theory suggests that the group is likely to make efforts to reduce goal difficulty (Campion & Lord, 1982), to change its mind about the importance of the goal, or to attribute the failure to other forces outside of their control (e.g. develop a defensive routine; Zander, 1968). Unclear goals or goals without strong group commitment will lead to more individual-oriented behaviors than group-oriented behaviors (Horwitz, 1968). This in turn creates a more competitive than cooperative group orientation (Deutsch, 1968), decreasing awareness about the group's accomplishments as a whole. For example, if group members are overly competitive with one another, this may encourage individuals to withhold important information for personal advantage, making it impossible for the group to uncover unique sources of knowledge held by individuals that other members are not aware of (cf. Stasser, Stewart, & Wittenbaum, 1995). In addition, if goals and standards are not clear and the group repeatedly receives ambiguous feedback that indicates the need for change, the group is likely to experience negative outcomes and develop evaluation apprehension (Allport, 1954). In other words, if a group routinely experiences ambiguous negative feedback and/or fails to reach its goals, the group is likely to be unclear as to which paths lead to success and decrease its motivation to make changes because members think they will not benefit and will get it wrong anyway. This creates a self-reinforcing downward spiral that decreases the chances a group will be able to successfully or objectively regulate their activities in the future.

In Summary

Successful group regulation is, of course, more complex than individual self-regulation because groups face a variety of unique internal conflicts and competing tensions. Groups consist of multiple individuals with differing perspectives, expectations, goals, needs, wants, and motivations (Homans, 1950; Wall & Nolan, 1986). Differences in individual preferences can lead to conflict over how to manage, or even recognize, competing group tensions. This creates a "balance beam" challenge for groups to stop themselves from either over-regulating on one side (e.g., groupthink & polarization) or ignoring the tension and creating process routines that work around the tensions. Conflict over how to manage group tensions is likely to decrease a group's ability to accurately interpret discrepancies between current performance and desired goals by increasing stress and reducing the cognitive capacity of individual members as they focus their attention on internal tensions rather than on important performance cues from external feedback (cf. Evan, 1965; Jehn & Mannix, 2001). If individual group members are not able to recognize goal-performance discrepancies, they will be unable to successfully incorporate feedback to revise work practices and will ultimately fail. Thus, performance failures come from the inability of the group to satisfy the three conditions of successful self-regulation as illustrated in Fig. 7.1.

LEADERSHIP AS FACILITATING GROUP REGULATION

Adopting a self-regulation perspective has a number of implications as a theoretical framework for the successful leadership of groups. First and foremost, this perspective outlines three broad strategies for leadership success that are each necessary but not sufficient in helping groups avoid regulatory failures: (a) promote self-awareness among group members, (b) set clear standards and goals for the group, and (c) motivate group members to make necessary change (cf. Carver & Scheier, 1982; Vancouver, 2000). While these are common themes in many existing leadership models, the group regulation perspective is able to incorporate competing explanations for success into a single model (e.g., goal setting vs. leadership style) by adopting a more dynamic systems approach. This approach is also able to incorporate internal and external forces that shape how leaders and groups interact, as well as different group designs and varying degrees of group autonomy into a single model. By directly addressing and recognizing competing tensions that can predispose a group to long-term failure, the group regulation perspective allows for a variety of leadership qualities and strategies that can be used to satisfy the three tenets of successful group regulation. In order to demonstrate how our group regulation perspective fits within the larger group dynamics and leadership literature, we draw guidance on successful tactics for accomplishing each of these tenets from the existing groups and leadership literature.

Promote Self-Awareness Among Group Members

In order to remain self-aware, groups must both monitor their internal process as well as incorporate feedback from the external organization into their work practices. We identify from the existing literature at least three ways in which leaders can accomplish this. The first way in which leaders raise self-awareness is to actively manage the flow of information within the group itself. This can be done by providing direct and private feedback to individual members about how well they are living up to their prescribed group roles and responsibilities in the form of praise, regular performance reviews, or performance rewards (Bass, 1990; Yukl, 1998). Leaders can also help to balance competing tensions by structuring meetings or discussions to ensure adequate, but not excessive, opportunities for voice or discussion of issues in the group. Opportunity for voice by all encourages creative or divergent thinking (Nemeth, 1986, 1992), promotes members sharing task-related information that has not already been discussed in a meeting (such as comparisons to past experiences or unique knowledge; Stasser, 1992), and stimulates members to foresee the consequences of what each of their alternatives might be (Hirokawa, 1988; Tubbs, 1998). Excess opportunities for voice (e.g., consensus decision rules) should be avoided, however, as it can lead to poor decision quality and inefficient use of time (Peterson, 1999). Finally, leaders may also promote awareness by inviting multiple subgroups to work on the same problem simultaneously and then compare outcomes, by bringing in outsiders/experts to evaluate and challenge preliminary group solutions, and by assigning at least one group member the role of devil's advocate (Herek, Janis, & Huth, 1987; Janis, 1982, 1989).

The second way in which leaders can promote self-awareness is to actively manage the flow and timing of information coming in from outside the group (e.g., the tension of how open or closed the group should be to the outside world). Groups usually have natural and recognized boundaries between themselves and the external environment, such as assigned membership and their purpose or task (Pasmore, Francis, & Haldeman, 1982). Successful groups need to be open to outside influences because they are reliant on the larger organizational environment in which they are embedded for deadlines, task assignments, and social recognition. There is a balance to strike with openness, however. Groups can become undifferentiated or overdifferentiated with the environment to the point that their unique task and purpose becomes unclear (Arrow et al., 2000). A leader can promote self-awareness by helping groups recognize how their external information-gathering strategies are inhibiting or helping them to accomplish their task. Ancona and Caldwell (1992) suggest that groups can get caught in negative external communication patterns that detract from the group accomplishing its task. They found, for example, that groups that engaged in external information-scouting activities throughout the entire cycle of task completion underperformed groups that engaged instead in activities such as helping the group coordinate resources with other departments to meet deadlines and representing their efforts to senior management (Ancona & Caldwell, 1992). A leader can help groups recognize when and what strategies are appropriate to the group's goal.

Another tactic leaders can use to promote self-awareness is to invite new people into the team who have important perspectives to add or, alternatively, to extend the invitation just for a meeting or two where their expertise is needed (George, 1980; Janis, 1982, 1989). Previous research suggests that an appropriate time for promoting self-awareness of goal clarity and the effectiveness of group procedures is at the mid-point of a group's task cycle because the pressure of deadlines encourages openness to alternatives (Gersick, 1988). In this way, the leader promotes self-awareness by encouraging self-discovery at the moment the group is most open to it.

The third way in which leaders raise self-awareness is to play a linking-pin role (Yukl, 1998) by bringing unique resources and information into the group discussion (Ancona, 1990). Past research has shown that leaders are well positioned to help groups do this because they are high status people with access to unique information; and as a result are often better able to identify problems than other group members because they are more in touch with what is happening outside of the group (Ridgeway, 1984). This role is reinforced because leaders are often held accountable for their group's performance (Moreland & Levine, 1992). Existing research has identified a number of ways in which leaders can put their unique information to work for the benefit of their groups. First, leaders can encourage self-awareness by providing the group with relevant inputs (advice, resources) to help the group examine whether changing their work practices and strategies will reduce the goal discrepancy, or whether the group needs to examine the deeper underlying reasoning behind the discrepancies (Argyris, 1977, 1994; Campion & Lord, 1982). For example, if the group encounters an individual who obstructs their work, the team leader may be in the best or most objective position to know whether the underlying problem is actually that individual, the culture of the organization, or the politics behind what the group is trying to accomplish.

Also in this role, leaders can use their access to external information to the group's advantage both within the group and in the broader external environment. Within the group they can promote self-awareness by (a) providing information about strategies or resources that similar groups are using, (b) helping the group forecast how their activities and efforts can stay in sync with how current organizational priorities are evolving, (c) assisting the group with understanding what the priorities might be in the future, and (d) providing information on how to interpret and understand how the group's tasks fit within broader organizational goals (Yukl,

1998; Yukl & Van Fleet, 1992). Leaders can promote awareness in the broader organizational context by (a) specifically advocating for the team (with upper management or other organizational groups), (b) helping to gather information about confusing or vague organizational policies or goals, (c) identifying underlying structures in the organization that are important for the group to work within or to ignore, and (d) helping filter the environmental noise from the group-relevant information coming from outside (Ancona, 1990; Cummings, 1978; Gladstein, 1984; Senge, 1990).

Set Clear Standards and Goals for the Group

Clear standards and goals have long been considered a bedrock ingredient for effective leadership. Clear goals are important because they are the comparator by which the group benchmarks its efforts and interprets feedback. A number of scholars have identified clear goals as key to helping any group create strong group norms of success, high collective efficacy, and ultimately positive performance spirals (Locke & Latham, 1990). If each group member is able to understand the group goal and recognize how his or her individual contribution toward that goal is of value in the group, that individual will be motivated to achieve their part of the group goal (Campion & Lord, 1982), the group will create a cooperative orientation, and is likely to perform better (Deutsch, 1949).

The existing literature also suggests a number of tactics for structuring decision-making processes and helping groups establish clear standards and goals. First, Hirokawa's (1985, 1988) early work shows that groups that take the time to go through goal planning and clarification *before* they begin discussion of the problem itself are more effective problem solvers, regardless of the work method later used. He also finds that determining the minimal characteristics any alternative must possess to be acceptable helps to clarify goals and standards before the group begins its work, and thus improves group performance (Gouran & Hirokawa, 1986, 1996). Similarly, Janis (1982; Herek et al., 1987) suggests that encouraging groups to survey the range of objectives they wish to achieve before they discuss a problem improves group decision quality. In short, by structuring decision-making processes and helping a group to reconcile changing external goal expectations and internal goal interpretations, the leader can help to reduce competing tensions among individual members about how to interpret and focus group activity.

A systems view of goal setting also maintains that a group will face multiple goals at any given time—and that those goals may change or fluctuate depending on other system influences (Campion & Lord, 1982; Locke et al., 1981). Therefore, leaders can play an important role in clarifying external expectations by helping groups gain an understanding of how their goals are distinct from and complementary to each other and broader organizational goals (Yukl & Van Fleet, 1992). Specific leader behaviors outlined in the literature include, (a) facilitating alignment of personal, group, and organizational goals, (b) elucidating how group resources relate to organizational goals, and (c) providing timelines and standards for measuring achievement (Bass, 1990; Yukl, 1998).

Motivate Group Members to Make Necessary Change

Once a group is aware of where it currently stands and is clear on its goals, the next step is to motivate group members to make the necessary changes to bring goals in line with current practice (i.e., in self-regulation terms, take action to reduce the discrepancy between goals and current performance). We identify two interdependent strategies from the existing literature by which leaders can do this. The first is by working to secure the necessary external resources for the group to succeed. Leaders should identify and seek to remedy any resource limitations or "ceiling effects" placed on the group by a lack of resources, both mechanical (e.g., old machinery, lack of technology, etc.; Goodman, Devadas, & Griffity-Hughson, 1988) as well as human (e.g., a lack of necessary skills and training; Benne & Sheats, 1948). Resource gathering is critical because fewer internal resource conflicts will help the group stay focused on the actual task (Pfeffer & Salancik, 1978). The leader can also increase the group's motivation to make changes by acting on its behalf in the external environment. For example, the leader can advocate for the group in the external environment to reinforce group's visibility and viability with upper management and other groups (Cohen & Bailey, 1997; Manz & Sims, 1987). Visibility in the larger organizational system may make it easier to secure resources, for the group itself to monitor its boundaries (if more people know about the group's activities then there are more sources of feedback available), and therefore for the group to be self-aware and motivated (Cummings, 1978; Howell, Bowen, Dorfman, & Podskaoff, 1990; Yukl, 1998). Advocacy may also result in the group being assigned to more interesting or challenging tasks, which may also motivate the group to maintain their success.

In working to provide the necessary resources, leaders also need to be especially attuned to when feedback is having the effect of frustration rather than motivation because the group views its goal boundaries as too broad or unattainable. When this is the case, the team leader should work with the group either to make the goal more attainable or to establish sub-goals (Campion & Lord, 1982). In doing so, the leader should give specific feedback about procedures and behaviors that will make it possible to accomplish these revised goals. One way to do this is to reframe or "redefine success and failure in terms of instructive feedback and learning. That is, success is not based on the outcome, but it comes from the information gained via the task attempt" (Lindsley et al., 1995, p. 662). This motivates groups to self-reflect and become more self-aware because they do not fear punishment (i.e., develop evaluation apprehension).

The second basic motivation strategy leaders can employ is trust building. Existing research indicates motivational losses in groups are often based in lack of trust due to perceived injustice and free riding by others (Kerr & Bruun, 1983; Kidwell, 1993; Latane, Williams, & Harkins, 1979; Lind & Tyler, 1988). Feeling of injustice can lead to a downward spiral of dissatisfaction, withdrawal, and shirking (Kerr & Bruun, 1983; Latane et al., 1979). Leaders generally have the authority to change group procedures, re-assign roles, or resolve conflicts. One effective method for building trust and motivation before this spiral starts is for the leader to provide "artifacts" of autonomy that represent faith in the group's ability (Schein, 1992)—for example, allowing group members to attend continuing education or skill development courses (Benne & Sheats, 1948; Manz & Sims, 1987), doing away with time cards, or allowing participation in the re-evaluation of reward systems (Goodman et al., 1988).

In sum, the leader must not only be aware of how the group and external environment are functioning (as well anticipate future changes), but must also be able to regulate the timing and impact of his or her own involvement with the team. Different tensions and regulatory errors require different teaching, intervention, and resources in order to get the group back on track (Tubbs, 1998). The leader must be aware of how to match his or her influence with each group situation, as well as the potential consequences an intervention might have.

Other Implications of Adopting a Self-Regulation Perspective

In addition to the tactics for achieving goal clarity, self-awareness, and motivation within the group that we were able to glean from the existing literature, there are a number of other significant implications for successful leadership that come from adopting a self-regulation perspective on groups. Each of these implications finds empirical support at the individual level, but as yet is largely untested at the group level. We suggest them here as testable hypotheses for scholars to pursue in the future:

1. *Leadership emerges from tactics to engage group awareness, goal clarity, and motivation of group members to address performance gaps.* Although there is an existing body of research on emergent and shared leadership (e.g., Hollander, 1980; Yukl, 1998), none of it comes from a group-regulation perspective. These perspectives do recognize the positive (i.e., motivation, innovation) aspects of autonomy and participation, but they do not address how groups can balance competing tensions in the absence of an authority to enforce, reward, or correct destructive group or individual activities or patterns. We suggest that individuals who are able to help groups satisfy the three tenets of group regulation will be ascribed leadership characteristics by other members because of their ability to help groups avoid regulatory pitfalls and correct and learn from regulatory problems. Some indirect evidence for this point already exists in the literature: (a) leaders with both technical and social skills have been found to be motivating to groups (Bass, 1990), (b) leaders that encourage self-criticism and evaluation were rated as most effective (Manz & Sims, 1987), and (c) leaders most able to build relationships on both sides of group boundaries led their teams to greater success (Druskat & Wheeler, 2001). In short, individuals who are able to balance social and technical tensions in groups will most likely inspire the confidence of others in the group and emerge as a leader.

2. *Individuals and groups who are high in conscientiousness are good at self-regulation and more likely to be good at group regulation.* Two recent studies suggest that individuals high in conscientiousness are more likely to set achievement goals and stick to them until accomplished, and thus perform better (Barrick & Mount, 1991; Sansone, Wiebe, & Morgan, 1999). They argue that high-conscientiousness individuals are better able to self-regulate because they are able to delay gratification. We suggest that this may also hold true for leaders and at the group level as well. There is some preliminary evidence to support this claim. For example, Barrick, Stewart, Neubert, and Mount (1998) found that groups with higher mean levels of conscientiousness were rated more highly by their supervisors. Also, Peterson, Smith, Martorana, and Owens (2003) found that leader conscientiousness was related to positive team dynamics and firm financial performance in top management teams.

3. *When goal attainment is slower than expected, groups will progress through the following sequence: (1) increase effort, (2) shift attention to other goals, and then (3) quit the goal entirely.* In a recent meta-analysis of the past 30 years of research on feedback interventions, Kluger and DeNisi (1996) suggest that individuals deal with negative feedback by first working harder to overcome the problem, then shift their attention to other goals they see as more achievable (e.g., subgoals), and then finally quit the goal entirely if it is not achieved in a certain amount of time. We suggest that this same process may work at the group level. Groups that are successfully self-regulating will be better at working their way through this process appropriately. Self-regulating groups will neither fail by shifting away from their goals too easily because of a lack of collective efficacy (e.g., Bandura, 1986); nor will they fail by persisting too long in their goals (e.g., Staw & Ross, 1987). In other words, successful self-regulation should lead to a reduction in susceptibility to common information processing errors.

4. *Leader feedback focused on the group task rather than individual contributions to the task are more likely to improve group performance.* In addition to their finding about the tactics that people engage in to address negative feedback, Kluger and DeNisi (1996) also found that feedback focused more toward the task rather than the individual is more likely to improve performance at the individual level because individual feedback can be personally threatening. Therefore, we hypothesize that feedback given at the group level is more likely to improve group performance when directed at the task rather than specific individuals. To be motivating, individual feedback is probably best given in private and also focused toward task activities rather than being personal critique. In this way the leader will not compound competing tensions between group members (e.g., need for recognition), but instead focus them more on regulating for strategies of task success.

5. *Chronic error of one kind should lead to reorganization or resetting of goals.* Building on Hypothesis 3, self-regulation theory suggests that repeated failure should lead to re-evaluation or resetting of goals in order to achieve success (Carver & Scheier, 1982; Vancouver, 2000). For the group level this may be the essence of vision in leadership, convincing the group to alter course in the face of repeated failure. This highlights the need for a leader to help a group recognize, learn from mistakes, and redefine their efforts as necessary. Successful group regulation means that errors are learned from, do not become chronic or routine, and that work practices and goals are appropriately adjusted.

6. *Groups can run without regulation interventions (i.e., leadership) only so long as the environment remains stable.* Once established with regular (successful) patterns of feedback and self-awareness raising, established norms and process routines should be sufficient for groups to function without leadership so long as the external and internal group environments remain relatively stable. Once operating conditions become unstable (e.g., negative feedback, team turnover, etc.), we would expect the re-activation of naturally competing tensions, as the group has to re-clarify and re-define how to focus internal activity. This re-activation predisposes the group to regulatory failure and it may need assistance to readjust goals (i.e., vision). Hence, the often heard call for greater leadership in uncertain times.

CONCLUSION

This chapter is intended to begin a discussion about leadership as group regulation. Specifically, we propose here that group regulation failures are natural and illustrate the need for leadership as a corrective tool for these failures. We are optimistic about the future of group regulation theory to provide fresh insight into effective leadership for two reasons. First, the notion of leadership as group regulation nicely organizes many existing findings in the leadership literature, which is large but extremely fragmented (see Bass, 1990). More importantly, however, we were able to generate a number of novel hypotheses from a rather basic application of self-regulation theory. Although our discussion here is preliminary, we believe a deeper analysis using group regulation theory will further elucidate these ideas and generate additional fresh perspective on why certain leadership behaviors are effective. Ultimately, of course, the real test of whether our application of self-regulation theory to group leadership is useful will be the results of future empirical tests of the novel hypotheses we generate from this perspective both here and in the future. We invite scholars interested in group decision making, leadership, or systems theory to join us in this effort.

ACKNOWLEDGMENTS

Both authors contributed equally to this chapter. We thank all of the participants in the "New Thoughts on the Psychology of Leadership" conference, but especially Richard Hackman, Rod Kramer, and Dave Messick for particularly helpful insights and suggestions on earlier versions of this chapter. Correspondence concerning this chapter should be addressed to Randall S. Peterson, London Business School, Regent's Park, London NW1 4SA, United Kingdom. E-mail should be sent to: RPeterson@london.edu.

REFERENCES

Allport, G. (1954). The historical background of modern psychology. In G. Lindzey (Ed.), *Handbook of social psychology* (Vol. 1, pp. 3–56). Cambridge, MA: Addison-Wesley.

Altman, I., Vinsel, A., & Brown, B. (Eds.). (1981). *Dialectic conceptions in social psychology: An application to social penetration and privacy regulation* (Vol. 14). New York: Academic Press.

Ancona, D. (1990). Outward bound: Strategies for team survival in an organization. *Academy of Management Journal, 33,* 334–365.

Ancona, D., & Caldwell, D. (1992). Bridging the boundary: External activity and performance in organizational teams. *Administrative Science Quarterly, 37,* 634–665.

Argyris, C. (1977). Double loop learning in organizations. *Harvard Business Review, 55,* 115–125.

Argyris, C. (1985). *Strategy, change, and defensive routines.* Marshfield, MA: Pitman Publishing Inc.

Argyris, C. (1994). Good communication that blocks learning. *Harvard Business Review, 72,* 77–85.

Arrow, H., McGrath, J., & Berdahl, J. (2000). *Small groups as complex systems: Formation, coordination, development, and adaptation.* Thousand Oaks, CA: Sage Publications.

Austin, J., & Vancouver, J. (1996). Goal constructs in psychology: Structure, process, and content. *Psychological Bulletin, 120,* 338–375.

Bandura, A. (1986). *Social foundations of thought and action: A social cognitive view.* Englewood Cliffs, NJ: Prentice-Hall.

Barrick, M. R., & Mount, M. K. (1991). The Big Five personality dimensions and job performance: A meta-analysis. *Personnel Psychology, 44,* 1–26.

Barrick, M. R., Stewart, G., Neubert, M., & Mount, M. (1998). Relating member ability and personality to work-team processes and team effectiveness. *Journal of Applied Psychology, 83,* 377–391.

Bass, B. (1990). *Bass & Stogdill's handbook of leadership: Theory, research, and managerial applications.* New York: The Free Press.

Baumeister, R. (1998). The self. In D. Gilbert, S. Fiske, & G. Lindzey (Eds.), *The handbook of social psychology* (4th ed., Vol. 1, pp. 680–740). Boston: McGraw-Hill.

Benne, K., & Sheats, P. (1948). Functional roles of group members. *The Journal of Social Issues, 4,* 41–49.

Blake, R., & Mouton, J. (1964). *The managerial grid.* Houston, TX: Gulf.

Campion, M., & Lord, R. (1982). A control systems conceptualization of the goal-setting and changing process. *Organizational Behavior and Human Performance, 30,* 265–287.

Carver, C., & Scheier, M. (1982). Control theory: A useful conceptual framework for personality-social, clinical, and health psychology. *Psychological Bulletin, 92,* 111–135.

Carver, C., & Scheier, M. (2000). On the structure of behavioral self-regulation. In M. Boekaerts, P. Pintirch, & M. Zeidner (Eds.), *Handbook of self-regulation* (pp. 41–84). San Diego: Academic Press.

Cohen, S., & Bailey, D. (1997). What makes teams work: Group effectiveness research from the shop floor to the executive suite. *Journal of Management, 23,* 239–290.

Cummings, T. (1978). Self-regulating work groups: A socio-technical synthesis. *Academy of Management Review, 3,* 625–634.

Deutsch, M. (1949). A theory of cooperation and competition. *Human Relations, 2,* 129–152.

Deutsch, M. (1968). The effects of cooperation and competition upon group process. In D. Cartwright & A. Zander (Eds.), *Group dynamics: Research and theory* (3rd ed., pp. 461–482). New York: Harper & Row.

Druskat, V., & Wheeler, J. (2001, August). *Managing from the boundary: The effective leadership of self-managing work teams.* Paper presented at the Academy of Management, Washington D.C.

Evan, W. (1965). Conflict and performance in R & D organizations. *Industrial Management Review, 7,* 37–46.

George, A. (1980). *Presidential decision making in foreign policy: The effective use of information and advice.* Boulder, CO: Westview.

Gersick, C. (1988). Time and transition in work teams: Toward a new model of group development. *Academy of Management Journal, 31,* 9–41.

Gladstein, D. (1984). Groups in context: A model of task group effectiveness. *Administrative Science Quarterly, 29,* 499–517.

Goodman, P., Devadas, R., & Griffity-Hughson, T. (1988). Groups and productivity: Analyzing the effectiveness of self-managing teams. In J. Campbell, R. Campbell & Associates (Eds.), *Productivity in organizations: New perspectives from industrial and organizational psychology* (pp. 295–327). San Francisco: Jossey-Bass.

Gouran, D., & Hirokawa, R. (1986). The role of communication in effective decision-making groups: A functionalist perspective. In M. Mander (Ed.), *Communications in transition* (pp. 168–185). New York: Praeger.

Gouran, D., & Hirokawa, R. (1996). Functional theory and communication in decision-making and problem-solving groups: An expanded view. In R. Hirokawa & M. S. Poole (Eds.), *Communication and group decision making* (pp. 55–80). Thousand Oaks, CA: Sage.

Guetzkow, H., & Gyr, J. (1954). An analysis of conflict in decision-making groups. *Human Relations, 7,* 367–381.

Guzzo, R., & Shea, G. (1992). Group performance and intergroup relations in organizations. In M. Dunnette & L. Hough (Eds.), *Handbook of industrial and organizational psychology* (2nd ed., Vol. 3, pp. 269–313). Palo Alto, CA: Consulting Psychologists Press.

Herek, G., Janis, I., & Huth, P. (1987). Decision making during international crises—Is quality of process related to outcome? *Journal of Conflict Resolution, 37,* 203–226.

Hirokawa, R. (1985). Discussion procedures and decision-making performance. *Human Communication Research, 12,* 203–224.

Hirokawa, R. (1988). Group communication and decision-making performance: A continued test of the functional perspective. *Human Communication Research, 14,* 487–515.

Hollander, E. (1980). Leadership and social exchange processes. In K. Gergen, M. Greenberg, & R. Willis (Eds.), *Social exchange: Advances in theory and research* (pp. 103–118). New York: Plenum Press.

Homans, G. (1950). *The human group.* New York: Harcourt, Brace and Company.

Horwitz, M. (1968). The recall of interrupted group tasks: An experimental study of individual motivation in relation to group goals. In D. Cartwright & A. Zander (Eds.), *Group dynamics: Research and theory* (3rd ed., pp. 444–460). New York: Harper & Row.

Howell, J., Bowen, D., Dorfman, P., & Podskaoff, P. (1990). Substitutes for leadership: Effective alternatives to ineffective leadership. *Organizational Dynamics,* 21–38.

Ilgen, D., Fisher, C., & Taylor, M. S. (1979). Consequences of individual feedback on behavior in organizations. *Journal of Applied Psychology, 64,* 349–371.

Janis, I. (1982). *Victims of Groupthink* (2nd edition). Boston: Houghton Mifflin Company.

Janis, I. (1989). *Crucial decisions: Leadership in policy-making and management.* New York: The Free Press.

Jehn, K., & Mannix, E. (2001). The dynamic nature of conflict: A longitudinal study of intragroup conflict and group performance. *Academy of Management Journal, 44,* 238–251.

Karoly, P. (1993). Mechanisms of self-regulation: A systems view. *Annual Review of Psychology, 44,* 23–52.

Kerr, N., & Bruun, S. (1983). Dispensability of member effort and group motivation losses: Free-rider effects. *Journal of Personality and Social Psychology, 44,* 78–94.

Kidwell, R. (1993). Employee propensity to withhold effort: A conceptual model to intersect three avenues of research. *Academy of Management Review, 18,* 429–456.

Kluger, A., & DeNisi, A. (1996). The effects of feedback interventions on performance: A historical review, a meta-analysis, and a preliminary feedback intervention theory. *Psychological Bulletin, 119,* 254–284.

Latane, B., Williams, K., & Harkins, S. (1979). Many hands make light work: The causes and consequences of social loafing. *Journal of Personality and Social Psychology, 37,* 822–832.

Lind, E. A., & Tyler, T. (1988). *The social psychology of procedural justice.* New York: Plenum Press.

Lindsley, D., Brass, D., & Thomas, J. (1995). Efficacy-performance spirals: A multilevel perspective. *Academy of Management Review, 20,* 645–678.

Locke, E., & Latham, G. (1990). *A theory of goal setting and task performance.* Upper Saddle River, NJ: Prentice-Hall.

Locke, E., Shaw, K., Saari, L., & Latham, G. (1981). Goal setting and task performance: 1969–1980. *Psychological Bulletin, 90,* 125–152.

Manz, C. C., & Sims, H. P. (1987). Leading workers to lead themselves: The external leadership of self-managing work teams. *Administrative Science Quarterly, 32,* 106–128.

McGrath, J. (1991). Time, interaction, and performance (TIP): A theory of groups. *Small Group Research, 22,* 147–174.

Moreland, R., & Levine, J. (1992). Problem identification by groups. In S. Worchel, W. Wood, & J. Simpson (Eds.), *Group process and productivity* (pp. 17–47). Newbury Park, CA: Sage Publications.

Nemeth, C. (1986). Differential contributions of majority and minority influence. *Psychological Review, 93,* 23–32.

Nemeth, C. (1992). Minority dissent as a stimulant to group performance. In S. Worchel, W. Wood, & J. Simpson (Eds.), *Group process and productivity* (pp. 95–111). Newbury Park, CA: Sage.

Pasmore, W., Francis, C., & Haldeman, J. (1982). Sociotechnical systems: A North American reflection on empirical studies of the seventies. *Human Relations, 35,* 1179–1204.

Peterson, R. (1999). Can you have too much of a good thing? The limits of voice for improving satisfaction with leaders. *Personality and Social Psychology Bulletin, 25,* 313–324.

Peterson, R. S., Smith, D. B., Martorana, P. V., & Owens, P. D. (2003). The impact of chief executive officer personality on top management team dynamics: One mechanism by which leadership affects organizational performance. *Journal of Applied Psychology, 88,* 795–808.

Pfeffer, J., & Salancik, G. R. (1978). *The external control of organizations: A resource dependence perspective.* New York: Harper & Row.

Ridgeway, C. L. (1984). Dominance, performance, and status in groups. A theoretical analysis. In E. J. Lawler (Ed.), *Advances in group process* (Vol. 1, pp. 59–93). Greenwich, CT: JAI Press.

Riess, M., Rosenfeld, P., Melbury, V., & Tedeschi, J. (1981). Self-serving attributions: Biased private perceptions and distorted public descriptions. *Journal of Personality and Social Psychology, 41,* 224–231.

Sansone, C., Wiebe, D., & Morgan, C. (1999). Self-regulating interest: The moderating role of hardiness and conscientiousness. *Journal of Personality, 67,* 701–732.

Schein, E. (1992). *Organizational culture and leadership* (2nd ed.). San Francisco: Jossey-Bass.

Senge, P. (1990). *The fifth discipline: The art and practice of the learning organization.* New York: Currency Doubleday.

Simons, T., & Peterson, R. (2000). Task conflict and relationship conflict in top management teams: The pivotal role of intragroup trust. *Journal of Applied Psychology, 83,* 102–111.

Smith, K., & Berg, D. (1987). *Paradoxes of group life: Understanding conflict, paralysis, and movement in group dynamics.* San Francisco: Jossey-Bass.

Stasser, G. (1992). Pooling of unshared information during group discussions. In S. Worchel, W. Wood, & J. Simpson (Eds.), *Group process and productivity* (pp. 48–67). Newbury Park, CA: Sage Publications.

Stasser, G., Stewart, D., & Wittenbaum, G. (1995). Expert roles and information exchange during discussion: The importance of knowing who knows what. *Journal of Experimental Social Psychology, 31,* 244–265.

Staw, B., & Ross, J. (1987). Behavior in escalation situations: Antecedents, prototypes, and solutions. *Research in Organizational Behavior, 19,* 39–79.

Steiner, I. (1972). *Group process and productivity.* New York: Academic Press.

Tubbs, S. (1998). *A systems approach to small group interaction* (6th ed.). Boston: McGraw-Hill.

Vancouver, J. (1996). Living systems theory as a paradigm for organizational behavior: Understanding humans, organizations, and social processes. *Behavioral Science, 41,* 165–204.

Vancouver, J. B. (2000). Self-regulation in organizational settings: A tale of two paradigms. In M. Boekaerts, P. R. Pintrich, & M. Zeidner (Eds.), *Handbook of self-regulation* (pp. 303–336). San Diego: Academic Press.

Wall, J. J., & Callister, R. R. (1995). Conflict and its management. *Journal of Management, 21,* 515–558.

Wall, V., & Nolan, L. (1986). Perceptions of inequity, satisfaction, and conflict in task-oriented groups. *Human Relations, 39,* 1033–1052.

Whyte, G. (1998). Recasting Janis's groupthink model: The key role of collective efficacy in decision fiascoes. *Organizational Behavior and Human Decision Processes, 73,* 185–209.

Whyte, G., & Peterson, R. S. (2001, August). *The role of efficacy perceptions in group decision failure.* Paper presented at the Academy of Management, Washington, DC.

Yukl, G. (1998). *Leadership in organizations* (4th ed.). Upper Saddle River, NJ: Prentice-Hall.

Yukl, G., & Van Fleet, D. (1992). Theory and research on leadership in organizations. In M. Dunnette & L. Hough (Eds.), *Handbook of industrial and organizational psychology* (2nd ed., Vol. 3, pp. 147–197). Palo Alto, CA: Consulting Psychologists Press.

Zander, A. (1968). Group aspirations. In D. Cartwright & A. Zander (Eds.), *Group dynamics: Research and theory* (3rd ed., pp. 418–430). New York: Harper & Row.

8

Process-Based Leadership: How Do Leaders Lead?

Tom R. Tyler
New York University

Leadership is the process by which a leader, by persuasion or example, induces followers to pursue their objectives for the group. In other words, it is "a process (act) of influencing the activities of an organized group in its efforts toward goal setting and goal achievement" (Stogdill, 1950, p. 3), or a "specialized form of social interaction . . . in which cooperating individuals are permitted to influence and motivate others to promote the attainment of group and individual goals" (Forsyth, 1999, p. 343). From each of these perspectives, leadership involves a "process of influence whereby the leader has an impact on others by inducing them to behave in a certain way" (Bryman, 1996, p. 276). These definitions have in common their emphasis on the view that leadership is linked to the ability to shape the behavior of those within one's group, organization, or society.

Furthermore, leadership involves more than being able to obtain changes in behavior that flow from coercion linked to the possession of power or enticement linked to the ability to reward ("command and control" models of motivation, see Tyler & Blader, 2000). Leadership involves the possession of qualities that lead others to want to follow the leader's directives, either because they feel obligated to do so, or because they desire to do so.

In other words, leadership is a characteristic that is voluntarily conferred upon a person by others and involves the ability of a person to engage the active and willing cooperation of followers. Leadership is, therefore, a process of influence that "depends more on persuasion than on coercion" (Hollander, 1978, pp. 1–2).

Of course, the ability to motivate group members, while clearly a key function of leadership, is not all that leadership involves. Leadership is also linked to the ability to set goals for the group ("vision"); goals whose attainment facilitates the continued success of the group. In addition, leadership involves being able to structure the organization so that it can effectively attain those goals ("implementation"). Further, the numerous theories of leadership that have developed since the earliest history of organized societies articulate a wide variety of other criteria of leadership, making any simple definition of leadership incomplete (see Bass, 1981).

This discussion of *process-based leadership* focuses on one aspect of leadership—the motivational function of leadership. I am concerned with the ability of the leader to gain voluntary cooperation from others in the group ("followers"). To address this issue, I draw upon prior examinations of the antecedents of cooperation by group members (Tyler, 1999). This prior work links the qualities of leaders and their behavior as leaders to their ability to obtain cooperative behaviors from their followers. Those leadership qualities are articulated in the *relational model of authority* (Tyler & Lind, 1992), and are linked to cooperative behavior in the *group engagement model* (Tyler & Blader, 2000).

COOPERATIVE BEHAVIOR

Leaders seek to gain two types of cooperative behavior from their followers. The first is rule-following behavior—that is, "compliance with the law" (Tyler, 1990). For leaders to be effective, they must be able to motivate their followers to follow group rules. For a group to work, the members of that group must limit their behavior in response to group guidelines prohibiting or limiting engagement in behaviors that harm the group. This type of limiting behavior is studied in the literature on social regulation, and is the focus of a considerable body of research in the area of law and in studies of the exercise of legal authority. For example, in the area of social regulation, the ability to gain compliance with rules and decisions is assumed to be the key to being an effective leader (Tyler, 1990).

The second type of behavior needed from group members is for followers to engage in behaviors that benefit the group. Such behavior involves proactively working in ways that promote the group's goals. A student needs to study and work hard to learn the material taught in their classes (proactive behavior), in addition to not cheating on tests or having someone write their terms papers (limiting behavior). Similarly, an employee needs to work hard at their job, in addition to not stealing office supplies. An employee who came into work and sat quietly at their desk all day, not stealing office supplies or sabotaging their workplace, would, from a social regulatory viewpoint, be an ideal employee. However, they would still be problematic in a larger sense, because they would not be doing anything positive for their group. Understanding how leaders can motivate these positive, proactive behaviors that promote group goals is the focus of much of the fields of organizational psychology and organizational behavior (Tyler & Blader, 2000).

My own research on leadership began in the area of social regulation with studies exploring how people could be motivated to comply with laws and with the directives of legal authorities. This early work did not examine the ability to leaders to promote proactive behaviors. Like most research on social regulation, it is directed at understanding the psychological dynamics of compliance.

Although I did not study the motivations underlying proactive behaviors in the political/legal arena, it is important to note that there are literatures that do study how to encourage proactive behavior in the political/legal arena. One is the literature on voting—a voluntary proactive behavior in the civic arena. Another is the literature on volunteerism, which examines when people join community groups and work proactively to solve problems in their communities. Such actions vary widely, ranging from working with a neighborhood block watch committee developed to help control crime in one's neighborhood to providing meals or companionship to the elderly and needy. In each case, the behavior involves a proactive action on the part of an individual or group that helps to meet social needs.

In the case of social regulation, efforts to describe how leaders might motivate rule-following behavior on the part of their followers are typically rooted in psychological models of human motivation. Most of the models that have dominated the study of motivation in the area of social regulation are instrumental or rational choice models, referred to as *strategies for deterrence* or *social control* (Tyler & Huo, 2002). These deterrence or social control models suggest that legal authorities can motivate compliance with the law via the threat of application of punishment—i.e., through the threat or implementation of a system of sanctioning (i.e., punishment).

These models assume that people's behavior is shaped by their judgments about their self-interest. Since rule breaking offers people an opportunity to engage in behavior from which they immediately gain, some counteracting force is needed to stop people from breaking rules. That counteracting force can involve providing some degree of expectation of punishment following rule breaking. So, a person must weigh the potential gain of stealing office supplies against the potential loss of their job and income if caught stealing. Leaders provide this counteracting force by creating systems of surveillance for detecting rule breaking and sanctioning systems that deliver punishments when rule violations are detected.

Studies of deterrence in real-world settings provide evidence that deterrence actually influences the rate of rule breaking. However, that evidence is far from unequivocal. Many, but not all, studies suggest that deterrence does shape rule-related behavior. However, even those studies that find effects support the conclusion that, if deterrence effects do occur, their magnitude is small. For example, MacCoun (1993) estimates that variations in the likelihood of being caught and punished for drug use explain approximately 5% of the variance in drug-related behavior. Similarly, Tyler and Blader (2000) estimate that in work settings cost/gain estimates explain approximately 10% of the variance in rule-following behavior.

Deterrence strategies also have social costs. One is that they lead to widespread sanctioning. The United States, for example, has one of the highest rates of imprisonment in the world. This high proportion of the population that is in prison is the result of the widespread application of severe sanctions for rule breaking, including the increasingly widespread use of lifetime imprisonment following several convictions.

Another social cost is the creation of hostility and resentment among citizens, who are subjected to negative experiences with legal authorities. These negative feelings create problems because they diminish the acceptance of legal authority and lower voluntary rule-following behavior. Hence, while deterrence strategies may reduce rule breaking, their use as a strategy of social regulation also has social costs.

Effective social regulation is a necessary element of leadership because groups cannot function if people do not limit their behavior in accordance with group rules. Therefore, group leaders must use whatever strategies they have available for motivating rule-following behavior. Although it does not work especially well, deterrence does work, and has therefore been used widely by leaders. The question I seek to address in my work is whether there is an alternative model of leadership that might also work, but without the negative social consequences associated with deterrence theory.

One theory is that leaders might be able to use their legitimacy to encourage rule following. Legitimate leaders are leaders that followers view as being, by virtue of their position or personal qualities, entitled to be obeyed. What this means is that when leaders make decisions or create rules, people feel personally responsible for following those rules. Hence, compliance becomes self-regulatory, and leaders do not need to use group resources to provide incentives or create systems of sanctioning to enforce rules. Irrespective of whether legitimacy is necessary for effective leadership, it clearly benefits the leader to be able to ensure that people follow rules without having to create and implement incentive or sanctioning systems. The empirical question is whether legitimacy in fact leads to voluntary rule following.

In Tyler (1990), I examined the influence of legitimacy on people's rule-following behavior. In this case, I studied a sample of citizens and looked at whether those citizens who view law and legal authorities as more legitimate are more likely to follow the law in their everyday lives. The results of the study suggest that legitimacy influences rule following. Furthermore, the influence of legitimacy is greater than is the influence of the perceived risk of being caught and punished for rule breaking. These findings suggest that effective leadership, in situations in which leadership involves being able to motivate rule following, as is the case with social regulatory authorities, is rooted in being viewed as a legitimate leader.

This finding is not confined to everyday obedience to the law. I have also examined the factors shaping people's willingness to defer to the decisions and policies of national level authorities. In a study of the United States Supreme Court I examined people's willingness to defer to the Court's abortion decision. My results suggest that the legitimacy of the Supreme Court shapes deference, and is more important than is agreement with the abortion decision (*Rowe v. Wade*) itself, or with decisions more generally. If people feel that the Court is a legitimate legal institution, which is entitled to interpret the meaning of the Constitution, they feel obligated to defer to its decisions even when they disagree with them (Tyler & Mitchell, 1994). Of course, people are not confronted with everyday instances of the need to comply with a Supreme Court decision. So, in this case, acceptance is more policy based. People who view the Court as a legitimate social institution feel that the policies of the Court ought to be accepted.

These findings illustrate what I regard as a key aspect of my work on leadership. I view effective leadership as being linked to the views of followers. To understand how someone can be an effective leader, we must try to understand why a follower would give up discretion over their own behavior to that leader. After all, rational choice models make the important point that, in general, people prefer to have freedom to determine their own behavior so that they can act in ways that maximize the desirability of their outcomes. As a result, people resist giving up control over their behavior to other people. Yet, in the context of groups, there is evidence that people defer to leaders. And, they do so voluntarily, without having to be rewarded or punished. The ability to secure such self-regulatory behavior is central to success as a leader.

This suggestion is consistent with the argument of Michelle Bligh and James Meindl that too much attention has been directed toward trying to understand the characteristics of leaders, and too little toward trying to understand the characteristics of situations and of followers (Bligh & Meindl, chap. 2, this volume). The concern here is with the characteristics of followers, and the argument is that it is the judgments of followers about the legitimacy of leaders, and the resultant self-imposed responsibility for following those leaders, that shapes leadership effectiveness in social regulation.

Of course, as I noted earlier, social regulation is focused on one set of issues—those linked to the willingness of people to defer to rules and to the decisions of social authorities. Being able to gain such willingness is one crucial aspect of being a leader. However, leadership is not only about gaining restraint from followers. Leadership also involves being able to stimulate group members to expend effort and to engage in the activities that enhance group viability. Recognition of this function of leadership suggests that leader effectiveness is linked to both the ability of leaders to limit undesirable behavior and to their ability to promote desired behavior.

Together with Steve Blader, I have proposed and tested the *group engagement model* in a work setting (Tyler & Blader, 2000). That model explores the mechanisms through which leaders can motivate the members of groups, organizations or societies both to limit their undesirable behavior and to increase their involvement in desirable behaviors that promote group goals. This model moves beyond my earlier work on motivating rule-following behaviors in several ways. First, as noted, it encompasses both rule following and proactive engagement in ingroup tasks within a single conceptual framework.

	Rule following (limiting behaviors that harm the group)	Working on behalf of the group (promoting behaviors that advance group goals)
Mandatory	Compliance with leaders, rules, decisions	In-role behavior
Discretionary	Deference to leaders, rules, decisions	Extra-role behavior

FIG. 8.1.   A behavioral typology of cooperation.

In addition, the *group engagement model* makes a distinction between two forms of each behavior: mandatory and discretionary (see Tyler & Blader, 2000). Mandatory behaviors are those that are required by one's role or by group rules. Discretionary behaviors are not formally required. For example, employees can do their jobs well or poorly. This is referred to as in-role behavior. They can also engage in actions not required by their role, often referred to as extra-role behaviors. When we combine these two distinctions, we end up with the four types of behavior shown in Fig. 8.1. The importance of this distinction is implied by the discussion of social regulatory approaches, but it is more overtly recognized and measured in this work than in those earlier studies.

MOTIVATIONS FOR COOPERATION

The task of the leader is to engage members of the group in the four types of cooperative behavior outlined in Fig. 8.1. There are two basic ways in which leaders might try to shape the motivations of the people in their group. These approaches seek to engage the two central sources of human motivation. These two types of motivation for social behavior in groups were first identified and articulated by Lewin in his field theory model of human motivation (Gold, 1999). That model views behavior as a function of the person and the environment $(B = f(p,e))$ (see Lewin, 1997).

First, leaders might alter the situation in which their followers are making rational behavioral decisions, either by creating incentives to reward desired behaviors, by punishing or threatening to punish those who engage in undesired behaviors, or by both strategies. This type of motivation has already been discussed in the context of deterrence or social control models for gaining compliance. Environmental motivational force reflects the incentives and risks that exist in the immediate environment. These environmental contingencies influence motivation because one core motivation underlying people's behavior is the desire to gain rewards and avoid punishments.

I have already discussed the influence of environmental forces on motivation. Of course, leaders can never completely control the environment. For example, criminal behavior is not only shaped by sanction risk. It is also shaped by whether a person is able to get a job, and has an alternative way to make a living, as well as by whether inviting criminal opportunities exist. Nonetheless, as already noted, the aspects of the environment that the leader can control do shape behavior and this provides an opportunity for leaders to shape the motivations of the people in the group.

Second, leaders might try to create or activate attitudes and values that would lead group members to voluntarily engage in desired types of behavior. This personal motivational force reflects the internal motivations that shape the behavioral direction that a person brings into a given setting—the things that the person feels that they ought to do (values) or want to do (attitudes).

VALUES AND COOPERATIVE BEHAVIOR

One aspect of the type of internal motivation that I have already outlined is that of social values, and reflects the influence of people's sense of responsibility and obligation on their cooperative behavior. Values are people's feelings about what is right and proper—what they "ought" to do. Values motivate people to cooperate by refraining from engaging in undesirable behaviors. People with values that support the group, for example, feel it is wrong to steal office supplies, to take long lunches, and to otherwise break work rules. Similarly, in society more generally, supportive values lead people to follow the law by not using drugs, not robbing banks, and not murdering their neighbors.

There are two basic types of values that are potentially relevant to cooperation in groups. The social value of concern here is legitimacy—the feeling of obligation to obey the rules, authorities, and institutions of a group. A group leader who has legitimacy can issue directives and the people in the group will follow them because they feel that the leader is entitled to be obeyed. Again, people are self-regulatory. They follow the directives of the leader because they feel that it is their personal responsibility to do so. Hence, the leader does not have to deploy incentive or sanctioning systems in order to gain cooperative behavior from group members.

The examples I have already outlined illustrate the value of having legitimacy. Studies similarly find that the laws with which people deal in their everyday lives vary in their legitimacy. Tyler (1990) found that the legitimacy of laws had a direct influence on whether or not people followed those laws in their everyday lives. Further, that influence was a more important influence on behavior than was the influence of the likelihood of being caught and punished for rule breaking behavior.

Tyler and Blader (2000) found similar results in work organizations in the case of work rules. Those who viewed work rules and managerial authorities as legitimate were more willing to follow those rules. Again, the influence of legitimacy was greater than the influence of sanctioning possibilities. Legitimacy had an especially strong influence on voluntary rule-following behavior (deference to rules).

The problem with legitimacy as a form of authority is that people are found to suspend their own personal moral values when dealing with legitimate authorities. They authorize those authorities to make decisions about what is appropriate and reasonable in a given situation (Kelman & Hamilton, 1989). As a consequence, legitimacy can lead group members to engage in immoral actions, actions that would typically be against their own sense of what is appropriate. In the classic experiments on obedience to authority conducted by Milgram, for example, people were willing to engage in behaviors that they thought were harming others when ordered to do so by a legitimate authority (Milgram, 1974). These findings suggest a need to be sensitive to the potentially socially destructive consequences of legitimacy.

Another set of values are those linked to personal morality. Personal moral values are internal representations of conscience that tell people which social behaviors are right or wrong to engage in within social contexts. Following moral rules is self-directed in that when people violate moral rules they feel guilt, an aversive emotional state (Hoffman, 2000). Consequently, people follow moral rules for internal motivational reasons, distinct from the contingencies in the environment.

Morality is an important force shaping people's compliance with rules (Robinson & Darley, 1995; Tyler, 1990). In fact, in the context of ordinary citizens' relationships with the law, morality has a greater influence on people's behavior than does the threat of being caught and punished for wrongdoing (Tyler, 1990). As a consequence, if the people in a group feel that it is morally wrong to break group rules, the level of rule-breaking behavior will diminish considerably. Leaders benefit from creating and sustaining a moral climate in which it is viewed as morally wrong to break group rules.

Despite the value of morality as a motivator of rule-following behavior, from the perspective of group leaders morality is a double-edged sword (see Tyler & Darley, 2000). If people's morality supports the group and group authorities, the group gains a powerful motivational force supporting group rules. However, if the moral values of the members of a group are linked to a different moral code, that undermines the leader of a group, since group members are internally motivated to deviate from group rules.

The classic example of such conflicts is the history of conflicts between government authority and the authority or religion and the church (Kelman & Hamilton, 1989). When government leaders can successfully gain the support of religious values for their policies, they gain a powerful motivational force, leading people to follow those policies. However, when religious principles oppose government policies, people have a set of moral values that motivate them to disobey the law. Draft resisters, for example, refuse to fight for their country because of their moral values (Levi, 1997), and soldiers refuse to carry out "legitimate" orders that they regard as immoral (Kelman & Hamilton, 1989).

ATTITUDES AND COOPERATION

Another type of internal motivation develops from attitudes—the things that a person wants to do. There are two types of attitude of particular relevance here. The first is intrinsic motivation. People like or enjoy certain types of activities and do those activities because of their intrinsic interest. People may like playing baseball, entertaining friends, or cleaning up their yard. These activities are rewarding in and of themselves, and people engage in them for internal reasons, not for external reward. Similarly, employees may like their jobs, family members may enjoy doing housework, and college professors may enjoy teaching introductory psychology.

An example of the motivating power of intrinsic motivation is provided by the recent golf victories of Tiger Woods. Woods is an excellent golfer, who has recently won many victories in major tournaments. His victories flow from a lifelong enthusiasm for golf, an enthusiasm that has led him to endless hours of practice to improve his performance. For example, following his recent Master's tournament victory, Woods immediately expressed interest in watching tapes of his performance to identify weaknesses that he might correct.

Although Woods receives financial rewards for his victories, his motivation for superior performance seems to be more than the goal of being wealthy. He appears to be motivated by enthusiasm for his chosen career, and a desire to excel at it. This intrinsic motivation leads him to continue to practice and strive to improve, even when his performance is at a high level. Woods is not unique. Many people strive to excel at their work because they are intrinsically excited about and motivated by their jobs. In another example, consider the many university professors who, although they have tenure (job security), work long hours motivated by enthusiasm for advancing their particular areas of research. Again, professors receive rewards for their performance, but their efforts are not only motivated by rewards. They are also motivated by interest in the topics they study and teach about. Law and business professors, for example, could quickly double or triple their financial rewards by abandoning academic positions for positions in the private sector, but they would lose some of their freedom to do the work that intrinsically motivates them.

A second type of attitude shaping cooperation is loyalty or commitment to the group or organization. People in groups come to identify with those groups, and to care about the well being of the group and its members. In fact, two of the key findings of social identity theory (Hogg & Abrams, 1988) are that: (a) people in groups come to identify with groups, merging their sense of themselves with the identity of the group and that (b) once people identify with groups, they put the welfare of the group above their own welfare. For example, when group members are given the choice of maximizing personal or group outcomes, they maximize group outcomes (Hogg & Abrams, 1988). So, acting in ways that benefit the group becomes an internal motivation, and people act in these ways without the expectation of personal reward.

An example of research demonstrating the impact of identification with a group is the work of Brann and Foddy (1988). Using a simulated commons dilemma, these authors examine how people react when they feel that a commonly held resource is being rapidly depleted in a community.

Those people low in loyalty to their group react by taking more of the remaining scarce resource for themselves ("hoarding"). Such behavior is personally rational, since, as a result of this behavior, the individual retains some of the collective resource for their own use when the pool is depleted, but it accelerates collective disintegration by more rapidly depleting a commonly held resource. This is especially destructive with self-renewing resources, such as fish or trees, since depletion of the resource leads to extinction of the resource. But, even with resources such as food in stores, the tendency to hoard during a crisis has damaging social consequences.

In contrast to those low in identification, people high in identification with the group took less of the resource for themselves in response to information that the collective resource was being rapidly depleted. Individuals high in identification with the group took a personal risk in an effort to slow the deterioration of the group occurring through the loss of a collective resource. Their response to a crisis was to take more personal risks on behalf of the group, not less. They put the welfare of the group first. Such individuals are motivated by the internal value of commitment to the group, and act in ways that are inconsistent with their own personal short-term self-interest, to preserve the group.

Of course, the social dilemma literature makes clear that acting in one's short-term self-interest is often harmful to one's long-term self-interest. By taking a short-term risk on the group, people may be increasing the prospects for their own long-term future. This is true because those people who hoard scarce resources only assure their well-being for a brief period of time. They can gather a set of rapidly disappearing resources, which will sustain them for a short period of time. However, once those resources are depleted, there are no more resources. The common pool of resources is gone. As already noted, this is especially true of resources that replenish themselves, resources such as fish and trees. Once a species is extinct, it cannot be renewed. It is, however, also true of social capital—the collective attitudes and institutions that sustain groups—which are difficult to develop and easy to diminish.

If, for example, the cooperative behavior of concern involves working to keeping one's neighborhood clean, the short-term self-interested tendency is to let other people do the work. However, such "free riding" undermines everyone's interest in this activity, and there is ultimately no effort to clean up the neighborhood. Fortunately, in such a situation it is possible to renew the institutions and motivations that lead to member efforts on behalf of the community. But, this renewal requires recreating the value of commitment to the community and its welfare.

So, intrinsic motivation and commitment to the group are two types of internal motivations that lead people to act on behalf of groups. In each case, people act in cooperative ways, without the need for incentives or sanctioning as a motivating force. Groups gain from such internally motivated behavior because the group, its authorities and its institutions, do not need to deploy group resources for resource-based motivational strategies. Instead, the members of the group act in cooperative ways due to their own internal motivations.

Clearly, supportive attitudes are important and valuable for groups, organizations, and societies. The question is how leaders might create and sustain these motivations. The clearest case is that of commitment to the group. Leaders play an important role in creating and sustaining a group with which members can identify and to which they become loyal and committed. This feeling of group identification encourages cooperation on behalf of the group because people merge their sense of themselves in the group and the welfare of the group becomes indistinguishable from personal welfare.

The literature in social psychology describes identification with the group as superordinate identification, and notes a variety of ways that such identification can be developed and sustained. Gaertner and Dovidio (2000) discuss this issue in the context of their "common ingroup identity model." They suggest that a range of factors can shape the strength of people's awareness of group boundaries as well as the degree to which people identify with their own group. A review of this literature is beyond the scope of this chapter, except to say that there are a variety of ways in which groups and their leaders can encourage people both to organize their perceptions of group boundaries in desired ways and to identify with their own group.

It is also clear that situational factors shape the development of intrinsic motivation. In particular, the use of incentives or sanctions to promote desired behavior diminishes or "crowds out" intrinsic motivation (Deci, 1975; Frey, 1997). This suggests that the use of these basic instrumental strategies, while promoting cooperative behavior in the immediate moment, also has the effect of undermining other motivations for that behavior. In the long term, the use of incentive or sanction-based strategies of motivation may diminish cooperation.

What promotes intrinsic motivation? Again, there is a large psychological literature on this issue, which cannot be fully considered here. It is clear, however, that leaders can encourage such motivation by the way that they structure groups and group tasks (Deci, 1975, 1980).

My point in this discussion is that efforts to stimulate cooperation by appealing to attitudes and values are more effective ways to encourage cooperation than are approaches that rely on the use of incentives or sanctions to achieve the same objectives. These approaches are found to be more influential in stimulating cooperation than are incentive- or sanction-based systems. Further, they have the advantage of being self-motivating. When acting in response to their attitudes, people are responding to their own feelings about what they like and want to do. So, people are motivated to engage in cooperative acts without focusing on the rewards for such actions. When responding to their values, people are focusing on their own sense of what is right, and their behavior is self-regulating.

The important role of attitudes and values in stimulating cooperation suggests the importance of creating a supportive culture or value climate within a group. Leaders need to stimulate intrinsic interest in group roles, identification with the group, and the development of moral values and feelings that group authorities are legitimate. Such a culture can then be drawn upon when authorities are seeking to motivate cooperative behavior within a group.

Because of the motivational power of legitimacy, leaders, who represent the group, are in a unique position of being able to call upon the members of the group to engage in behaviors that involve risks and sacrifices in the name of the group. Such legitimate authority is typically associated with formal leaders and authorities. While it can be developed by informal leaders in spontaneous and temporary groups, legitimacy is not easily acquired, nor are people especially willing to forgo personal gains in deference to the directives of others.

Because of the unique ability of authorities to use legitimacy as a motivational force, leadership is likely to be most important when a situation calls for restraint on the part of group members—in particular the willing deference to group rules. Such motivation is different from the willingness to make personal sacrifices for the group that may flow from attitudes of commitment and loyalty, and may lead to volunteerism.

COOPERATIVE BEHAVIOR
IN WORK SETTINGS

This discussion of leadership began by looking at work on social regulation. That work shows that in legal settings legitimacy is an important attribute associated with successful leadership. When authorities are legitimate, people obey the rules they enforce. We can extend our test of this basic argument into the arena of work organizations by examining the results of a study of 404 employees interviewed about their behavior in their work organization (see Tyler & Blader, 2000, for a detailed discussion of the results of this study).

One reason that people might participate in and cooperate with groups is to gain the resources associated with group membership. Traditional explanations of people's choices among possible behaviors they might engage in within groups or organizations; their decisions about whether or not to stay or leave a group or organization; their decisions about the extent to which they will enact organizational roles; and their decisions about the degree to which they will follow rules all suggest that these decisions are shaped by estimates of gain and loss (as defined within social exchange theory; see Thibaut & Kelley, 1959).

Social exchange theory suggests that people's orientation toward organizations reflects their views about the favorability of the exchange of effort and resources between them and that organization. If people feel that they are receiving favorable resources from the organization, they stay within it, performing their organizational roles and following organizational rules.

Gain/loss arguments have also been used by a variety of social psychologists as possible explanations for the motivations underlying people's willingness to help others in groups. The willingness to help others has been linked to the perceived benefits and costs of helping (Latane & Darley, 1970; Piliavin, Piliavin, & Rodin, 1975), while cooperation within groups has been linked to estimates of the likelihood that others will reciprocate such cooperative behavior (Komorita & Parks, 1994; Rousseau, 1995; Tyler & Kramer, 1996; Williamson, 1993). Expectancy theory similarly links work motivation to expected payoffs (Vroom, 1964), as does goal setting theory (Locke & Latham, 1990).

An example of the application of social exchange theory to behavior within groups and organizations is provided by the work of Rusbult on the investment model. The investment model explores loyalty to long-term relationships with other people, groups and organizations (Rusbult & Van Lange, 1996). The key issue that is predicted by the investment model to shape personal decisions about whether to exit a group or to remain loyal to it is how dependent an individual feels they are on the organization for obtaining personally valued resources.

Studies based on the investment model suggest that greater dependence on an organization leads to heightened loyalty, with people being less willing to leave organizations that provide them with high levels of desired resources, that provide more resources than available alternatives, and/or in which they have invested time, energy, or resources. These studies support the argument that one way to understand people's behavior in organizations is via an instrumental perspective focusing on long-term assessments of resources likely to be obtained from the group.

Making use of the distinction between mandatory and discretionary behavior, we can focus directly on voluntary deference to authority (Tyler, 1990, only examines mandated behavior—i.e., compliance). When we do so we find that both the risks associated with rule breaking and the legitimacy of organizational rules influence whether employees defer to organizational rules. Of these two factors, legitimacy is more important. It explains 21% of the variance in deference to rules beyond what can be explained by risk judgments. In contrast, risk judgments explain one percent of the variance in deference to organizational rules beyond that which can be explained by legitimacy. The key factor shaping deference to rules, in other words, is the legitimacy of those rules. Hence, like legal authorities, managerial authorities need legitimacy to effectively manage the rule-related behavior of employees.

The advantage of studying the work environment is that it allows the full range of the group engagement model to be tested. When such a test is conducted, using the sample of employees already outlined, the results shown in Fig. 8.2 are obtained (this figure is taken from Tyler & Blader, 2000, p. 191, and a fuller description of the study is provided there).

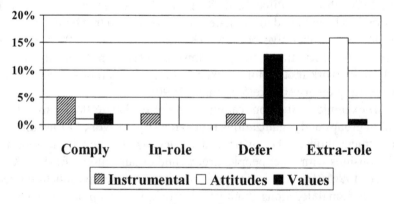

FIG. 8.2.   The influence of instrumental judgments, attitudes, and values on cooperation (entries are the unique contribution of each factor in explaining the behavior). From *Cooperation in Groups*, by T. R. Tyler and S. L. Blader, 2000. Copyright © 2000 by Psychology Press. Reprinted with permission of Routledge/Taylor & Francis Books, Inc.

The results shown in Fig. 8.2 support several arguments. First, they suggest that it is important to distinguish between external and internal sources of motivation. Internal sources of motivation—attitudes and values—are especially important in shaping discretionary behavior. Further, attitudes are central to proactive behavior, in the form of extra-role behavior, while values are the key antecedent of deference to organizational rules. Hence, attitudes and values both have an important influence on discretionary cooperative behavior, but the nature of their influence differs greatly, depending on which type of cooperative behavior is being considered.

These findings suggest that leaders gain a great deal when they can appeal to attitudes and values among their followers. The existence of those attitudes and values provides a motivating force for discretionary behavior of two types: deference to rules and extra-role behavior. The question, to be addressed later in this discussion, is how such attitudes and values can be activated. In other words, what leadership or management practices lead to cooperative behavior among group members?

THE ANTECEDENTS OF EFFECTIVE LEADERSHIP

As I have noted, many theories of leadership argue that leaders exercise influence through their control of incentives and sanctions. The literature on motivations for following leaders often argues that leader–follower relations depend on the exchange of rewards. According to this perspective, if leaders make good decisions that lead to success and to the gain of resources for group members, followers respond by obeying the directives of their leaders (Levine & Moreland, 1995). For example, some studies of leaders emphasize the importance of their task competence (Hollander, 1980; Hollander & Julian, 1978; Ridgeway, 1981), suggesting that people will follow those leaders that they feel can solve group problems in a way that will lead to personal gain for group members.

Similarly, transactional theories of leadership suggest that leader–follower relations depend on resources received from leaders in the past or expected in the future (Bardach & Eccles, 1989; Dasgupta, 1988; Komorita, Chan, & Parks, 1993; Komorita, Parks, & Hulbert, 1992; Wayne & Ferris, 1990; Williamson, 1993). One example of such a theory of leadership is vertical dyad linkage theory (Dansereau, Graen, & Haga, 1975) that explores the nature of the exchange relationships between organization members and their leaders (Chemers, 1983, 1987; Duchon, Green, & Taber, 1986; Vecchio & Gobdel, 1984). Such exchanges vary in the nature of the resources exchanged, although theories typically focus on material rewards and costs (Dansereau et al., 1975; Dienesch & Liden, 1986; Graen & Cashman, 1975; Graen, Wakabayashi, Graen, & Graen, 1990; Liden & Graen, 1980).

Of course, expected gain and loss judgments in organizational settings are not only made about the immediate situation. People have long-term relationships with groups and they make long-term judgments about the expected costs and benefits of group membership. In the context of ongoing groups, these more long-term judgments of expected rewards/costs guide people's behavior within their group. In making such long-term judgments about what types of behavior will be rewarding, people evaluate the overall quality of the outcomes they are receiving from the group, across situations, relative to their available alternatives, as well as by judging the degree to which they have already invested resources in the group.

An example of the application of long-term resource-based approaches to the study of behavior in groups is provided by the investment model (Rusbult & Van Lange, 1996), which studies the factors shaping people's decisions to leave or remain within groups (their "loyalty" to the group). The investment model predicts that the key factor shaping personal decisions about whether to exit a group is how dependent an individual feels they are on the group for obtaining personally valued resources. Dependence judgments involve considerations of one's immediate and expected long-term reward level, the quality of one's alternatives, and the amount that one has invested in a group.

Studies based on the investment model suggest that greater dependence on a group or relationship leads to heightened loyalty, with people less willing to leave groups that provide them with high levels of desired resources and/or in which they have already invested resources. These studies support the argument that one way to understand people's behavior in groups is through an instrumental perspective. They emphasize the value of such an instrumental approach being linked to overall and long-term assessments of resources obtained from the group, as well as to the immediate gains or risks found within any particular situation.

All of these models support the argument already outlined in suggesting that leaders shape the motivations and behaviors of followers via their control of incentives and sanctions. Hence, they all argue for the role, at least in the short-term, of expectations of gain and loss.

JUSTICE MODELS

In contrast to these outcome models, in my work I argue that effective leadership is based on the judgment by followers that a leader is exercising authority through fair procedures—the procedural justice based model of authority dynamics that I earlier labeled the *relational model of authority* (Tyler & Lind, 1992).

In my earlier work on social regulation I found that the legitimacy of social regulatory leaders is rooted in judgments about the justice of their decision-making procedures. In Tyler (1990) I explored the influence of different aspects of personal experience with police officers and judges on judgments about the legitimacy of legal authority. That study showed that the primary aspect of experience shaping people's views about legitimacy was their evaluation of the fairness of the procedures used by the authority involved.

In addition, a second study of legal authority, which examined the basis of the legitimacy of the Supreme Court similarly found that institutional legitimacy is linked to evaluations of the fairness of Court decision-making procedures. This is not only a feature of the Court. Evaluations of Congress also find strong influences of procedural justice (Tyler, 2001). In other words, irrespective of whether we consider personal experiences or institutional level evaluations, the roots of legitimacy lie in procedural justice.

Again, in my more recent work I have extended this analysis to the area of work organizations, using the previously outlined sample of employees (Tyler & Blader, 2000). In that study we compare the influence of general evaluations of the fairness of organizational procedures to the influence of general evaluations of the favorability and fairness of the outcomes of those procedures. We explore the influence of these three factors on attitudes, values, and mandatory and discretionary behaviors.

The results of this workplace analysis are shown in Fig. 8.3 (from Tyler & Blader, 2000, p. 193). The results suggest several conclusions. First, procedural justice is the key antecedent of attitudes and values. Second, procedural justice is the key antecedent of discretionary behavior. Taken together, these findings support our argument that procedural justice is the key to promoting discretionary behavior. In this case, however, discretionary behavior is not only deference to rules; it also involves extra-role behavior.

These findings suggest that leadership rests upon the judgments of followers that the leader is making decisions using fair procedures. When

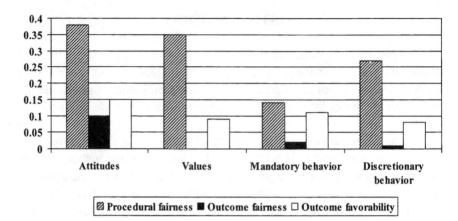

FIG. 8.3. The influence of outcome favorability, outcome fairness, and procedural fairness on attitudes, values, and cooperative behavior (beta weights showing independent influence). From *Cooperation in Groups*, by T. R. Tyler and S. L. Blader, 2000. Copyright © 2000 by Psychology Press. Reprinted with permission of Routledge/Taylor & Francis Books, Inc.

followers believe that this is true, their intrinsic job motivation, their commitment to the organization, and their view that the organization's rules are legitimate and ought to be obeyed all increase. As we have already noted, these internal motivations are the key to discretionary behavior. As we would expect, in such a situation, we find a direct influence of procedural justice on discretionary behavior.

WHAT IS A FAIR PROCEDURE?

If, as I am suggesting here, the roots of effective leadership lie in leading via the use of procedures that people will experience as fair, then we have substantial support for a model of the type of *process-based leadership* that is the title of this chapter. Process-based leadership is based on the idea that an important part of the way that leaders lead is by motivating group members to act on their attitudes and values, leading to self-motivating and self-regulating behavior on the part of group members. The findings I outline here support the suggestion that both people's willingness to follow rules and their willingness to work on behalf of their groups or organizations are linked to their judgment that the leaders of their group are exercising authority using procedures that followers understand to be fair. To implement a strategy of leadership based on these findings, it is important to understand what people mean by a fair procedure.

Research based on personal interactions with legal authorities suggests that procedural justice is a multidimensional construct with at least eight independent factors shaping overall judgments about the fairness of the methods used by leaders to exercise authority (Tyler, 1988, 1990). Central to such procedural justice evaluations are evaluations of the neutrality of decision-making procedures, the degree to which leaders treat followers with dignity and respect, and the extent to which followers think that leaders are trustworthy and benevolent (Tyler & Lind, 1992).

Interestingly, this conclusion is echoed in a recent study of the exercise of legal authority focusing on the willingness of people to accept the decisions made by police officers and judges. In that study, detailed in Tyler and Huo (2002), a large sample of citizens in Oakland and Los Angeles, California, are interviewed about their recent personal experiences with police officers or judges. The results of the study suggest that the quality of the treatment that people receive from those legal authorities is central to the willingness of people to voluntarily defer to their decisions.

The results of that analysis are shown in Table 8.1. These results make clear that quality of treatment is central to the willingness of people to

TABLE 8.1
The Procedural Factors Shaping Decision Acceptance With Legal Authorities

| | Decision Acceptance in Personal Experiences With Police Officers/Judges | | Obligation to Obey Legal Authorities | Trust in Legal Authorities |
	Voluntary Experience	Not Voluntary Experience		
Beta weights				
Quality of decision making	.20***	.14***	.20***	.28***
Quality of treatment	.53***	.65***	.29***	.30***
Distributive justice	.11***	.04	−.13***	−.02
Outcome favorability	.11***	.06*	.13***	.08
Adjusted proportion of the variance explained	67%	65%	23%	33%

Note. From Tyler and Huo (2002), *Trust and the Rule of Law.* New York: Russell Sage Foundation.

$*p < .05.$ $**p < .01.$ $***p < .001.$

accept the decisions of legal authorities. This supports the argument that one of the most important ways that people judge authorities is by how those authorities treat the people within their group. Such issues of treatment are often more central to reactions to authorities than are evaluations of the quality of decision making. They are certainly more central than are evaluations of outcome favorability or outcome fairness.

More recently, we examined the antecedents of procedural justice in work settings, using our previously described sample of employees (Tyler & Blader, 2000). To conduct that analysis we drew upon a new conceptualization of the potential antecedents of procedural justice that identifies four potential antecedents of procedural justice: the fairness of the decision-making procedures; the quality of the treatment that people receive from group leaders; the fairness of the outcomes received; and the favorability of the outcomes received from the organization and its leaders. This model is referred to as the *two component model of procedural justice* because it divides the antecedents of justice into two basic components (see Blader & Tyler, 2003).

The results of the previously outlined analysis are shown in Table 8.2. Those results suggest that there are two key antecedents of procedural justice evaluations. Those are judgments about the fairness of decision-making procedures and judgments about the quality of the treatment that followers receive from leaders. In other words, both of the components of procedural justice that we expected to matter make important independent contributions to judgments about the fairness of procedures.

It is similarly possible to examine the influence of these elements on the attitudes, values, and behaviors already outlined. To conduct such an analysis we created two summary indices reflecting orientation toward

TABLE 8.2

The Elements of a Fair Procedure in Work Settings

Beta weights	
Quality of decision-making	.49***
Quality of treatment	.38***
Distributive justice	.13*
Outcome favorability	.00
Adjusted proportion of the variance explained	80%***

Note. From Tyler and Blader (2000), *Cooperation in Groups.* Copyright © 2000.
$*p < .05. **p < .01. ***p < .001.$

TABLE 8.3

The Influence of Procedural Elements
on Cooperative Behavior

	Orientation Toward Limiting Behavior	Orientation Toward Promotive Behavior
Beta weights		
Quality of decision-making	.23***	−.12
Quality of treatment	.10*	.49***
Distributive justice	.00	−.03
Outcome favorability	.01	.11*
Adjusted proportion of the variance explained	10%	23%

*$p < .05.$ **$p < .01.$ ***$p < .001.$

limiting behavior (summarizing legitimacy, compliance, and deference) and orientation toward promotive behavior (summarizing commitment, in-role behavior, extra-role behavior). We then examined the influence of the four elements of organizations on these two key motivational indices.

The results are shown in Table 8.3. They support the argument that both the quality of decision making and the quality of treatment are central elements of procedures. Further, the results suggest that quality of decision making is most important in the case of encouraging limiting behavior, while quality of treatment is central to motivating promotive behavior.

If leaders want people to be willing to self-regulate, and to voluntarily defer from engaging in personally rewarding behaviors that break organizational rules, they need to make clear that they are making their decisions fairly. They do so by making clear that their decisions are made neutrally, based on objective facts and without bias or favoritism.

If leaders want people to be motivated toward working on behalf of the group, and they want them to engage in voluntary behaviors that promote the organization's welfare, then they should communicate clearly that they respect the members of their group and the members' rights. They do so by treating people with dignity and respect. The issue of quality of treatment dominates reactions to authorities.

Of the findings outlined, the most striking is the central role of the quality of treatment that people receive on their views about the fairness of procedures, and on their willingness to engage behaviorally in groups and organizations. This is especially true when we are exploring people's orientation toward promotive behavior, such as in-role or extra-role behavior in work organizations. When people feel valued as people, they actively involve themselves in activities that benefit their group, organization, or society.

IMPLICATIONS

Leaders are typically trained in the specialized knowledge and skills that they need to attain technical competence in their field. This set of skills allows them to make decisions that are of high quality, when evaluated against objective criteria of good and bad decision making. The equation of leadership to technical competence and expertise is widespread, and flows from the certification of authorities through training programs that emphasize technical skills.

The findings outlined here show that the quality of the decision making that people experience when dealing with leaders is important. It plays an especially important role in shaping people's willingness to follow social rules. However, the quality of the treatment that people receive is the key antecedent to their willingness to engage themselves proactively in tasks that help the group. Hence, the ability to make decisions well is only one element of effective leadership.

One implication of this finding is that people judge leaders using a broad set of criteria, only some of which involve their competence. In addition to making decisions through appropriate and reasonable procedures, authorities also have to be concerned about how they treat the people with whom they are dealing.

These findings suggest that leaders need to focus on a two-pronged approach to *process-based leadership*. The first prong involves fair decision making. People are sensitive to a variety of issues about decision making, including whether or not the decision maker is unbiased and neutral, uses facts and objective information, and treats people consistently. The second prong involves the quality of people's treatment during the decision-making process. People are sensitive to whether or not they are treated with dignity and respect, whether their rights are acknowledged, and whether their needs and concerns are considered.

Interestingly, both of the prongs of *process-based leadership* that I have outlined are distinct from the favorability or the fairness of people's outcomes. In each case, people's reactions to the actions of their leaders are linked to the manner in which those leaders behave, rather than to the outcomes of their behavior. Hence, the ability of leaders to motivate their followers is rooted largely in the process by which they lead, rather than in the outcomes they deliver.

This finding is consistent with the findings that emerge in studies of trust in authorities (see Tyler & Degoey, 1996). In such studies, trust in authorities is divided into two distinct elements: trust in the competence of authorities to solve problems and deliver favorable outcomes and trust in the benevolence and caring of leaders. When that division is made, trust in motives (benevolence, caring) is found to be the key antecedent of the willingness to accept the decision of leaders. Again, it is not the outcomes that leaders can or do deliver that shapes people's responses to those leaders.

REFERENCES

Bardach, J. L., & Eccles, R. G. (1989). Price, authority, and trust. *Annual Review of Sociology, 15,* 97–118.

Bass, B. M. (1981). *Stogdill's handbook of leadership: A survey of theory and research.* NY: The Free Press.

Blader, S. L., & Tyler, T. R. (2003). A four-component model of procedural fairness. *Social Psychology Bulletin, 29,* 747–758.

Brann, P., & Foddy, M. (1988). Trust and consumption of a deteriorating common resource. *Journal of Conflict Resolution, 31,* 615–630.

Bryman, A. (1996). Leadership in organizations. In S. R. Clegg, C. Hardy, & W. R. Nord (Eds.), *Handbook of organization studies* (pp. 276–292). Thousand Oaks: Sage.

Chemers, M. M. (1983). Leadership theory and research: A systems-process integration. In P. B. Paulus (Ed.), *Basic Group Processes* (pp. 9–39). New York: Springer-Verlag.

Chemers, M. M. (1987). Leadership processes: Intrapersonal, interpersonal, and societal influences. In C. Hendrick (Ed.), *Review of personalty and social psychology* (Vol. 8, pp. 252–277). Newbury Park, CA: Sage.

Dansereau, F., Graen, G., & Haga, W. J. (1975). A vertical dyad linkage approach to leadership within formal organizations: A longitudinal investigation of the role making process. *Organizational Behavior, 13,* 46–78.

Dasgupta, P. (1988). Trust as a commodity. In D. Gambetta (Ed.), *Trust: Making and breaking cooperative relations* (pp. 49–72). Oxford: Basil Blackwell.

Deci, E. L. (1975). *Intrinsic motivation.* New York: Plenum.

Deci, E. L. (1980). *The psychology of self-determination.* Lexington, MA.: Lexington Books.

Dienesch, R. M., & Liden, R. C. (1986). Leader–member exchange model of leadership: A critique and further development. *Academy of Management Review, 11,* 618–634.

Duchon, D., Green, S., & Taber, T. D. (1986). Vertical dyad linkage: A longitudinal assessment of antecedents, measures, and consequences. *Journal of Applied Psychology, 71,* 56–60.

Forsyth, D. R. (1999). *Group dynamics* (3rd ed.). New York: Brooks/Cole-Wadsworth.

Frey, B. S. (1997). *Not just for the money: An economic theory of personal motivation.* Cheltenham, UK: Edward Elger.

Gaertner, S. L., & Dovidio, J. F. (2000). *Reducing intergroup bias: The common ingroup identity model.* Philadelphia: Psychology Press.

Gold, M. (Ed.). (1999). *The complete social scientist: A Kurt Lewin Reader.* Washington, DC: American Psychological Association.

Graen, G., & Cashman, J. (1975). A role-making model of leadership in formal organizations. In J. G. Hunt & L. L. Larson (Eds.), *Leadership frontiers* (pp. 143–165). Kent, OH: Kent State University Press.

Graen, G., Wakabayashi, M., Graen, M. R., & Graen, M. G. (1990). International generalizability of American hypotheses about Japanese management progress. *Leadership Quarterly, 1,* 1–23.

Hoffman, M. L. (2000). *Empathy and moral development.* Cambridge, UK: Cambridge University Press.

Hogg, M., & Abrams, D. (1988). *Social identifications: A social psychology of intergroup relations and group processes.* London: Routledge.

Hollander, E. (1978). *Leadership dynamics: A practical guide to effective relationships.* New York: The Free Press.

Hollander, E. (1980). Leadership and social exchange processes. In K. Gergen, M. S. Greenberg, & R. H. Willis (Eds.), *Social exchange.* New York: Plenum.

Hollander, E., & Julian, J. W. (1978). Studies in leader legitimacy, influence, and innovation. In L. Berkowitz (Ed.), *Group processes.* New York: Academic.

Kelman, H. C., & Hamilton, V. L. (1989). *Crimes of obedience.* New Haven: Yale.

Komorita, S. S., Chan, D. K. S., & Parks, C. D. (1993). The effects of reward structure and reciprocity in social dilemmas. *Journal of Experimental Social Psychology, 29,* 252–267.

Komorita, S. S., & Parks, C. D. (1994). *Social dilemmas.* Madison, WI: Brown and Benchmark.

Komorita, S. S., Parks, C. D., & Hulbert, L. G. (1992). Reciprocity and the induction of cooperation in social dilemmas. *Journal of Personality and Social Psychology, 62,* 607–617.

Latane, B., & Darley, J. (1970). *The unresponsive bystander: Why doesn't he help?* New York: Appleton-Century-Crofts.

Levi, M. (1997). *Consent, dissent, and patriotism.* Cambridge, UK: Cambridge University Press.

Levine, J. M., & Moreland, R. L. (1995). Group processes. In A. Tesser (Ed.), *Advanced social psychology* (pp. 419–466). New York: McGraw-Hill.

Lewin, K. (1997). *Resolving social conflicts and field theory in social science.* Washington, DC: American Psychological Association.

Liden, R. C., & Graen, G. (1980). Generalizability of the vertical dyad linkage model of leadership. *Academy of Management Journal, 23,* 451–465.

Locke, E. A., & Latham, G. P. (1990). *A theory of goal setting and performance.* Englewood Cliffs, NJ: Prentice-Hall.

MacCoun, R. J. (1993). Drugs and the law. *Psychological Bulletin, 113,* 497–512.

Milgram, S. (1974). *Obedience to authority.* New York: Harper and Row.

Piliavin, I. M., Piliavin, J. A., & Rodin, J. (1975). Cost, diffusion, and the stigmatized victim. *Journal of Personality and Social Psychology, 32,* 429–438.

Ridgeway, C. L. (1981). Nonconformity, competence, and influence in groups. *American Sociological Review, 46,* 333–347.

Robinson, P., & Darley, J. (1995). *Justice, liability, and blame.* Boulder, CO: Westview.

Rousseau, D. M. (1995). *Psychological contracts in organizations: Understanding written and unwritten agreements.* Thousand Oaks, CA: Sage.

Rusbult, C., & Van Lange, P. (1996). Interdependence processes. In E. T. Higgins & A. W. Kruglanski (Eds.), *Social psychology* (pp. 564–596). New York: Guilford.

Stogdill, R. M. (1950). Leadership, membership and organization. *Psychological Bulletin, 47,* 1–14.

Thibaut, J., & Kelley, H. H. (1959). *The social psychology of groups.* New York: Wiley.

Tyler, T. R. (1988). What is procedural justice? *Law and Society Review, 22,* 103–135.

Tyler, T. R. (1990). *Why people obey the law.* New Haven: Yale.

Tyler, T. R. (1999). Why do people help organizations? Social identity and pro-organizational behavior. In B. Staw & R. Sutton (Eds.), *Research on organizational behavior* (Vol. 21, pp. 201–246). Greenwich, CT: JAI.

Tyler, T. R. (2001). A psychological perspective on the legitimacy of institutions and authorities. In J. T. Jost & B. Major (Eds.), *The psychology of legitimacy: Emerging perspectives on ideology, justice, and intergroup relations* (pp. 416–436). Cambridge, UK: Cambridge University Press.

Tyler, T. R., & Blader, S. L. (2000). *Cooperation in groups*. Philadelphia: Psychology Press.

Tyler, T. R., & Darley, J. (2000). Building a law-abiding society: Taking public views about morality and the legitimacy of legal authorities into account when formulating substantive law. *Hofstra Law Review, 28,* 707–739.

Tyler, T. R., & Degoey, P. (1996). Trust in organizational authorities: The influence of motive attributions on willingness to accept decisions. In R. Kramer & T. R. Tyler (Eds.), *Trust in organizations* (pp. 331–356). Thousand Oaks, CA: Sage.

Tyler, T. R., & Huo, Y. J. (2002). *Trust and the rule of law*. New York: Russell Sage Foundation.

Tyler, T. R., & Kramer, R. (1996). *Trust in organizations*. Thousand Oaks: Sage.

Tyler, T. R., and Lind, E. A. (1992). A relational model of authority in groups. *Advances in Experimental Social Psychology, 25,* 115–191.

Tyler, T. R., & Mitchell, G. (1994). Legitimacy and the empowerment of discretionary legal authority. *Duke Law Journal, 43,* 703–814.

Vecchio, R. P., & Gobdel, B. C. (1984). The vertical dyad linkage model of leadership: problems and prospects. *Organizational Behavior, 34,* 5–20.

Vroom, V. H. (1964). *Work and motivation*. New York: Wiley.

Wayne, S. J., & Ferris, G. R. (1990). Influence tactics, affect, and exchange quality in supervisor-subordinate interactions. *Journal of Applied Psychology, 75,* 487–499.

Williamson, O. E. (1993). Calculativeness, trust, and economic organization. *Journal of Law and Economics, 36,* 453–486.

9

Claiming Authority: Negotiating Challenges for Women Leaders

Hannah R. Bowles
Kathleen L. McGinn
Harvard University

Style isn't women's problem. The most recent research on gender in leadership indicates that while women tend to adopt different leadership styles than men, they are rated to be just as—if not more—effective on important leadership dimensions. Meta-analytic research shows that women tend to be relatively more democratic (as opposed to autocratic) leaders than are their male peers (Eagly & Johnson, 1990). These statistical effects are enlivened by the testimonies of accomplished women who celebrate the development of what they claim is a distinctive voice for women leaders (Rosener, 1990). In a style that fits comfortably for them, women leaders have donned agilely the traditionally male leadership mantle. The popular press cheers that "women rule" as leaders (Sharpe, 2000), and the most recent meta-analytic research on gender and leadership supports their claim (Eagly, Johannesen-Schmidt, & van Engen, 2002, p. 36).

So, why—if both men and women have what it takes to be effective leaders—are women lagging so far behind men in the race to the top? We propose that the gender gap in leadership is not about leading per se, but rather about claiming positions of authority. Where the most significant gender differences in relation to leadership occur is in the claiming of authority—men claim and hold a greater number of leadership positions than do women—not in what men and women do once they achieve that authority.

In this chapter, we explore four dominant explanations for the gender gap in claiming authority: gender bias, lack of experience, lack of motivation, and familial responsibility. There is validity to each of these explanations, but there are limitations as well. Each explanation suggests both barriers and opportunities. We argue that each potential barrier is surmountable through capitalizing on opportunities for negotiation. Drawing on recent developments in research on gender in negotiation, we propose an explanation for why the types of negotiations involved in claiming positions of authority are precisely those types of negotiations in which gender differences favoring males tend to emerge. We suggest future research to further explore the barriers and opportunities encountered by women negotiating to claim authority.

DOMINANT EXPLANATIONS FOR THE GENDER GAP IN LEADERSHIP

Four explanations for why women are underrepresented in positions of leadership emerge out of the gender and work literature. Each suggests barriers and opportunities for women attempting to claim authority. One leading explanation is that gender bias in the workplace poses active constraints on women advancing to higher levels of authority (Eagly & Karau, 2002; Kolb & Williams, 2000). Another explanation is that women lack the specific types of experience and skills to be serious contenders for the top job (Catalyst, 1998; Wirth, 2001). In spite of the fact that nearly half of all managers are women, only a small minority of senior women managers carry the types of profit-and-loss or revenue-generating responsibilities that lead to the very top (Wirth, 2001, p. 39). A third explanation is that women do not seem as interested as men in gaining the necessary experience and taking the initiative to lead (Wellington & Giscombe, 2001). Finally, and related to the question of whether women really want to lead, is the issue of women assuming primary responsibility for household and family and being less able or willing than men to balance personal life demands with the demands of top leadership positions.

GENDER BIAS

Barriers to Claiming Authority

Occupational positions dominated by one sex tend to be imbued with gender-consistent attributes for success (Cejka & Eagly, 1999; Eagly & Steffen, 2000), and the overwhelming majority of top leadership positions in American society are held by men. In 2002, less than 16% of the corporate officers in America's 500 largest companies were women. While 60 of the largest 500 companies had filled at least 25% of their corporate officers ranks with women, 71 of the 500 did not have one woman corporate officer (Catalyst, 2002). Looking to the public sector, there were only six U.S. states with women governors in 2003, and half of the states had no women representatives in the 108th U.S. Congress (Center for American Women and Politics, 2002). We are accustomed to seeing, and therefore tend to expect to see, men in charge.

Women's prospects for leadership may be obstructed by sex-typed images of leadership (Schein, 2001; Valian, 1999). We anticipate that men will assume leadership in mixed-sex groups, and tend to work together and interact socially in ways that reinforce those gender-based social roles (Dovidio, Ellyson, Keating, & Heltman, 1988; Wood & Karten, 1986). As the ratio of women to men decreases—as is generally the case as one rises through organizational ranks—resistance to women's claiming of authority increases (M. Heilman, 1980, 1995; Kanter, 1977b). Women who defy the social rules of the situation and attempt to assert their authority in the absence of external validation are likely to meet with social disapproval from their counterparts (Ridgeway, 2001; Ridgeway & Smith-Lovin, 1999; Rudman & Glick, 1999; Valian, 1999).

Once women manage to establish themselves in positions of authority, gender-based social roles inform how others—and the women themselves—think they should behave (Eagly, 1987; Eagly & Johannesen-Schmidt, 2001). Gender differences (favoring males) in the evaluation of leaders are most significant when leaders take on stereotypically masculine roles (Eagly, Makhijani, & Klonsky, 1992). Women who adopt stereotypically masculine behaviors violate the norms of female niceness, and are negatively socially sanctioned for it (Branson, 2002; Rudman & Glick, 1999). It is no wonder, perhaps, that men and women have tended to adopt distinct leadership styles (Eagly & Johannesen-Schmidt, 2001; Eagly & Johnson, 1990).

Opportunities for Claiming Authority

Even if gender biases create constraints in the style of leadership women adopt, many studies provide evidence that women's leadership styles are just as, if not more, effective than those of their male peers. In Burns' (1978) theory of "transformational" and "transactional" leaders, transactional leaders motivate followers by appealing to their existing preferences by coercion or reward, including contingent rewards based on performance. Transformational leaders, in contrast, "engage with others in such a way that leaders and followers raise one another to higher levels of motivation and morality" (Burns, 1978, p. 20). Recent meta-analytic research has established a significant positive correlation between leadership effectiveness and indicators of transformational leadership and the contingent reward dimensions of transactional leadership (Eagly et al., 2002; Lowe, Kroeck, & Sivasubramaniam, 1996).

In her most recent meta-analytic study of gender and leadership, Alice Eagly and her colleagues tested whether gender differences in leadership style would map onto measures of transformational and transactional leadership styles. They proposed that women might rely more heavily than men on "transformational" leadership styles and positive reward aspects of "transactional" leadership, because these behaviors would pose less of a gender role conflict than would other more control-oriented or coercive leadership styles. In a meta-analysis of 45 studies, Eagly and colleagues found that women were rated significantly higher than men on nearly all of the indicators of transformational leadership, as well as the contingent reward dimension of transactional leadership (Eagly et al., 2002). There were no significant gender differences observed in leaders' ability to inspire pride and respect. Furthermore, other research by Eagly and colleagues has demonstrated that gender roles are malleable, bending—albeit slowly— with changes in social conventions and the division of labor within society (Diekman & Eagly, 2000; Wood & Eagly, 2002). By taking on and succeeding in leadership roles in ever-greater numbers, women have the ability to erode stereotype-based assumptions that leadership is a man's job.

LACK OF EXPERIENCE

Barriers to Claiming Authority

One of the oft-cited barriers to women's advancement into senior management positions is a lack of critical management experiences. Although women in the United States hold 47% of executive and managerial positions, they tend to be concentrated in the "velvet ghetto" of human resource management, education and accounting (Bureau of Labor Statistics, 2002; Wirth, 2001; Woodall, Edwards, & Welchman, 1995). The route to the highest echelons of corporate America tends to not to flow through these "non-strategic" departments but rather through line management positions that carry relatively more revenue-generating responsibilities and higher profile influence within the corporation. In 1999, women in the United States held just over 6% of the corporate line jobs and, correspondingly, about 5% of the highest ranking corporate positions (e.g., chairperson, CEO, president, etc.; Wirth, 2001, p. 39).

Opportunities for Claiming Authority

When Catalyst asked CEOs what they thought would be the most effective corporate strategies for advancing women to senior management positions, 74% responded "giving women high visibility assignments" (Catalyst, 1996, p. 32). Many CEOs underscore the importance of women taking the initiative in letting their managers know they are interested in career-enhancing opportunities and point out that the organizational pipeline is stacked with women poised to rise to the highest ranks (Wellington & Giscombe, 2001). With broad-based recognition of the types of management experience that women need to obtain and a deep pool of prospective women competitors for those slots, the time should be ripe for women to fill those higher visibility, strategic management positions in ever greater numbers.

LACK OF MOTIVATION

Barriers to Claiming Authority

Another broadly espoused explanation for why there are not more women in leadership positions is that women are not hungry for leadership positions; opportunities abound, but women do not aggressively pursue them. Research supports the notion that many women shy away from promoting themselves for leadership positions. Qualitative studies suggest that women often take on informal as opposed to official leadership roles, tending to team cohesion and group conflict behind the scenes (Fletcher, 2001; Kolb, 1992; Neubert, 1999). Other research suggests that women may actually avoid the term "leader," in favor of less self-serving titles such as "facilitator," "organizer," or "coordinator" (Andrews, 1992). Consistent with the propositions of the qualitative researchers, meta-analytic research from lab and field studies on the emergence of leaders in initially leaderless groups has shown men to be significantly more likely than women to emerge as work group leaders, while women are more likely than men to be recognized as social facilitators (Eagly & Karau, 1991).

As discussed in the sections on gender biases, social incentives motivate women to downplay rather than explicitly promote their desires for and competence in positions of authority. Work by Laura Rudman on the dilemmas of self-promotion shows that if a man and a woman self-promote in a job situation, both communicate their professional competence successfully but the woman comes off as socially incompetent and undesirable for the position (Rudman, 1998). Even if a woman desires to run the show, she may be inhibited from asserting her authority by her own socialization and the expectations of others (Ridgeway, 2001).

Opportunities for Claiming Authority

However pervasive the effects of gender-based social roles and expectations may be on the motivation to claim authority, these effects are moderated by situational factors. Research by Eagly and colleagues, for instance, shows that women are more likely to emerge as leaders the longer the group interacts together and the more complex the level of social interaction becomes (Eagly & Karau, 1991). Numerous studies have shown that the gender distribution within occupations also moderates the extent to which gender influences workplace behavior, expectations and opportunities (Cohen, Broschak, & Haveman, 1998; Ely, 1994, 1995; Heilman, 1995; Heilman, 1980; Kanter, 1977a; Lee, 2001). Gender is more likely to influence leadership emergence if there is a highly asymmetric sex distribution in leadership positions; in most large organizational settings, this is a structural condition likely to favor male over female leadership candidates.

An intuitive and/or experience-based awareness of these situational constraints may explain why so many ambitious women are leaving large organizations to start their own ventures (Wirth, 2001). From the mid-1980s to the mid-1990s, the number of women-owned businesses increased by 78%, with survival rates exceeding the national average. Although the largest share (estimated 52%) of women-owned businesses have been in the service sector, the top growth industries for women-owned businesses from 1987–1996 were in traditionally male sectors such as construction, wholesale trade, transportation, agribusiness and manufacturing. From 1987–1996, women-owned business with 100 or more workers increased employment by 158%, which was more than double the rate for all U.S. firms of similar size. Employment growth in women-owned businesses beat the national average in nearly every major industry and U.S. region (Small Business Administration, 2001). It is hard to argue that women do not have the drive to lead. Women entrepreneurs have gone out and shaped organizations in ways that allow them to flourish and lead effectively. What we need now is research investigating and collecting the accumulated learning from the entrepreneurs leading women-owned businesses, to help instruct "intrapreneurs" to follow their lead by claiming higher positions of authority in traditional organizations.

FAMILIAL RESPONSIBILITY

Barriers to Claiming Authority

Many argue that the most obvious and difficult barrier to women achieving leadership positions is that they bear a disproportionate share of childrearing and household management responsibilities (Mahoney, 1996). Working moms tend to feel they have primary responsibility for child care and household duties and experience significantly more guilt than male partners over family–work conflicts. For example, in a study of 139 married couples with young children and relatively equal-status careers in business or academia, researchers observed "considerable, traditional inequity in the distribution of child-care tasks and chore responsibility" (Biernat & Wortman, 1991, p. 844). In spite of carrying a disproportionate share of the at-home workload, the women in the study reported being generally satisfied with their husbands' contribution to the domestic labor and relatively critical of their own household performance (Biernat & Wortman, 1991).

Role conflicts and time constraints created by simultaneous responsibilities at work and at home carry substantial implications for women's life choices and career trajectories. Some women cope by eliminating traditional roles, not marrying or choosing not to have children (Hall, 1972; Hewlett, 2002; Nieva & Gutek, 1981). A 2001 survey found that, among "ultra high-achieving women" in corporate America (i.e., with annual earnings of $100,000 or higher) 49% had no children by the age of 40.

This figure compares to 19% for "ultra-high achieving men" (i.e., with annual earnings of $200,000 or higher; Hewlett, 2002)—and to approximately 20% for the general population of American women age 40 (Bachu & O'Connell, 2001). A 2001 study of Harvard Business School graduates from the classes of 1981, 1986, and 1991 found that only 38% of the female graduates were working full time. The majority of the women from the HBS graduating classes had substantially or completely disengaged from the work force to spend more time with their children and spouses (Blagg & Young, 2002).

One strategy that working mothers adopt is the "superwoman" approach: "coping through reactive role behavior . . . whose aim is to meet all of the role demands experienced" (Hall, 1972, p. 479). For many woman, this is an impossible standard to which to hold themselves and one that places the entire overload problem on women's shoulders (Nieva & Gutek, 1981, p. 49). Beyond wearing women down, "double-duty" (Biernat & Wortman, 1991; Hochschild, 1990) places constraints on women's social lives. Without time to spare, "superwomen" have few opportunities to deepen and broaden their informal networks and thereby accumulate the social capital needed to leverage themselves into high-profile positions (Ibarra, 1992, 1993; Nieva & Gutek, 1981; Wellington & Giscombe, 2001).

An alternative to becoming "superwoman" is to cope with work–home role and time conflicts by reducing work-force attachment and choosing an intermittent or part-time work style. Women who choose this alternative tend to readjust their career aspirations (Hall, 1972; Nieva & Gutek, 1981). When they reenter the work force, it tends to be at lower level positions than they departed from earlier in their careers (Nieva & Gutek, 1981) and to be at lower levels of pay as compared to women who had continued working (Waldfogel, 1998). This is in part because reentry women find their training or skills to be outdated, but also because they have a diminished self-concept with regard to their workplace skills, abilities and leadership potential (Nieva & Gutek, 1981; Padula, 1994).

Opportunities for Claiming Authority

A potentially more productive response to work–family barriers than reactive role management (e.g., playing superwoman) or personal role redefinition (e.g., choosing between home/family or career) is "structural role redefinition" (Hall, 1972, p. 477). Structural role redefinition involves engaging with family and work partners to renegotiate role-based expectations and resources (Hall, 1972, p. 477). At home, this means negotiating a workable distribution of household labor between spouses, partnering with friends and extended family, and hiring additional support to fill in where there are not the resources within the family to cover all responsibilities.

Again the example of women entrepreneurs suggests numerous potential models for how to restructure workplaces to better enable women to pursue their ideals at home and at work. High-achieving self-employed women are significantly less likely to be childless than high-achieving corporate women (22% v. 42%; Hewlett, 2002). The percentage of women entrepreneurs with children (78%) is very close to the national average for all women of age 40 (80%; Bachu & O'Connell, 2001).

Even within larger organizations, there is increasing evidence that family-friendly institutional reforms can carry significant benefits for women's work-force participation after childbirth. The study of organizations with and without job-protected maternity leave in the United States and the United Kingdom shows that women who had leave coverage and returned to work after childbirth received a wage premium that offset the commonly observed "family gap" favoring women without children (Waldfogel, 1998). By instituting work arrangements that take into account that work and family demands have to be managed in concert, organizations are more likely to retain working mothers on leadership tracks. With the benefit of higher levels of work experience, job tenure, and pay, we are likely to see more working mothers competing for top slots.

TAKING STOCK: NEGOTIATING
TO CLAIM AUTHORITY

Although there is certainly some validity to each of these four dominant explanations, none of them poses an insurmountable barrier to women claiming greater levels of authority. An analysis of each of the four explanations points to clearly negotiable opportunities for change. Although gender-based social roles and stereotypes are dense and constraining, they are not intractable. Norms, beliefs, and behavior are part of a negotiated order, and, as eloquently stated by Constance Buchanan, founding director of the Harvard Divinity School's Women's Studies in Religion program: "Women especially possess the will to take the initiative in this social reorganization. . . . Pressed to rearrange the meaning and structure of their own lives, they can more easily notice and question the institutional and work norms to which most men have become habituated" (Hartman, 1999,

p. 19). If it takes particular types of work experience and/or high-profile work opportunities to make it to the top, women can negotiate for those positions. If women want to be leaders, they can find ways to make their preferences known and to ask for others' support in achieving their aims. If the complexity of work and family life creates constraints, women can renegotiate their own and others' role expectations and claim the necessary resources and assistance.

But, if these opportunities to renegotiate gendered assumptions, work experiences, leadership opportunities, and role constraints are so clear, why haven't women seized them already? We propose that recent developments in the study of gender in negotiation may shed light on the gender gap in the claiming of authority.

GENDER IN NEGOTIATION

Recent developments in the study of gender in negotiation have shown that the effects of gender on negotiation outcomes are contingent on situational factors (Bowles, Babcock, & McGinn, 2003; Kray, Thompson, & Galinsky, 2001; Walters, Stuhlmacher, & Meyer, 1998). More specifically, this research suggests that sex differences are more likely to emerge when there is ambiguity about the bargaining range and the appropriate standards for negotiated agreement, and when gender is relevant and salient to behavior or performance expectations (Bowles et al., 2003). We propose that insights from these recent developments in the study of gender in negotiation may help to illuminate why women are finding it so difficult to negotiate their way past the barriers we have described.

MODERATORS OF GENDER EFFECTS IN NEGOTIATION: AMBIGUITY AND GENDER TRIGGERS

Ambiguity

Ambiguity about the bargaining range and the appropriate standards for agreement opens the door for gender-based norms and preconceptions to influence negotiation expectations and outcomes (Bowles et al., 2003). We rely on past experience and preconceptions to fill in the blanks when there are no clear external standards to use to judge or interpret a situation. For instance, there is extensive evidence from field and laboratory studies that sex biases in performance evaluations and hiring decisions are positively associated with the amount of subjective inference required by the evaluator; the more job-relevant information that is available, the less likely it is that the worker's sex will inform the evaluator's judgment (Chang, 2000; Foddy & Smithson, 1999; Heilman, 1984, 1995; Heilman, Martell, & Simon, 1988; Lenney, Mitchell, & Browning, 1983; Pfeffer, 1977; Pheterson, Kiesler, & Goldberg, 1971; Tosi & Einbender, 1985). Ambiguity has also been shown to play a role in men and women's own expectations for themselves. Research on the entitlement effect, for instance, shows that women (as compared to men) will expect less pay for equal labor and work longer and with fewer errors for equal pay, but only in the absence of clear pay comparison information (Callahan-Levy & Messe, 1979; Major, McFarlin, & Gagnon, 1984). When comparison standards for compensation are made clear, there is no significant gender difference in what men and women believe they should be paid (Major & Forcey, 1985). This effect is partially explained by evidence that, when compensation standards are unclear, men and women will tend to compare themselves to similar (viz., same-gender) others for information on how to compensate themselves. In a society where men tend to be granted more compensation and other material resources than women, and members of both groups compare their own resources with those held by others of the same gender group, it is reasonable for men and women anchor on different reference points when setting their compensation expectations in ambiguous situations (Crosby, 1982; Major & Forcey, 1985).

Gender Triggers

"Gender trigger" encapsulates the notion that there are circumstances in which gender becomes relevant and salient to behavior or performance expectations. Gender triggers reflect sex-based stereotypes and social roles that are embedded in our social fabric (Kolb & Williams, 2000). Because of this embeddedness, they do not need to be embraced or consciously considered in order to shape expectations or behavior (Eagly, 1987; Steele, 1997). Gender triggers influence negotiation by prescribing distinct behavioral scripts and outcome expectations for male and female negotiators (Bowles et al., 2003; Kolb & Williams, 2000). Negotiation research has identified three examples of potential gender triggers in bargaining: competitive versus integrative negotiation, negotiating for the self versus others, and the activation of implicit stereotypes.

Competitive Versus Integrative Negotiation. Competitive negotiations are consistent with norms for appropriate masculine behavior
(e.g., being agentic, self-promoting) and they contradict the norms for appropriate feminine behavior (e.g., maintaining a communal- as opposed
to self-orientation; Bakan, 1966). Integrative negotiations, in contrast, call
for a mix of value-creating and value-claiming behavior (Lax & Sebenius, 1986), which does not clearly contradict or conform to either gender
stereotype. Because competitive bargaining is a relatively masculine domain, male negotiators are likely to have more confidence and higher performance expectations in competitive negotiations than are female negotiators (Beyer, 1990; Beyer & Bowden, 1997; Lenney, 1981). Consistently,
much of the evidence that gender has the potential to influence negotiation
expectations and performance is based on studies of competitive negotiations, such as the ultimatum game (Solnick, 2001), sale price (Ayres, 1991;
Kray et al., 2001), and salary negotiations (Bowles et al., 2003; Gerhart &
Rynes, 1991; Stevens, Bavetta, & Gist, 1993).

Negotiating for Self Versus Other. Western norms for feminine
behavior prescribe that women behave in other-oriented as opposed self-
interested ways. Because of this, women are likely to be particularly
inhibited by competitive negotiations for the self as opposed to those for
others. One recent experimental study showed that women's negotiating intentions were moderated by whether the negotiation concerned the
negotiator's own wage or the wage to be received by an anonymous other.
When negotiating for someone else, female negotiators reported that they
would ask for 22% more on average than they would when they were
negotiating for themselves. Negotiating for self or other had no influence
on males' negotiating intentions (Bowles et al., 2003).

Activation of Implicit Stereotypes. Motivated by Claude Steele's
work on stereotype threat, negotiation researchers have shown that the
implicit priming of gender-based stereotypes can lead negotiators to fulfill stereotype-based expectations (Kray et al., 2001). For example, Steele
and colleagues administered a math test to mathematically inclined young
women and men. When the researchers' introduction to the exam mentioned that there tended to be gender differences in test performance,
women performed significantly worse than men. When the researchers
mentioned that the tests tended not to produce gender differences, there
was no significant difference in performance by sex (Spencer, Steele, &
Quinn, 1999). Applied to negotiation, Kray and her colleagues showed that

the threat of negative stereotype confirmation could undermine women's negotiating performance. Stating that negotiation outcomes are evaluative of "true" negotiating ability (vs. non-evaluative) or presenting the negotiation task in gendered (vs. neutral) language negatively affected women's negotiating performance relative to men's (Kray et al., 2001).

These recent developments in the research on gender in negotiation shed new light on the gender gap in leadership positions: the race to claim authority calls for just those types of negotiations in which gender differences tend to emerge. In negotiations to claim greater authority, exactly what is up for negotiation can be *highly ambiguous*, and women are called to negotiate *competitively for themselves* in domains that are rife with *negative gender-based stereotypes*. To compete more effectively for leadership positions, women need to be successful in precisely the types of negotiations that are likely to be relatively inhibiting and challenging for women.

CONCLUSION

Psychological researchers may gain new insights into the study of gender in leadership by building on recent developments in the study of gender in negotiation. It seems unlikely that the relatively small gender differences—sometimes favoring males, sometimes favoring females or neither—observed in leadership style and effectiveness can account for the relatively dramatic gender gap in leadership positions. In order to understand the gender gap in leadership, we propose that psychological researchers refocus their attention away from what men and women tend to do or how well they perform once they reach those positions, and toward how women can negotiate to achieve the experience and resources that lie on the path to leadership positions.

This new research direction we propose is consistent with and complementary to the most recent developments in the psychological study of gender and leadership. Following more than a decade of research on gender and leadership, Alice Eagly has proposed the pursuit of new research on prejudice as a barrier to women's advancement into leadership positions (Eagly & Karau, 2002). Eagly and Karau propose that perceived incongruity between female gender roles and leadership roles leads women to be undervalued as potential leadership candidates. We embrace the notion that gender-based social roles and sex-stereotypes have the potential to color both prospective leaders' aspirations and observers' judgments of leadership candidates. We propose to focus on the influence of these "gender triggers" in negotiations to claim authority, because we believe that negotiations over the resources and opportunities to gain positions of authority make up a particularly influential set of social interactions in determining who becomes a leader.

The study of negotiations to claim authority will benefit from further research in both the laboratory and the field. Laboratory researchers could test whether manipulation of ambiguity and "gender triggers" (e.g., perceived gender role incongruity) moderates gender differences in expectations and outcomes in negotiations over leadership-relevant resources (e.g., work opportunities, votes or funds for task completion). Field research could test when and how gender differences emerge in prospective leaders' negotiation expectations over leadership-relevant resources. Research within organizations could also explore gender differences in the frequency of negotiations over leadership-relevant resources and also whether men and women have qualitatively different information and/or opportunities for these negotiations. Finally, ethnographic work could explore inductively the work arrangements of women entrepreneurs to see if they suggest negotiable alternatives for enhancing the leadership potential of women in larger organizational settings.

The gender gap in leadership positions can be reduced through negotiation. The study of gender in negotiation carries the potential to generate useful prescriptive suggestions for individuals who aspire to leadership positions. Such micro-level prescriptions provide individuals with options for changing situations to their own advantage in the short term rather than waiting for macro-level developments, such as the reduction of prejudice and/or the feminization of leadership (Eagly & Karau, 2002). Although women face legitimate barriers in their negotiations to claim authority, the playing field is ripe with opportunities for women to enhance their negotiating power and to reshape negotiating situations in their own favor—and ultimately to claim the authority they seek.

REFERENCES

Andrews, P. H. (1992). Sex and gender differences in group communication: Impact on the facilitation process. *Small Group Research, 23*(1), 74–94.

Ayres, I. (1991). Fair driving: Gender and race discrimination in retail car negotiations. *Harvard Law Review, 104,* 817.

Bachu, A., & O'Connell, M. (2001). *Fertility of American women: June 2000.* Washington, DC: U.S. Census Bureau.

Bakan, D. (1966). *The duality of human existence.* Chicago: Rand McNally.

Beyer, S. (1990). Gender differences in the accuracy of self-evaluations of performance. *Journal of Personality and Social Psychology, 59,* 960–970.

Beyer, S., & Bowden, E. M. (1997). Gender differences in self-perceptions: Convergent evidence from three measures of accuracy and bias. *Personality and Social Psychology Bulletin, 23,* 157–172.

Biernat, M., & Wortman, C. B. (1991). Sharing of home responsibilities between professionally employed women and their husbands. *Journal of Personality and Social Psychology, 60*(6), 844–860.

Blagg, D., & Young, S. (2002). Redefining success: Women and work. *Harvard Business School Bulletin, 78,* 32–37.

Bowles, H. R., Babcock, L., & McGinn, K. L. (2003). *When does gender matter in negotiation?* (Working Paper). Cambridge, MA: Harvard University.

Branson, L. (2002, March 17). Reform of the bully broads. *The Boston Globe Magazine,* pp. 12–17.

Bureau of Labor Statistics. (2002). *Highlights of women's earnings in 2001* (p. 960). Washington, DC: U.S. Department of Labor.

Burns, J. M. (1978). *Leadership.* New York: Harpertorch Books.

Callahan-Levy, C., & Messe, L. A. (1979). Sex differences in the allocation of pay. *Journal of Personality and Social Psychology, 37*(3), 433–446.

Catalyst. (1996). *Catalyst — Working with business and the professions to effect change for women.* New York: Catalyst.

Catalyst. (1998). *Advancing women in business — The Catalyst guide to best practices from the corporate leaders.* San Francisco: Jossey-Bass.

Catalyst. (2002, November 19). *Catalyst census marks gains in numbers of women corporate officers in America's largest 500 companies.* Retrieved January 23, 2003, from http://www.catalystwomen.org/press_room/press_releases/2002_cote.htm

Cejka, M. A., & Eagly, A. H. (1999). Gender-stereotypic images of occupations correspond to the sex segregation of employment. *Personality and Social Psychology Bulletin, 25*(4), 413–423.

Center for American Women and Politics. (2002). *Women who will serve in the 108th congress 2003–05.* Eagleton Institute of Politics, Rutgers, The State University of New Jersey. Retrieved January 23, 2003, from http://www.cawp.rutgers.edu/facts/cong-03.html

Chang, P. M. Y. (2000). *Discrimination by design: The effects of organizational design on the exercise of gender discrimination in denominational labor markets* (working paper). Chesnut Hill, MA: Boston College.

Cohen, L. E., Broschak, J. P., & Haveman, H. A. (1998). And then there were more? The effect of organizational sex composition on the hiring and promotion of managers. *American Sociological Review, 63,* 711–727.

Crosby, F. (1982). *Relative deprivation and working women.* New York: Oxford University Press.

Diekman, A. B., & Eagly, A. H. (2000). Stereotypes as dynamic constructs: Women and men of the past, present, and future. *Personality and Social Psychology Bulletin, 26*(10), 1171.

Dovidio, J. F., Ellyson, S. L., Keating, C. F., & Heltman, K. (1988). The relationship of social power to visual displays of dominance between men and women. *Journal of Personality and Social Psychology, 54,* 233–242.

Eagly, A. H. (1987). *Sex difference in social behavior: A social-role interpretation.* Hillsdale, NJ: Lawrence Erlbaum Associates.

Eagly, A. H., & Johannesen-Schmidt, M. C. (2001). The leadership styles of women and men. *Journal of Social Issues, 57*(4), 781–797.

Eagly, A. H., Johannesen-Schmidt, M. C., & van Engen, M. L. (2003). Transformational, transactional and laissez-faire leadership styles: A meta-analysis comparing men and women. *Psychological Bulletin, 129*(4), 569–591.

Eagly, A. H., & Johnson, B. T. (1990). Gender and leadership style: A meta-analysis. *Psychological Bulletin, 108*(2), 233–256.

Eagly, A. H., & Karau, S. J. (1991). Gender and the emergence of leaders: A meta-analysis. *Journal of Personality and Social Psychology, 60*(5), 685–710.

Eagly, A. H., & Karau, S. J. (2002). Role congruity theory of prejudice toward female leaders. *Psychological Review, 109*(3), 573–598.

Eagly, A. H., Makhijani, M. G., & Klonsky, B. G. (1992). Gender and the evaluation of leaders: A meta-analysis. *Psychological Bulletin, 111*(1), 3–22.

Eagly, A. H., & Steffen, V. J. (2000). Gender stereotypes stem from the distribution of women and men into social roles. In C. Stangor (Ed), *Stereotypes and prejudice: Essential readings. Key readings in social psychology* (pp. 142–160). Philadelphia, PA: Psychology Press/Taylor & Francis.

Ely, R. J. (1994). The effects of organizational demographics and social identity on relationships among professional women. *Administrative Science Quarterly, 39*(2), 203–238.

Ely, R. J. (1995). The power of demography: Women's social constructions of gender identity at work. *Academy of Management Journal, 38*(3), 589–635.

Fletcher, J. K. (2001). *Disappearing acts: Gender, power and relational practice at work.* Boston: MIT Press.

Foddy, M., & Smithson, M. (1999). Can gender inequalities be eliminated? *Social Psychology Quarterly, 62*(4), 307–324.

Gerhart, B., & Rynes, S. (1991). Determinants and consequences of salary negotiations by male and female MBA graduates. *Journal of Applied Psychology, 76*(2), 256–262.

Hall, D. T. (1972). A model of coping with role conflict: The role behavior of college educated women. *Administrative Science Quarterly, 17*(4), 471–486.

Hartman, M. S. (1999). *Talking leadership: Conversations with powerful women.* New Brunswick, NJ: Rutgers University Press.

Heilman, M. E. (1980). The impact of situational factors on personnel decisions concerning women: Varying the sex composition of the applicant pool. *Organizational Behavior and Human Performance, 26*(3), 286–295.

Heilman, M. E. (1984). Information as a deterrent against sex discrimination: The effects of applicant sex and information type on preliminary employment decisions. *Organizational Behavior and Human Performance, 33*(2), 174–186.

Heilman, M. E. (1995). Sex stereotypes and their effects in the workplace: What we know and what we don't know. *Journal of Social Behavior and Personality, 10*(6), 3–26.

Heilman, M. E., Martell, R. F., & Simon, M. C. (1988). The vagaries of sex bias: Conditions regulating the undervaluation, equivaluation, and overvaluation of female job applicants. *Organizational Behavior and Human Decision Processes, 41*(1), 98–110.

Hewlett, S. A. (2002). *Creating a life: Professional women and the quest for children.* New York: Talk Miramax Books.

Hochschild, A. R. (1990). *The second shift: Inside the two-job marriage.* New York: Morrow/Avon.

Ibarra, H. (1992). Homophily and differential returns: Sex differences in network structure and access in an advertising firm. *Administrative Science Quarterly, 37*(3), 422–447.

Ibarra, H. (1993). Network centrality, power, and innovation involvement: Determinants of technical and administrative roles. *Academy of Management Journal, 36*(3), 471–500.

Kanter, R. M. (1977a). *Men and women of the corporation.* New York: Basic Books.
Kanter, R. M. (1977b). Some effects of proportions on group life: Skewed sex ratios and responses to token women. *American Journal of Sociology, 82*(5), 965–990.
Kolb, D. M. (1992). Women's work: Peacemaking in organizations. In D. M. Kolb & J. M. Bartunek (Eds.), *Hidden conflict in organizations: Uncovering behind-the-scenes disputes* (pp. 63–91). Newbury Park, CA: Sage Publications.
Kolb, D. M., & Williams, J. (2000). *The Shadow Negotiation: How women can master the hidden agendas that determine bargaining success.* New York: Simon and Schuster.
Kray, L. J., Thompson, L., & Galinsky, A. (2001). Battle of the sexes: Gender stereotype confirmation and reactance in negotiations. *Journal of Personality and Social Psychology, 80*(6), 942–958.
Lax, D., & Sebenius, J. (1986). *The manager as negotiator: Bargaining for cooperation and competitive gain.* New York: The Free Press.
Lee, L.-E. (2001). *Feeling well-paid: The effect of labor market structure and social comparisons on pay evaluation* (Qualifying Paper submitted to Department of Sociology). Cambridge, MA: Harvard University.
Lenney, E. (1981). What's fine for the gander isn't always good for the goose: Sex differences in self-confidence as a function of ability area and comparison with others. *Sex Roles, 7,* 905–923.
Lenney, E., Mitchell, L., & Browning, C. (1983). The effect of clear evaluation criteria on sex bias in judgments of performance. *Psychology of Women Quarterly, 7*(4), 313–328.
Lowe, K. B., Kroeck, K. G., & Sivasubramaniam, N. (1996). Effectiveness correlates of transformational and transactional leadership: A meta-analytic review of the MLQ literature. *Leadership Quarterly, 7,* 385–425.
Mahoney, R. (1996). *Kidding ourselves: Breadwinning, babies, and bargaining power.* New York: Basic Books.
Major, B., & Forcey, B. (1985). Social comparisons and pay evaluations: Preferences for same-sex and same-job wage comparisons. *Journal of Experimental Social Psychology, 21*(4), 393–405.
Major, B., McFarlin, D. B., & Gagnon, D. (1984). Overworked and underpaid: On the nature of gender differences in personal entitlement. *Journal of Personality and Social Psychology, 47,* 1399–1412.
Neubert, M. J. (1999). Too much of a good thing or the more the merrier? Exploring the dispersion and gender composition of informal leadership in manufacturing teams. *Small Group Research, 30*(5), 635–646.
Nieva, V. F., & Gutek, B. A. (1981). *Women and work: A psychological perspective.* New York: Praeger Publishers.
Padula, M. A. (1994). Reentry women: A literature review with recommendations for counseling and research. *Journal of Counseling and Development, 73*(1), 10–16.
Pfeffer, J. (1977). Toward an examination of stratification in organizations. *Administrative Science Quarterly, 22*(4), 553–567.
Pheterson, G. I., Kiesler, S., & Goldberg, P. A. (1971). Evaluation of the performance of women as a function of their sex, achievement, and personal history. *Journal of Personality and Social Psychology, 19,* 114–118.
Ridgeway, C. L. (2001). Gender, status and leadership. *Journal of Social Issues, 57*(4), 637–655.
Ridgeway, C. L., & Smith-Lovin, L. (1999). Gender and interaction. In J. S. Chafetz (Ed.), *Handbook of the sociology of gender* (pp. 247–274). New York: Kluwer Academic/Plenum Publishers.
Rosener, J. B. (1990). Ways women lead. *Harvard Business Review* (November-December), 119–126.

Rudman, L. A. (1998). Self-promotion as a risk factor for women: The costs and benefits of counterstereotypical impression management. *Journal of Personality and Social Psychology, 74*(3), 629–645.

Rudman, L. A., & Glick, P. (1999). Feminized management and backlash toward agentic women: The hidden costs to women of a kinder, gentler image of middle managers. *Journal of Personality and Social Psychology, 77*(5), 1004–1010.

Schein, V. E. (2001). A global look at psychological barriers to women's progress in management. *Journal of Social Issues, 57*(4), 675–688.

Sharpe, R. (2000, November 20). As leaders, women rule. *Business Week,* p. 74.

Small Business Administration, U. G. (2001, August 10, 2001). *Startling new statistics.* SBA Online Women's Business Center. Retrieved December 6, 2002, from http://www.onlinewbc.gov/docs/starting/new_stats.html

Solnick, S. J. (2001). Gender differences in the ultimatum game. *Economic Inquiry, 39*(2), 189–200.

Spencer, S. J., Steele, C. M., & Quinn, D. M. (1999). Stereotype threat and women's math performance. *Journal of Experimental Social Psychology, 35*(1), 4–28.

Steele, C. M. (1997). A threat in the air: How stereotypes shape intellectual ability and performance. *American Psychologist, 52,* 613–629.

Stevens, C. K., Bavetta, A. G., & Gist, M. E. (1993). Gender differences in the acquisition of salary negotiation skills: The role of goals, self-efficacy, and perceived control. *Journal of Applied Psychology, 78*(5), 723–735.

Tosi, H. L., & Einbender, S. W. (1985). The effects of the type and amount of information in sex discrimination research: A meta-analysis. *Academy of Management Journal, 28*(3), 712–723.

Valian, V. (1999). *Why so slow? The advancement of women.* Cambridge, MA: MIT Press.

Waldfogel, J. (1998). The family gap for young women in the United States and Britain: Can maternity leave make a difference? *Journal of Labor Economics, 16*(3), 505–545.

Walters, A. E., Stuhlmacher, A. F., & Meyer, L. L. (1998). Gender and negotiator competitiveness: A meta-analysis. *Organizational Behavior and Human Decision Processes, 76*(1), 1–29.

Wellington, S., & Giscombe, K. (2001). Women and leadership in corporate America. In C. B. Costello & A. J. Stone (Eds.), *The American woman 2001–2002: Getting to the top.* New York: W. W. Norton & Company.

Wirth, L. (2001). *Breaking through the glass ceiling: Women in management.* Geneva, Switzerland: International Labour Office.

Wood, W., & Eagly, A. H. (2002). A cross-cultural analysis of the behavior of women and men: Implications for the origins of sex differences. *Psychological Bulletin, 128*(5), 699–727.

Wood, W., & Karten, S. J. (1986). Sex differences in interaction style as a product of perceived sex differences in competence. *Journal of Personality and Social Psychology, 50*(2), 341–347.

Woodall, J., Edwards, C., & Welchman, R. (1995). Winning the lottery? Organizational restructuring and women's managerial career development. *Women in Management Review, 10*(3), 32–39.

10

Why David Sometimes Wins: Strategic Capacity in Social Movements

Marshall Ganz
Harvard University

And there went out a champion out of the camp of the Philis-
tines, named Goliath . . . whose height was six cubits and a
span. And he had a helmet of brass upon his head, and he was
armed with a coat of mail . . . and he had greaves of brass upon
his legs . . . and the staff of his spear was like a weaver's beam;
and his spear's head weights six hundred shekels of iron. . . .
And he stood and cried to the armies of Israel. . . . "Choose you
a man for you. . . . If he be able to fight with me, and to kill me,
then will we be your servants; but if I prevail against him, and
kill him, then shall ye be our servants. . . . Give me a man that
we may fight together." When Saul and all Israel heard those
words of the Philistine, they were dismayed and greatly afraid.
And David said unto Saul, Let no man's heart fail because of him;
thy servant will go and fight with this Philistine. And Saul said to
David, Thou art not able to go against this Philistine to fight with
him: for thou art but a youth, and he a man of war from his youth.
. . . David said . . . The Lord that delivered me out of the lion, and
out of the paw of the bear, he will deliver me out of the hand of this
Philistine. And Saul said unto David, Go, and the Lord be with thee.

And Saul armed David with his armour, and he put an helmet of
brass upon his head; also he armed him with a coat of mail. And
David girded his sword upon his armour, and he assayed to go; for
he had not proved it. And David said unto Saul, I cannot go with
these; for I have not proved them. And David put them off him. And
he took his staff in his hand, and chose him five smooth stones out
of the brook, and put them in a shepherd's bag which he had . . . ;
and his sling was in his hand: and he drew near unto the Philistine.
. . . And the Philistine looked about, and saw David, he disdained
him: for he was but a youth, and ruddy, and of a fair countenance.
. . . And then said David to the Philistine, Thou comest to me with
a sword, and with a spear, and with a shield; but I come to thee in
the name of the Lord of hosts . . . and David put his hand in his bag,
and took thence a stone, and slang it, and smote the Philistine in his
forehead . . . and he fell upon his face to the earth.
       —*The Holy Bible,* 1 Sam 17:4–49 (King James Version)

INTRODUCTION:
HOW DAVID BEAT GOLIATH

The belief that strategic resourcefulness can overcome institutionalized resources is an ancient one. Tales of young, guileful, courageous under-dogs who overwhelm old, powerful, and confident opponents occupy a mythic place in Western culture. When Goliath, a veteran warrior, victor of many battles, arrayed in full battle gear, challenges the Israelites, their military leaders cower in fear. It is David, the young shepherd boy, to whom God gives the courage to face the giant. David's success begins with his courage, his commitment, and his motivation.

But it takes more than courage to bring David success. David thinks about the battle differently. Reminded by five stones he finds in a brook, he reflects on previous encounters in which he protected his flock from bears and lions. Based on these recollections he reframes this new battle in a way that gives him an advantage. Pointedly rejecting the king's offer of shield, sword, and armor as weapons he cannot use effectively against a master of these weapons, David conceives a plan of battle based on his five smooth stones, his skill with a sling, and the giant's underestimation of him.

The story of David and Goliath dramatizes questions about which many remain intensely curious: How have insurgents successfully challenged those with power over them? How can we challenge those with power over us? How can we change powerful institutions that shape our very lives?

Over the course of the last 50 years there have been many such challenges in the United States and around the world: the civil rights movement, the women's movement, the environmental movement, the democracy movements of Eastern Europe, the South African liberation movement, and so forth. Social scientists tend to account for these events, however, by arguing one version or another of "the time for change was right" while many historians attribute success to the intervention of gifted, charismatic individuals. Few analysts explore relationships among the times, the people who act upon them, and the organizational settings in which they act, to learn why "Davids" succeed when they do.

Failure to focus on the contribution of strategic leadership to social movement outcomes is a particularly serious shortcoming of social movement theory (Jasper, 1997; Morris & Staggenborg, 2002). Explanations of the emergence, development, and outcomes of social movements based on variation in access to resources and opportunities stress the influence of environmental changes on actors (McAdam, McCarthy, & Zald, 1996). In this view, social movements unfold when actors predictably respond to new political opportunities or newly available resources. But theorists who emphasize opportunity explain little of why one actor should make better use of the same opportunity than another. Yet it is often in the differences in how actors use their opportunities that social movement legacies are shaped (Sewell, 1992). Other scholars, who rely on variation in resources to explain why some movements are more successful than others, fail to explain how actors with fewer resources can defeat those with more resources (McCarthy & Zald, 1977). But when insurgents overcome well-established rivals or opponents this is most often the case. Students of strategy and tactics offer accounts of their sources, their logic and their effect on outcomes, but do not explain why one organization would be likely to devise more effective tactics than another (Freeman, 1979; Gamson, 1975; Lipsky, 1968; McAdam, 1983; Tilly, 1981). And much of the discussion of the meaning that social movement actors give to what they do, which has been dealt with under the general rubric of "framing," focuses on one aspect of strategy—how social movements interpret themselves— but tells us little of how framing is actually done, who does it, or why one organization would do a better job of it than another (Benford, 1997; Benford & Snow, 2000; Davis, 2002; Snow, Rochford, Burke, Worden, & Benford, 1986). And finally, scholars who invoke "culture" to correct for the weaknesses in structural accounts of social movements often remain quite structuralist in their analyses, only shifting the focus from political or economic structures to cultural ones (Johnston & Klandermans, 1995); but they fail to explain variation in the agency actors exercise with respect to cultural, political or economic structures. Yet it is the exercise of agency that is at the heart of strategy.

Students of strategic leadership, on the other hand, even in management, military, and political studies, focus more on what leaders do and how strategy works than on explaining why leaders of some organizations devise more effective strategy than others. Popular accounts of insurgent success attribute effective strategy to uniquely gifted leaders rather than offering systematic accounts of conditions under which leaders are more or less likely to devise effective strategies (Howell, 1990; Westley & Mintzberg, 1988). In part, this is because good strategy is often anything but obvious. Based on the innovative, often guileful, exercise of agency, strategy can be hard to deduce from objective configurations of resources and opportunities because it may be based on a novel assessment of them. Although effects attributed to charismatic leaders—attracting followers, enhancing their sense of self-esteem, and inspiring them to exert extra effort—can be invaluable organizational resources, they are distinct from good strategy (Hollander & Offermann, 1990; House, Spangler, & Woycke, 1991). In social movement settings, especially at times of crisis, talented leaders may also be transformed into symbols of a new community of identity, a source of their charisma (Collins, 1981; Durkheim, 1964; Pillai, 1996; Weber, 1978a).[1] But as sociologists of religion and others have documented, many groups have charismatic leaders but few devise strategy effective enough to achieve institutional stability, much less to become successful social movement organizations (Carlton-Ford, 1992; Stark & Bainbridge, 1985).[2]

---

[1] Although charisma is often viewed as a personality attribute, it is better understood as an interaction between leader and constituency. Weber (1978b) attributes the "charismatic" authority of religious leaders to their followers' experience of the "divine" sources of their authority. Durkheim (1964) describes the role of mythic leaders or "civilizing heroes" as communal symbols. Collins (1981) argues that charismatic leaders are "individuals who have become the focal point of an emotion-producing ritual that links together a large coalition; their charisma waxes and wanes according to the degree to which the aggregate conditions for the dramatic predomination of that coalition are met." And Pillai (1996) offers empirical data that links the emergence of charismatic leaders to a group's experience of crisis.

[2] Stark and Bainbridge (1985), for example, report that in 1978 California was home to 167 of the nation's some 450 cults, most of which had charismatic leaders, and Carlton-Ford (1992) reports 22 of 44 urban communes studied had charismatic leaders.

Explaining social movement outcomes, then, often requires accounting for the fact that different actors act in different ways, some of which influence the environment more than others. Some see political opportunities where others do not, mobilize resources in ways others do not, and frame their causes in ways others do not.

But strategy is not purely subjective. Strategic thinking is reflexive and imaginative, based on ways leaders learn to reflect on the past, attend to the present, and anticipate the future (Bruner, 1990). Leaders—like all of us—are influenced by their life experiences, relationships, and practical learning that provide them with lenses through which they see the world (Banaszak, 1996; Bandura, 1989; DiMaggio, 1997; DiMaggio & Powell, 1991; Zerubavel, 1997),[3] and by the organizational structures within which they interact with each other and with their environments (Rogers, 1995a; Van de Ven, Polley, Garud, & Venkataraman, 1999; Weick, 1979). In this chapter, I discuss how the strategic capacity of a leadership team— conditions that facilitate the development of effective strategy—can help explain why "David" sometimes wins (Ganz, 2000a, 2000b).

UNDERSTANDING STRATEGY

In our interdependent world of competition and cooperation, achieving one's goals often requires mobilizing and deploying one's resources to influence the interests of others who control resources we need—the use of power (Dahrendorf, 1958; Emerson, 1962; Lukes, 1975; Michels, 1962; Oberschall, 1973; Salancik & Pfeffer, 1977; Tilly, 1978; Weber, 1946).[4] By resources I mean political, economic and cultural—or moral—assets actors can use to realize their goals (Bourdieu, 1986; Emerson, 1962;

---

[3] A number of scholars offer psychological or sociological versions of what Bandura (1989) calls "the emergent interactive agency" that he contrasts with "pure autonomous agency" or "mechanistic agency," including DiMaggio and Powell (1991), Banaszak (1996), Zerubavel (1997), and DiMaggio (1997).

[4] This concept of power derives from Weber's (1946) view of stratification as power relations emergent from competition and collaboration among actors within economic, status and political markets, a view more recently articulated by Dahrendorf (1958). Oberschall (1973) and Tilly (1978) introduced this view of power to the study of social movements. Lukes (1975) shows how the power relations with which social movements contend become institutionalized. And at the micro level, Emerson (1962) develops a similar concept of power as growing out of exchange relations among individuals in terms of their interests and resources. To conceptualize power relations within organizations I draw on a tradition originating with Michels (1962), more recently articulated by Salancik and Pfeffer (1977).

Hall, 1997; Mann, 1986; Oberschall, 1973; Tilly, 1978; Weber, 1946).[5] Although no one is entirely without resources, people do not have power if they are unable to mobilize or deploy their resources in ways that influence the interests of others. Bus fare, for example, can become a source of power if mobilized collectively in a bus boycott. Strategy is how actors translate their resources into power—to get "more bang for the buck."

Opportunities occur at moments when actors' resources acquire more value because of changes in the environmental context. Actors do not suddenly acquire more resources or devise a new strategy, but find that resources they already have give them more leverage in achieving their goals. A full granary, for example, acquires greater value in a famine, creating opportunity for its owner. Similarly, a close election creates opportunity for political leaders who can influence swing voters. A labor shortage creates opportunity for workers to get more compensation for their labor. This is one reason timing is such an important element of strategy.

Actors have unequal access to resources, in part because of the ways in which the outcomes of prior competition and collaboration become institutionalized, influencing the distribution of resources and reshaping rules by which actors compete and arenas within which they can do so (Gamson, 1975; Lukes, 1975; North, 1990; Skocpol, 1985). A critical strategic goal of those contesting power is to find ways to turn short-term opportunities into long-term gains by institutionalizing them, for example, as formal organizations, collective bargaining agreements, or legislation. Assessing strategic effectiveness thus requires taking a "long view," a reason for studying the development of strategy over time (Andrews, 1997).

Strategy is how we turn what we have into what we need to get what we want. It is how we transform our resources into the power to achieve our purposes. It is the conceptual link we make between the targeting, timing, and tactics with which we mobilize and deploy resources and the outcomes we hope to achieve (Brown & Eisenhardt, 1998; Clausewitz, 1968; Hamel & Prahalad, 1989; Porter, 1996). Although we often do not act rationally and our actions can yield unintended outcomes, we do act purposefully (Bruner, 1990; Cohen, March, & Olson 1972; Crow, 1989; Salancik & Pfeffer, 1977; Watson, 1990; Weick, 1979). Strategy is effective when we realize our goals through its use. Studying strategy is a way to discern the patterns in the relationship among intention, action and outcome.

---

[5] Although resources are often construed in narrow economic terms, Weber's multidimensional view is echoed in Mann's (1986) account of ideological, economic, military, and political sources of power, Bourdieu's analysis of "cultural capital," and Hall's (1997) "moral authority as a power resource."

Our strategy frames our choices about targeting, timing, and tactics. As schema theorists have shown, we attribute meaning to specific events by locating them within broader frameworks of understanding (D'Andrade, 1992; DiMaggio, 1997; Fiske & Taylor, 1991; Gamson, 1992; Gamson & Meyer, 1996; Goffman, 1974; Snow et al., 1986). The strategic significance of the choices we make about how to target resources, time initiatives, and employ tactics depends on how we frame them relative to other choices in a path toward our goals. One reason it is difficult to study strategy is that although choices about targeting, timing, and tactics can be directly observed, the strategy that frames these choices—and provides them with their coherence—must often be inferred, using data drawn from interviews with participants, oral histories, correspondence, memoirs, charters, constitutions, organizational journals, activity reports, minutes of meetings, and participant observation.

Because strategy orients current action toward future goals, it develops in interaction with an ever-changing environment, especially the actions and reactions of other actors (Alinsky, 1971; Brown & Eisenhardt, 1997; Burgelman, 1991; Hamel, 1996; Mintzberg, 1987; Weick, 1979).[6] In fixed contexts in which rules, resources, and interests are given, strategy can, to some extent, be understood in the analytic terms of game theory (Schelling, 1960). But in settings in which rules, resources, and interests are emergent—such as social movements—strategy has more in common with creative thinking (Brown & Eisenhardt, 1997; Hamel, 1996; Morris, 1984). Strategic action can thus best be understood as an ongoing creative process of understanding and adapting new conditions to one's goals (Brown & Eisenhardt, 1998).

The relationship of strategy to outcomes can be clarified by the distinction that game theorists make among games of chance, skill, and strategy (Schelling, 1960). In games of chance, winning depends on the luck of the draw. In games of skill, it depends on behavioral facility, like hitting a tennis ball. In games of strategy, it depends on cognitive discernment—in interaction with other players—of the best course of action, as in the game of Go. In most games, all three elements come into play. Poker, for example, involves chance (deal of the cards), skill (estimating probabilities), and strategy (betting decisions). Although chance may be

---

[6]Community organizer Saul Alinsky (1971) summarized this view of emergent strategy as "the action is in the reaction." Weick (1979) articulates a scholarly version of this perspective— one that since the business environment has become more turbulent has supplanted "strategic planning" in the work of Mintzberg (1987, 1994), Burgelman (1991), Hamel (1996), and Brown and Eisenhardt (1997).

dispositive in any one hand, or even one game, in the long run skill and strategy distinguish excellent players—and their winnings—from others. Similarly, environmental developments can be seen as "chance" in so far as any one actor is concerned. But, in the long run, some actors are more likely to achieve their goals than others because they are better able to take advantage of these chances. Environmental change may generate the opportunities for social movements to emerge, but the outcomes and legacies of such movements have more to do with the strategies actors devise to turn these opportunities to their purposes, thus reshaping their environment.

A THEORY OF STRATEGIC CAPACITY

Strategy is articulated in decisions organizational leaders make as they interact with their environment. The likelihood that their strategy will be effective increases with their motivation, access to salient knowledge, and the quality of the heuristic processes they employ in their deliberations— their strategic capacity.

In explaining sources of effective strategy, I focus on why one organization is more likely to develop a series of effective tactics than another, not why one tactic is more effective than another. Unlike studies of the effectiveness of particular tactics by social movement, military, political or management scholars, identification of factors that influence effective strategizing requires studying the same organizations over time. (Gamson, 1975; Lipsky, 1968; McAdam, 1983). Although strategic capacity, strategy, and outcomes are distinct links in a probabilistic causal chain, greater strategic capacity is likely to yield better strategy, and better strategy is likely to yield better outcomes.

Variation in strategic capacity may also explain differences in what actors make of unique moments of opportunity that demand rapid decisions—especially moments of extraordinary flux when sudden reconfigurations of leadership and organization may faciliate the emergence of social movements. And because the strategic capacity of organizations can grow or atrophy, such variation may help explain changes in organizational effectiveness over time—why some new organizations overcome the "liability of newness" to succeed while other old organizations suffer from a "liability of senescence" and fail.

I do not claim to have found a key variable sufficient to account for all differences in observed outcomes. Rather, I argue that the outcome I try to explain—one group devises more effective strategy than another—is more or less likely to the extent that conditions specified in this model are met. In poker, chance may determine the outcome of any one hand, or even a game, but in the long run, some players are more likely be winners than others. An organization can stumble on opportunity, but I argue that the likelihood that the organization will make strategic use of it depends on factors I specify here.

In viewing strategy as a kind of creative thinking, as shown in Fig. 10.1, I build on the work of social psychologists who hypothesize three key influences on creative output: task motivation, domain-relevant skills, and heuristic processes (Amabile, 1996).[7] In this view, creativity is enhanced by motivation generated by rewards that are intrinsic to task performance, rather than extrinsic to it. Although domain-relevant skills faciliate the implementation of known algorithms to solve familiar problems, hueristic processes are required to generate new algorithms to solve novel problems (Amabile, 1996a; J. R. Hackman & Morris, 1975).

Whereas creativity is an individual phenomenon, strategy is more often than not the creative output of a leadership team. The conditions under which a leadership team interacts contribute social influences that may be more or less supportive of the creativity of its individual members (Amabile, 1988, J. R. Hackman & Morris, 1975; McGrath, 1984; 1996; Nemeth & Straw, 1989; Van de Ven et al., 1999). Furthermore, the task of devising strategy in complex, changing environments may require interaction among team members like the performance of a jazz ensemble. As a kind of distributed cognition, it may require synthesizing skills and information beyond the ken of any one individual, making the terms of that interaction particularly important (Hutchins, 1991; Rogers, 1995; Van de Ven et al., 1999).

Motivation

David committed to fight Goliath before he knew how he would do it. He knew *why* he *had* to do it before he knew *how* he *could* do it. Motivation influences creative output because it affects the focus one brings to one's work, the ability to concentrate for extended periods of time, persistence, willingness to take risks, and ability to sustain high energy

---

[7]I am particularly indebted to Amabile's (1996) fine work on creativity that provides links between micro-behaviors and macro-outcomes. In adapting her work to an understanding of strategy, I substitute the term *salient knowledge* for *domain-relevant skills* to better capture the importance of environmental information to strategic thinking and I consider a broader range of motivational sources.

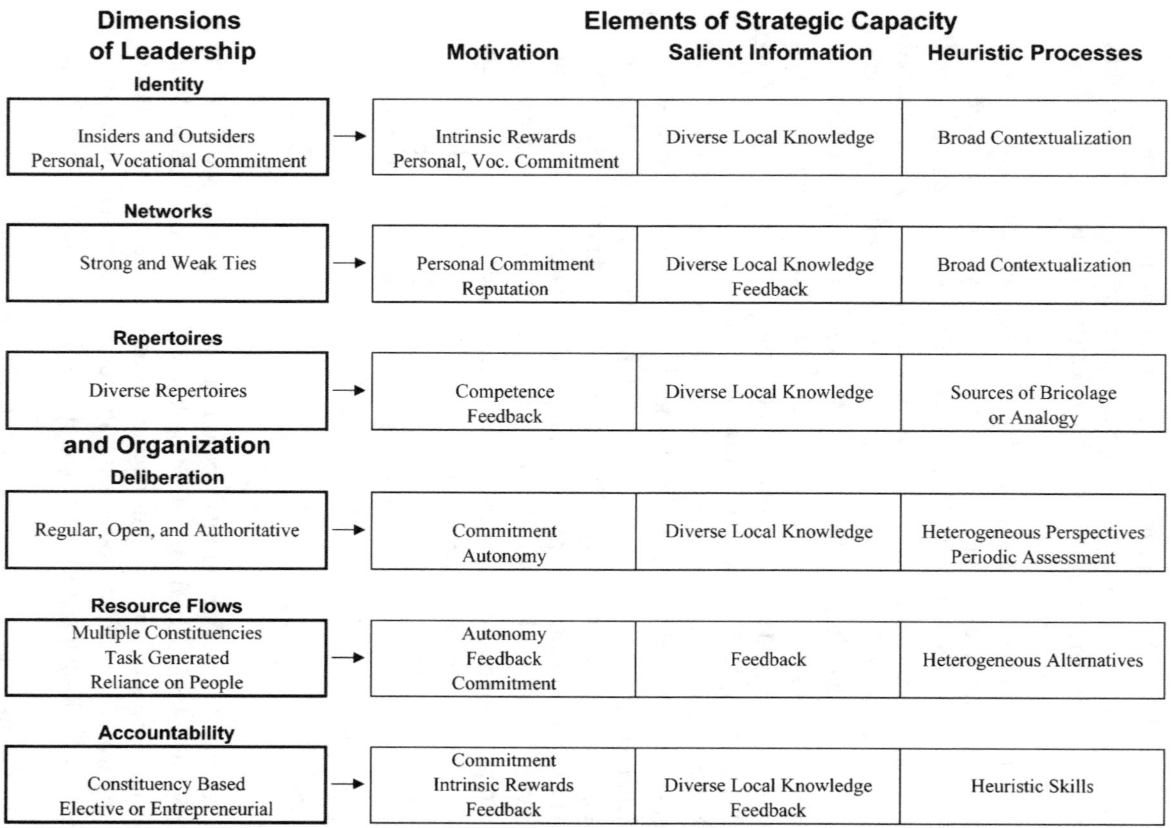

Elements of Strategic Capacity

Dimensions of Leadership		Motivation	Salient Information	Heuristic Processes
Identity				
Insiders and Outsiders Personal, Vocational Commitment	→	Intrinsic Rewards Personal, Voc. Commitment	Diverse Local Knowledge	Broad Contextualization
Networks				
Strong and Weak Ties	→	Personal Commitment Reputation	Diverse Local Knowledge Feedback	Broad Contextualization
Repertoires				
Diverse Repertoires	→	Competence Feedback	Diverse Local Knowledge	Sources of Bricolage or Analogy
and Organization				
Deliberation				
Regular, Open, and Authoritative	→	Commitment Autonomy	Diverse Local Knowledge	Heterogeneous Perspectives Periodic Assessment
Resource Flows				
Multiple Constituencies Task Generated Reliance on People	→	Autonomy Feedback Commitment	Feedback	Heterogeneous Alternatives
Accountability				
Constituency Based Elective or Entrepreneurial	→	Commitment Intrinsic Rewards Feedback	Diverse Local Knowledge Feedback	Heuristic Skills

FIG. 10.1.   This chart illustrates leadership and organizational sources (left column) of strategic capacity (right three columns). The influence is meant to be simultaneous, not sequential.

(Bergman, 1979; Glover & Sautter, 1977; Prentky, 1980; Ruscio, Whitney, & Amabile, 1995; Walberg, 1971). Motivated individuals are more likely to do the work required to acquire needed knowledge and skills (Conti, Amabile, & Pokkok, 1995). They are also able to override programmed modes of thought in order to think more critically and reflectively if they are intensely interested in a problem, dissatisfied with the status quo, or experiencing a schema failure as a result of sharp breaches in expectations and outcomes (Abelson, 1981; Bourdieu, 1990; DiMaggio, 1997; Garfinkel, 1984; Moscovici, 1984; Swidler, 1986). To the extent that success enhances motivation, it not only generates more resources but may encourage greater creativity (Chong, 1991).

Psychologists locate the sources of creative motivation primarily in the intrinsic rewards derived from work one loves to do (Amabile, 1996). While some emphasize the rewards derived from stimulation of novelty, feelings of mastery, and feelings of control experienced in the competent performance of a task (Berlyne, 1960; Deci & Ryan, 1985; Harter, 1978; Hebb, 1953; White, 1959), others emphasize the "meaningfulness" attributed to the task by the person doing it (J. R. Hackman & Oldham, 1976). I argue that for social movement leaders, motivation deriving from identity-forming values or the "moral sources" (Taylor, 1989) that infuse one's life with meaning and one's work with meaningfulness are of particular importance (Bruner, 1990; D'Andrade, 1992; Peterson, 1999; R. Turner & Killian, 1987; Weber, 1946).[8] Work that is expressive of identity can be viewed as a "vocation," and work at one's vocation promises more motivational reward than work at a "job" (Weber, 1958).

In the group work setting of a leadership team that is devising strategy, individual motivation is enhanced when people enjoy autonomy, receive positive feedback from peers and superiors, and are part of a team competing with other teams. It is dampened when they enjoy little autonomy, get no feedback or only negative feedback from peers and superiors, or face intense competition within the team (Amabile, 1988; R. Hackman, 1990).

Salient Knowledge

David did not know how to use King Saul's weapons, but he did know how to use stones as weapons. A second element of creativity is possession of

---

[8] I acknowledge that "interests" influence behavior, but follow Weber's (1946) "switch-man" metaphor according to which values shape people's understanding of their interests—a view shared by R. Turner and Killian (1987), Bruner (1990), D'Andrade (1992), and Peterson (1999).

domain-relevant skills, mastery of which is requisite to developing novel applications. Creative jazz piano players have learned how to play the piano very well. Picasso mastered the styles of his predecessors before painting *Les Demoiselles d'Avignon.*

In terms of strategy, mastery of specific skills—or how to strategize— is relevant, but so is access to local knowledge of the constituencies, opponents, and third parties with which one is interacting. We expect effective military srategists to have command not only of the art of strategy but also to possess an understanding of the troops, enemy, battlefield, and so forth. Salient knowledge includes both skills and information about the settings in which those skills are applied. The better our information about how to work within a particular domain—our local knowledge—the more likely we are to know how to deal with problems arising within that domain. When problems are routine, mastery of known algorithms, or, in the language of social movement theory, repertoires of collective action, facilitate effective problem solving. But since environments can change in response to our initiatives, especially volatile social movement environments, regular feedback is important in evaluating responses to these initiatives (Zaltman, Duncan, & Holbeck, 1973). When problems are novel, we must sort through our "repertoire" to find that which can be useful to us in learning how to innovate a response.

Heuristic Processes

David found his skill with stones useful because he could imaginatively recontextualize the battlefield, transforming it into a place where, as a shepherd, he knew how to protect his flock from wolves and bears. An outsider to the battle, he saw resources others did not see and opportunities they did not grasp. Goliath, on the other hand, the insider, failed to see this shepherd boy as a threat.

When we face new problems, we innovate solutions by using heuristic methods to imaginatively recontextualize data or synthesize it in new ways (Amabile, 1996; Bernstein, 1975; Langer, 1978; Langer & Imber, 1979; March & Olsen, 1976). To think creatively, we must recognize our problems as new ones, at least to us, that require new solutions. To find new solutions we use our gift for analogy to reframe data in ways that make novel interpretations and new pathways conceivable, combining familiar elements in new ways as bricoleurs (J. Campbell, 1997; Douglas, 1986; Gentner, 1989; Lakoff & Johnson, 1980; Langer, 1989; Levi-Strauss, 1966; Strang & Meyer, 1994). Because it requires fresh perspectives and novel approaches, innovative thinking is facilitated by encounters with diverse points of view—within one's own life experience or combined experience of the members of a group (Bernstein, 1975; DiMaggio, 1997; Kasperson, 1978; Langer, 1989; Nemeth, 1986; Piore, 1995; Rogers, 1995; Rosaldo, 1989; Senge, 1990; Weick, 1979; Van de Ven et al., 1999). Access to a diversity of approaches not only offers multiple routines from which to choose, but also contributes to the "mindfulness" that multiple solutions are possible (Langer, 1989) and that most known solutions are "equivocal" (Weick, 1979). And at the most basic level, the more ideas that are generated, the greater the likelihood that there will be good ones among them (D. Campbell, 1960; Simonton, 1988).

Creative problem solving by teams is challenging because minorities tend to conform to majorities and persons with less authority tend to conform their views to those of persons with more authority (Asch, 1952; J. R. Hackman & Morris, 1975; Janis, 1972; McGrath, 1984; Milgram, 1974). Expression of minority views, however, can encourage better problem solving because it stimulates divergent thought about issues, causing decision makers to attend to more aspects of the situation and reexamine their premises (Nemeth, 1986). And solving certain problems, such as strategizing in a complex and changing environment, may require access to a range of knowledge, skill, and experience broader than that which is available to any one person.

Teams thus composed of persons with heterogeneous perspectives are more likely to make good decisions than homogeneous teams, especially in solving novel problems, because they can access greater resources, bring a broader range of skills to bear on decision making, and marshal a diversity of views (Nemeth & Staw, 1989). Heterogeneity may grow out of the life experience of team members, their affiliation with diverse relational networks, or their knowledge of distinct action repertoires.

To take advantage of heterogeneity, however, a team must learn both to foster minority expression that encourages divergent thinking associated with creativity—learning by discovery—and to switch to convergent thinking required to make decisions—learning by testing. Managing these tensions is especially challenging when planning and action occur simultaneously, as in the process of innovation (Van de Ven et al., 1999). They are managed more successfully by leaders who are tolerant of ambiguity, who employ distinct organizational mechanisms for creative deliberation and decision making, rely on multiple sources of resources and authority, and resolve conflict by negotiation rather than by fiat or by consensus (Bartunek, 1993; Levinthal, 1997; Nemeth & Staw, 1989; Osborn, 1963).

SOURCES OF STRATEGIC CAPACITY:
LEADERSHIP AND ORGANIZATION

Having proposed a mechanism by which strategy is generated, I turn to the "input" to that mechanism, the sources of its strategic capacity—leadership and organization. As a unit of analysis, I focus on leadership teams— those persons who formally or informally participate in making authoritative strategic choices for an organization or units of an organization (Oberschall, 1973; Porter, 1996). I do not try to evaluate their qualities of leadership as such, but rather their contribution to the formulation of strategy. Although the "person in charge" plays a uniquely important leadership role, especially in forming, coaching and sustaining a team (Bartunek, 1993; J. R. Hackman & Walton, 1986), strategy, like innovation, is more often a result of the interaction among leaders than organizational myths usually acknowledge (Van de Ven et al., 1999). Understanding strategic capacity may also help to explain why some groups are better able to take advantage of moments of opportunity than others and to specify the conditions under which the effectiveness of an organizational strategy will grow or atrophy.

As shown in Fig. 10.1, the strategic capacity of a leadership team is enhanced when it includes people who are insiders to some constituencies, but outsiders to others; who have strong ties to some constituencies, but weak ties to others; and who have learned diverse collective action repertoires. Leadership teams make the most of these attributes if they conduct regular, open, and authoritative deliberations and are held accountable by multiple, salient constituencies from whom they also draw their resources.

Leadership

Leaders devise strategy in interaction with their environments. Scholars who recognize biographical experience as the primary source of cognitive socialization (Bernstein, 1975; DiMaggio, 1997; Zerubavel, 1997), cultural perspective (Jasper, 1997; Rosaldo, 1989), and motivation (D'Andrade, 1992) link leaders' psychological, professional, organizational, and generational backgrounds to specific strategies. Few, however, have explored links between leaders' backgrounds and their potential to develop *effective* strategy (Chandler, 1962, 1977; Freeman, 1979; Kuhn, 1962; Oberschall, 1973; Ross, 1983; Wickham-Crowley, 1992). But leaders' identities, sociocultural networks, and tactical repertoires—or who they are, whom they know, and what they know—do influence their strategic capacity.

Leadership teams that include "insiders" and "outsiders" have more strategic capacity that those that do not, as shown in the first row of Fig. 10.1, "Identity." Leaders' "identities" derive from their backgrounds as to race, class, gender, generation, ethnicity, religious beliefs, family background, education, and professional training. Teams of "insiders" and "outsiders" can thus combine access to a diversity of salient knowledge with the facility to recontextualize this knowledge creatively (Bernstein, 1975; Hamel, 1996; Rogers, 1995; Senge, 1990; Weick, 1979). Individuals with the "borderland" life experience of straddling cultural or institutional worlds are more likely to make innovative contributions than those without such experience (Kuhn, 1962; Piore, 1995; Rickards & Freedman, 1978; Rosaldo, 1989; Weick, 1979). Insiders who identify personally with their constituencies or outsiders whose vocation entails serving those constituencies are likely to derive more intrinsic rewards from their work than those whose motivation is solely instrumental or occupational (Howell, 1990; Meyer & Allen, 1997; Weick, 1979). Teams composed of persons with heterogeneous perspectives are likely to make better decisions than homogeneous teams, especially in solving novel problems, because they can access more resources, bring a broader range of skills to bear on decision making, and benefit from a diversity of views (Nemeth & Staw, 1989; Sutcliffe, 2000).

Leadership teams that include people networked by "strong" ties to some constituencies and by "weak" ties to others will have more strategic capacity than those that do not, as shown in the second row of Fig. 10.1, "Networks." Sociocultural networks are sources of ideas about what to do and how to do it (Emirbayer & Goodwin, 1994), mechanisms through which social movements recruit (Granovetter, 1973; McAdam & Paulsen, 1993; Stark & Bainbridge, 1985), sources of social capital (Chong, 1991; Coleman, 1990; Putnam, 1993), and incubators of new collective identities (Gamson, 1991; Taylor & Whittier, 1992). Sociologists distinguish between the "strong" ties within homogeneous networks and "weak" ties within heterogeneous networks. Leaders with strong constituency ties are more likely to know where to find local resources, whom to recruit, what tactics to use, and how to encourage constituents to identify with the organization than those without such ties (Morris, 1984). On the other hand, leaders with weak ties with multiple constituencies are more likely to know how to access a diversity of people, ideas, and routines that facilitate broad alliances. Combinations of strong ties and weak ties are associated with social movement recruitment because they link access with commitment, just as they are associated with innovation because they link information with influence (Rogers, 1995). Diverse ties, like diverse life experiences, facilitate the creative recontextualization of strategic choices. But strong ties strengthen a leader's motivation, due to his or her personal commitment to and identification with those whose lives are influenced by the choices he or she makes and among whom he or she earns his or her reputation (Chong, 1991).

Leadership teams that include persons with knowledge of diverse collective action repertoires have more strategic capacity than those without such knowledge, as shown in the third row of Fig. 10.1, "Repertoires." Knowledge of diverse collective action repertoires affords a leadership team greater strategic flexibility than those without that knowledge (Alexander, 1998; Hamel, 1996; Moore, 1995). Collective action repertoires are useful because of their practical (people know what to do), normative (people think they are right), and institutional (they attach to resources) utility in mobilizing people familiar with them (Clemens, 1996; Tilly, 1981). Tactics drawn from repertoires known to one's constituency but not to one's opposition are particularly useful (Alinsky, 1971). And knowledge of multiple repertoires not only widens leaders' range of possible choices, but affords them the opportunity to adapt to new situations through heuristic processes of bricolage or analogy. The motivation of leaders who are adept in such repertoires is enhanced by the competence they experience in their use and by positive feedback from constituencies who find these repertoires familiar.

Organization

Leaders interact with their environment from within organizational structures. A structure is created by commitments among founders who enact ways to interact with each other and with their environment (Weick, 1993). It defines patterns of legitimacy (DiMaggio & Powell, 1991; Weber, 1978c), power (Emerson, 1962; Perrow, 1986; Salancik & Pfeffer, 1977), and deliberation (March & Olson, 1976). Although organizational form may be a founders' strategic choice (Child, 1972; Clemens, 1996; Eisenhardt & Schoonhoven, 1990; Oliver, 1988; Weick, 1993), once established, it has a profound influence on subsequent innovation (Damanpour, 1991; Zaltman et al., 1973) and strategy (Bower, 1970; Chandler, 1962). In the development of strategy venues of deliberation, mechanisms of accountability, and resource flows are particularly important.

Leadership teams that conduct regular, open and authoritative deliberation have more strategic capacity than those that do not, as depicted in the fourth row of Fig. 10.1, "Deliberation." Leadership teams conducting regular, open, and authoritative deliberation enhance their strategic capacity because they acquire access to salient information, participate in a creative process by means of which they explore new ways to use this information, and are motivated by commitment to choices they participated in making and upon which they have the autonomy to act (Duncan, 1973; R. Hackman, 1990; Ruscio et al., 1995). Regular deliberation facilitates initiative by encouraging the periodic assessment of activities, regardless of whether or not there is a crisis (Brown & Eisenhardt, 1997, 1998). And deliberation open to heterogeneous points of view—or "deviant" perspectives—facilitates better decisions (Nemeth & Staw, 1989), encourages innovation (McCleod, 1992), and develops group capacity to perform cognitive tasks more creatively and effectively (Hutchins, 1991). To realize these benefits, leaders must develop deliberative practices encouraging the divergent thinking that grows out of the expression of diverse views as well as the convergent thinking required to make decisions to act upon them. For this purpose, conflict resolution by negotiation, accompanied by voting, may be preferable to either fiat or consensus because it preserves difference yet makes collective action possible (Bartunek, 1993). Deliberation resulting in actionable decisions motivates actors to take part in and to implement that which was decided upon (R. Hackman, 1990; Mintzberg & McHugh, 1985).

Leadership teams that mobilize resources, especially human resources, that are generated by an organizational program serving multiple constituencies, develop more strategic capacity than those that do not, as shown in the fifth row of Fig. 10.1, "Resource Flows." Leaders who mobilize resources from constituents must devise strategy to which constituents will respond (Knocke & Wood, 1981; Mansbridge, 1986; Pfeffer & Salancik, 1978). If membership dues are a major source of support, leaders learn to do what they have to do to get members to pay their dues. Reliance on resources drawn primarily from outside one's core constituency—even when those resources are internal to the organization, such as an endowment—may dampen leaders' motivation to devise effective strategy. As long as they attend to the politics that keep the bills paid, they can keep doing the same thing "wrong." At the same time, leaders who draw resources from multiple constituencies acquire the strategic flexibility that goes with gereater autonomy of greater room to maneuver (Alexander, 1998; Powell, 1988). Resources drawn from multiple sources may also encourage expression of the diverse views that are important for creative thinking (Levinthal, 1997). Leaders' choices about which constituencies from whom to mobilize resources can thus have an important influence on subsequent strategy (Oliver & Marwell, 1992). Relying more on people than on money facilitates growth in strategic capacity to the extent that it encourages development of more leaders who know how to strategize. The more capable strategists to which an organization has access, the greater the flexibility with which the organization can pursue its objectives and the larger scale on which it can do so (Weick, 1979).

Leadership teams that are self-selected or elected by constituencies to whom they are accountable have more strategic capacity than those selected bureaucratically, as shown in the sixth row of Fig. 10.1, "Accountability." Accountability structures influence strategy by establishing routines for leadership selection and defining loci of responsiveness. Leaders who are accountable to those outside their core constituency may have been selected based on criteria that have little to do with knowledge of or motivational connection with that constituency. As innovation scholars have shown, interaction with one's constituency (or customers) is a particularly important source of salient new ideas (Utterback, 1971; Von Hippel, 1988). Leaders selected bureaucratically are more likely to possess the skills and motivations compatible with bureaucratic success than with the creative work that innovation requires. Elected leaders are at least likely to have useful knowledge of the constituency that elected them and the political skills to have been elected. Entrepreneurial or self-selected leaders—at whose initiative the undertaking takes place—are more likely to possess skills and intrinsic motivations associated with creative work (Chambers, 1973; Getzels & Csikszentmihalyi, 1976; MacKinnon, 1965). Although elective and entrepreneurial leadership selection processes may be in tension with one another, either is likely to yield more strategic capacity than bureaucratic leadership selection.

Timing

Strategic choices are made not only in certain places but also at certain moments in time. Yet moments of opportunity come and go, and the choices that actors make at some moments have far greater influence than those made at other moments. What influence, if any, does strategic capacity have on actors' ability to act not only in appropriate ways but in timely ones?

Sociologists, organizational behavior scholars, and cultural analysts note that some moments have greater causal significance for subsequent events than other moments. Some sociologists emphasize the significance of "critical junctures," moments when events unfolding along distinct causal pathways interact to yield unique opportunities (Skocpol, 1984). Others identify as "focusing moments" events that create unique opportunities for mobilization by drawing attention to particular issues (Lofland, 1996). Others cite the "eventful temporality" of unique events that alter the deep context in which subsequent events unfold (Sewell, 1996). Organizational scholars identify portentous moments of organizational development as midway points toward realization of particular goals and other moments of high contingency (Gersick, 1994; Weick, 1979, 1993). Cultural scholars point to moments of crisis or "role transition" in the lives of individuals or communities at which norms, identities, and values become fluid or liminal, compared with other times when they are relatively resilient (Jasper, 1997; Morris, 1993; Smelser, 1962; Swidler, 1986; V. Turner, 1966; Turner & Killian, 1987). Moments of historical, cultural and organizational fluidity may occur singly or together—what scholars call *entrainment*—alignment of internal and external rhythms of change (Ancona & Chong, 1996).

Ironically, those moments when actors' strategic choices may matter most may also be moments of radical uncertainty, particularly in the case of social movements. Breakthrough events may alter the affected individuals, organizations, and environments so deeply that their consequences depend almost entirely on what actors make of them. Victories may be moments when strategic choices matter most, not times to "rest on one's laurels," but rather to make the most of one's successes. Victories may be moments of greatest risk.

Because of their radical uncertainty, these are conditions under which strategic capacity may matter most. It may be when the value of reliance on known algorithms is most limited that creative capability is most important (Tushman & Murmann, 1997). Leadership teams with more strategic capacity can make not only more informed choices, but quicker ones, allowing them to take greater advantage of unique moments of opportunity. And leadership teams with more strategic capacity can take advantage of moments of unique opportunity to reconfigure their own leadership and structure in ways that allow them to enhance their strategic capacity further.

Dynamics

Since strategic capacity is the result of a relationship among leaders, organization, and environment, failure to adapt to environmental change can lead to atrophy. On the other hand, if organizations adapt their leadership to changes in their environment and continue interacting with it, their strategic capacity can grow. Because established organizations rely on their resources for institutional power, their loss of resourcefulness may only become apparent when they are required to face new challenges in unfamiliar environments. That strategic capacity can atrophy helps explain not only why David can sometimes win but also why Goliath can sometimes lose.

Scholars note that organizations institutionalize as environments change (Hannan & Freeman, 1984; Stinchcombe, 1965). Processes of organizational inertia inhibit adaptation by old organizations to new environments, thus creating niches within which new organizations can emerge—a liability of aging or senescence (Aldrich & Auster, 1986). Leaders of the newer organizations were recently selected, have more organizational flexibility, and work in closer articulation with the environment. Leaders of older organizations were often selected in the past, are constrained by institutional routines, and may have resources that allow them to operate in counterproductive insulation from the environment. As leaders persist, they form bonds among themselves, develop common understandings of "how things work" and select others like themselves to lead. Access to internal organizational resources can insulate them, in the short run, from environmental change. For a time, these resources may even give them the power to shape that environment—but only for a time. Changes in organizational structure that reduce leaders' accountability to constituents, or the need to mobilize resources from constituents—or changes in deliberative processes that suppress dissent—can diminish strategic capacity, even as resources grow. The strategic capacity of an organization can thus grow over time if it adjusts its leadership team to reflect environmental change, multiplies deliberative venues, remains accountable to salient constituencies, and derives resources from them. Similarly, strategic capacity may atrophy if an organization fails to adjust its leadership, limits deliberative venues, loses accountability to salient constituencies, and relies on internal resources. Older organizations are likely to have less strategic capacity than newer ones.

Strategic Process Model

As summarized in Fig. 10.2, "Strategic Process Model," then, I argue that outcomes are influenced by strategy, the effectiveness of which is, in turn, the result of the strategic capacity of a leadership team. And the strategic

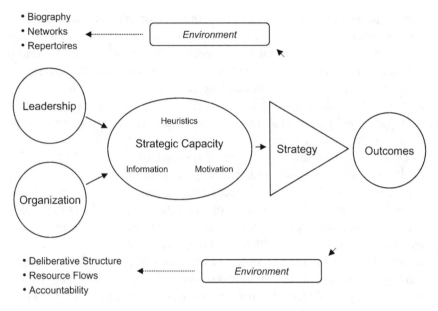

FIG. 10.2.   Strategic process.

capacity of a leadership team is the result of who its members are and how they structure their interaction with each other and with their environment, as explained previously.

EVALUATING STRATEGIC CAPACITY

Although elsewhere I show that variation in strategic capacity can explain the success of the United Farm Workers as compared with its rival organizations, the AFL-CIO's Agricultural Workers Organizing Committee (AWOC) and the International Brotherhood of Teamsters, in this chapter I've focused on articulating strategic capacity as a conceptual tool to help explain other cases of David-like success, or failure. How generalizable—and therefore, useful—can we expect this concept to be?

The core argument on which strategic capacity rests is the claim that under conditions of uncertainty, the capability to generate new algorithms, when rooted in deep understanding of the environment, is more strategically valuable than the capability to apply known algorithms, no matter how expertly. In other words, under conditions in which rules, resources, and interests are highly institutionalized and links betweens ends and means are certain, as in the world of game theory, the relationship between resources and success should be predictable, especially when expertise at how to play the game is factored in. Strategic capacity is thus more useful explaining outcomes in turbulent environments where rules, resources, and interests are emergent and links between ends and means are uncertain. This suggests that although it was developed in the context of social movement insurgency, strategic capacity as an analytic concept could be useful in explaining outcomes in any such environment—political, economic, or social.

One way the explanatory power of strategic capacity could be evaluated is with sets of cases in which strategic capacity and resources vary, as shown in Fig. 10.3. Strategic capacity adds the most explanatory value in cases falling into the upper left quadrant (little resources, lots of strategic capacity) and lower right quadrant (lots of resources, little strategic capacity). But it could be tested with respect to any set of cases not limited to the lower left quadrant (little resources, little strategic capacity) or the upper right quadrant (lots of resources, lots of strategic capacity). Although strategic capacity would have the least explanatory value for cases confined to the lower left quadrant (little resources, little strategic capacity) or upper right quadrant (lots of resources, lots of strategic capacity), these are quadrants in which we expect to find the most cases with the most predictable outcomes—that is, challengers with little resources and strategic capacity, or incumbents with lots of resources and strategic capacity. The unique contribution of a theory of strategic capacity is to offer a way to explain the

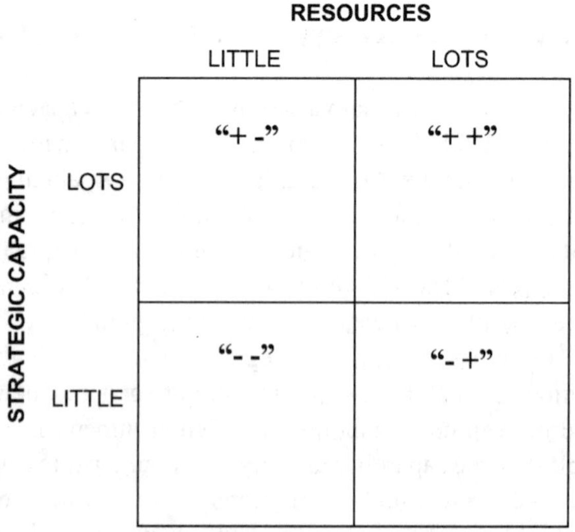

RESOURCES

	LITTLE	LOTS
LOTS	"+ -"	"+ +"
LITTLE	"- -"	"- +"

STRATEGIC CAPACITY

FIG. 10.3.   Strategic capacity and resources.

less frequent but—from a social movement point of view—more interesting outcomes of David winning and Goliath losing without resorting to accounts grounded in opportunity and resources that rob actors of their agency. By selecting cases based on variation in resources and strategic capacity we avoid the problem of selection on the dependent variable, success. Strategic capacity could be tested by comparing a set of cases with observable variation in independent variables of resources and strategic capacity and the dependent variable of success. To the extent that strategic capacity co-varies with success, the theory would be upheld. To the extent it does not, it would be falsified.

CONCLUSION

This chapter began by asking why "David" sometimes wins. Organizations can compensate for lack of economic, political, or cultural resources with creative strategy, a function of the motivation, access to a diversity of salient information, and heuristic facility with which their leadership teams interact with their environment. Changing environments generate opportunities and resources, but the significance of those opportunities or resources—and even what constitutes them—emerges from the hearts, heads, and hands of the actors who develop the means of putting them to work. People can generate the power to resolve grievances not only if those with power decide to use it on their behalf, but also if they can develop the capacity to outthink and outlast their opponents—a matter of leadership and organization. As an "actor-centered" approach, analysis of strategic capacity suggests ways to design leadership teams and structure organizations that increase the chances of devising effective strategies to deal with the challenges of organizing, innovation, and social change today. As students of "street smarts" have long understood, resourcefulness can sometimes compensate for a lack of resources. Although learning about how the environment influences actors is important, learning more about how actors influence the environment is the first step not only to understanding the world, but changing it.

REFERENCES

Abelson, R. P. (1981). Psychological status of the script concept. *American Psychologist, 36,* 715–29.

Aldrich, H. E., & Auster, E. R. (1986). Even dwarfs started small: Liabilities of age and size and their strategic implications. In B. M. Staw & L. L. Cummings (Eds.), *Research in organizational behavior* (Vol. 8, pp. 165–198). Greenwich, CT: JAI.

Alexander, V. D. (1998). Environmental constraints and organizational strategies: Complexity, conflict and coping in the nonprofit sector. In W. Powell & E. Clemens (Eds.), *Private action and the public good* (pp. 272–290). New Haven, CT: Yale University Press.

Alinsky, S. D. (1971). *Rules for radicals.* New York: Vintage.

Amabile, T. M. (1988). A model of organizational innovation. In B. M. Staw & L. L. Cummings (Eds.), *Research in organizational behavior* (Vol. 10, pp. 123–167). Greenwich, CT: JAI Press.

Amabile, T. M. (1996). *Creativity in context.* Boulder, CO: Westview Press.

Ancona, D., & Chong, C.-L. (1996). Entrainment: Cycles and synergy in organizational behavior. In B. M Staw & L. L. Cummings (Eds.), *Research in organizational behavior* (pp. 251–284). Greenwich, CT: JAI Press.

Andrews, K. (1997). The impacts of social movements on the political process: The civil rights movement and Black electoral politics in Mississippi. *American Sociological Review, 62,* 800–819.

Asch, S. (1952). *Social psychology.* Englewood Cliffs, NJ: Prentice-Hall.

Banaszak, L. A. (1996). *Why movements succeed or fail: Opportunity, culture and the struggle for woman suffrage.* Princeton, NJ: Princeton University Press.

Bandura, A. (1989). Human agency in social cognitive theory. *American Psychologist, 44*(9), 1175–1184.

Bartunek, J. M. (1993). Multiple cognition and conflicts associated with second order organizational change. In J. K. Murnighan (Ed.), *Social psychology in organizations* (pp. 337–343). Englewood Cliffs, NJ: Prentice-Hall.

Benford, R. D. (1997). An insider's critique of the social movement framing perspective. *Sociological Inquiry, 67,* 409–430.

Benford, R. D., & Snow, D. A. (2000). Framing processes and social movements: An overview and assessment. *Annual Review of Sociology, 26,* 611–639.

Bergman, J. (1979). Energy levels: An important factor in identifying and facilitating the development of giftedness in young children. *Creative Child and Adult Quarterly, 4,* 181–188.

Berlyne, D. E. (1960). *Conflict, arousal, and curiosity.* New York: McGraw-Hill.

Bernstein, B. (1975). Social class, language and socialization. In *Class, codes, and control: Theoretical studies towards sociology of language* (pp. 170–189). New York: Schocken Books.

Bourdieu, P. (1986). *Distinction: A social critique of the judgement of taste.* Cambridge, MA: Harvard University Press.

Bourdieu, P. (1990). *The logic of practice.* Palo Alto, CA: Stanford University Press.

Bower, J. L. (1970). *Managing the resource allocation process: A study of corporate planning and investment.* Homewood, IL: Richard D. Irwin, Inc.

Brown, S. L., & Eisenhardt, K. M. (1997). The art of continuous change: Linking complexity theory and time-paced evolution in relentlessly shifting organizations. *Administrative Science Quarterly, 42*(1), 34–56.

Brown, S. L., & Eisenhardt, K. M. (1998). *Competing on the edge: Strategy as structured chaos.* Boston: Harvard Business School Press.

Bruner, J. (1990). *Acts of meaning.* Cambridge, MA: Harvard University Press.

Burgelman, R. A. (1991). Intraorganizational ecology of strategy making and organizational adaptation: Theory and field research. *Organization Science, 2*(3), 239–262.

Campbell, D. T. (1960). Blind variation and selective retention in creative thought as in other knowledge processes. *Psychological Review, 67,* 380–400.

Campbell, J. L. (1997). Mechanisms of evolutionary change in economic governance: Interaction, interpretation, and bricolage. In L. Magnusson & J. Ottosson (Eds.), *Evolutionary economics and path dependence* (pp. 10–32). Cheltenham, England: Edward Elgar.

Carlton-Ford, S. L. (1992). Charisma, ritual, collective effervescence and self-esteem. *Sociological Quarterly, 33*(3), 365–388.

Chambers, J. A. (1973). Relating personality and biographical factors to scientific creativity. *Psychological Monographs, 78*(7).

Chandler, A. D. (1962). *Strategy and structure: Chapters in the history of the American industrial enterprise.* Cambridge, MA: MIT Press.

Chandler, A. D. (1977). *The visible hand: The managerial revolution in American business.* Cambridge, MA: Belknap Press.

Child, J. (1972). Organizational structure, environment and performance: The role of strategic choice. *Sociology, 6*(1), 1–22.

Chong, D. (1991). *Collective action and the civil rights movement.* Chicago: University of Chicago Press.

Clausewitz, C. von. (1968). *On war.* London: Penguin Books. (Original work published 1832)

Clemens, E. (1996). Organizational form as frame: Collective identity and political strategy in the labor movement, 1880–1920. In D. McAdam, J. McCarthy, & M. Zald (Eds.), *Comparative perspectives on social movements* (pp. 205–226). Cambridge, UK: Cambridge University Press.

Cohen, M. D., March, J. G., & Olson, J. P. (1972). Garbage can model of organizational choice. *Administrative Science Quarterly, 17,* 1–25.

Coleman, J. (1990). *Foundations of social theory.* Cambridge, MA: Belknap Press of Harvard University Press.

Collins, R. (1981). On the microfoundations of macrosociology. *American Journal of Sociology, 86,* 984–1013.

Conti, R., Amabile, T. M., & Pokkok, S. (1995, April). *Problem solving among computer science students: the effects of skill, evaluation expectation and personality on solution quality.* Paper presented at the annual meeting of the Eastern Psychological Association, Boston, MA.

Crow, G. (1989). The use of the concept of "strategy" in recent sociological literature. *Sociology, 23*(1), 1–24.

Dahrendorf, R. (1958). *Class and conflict in industrial society.* Palo Alto, CA: Stanford University Press.

Damanpour, F. (1991). Organizational innovation: A meta-analysis of effects of determinants and moderators. *Academy of Management Journal, 34*(3), 555–590.

D'Andrade, R. G. (1992). Schemas and motivation. In R. D'Andrade & C. Strauss (Eds.), *Human motives and cultural models* (pp. 23–44). New York: Cambridge University Press.

Davis, J. E. (2002). Narrative and social movements: The power of stories. In J. E. Davis (Ed.), *Stories of change: Narrative and social movements.* New York: State University of New York Press.

Deci, E. L., & Ryan, R. M. (1985). *Intrinsic motivation and self-determination in human behavior.* New York: Plenum Press.

DiMaggio, P. (1997). Culture and cognition. *Annual Review of Sociology, 23,* 263–287.

DiMaggio, P. J., & Powell, W. (1991). Introduction. In W. Powell & P. J. DiMaggio (Eds.), *The new institutionalism in organizational analysis* (pp. 1–38). Chicago: University of Chicago Press.

Douglas, M. (1986). *How institutions think.* Syracuse, NY: Syracuse University Press.

Duncan, R. B. (1973). Multiple decision making structures in adapting to environmental uncertainty: The impact on organizational effectiveness. *Human Relations, 26*(3), 273–292.

Durkheim, E. (1964). *Elementary forms of religious life.* New York: Macmillan.

Eisenhardt, K. M., & Schoonhoven, C. B. (1990). Organizational growth: Linking founding team, strategy, environment, and growth among U.S. semiconductor ventures, 1978–1988. *Administrative Science Quarterly, 35,* 504–529.

Emerson, R. (1962). Power-dependence relations. *American Sociological Review, 27,* 31–44.

Emirbayer, M., & Goodwin, J. (1994). Network analysis, culture, and the problem of agency. *American Journal of Sociology, 99,* 1411–1454.

Fiske, S., & Taylor, S. E. (1991). *Social cognition.* New York: McGraw-Hill.

Freeman, J. (1979). Resource mobilization and strategy: A model for analyzing social movement organizations. In M. N. Zald & J. D. McCarthy (Eds.), *The dynamics of social movements: Resources mobilization, social control, and tactics* (pp. 167–189). Cambridge, MA: Winthrop.

Gamson, W. (1975). *The strategy of social protest.* Belmont, CA: Wadsworth Publishing.

Gamson, W. (1991). Commitment and agency in social movements. *Sociological Forum, 6*(1), 27–50.

Gamson, W. (1992). *Talking politics.* New York: Cambridge University Press.

Gamson, W., & Meyer, D. (1996). Framing political opportunity. In D. McAdam, J. McCarthy, & M. Zald (Eds.), *Comparative perspectives on social movements.* New York: Cambridge University Press.

Ganz, M. (2000a). *Five smooth stones: Strategic capacity in the unionization of California agriculture.* Unpublished doctoral dissertation, Harvard University, Cambridge, MA.

Ganz, M. (2000b). Resources and resourcefulness: Strategic capacity in the unionization of California agriculture (1959–77). *American Journal of Sociology, 105*(4), 1003–1062.

Garfinkel, H. (1984). *Studies in ethnomethodology.* Cambridge, UK: Polity Press.

Gentner, D. (1989). Mechanisms of analogical learning. In S. Vosiadou & A. Ortony (Eds.), *Similarity and analogical reasoning* (pp. 199–239). Cambridge, UK: Cambridge University Press.

Gersick, C. J. (1994). Pacing strategic change: The case of a new venture. *Administrative Science Quarterly, 29,* 499–518.

Getzels, J., & Csikszentmihalyi, M. (1976). *The creative vision: A longitudinal study of problem finding in art.* New York: Wiley-Interscience.

Glover, J. A., & Sautter, F. (1977). Relation of four components of creativity to risk-taking preferences. *Psychological Reports, 41,* 227–230.

Goffman, E. (1974). *Frame analysis.* New York: Harper and Row.

Granovetter, M. (1973). The strength of weak ties. *American Journal of Sociology, 78,* 1360–1380.

Hackman, J. R., & Morris, C. G. (1975). Group tasks, group interaction process, and group performance effectiveness: A review and proposed integration. In L. Berkowitz (Ed.), *Advances in experimental social psychology* (pp. 45–99). New York: Academic Press.

Hackman, J. R., & Oldham, G. R. (1976). Motivation through the design of work: Test of the theory. *Organizational Behavior and Human Performance, 16,* 250–279.

Hackman, J. R., & Walton, R. (1986). Leading groups in organizations. In P. Goodman (Ed.), *Designing effective work groups* (pp. 72–119). San Francisco: Jossey-Bass.

Hackman, R. (1990). *Groups that work.* San Francisco: Jossey-Bass.

Hall, R. B. (1997). Moral authority as a power resource. *International Organizations, 51*(4), 591–622.

Hamel, G. (1996). Strategy as revolution. *Harvard Business Review, 74*(69), 69–78.

Hamel, G., & Prahalad, C. K. (1989). Strategic intent. *Harvard Business Review, 67*(3), 63–77.

Hannan, M. T., & Freeman, J. (1984). Structural inertia and organizational change. *American Sociological Review, 49*(2), 149–164.

Harter, S. (1978). Effectance motivation reconsidered: Toward a developmental model. *Human Development, 21,* 34–64.

Hebb, D. O. (1953). Drives and the CNS. *Psychological Review, 62,* 243–254.

Hollander, E. P., & Offermann, L. R. (1990). Power and leadership in organizations: Relationships in transition. *The American Psychologist, 45*(2), 179–190.

House, R. J., Spangler, W. D., & Woycke, J. (1991). Personality and charisma in the U.S. presidency: A psychological theory of leader effectiveness. *Administrative Science Quarterly, 36*(3), 364–397.

Howell, J. M. (1990). Champions of technological innovation. *Administrative Science Quarterly, 35*(2), 317–339.

Hutchins, E. (1991). The social organization of distributed cognition. In L. B. Resnick, J. M. Levine, & S. D. Teasley (Eds.), *Perspective on socially shared cognition* (pp. 283–307). Washington, DC: American Psychological Association.

Janis, I. (1972). *Victims of groupthink.* Boston: Houghton-Mifflin.

Jasper, J. M. (1997). *The art of moral protest: Culture, biography and creativity in social movements.* Chicago: University of Chicago Press.

Johnston, H., & Klandermans, B. (Eds). (1995). *Social movements and culture.* Minneapolis, MN: University of Minnesota Press.

Kasperson, C. J. (1978). Scientific creativity: A relationship with information channels. *Psychological Reports, 42,* 691–694.

Knocke, D., & Wood, J. R. (1981). *Organized for action: Commitment in voluntary associations.* New Brunswick, NJ: Rutgers University Press.

Kuhn, T. S. (1962). *The structure of scientific revolutions.* Chicago: University of Chicago Press.

Lakoff, G., & Johnson, M. (1980). The metaphorical structure of the human conceptual system. *Cognitive Science, 4,* 195–208.

Langer, E. (1978). Rethinking the role of thought in social interaction. In W. Ickes, R. Kidd, & J. Harvey (Eds.), *New directions in attribution research* (Vol. 2, pp. 35–58). Hillsdale, NJ: Lawrence Erlbaum Associates.

Langer, E. (1989). *Mindfulness.* Reading, MA: Addison-Wesley.

Langer, E., & Imber, L. (1979). When practice makes imperfect: Debilitating effects of overlearning. *Journal of Personality and Social Psychology, 37,* 2014–2024.

Levinthal, D. (1997). Three faces of organizational learning: Wisdom, inertia, and discovery. In R. Garud, P. Nayyar, & Z. Shapira (Eds.), *Technological innovation: Oversights and foresights* (pp. 167–180). Cambridge: Cambridge University Press.

Levi-Strauss, C. (1966). *The savage mind* (G. Weidenfield, Trans.). London: Weidenfeld and Nicolson. (Original work published 1962)

Lipsky, M. (1968). Protest as a political resource. *American Political Science Review, 62*(48), 1144–1158.

Lofland, J. (1996). *Social movement organizations.* New York: Walter deGruyter.

Lukes, S. (1975). *Power: A radical view.* New York: Macmillan.

MacKinnon, D. W. (1965). Personality and the realization of creative potential. *American Psychologist, 20*(2), 273–281.

Mann, M. (1986). A history of power from the beginning to A.D. 1760. In *The sources of social power* (Vol. 1, pp. 1–33). New York: Cambridge University Press.

Mansbridge, J. (1986). *Why we lost the ERA.* Chicago: University of Chicago Press.

March, J., & Olsen, J. (1976). *Ambiguity and choice in organizations.* Bergen, Norway: Universeitetsforiaget.

McAdam, D. (1983). Tactical innovations and the pace of insurgency. *American Sociological Review, 48,* 735–754.

McAdam, D., McCarthy, J., & Zald, M. (1996). Opportunities, mobilizing structures, and framing processes—Toward a synthetic comparative perspective on social movements. In D. McAdam, J. McCarthy, & M. Zald (Eds.), *Comparative perspectives on social movements* (pp. 1–22). New York: Cambridge University Press.

McAdam, D., & Paulsen, R. (1993). Specifying the relationships between social ties and activism. *American Journal of Sociology, 98,* 640–667.

McCarthy, J. D., & Zald, M. N. (1977). Resource mobilization and social movements: A partial theory. *American Journal of Sociology, 8*(6), 1212–1241.

McCleod, P. L. (1992). The effects of ethnic diversity on idea generation in small groups. In *Best Paper Proceedings,* Academy of Management Convention, Las Vegas, NV.

McGrath, J. (1984). *Groups: Interaction and performance*. Englewood Cliffs, NJ: Prentice-Hall.

Meyer, J. P., & Allen, N. J. (1997). *Commitment in the workplace: Theory, research and application*. Thousand Oaks, CA: Sage Publications.

Michels, R. (1962). *Political parties: A sociological study of oligarchical tendencies of modern democracy*. New York: Collier.

Milgram, S. (1974). *Obedience to authority*. New York: Harper & Row.

Mintzberg, H. (1987). Crafting strategy. *Harvard Business Review, 65*(4), 66–76.

Mintzberg, H. (1994). The rise and fall of strategic planning. *Harvard Business Review, 72*(1), 107–115.

Mintzberg, H., & McHugh, A. (1985). Strategy formation in an adhocracy. *Administrative Science Quarterly, 30*(2), 160–198.

Moore, M. H. (1995). *Creating public value: Strategic management in government*. Cambridge, MA: Harvard University Press.

Morris, A. (1984). *Origins of the civil rights movement: Black communities organizing for change*. New York: The Free Press.

Morris, A. (1993). Birmingham confrontation reconsidered: An analysis of the dynamics and tactics of mobilization. *American Sociological Review 58*, 621–636.

Morris, A., & Staggenborg, S. (2002). Leadership. In D. Snow, S. Soule, & H. Kresii (Eds.), *Social movements in the Blackwell companion to social movements* (pp. 171–196). Boston: Blackwell Publishers.

Moscovici, S. (1984). The phenomenon of social representations. In S. Moscovici & R. M. Moscovici-Farr (Eds.), *Social representation* (pp. 3–69). New York: Cambridge University Press.

Nemeth, C. J. (1986). Differential contributions of majority and minority influences. *Psychological Review, 93*(1), 22–32.

Nemeth, C. J., & Staw, B. M. (1989). The tradeoffs of social control and innovation in groups and organizations. In L. Berkowitz (Ed.), *Advances in experimental social psychology* (pp. 722–730). New York: Academic Press.

North, D. C. (1990). *Institutions, institutional change and economic performance*. New York: Cambridge University Press.

Oberschall, A. (1973). *Social conflict and social movements*. Englewood Cliffs, NJ: Prentice-Hall.

Oliver, C. (1988). The collective strategy framework: An application to competing predictions of isomorphism. *Administrative Science Quarterly, 33*(4), 543–561.

Oliver, P. E., & Marwell, G. (1992). Mobilizing technologies for collective action. In A. D. Morris & C. M. Mueller (Eds.), *Frontiers of social movement theory* (pp. 251–272). New Haven, CT: Yale University Press.

Osborn, A. (1963). *Applied imagination: Principles and procedures of creative thinking*. New York: Scribners.

Perrow, C. (1986). *Complex organizations: A critical essay*. New York: McGraw-Hill.

Peterson, J. (1999). *Maps of meaning: The architecture of belief*. New York: Routledge.

Pfeffer, J., & Salancik, G. (1978). *The external control of organizations: A resource dependence perspective*. New York: Harper and Row.

Pillai, R. (1996). Crisis and the emergence of charismatic leadership in groups: An experimental investigation. *Journal of Applied Social Psychology, 26*(6), 543–563.

Piore, M. (1995). *Beyond individualism*. Cambridge, MA: Harvard University Press.

Porter, M. E. (1996). Making strategy. *Harvard Business Review, 74*(6), 61–77.

Powell, W. W. (1988). Institutional effects on organizational structure and performance. In L. G. Zucker (Ed.), *Institutional patterns and organizations* (pp. 115–136). Cambridge, MA: Ballinger Publishing Co.

Prentky, R. A. (1980). *Creativity and psychopathology.* New York: Praeger.

Putnam, R. (1993). *Making democracy work.* Princeton, NJ: Princeton University Press.

Rickards, T., & Freedman, B. L. (1978). Procedures for managers in idea-deficient situations: Examination of brainstorming approaches. *Journal of Management Studies, 15,* 43–55.

Rogers, E. (1995). *Diffusion of innovations.* New York: The Free Press.

Rosaldo, R. (1989). *Culture and truth: The remaking of social analysis.* Boston: Beacon Press.

Ross, R. J. (1983). Generational change and primary groups in a social movement. In J. Freeman (Ed.), *Social movements of the sixties and seventies* (pp. 177–187). New York: Longman.

Ruscio, J., Whitney, D., & Amabile, T. M. (1995). *How do motivation and task behaviors affect creativity? An investigation in three domains.* Waltham, MA: Brandeis University.

Salancik, G. R., & Pfeffer, J. (1977). Who gets power—and how they hold on to it: A strategic contingency model of power. *Organizational Dynamics, 2*(21), 2–21.

Schelling, T. C. (1960). *The strategy of conflict.* Cambridge, MA: Harvard University Press.

Senge, P. (1990). *The fifth discipline: The art and practice of the learning organization.* New York: Doubleday.

Sewell, W. (1992). A theory of structure: Duality, agency and transformation. *American Journal of Sociology, 98,* 1–29.

Sewell, W. (1996). Three temporalities: Toward an eventful sociology. In T. J. McDonald (Ed.), *The historic turn in the human sciences* (pp. 245–280). Ann Arbor: University of Michigan Press.

Simonton, D. K. (1988). Creativity, leadership and chance. In R. J. Sternberg (Ed.), *The nature of creativity: Contemporary psychological perspectives* (pp. 386–426). Cambridge, UK: Cambridge University Press.

Skocpol, T. (1984). Emerging agendas and recurrent strategies in historical sociology. In T. Skocpol (Ed.), *Vision and method in historical sociology* (pp. 356–391). New York: Cambridge University Press.

Skocpol, T. (1985). Bringing the state back in: Strategies and analysis in current research. In P. Evans, D. Rueschemeyer, & T. Skocpol (Eds.), *Bringing the state back in* (pp. 3–37). New York: Cambridge University Press.

Smelser, N. J. (1962). *Theory of collective action.* New York: The Free Press.

Snow, D. A., Rochford, E. B., Worden, S. K., & Benford, R. D. (1986). Frame alignment processes, micromobilization, and movement participation. *American Sociological Review, 51,* 464–481.

Stark, R., & Bainbridge, W. (1985). *The future of religion: Secularization, revival and cult formation.* Berkeley, CA: University of California Press.

Stinchcombe, A. (1965). Social structure and organizations. In J. G. March (Ed.), *Handbook of organizations* (pp. 143–153). Chicago: Rand McNally.

Strang, D., & Meyer, J. (1994). Institutional conditions for diffusion. In W. R. Scott & J. W. Meyer (Eds.), *Institutional environments and organizations* (pp. 100–112). Beverly Hills, CA: Sage.

Sutcliffe, K. M. (2000). What executives notice: Accurate perceptions in top management teams. *Academy of Management Journal, 37,* 1360–1378.

Swidler, A. (1986). Culture in action: Symbols and strategies. *American Sociological Review, 51*(2), 273–286.

Taylor, C. (1989). *Sources of the self.* Cambridge, MA: Harvard University Press.

Taylor, V., & Whitter, N. E. (1992). Collective identity in social movement communities: Lesbian feminist mobilization. In A. D. Morris & C. M. Mueller (Eds.), *Frontiers in social movement theory* (pp. 104–130). New Haven, CT: Yale University Press.

Tilly, C. (1978). *From mobilization to revolution.* Reading, MA: Addison-Wesley.

Tilly, C. (1981). *Class, conflict, and collective action.* Beverly Hills, CA: Sage.

Turner, R., & Killian, L. (1987). Culture in action. In *Collective behavior* (3rd ed., pp. 273–286). Englewood Cliffs, NJ: Prentice-Hall.

Turner, V. (1966). *The ritual process: Structure and anti-structure.* Ithaca, NY: Cornell University Press.

Tushman, M., & Murmann, P. (1997). Organization responsiveness to environmental shock as an indicator of organizational foresight and oversight: The role of executive team characteristics and organization context. In R. Garud, P. Nayyoi, & Z. Shapira (Eds.), *Technological innovation: Foresights and oversights* (pp. 260–278). New York: Cambridge University Press.

Utterback, J. M. (1971). The process of technological innovation within the firm. *Academy of Management Journal, 14,* 75–88.

Van de Ven, A. H., Polley, D. E., Garud, R., & Venkataraman, S. (1999). *The innovation journey.* New York: Oxford University Press.

Von Hippel, E. (1988). *The sources of innovation.* New York: Oxford University Press.

Walberg, H. J. (1971). Varieties of adolescent creativity and the high school environment. *Exceptional children, 38,* 111–116.

Watson, W. (1990). Strategy, rationality, and inference: The possibility of symbolic performances. *Sociology, 24*(3), 480–514.

Weber, M. (1946). *From Max Weber: Essays in sociology* (H. H. Gerth & C. Wright Mills, Eds. and Trans.). New York: Oxford University Press. (Original work published 1920)

Weber, M. (1958). *The Protestant ethic and the spirit of capitalism.* New York: Charles Scribner's Sons.

Weber, M. (1978a). The types of legitimate domination. In G. Roth & C. Wittich (Eds.), *Economy and society* (Vol. 1, pp. 215–216, 241–245). Berkeley, CA: University of California Press. (Original work published 1914)

Weber, M. (1978b). Charisma and its transformation. In G. Roth & C. Wittich (Eds.), *Economy and society* (Vol. 2, pp. 1111–1157). Berkeley, CA: University of California Press. (Original work published 1914)

Weber, M. (1978c). Basic sociological terms. In G. Roth & C. Wittich (Eds.), *Economy and society* (Vol. 1, pp. 12–15, 48–52, 212–301). Berkeley, CA: University of California Press. (Original work published 1914)

Weick, K. E. (1979). *The social psychology of organizing.* New York: McGraw-Hill.

Weick, K. E. (1993). Sensemaking in organizations: Small structures with large consequences. In J. K. Murnighan (Eds.), *Social psychology in organizations* (pp. 10–37). Englewood Cliffs, NJ: Prentice-Hall.

Westley, F. R., & Mintzberg, H. (1988). Profiles of strategic vision: Levesque and Iacocca. In J. A. Conger & R. N. Kahungo (Eds.), *Charismatic leadership: The elusive factor in organizational effectiveness.* San Francisco: Jossey-Bass.

White, R. (1959). Motivation reconsidered: The concept of competence. *Psychological Review, 66,* 297–323.

Wickham-Crowley, T. (1992). *Guerrillas and revolution in Latin America: A comparative study of insurgents and regimes since 1956.* Princeton, NJ: Princeton University Press.

Zaltman, G., Duncan, R., & Holbeck, J. (1973). *Innovations and organizations.* New York: John Wiley and Sons.

Zerubavel, E. (1997). *Social mindscapes: An invitation to cognitive sociology.* Cambridge, MA: Harvard University Press.

III

Consequences of Leadership

11

The Perception of Conspiracy: Leader Paranoia as Adaptive Cognition

Roderick M. Kramer
Dana Gavrieli
Stanford University

There were serious men who had given up satisfying jobs on the outside because they were convinced Nixon stood on the threshold of greatness. To them, Nixon was the real thing, a genuine and inspired leader. . . . But there was another side to his nature—insecure, secretive, angry, vindictive—that lurked beneath the surface. . . . Nixon knew it was there and thought there were times when he needed to be mean in order to retain power in the face of countless hostile forces.

—David Gergen, 2000, p. 31

We often hear that someone worries too much. But in some fields like politics, you can't worry too much. If worrying means recognizing that things may go wrong and planning how to deal with these inevitable setbacks. Those blissful souls who speed so self-confidently along life's straight, smooth highways are often the ones who end up in the ditch when the road suddenly veers.

—Former Texas Governor John Connolly, commenting on Lyndon
  Johnson's seeming paranoia as President (quoted in Grubin, 1991)

In January 1998, First Lady Hillary Clinton attracted national attention when she asserted, during the course of an interview on a prominent national television show, that her husband, President Bill Clinton, was the victim of a "vast right-wing conspiracy." The First Lady's remarks were dismissed as merely fanciful by some commentators, and portrayed as a clever diversionary ploy by others. Few administration insiders, however, doubted that both the President and First Lady felt genuinely besieged by a cabal of powerful political enemies engaged in a concerted effort to tarnish and, ultimately, topple the Clinton presidency (Kurtz, 1998).

Although Hillary Clinton's fantastic pronouncement/proclamations provoked much bemused commentary, the conviction of political leaders that they are victims of elaborate, well-orchestrated conspiracies turn out to be far from rare, historically. A number of recent presidents, for example, have expressed paranoid-like suspicions during their tenure in the White House. U.S. presidents have often expressed—either in private ruminations with their aides or in public statements—the belief that they were the targets of vicious conspiracies involving either their political enemies or the national media. For example, as President Lyndon Johnson found all of his efforts to forge a victory in Vietnam frustrated, he came to believe that powerful domestic and foreign conspiracies were thwarting him at every turn (Goodwin, 1988). Similarly, as President Richard Nixon's inability to deflect national attention from the Watergate scandal persisted, he was sure he could discern the hidden hands of his enemies as they tirelessly worked the political and media levers in order to bring him to his knees (Ambrose, 1991, p. 285). As Admiral Elmo Zumwalt, Chief of Naval Operations during the Nixon presidency, observed, "The President [Richard Nixon] . . . saw the various attacks on him as part of a vast plot by intellectual snobs to destroy a president who was representative of the man in the street . . . he perceived himself as a fighter . . . involved in mortal battle with the forces of evil" (Ambrose, 1991, p. 285).

It would be easy to dismiss such instances of leader paranoia as extreme and, at best, rather curious psychological phenomena. Being a bit paranoid, it might be argued, simply comes with the territory. Unfortunately, in addition to being far from infrequent, the consequences of leaders' paranoia have often proven far from benign (see, e.g., Graumann, 1987; Robins & Post, 1997). On the basis of the conviction that others are out to get them, leaders have engaged in actions that have proven not only individually self-destructive, but also enormously costly to the organizations and societies they lead. For example, President Johnson's belief that opposition to the Vietnam War was fueled by a conspiracy involving both his domestic political enemies and foreign influences prompted him to obsess about ferreting out and destroying his political enemies, diverting precious attention away from pursuit of fulfillment of his domestic dream of a Great Society. Without intending to, he drove away some of the "best and brightest" in his administration, paralyzing much of his presidency. In the space of a few short years, he went from being one of the most beloved American presidents—re-elected to the presidency in 1964 by the then-largest popular mandate in U. S. history and compared in the press to Lincoln and Roosevelt—to one of its most reviled.

In a similar fashion, President Richard Nixon's conviction that he was the victim of a powerful political conspiracy caused him to engage in a reckless and ultimately self-destructive course of action as President. Because he believed he confronted ruthless opponents who would stop at nothing, he was able to justify a concerted program of massive wire-tapping, political sabotage, burglary, and other illegal covert acts—all of which were aimed at striking back and getting even with his presumed enemies. The scope of efforts at retaliation and retribution was massive: the National Archives and Records Administration alone has declassified over 204 hours of secretly recorded White House tapes devoted solely to "abuses of governmental power" by President Nixon and his aides (National Archives and Records Administration, 2001).

Despite their provocative nature and obvious importance, there has been surprisingly little systematic theory and research on the origins of leader conspiracy theories. How is it that experienced and often quite sophisticated leaders, often noted for their social perceptiveness and ability to pragmatically assess their political environments, fall prey to such seemingly extreme beliefs and irrational fears? Where do conspiracy theories come from? How do they develop, and what sustains them? A primary purpose of the present chapter is to examine these important questions in more detail.

INTENT AND SCOPE OF THE PRESENT ANALYSIS

The study of leader paranoia, it should be noted, has not been a completely neglected topic in the social science literature. Over the past few decades, there have been a number of attempts to trace the origins and dynamics of such paranoia. However, these past efforts have tended to adopt, almost without exception, a rather narrow psychobiographical approach (see Bullock, 1993; Robins & Post, 1997, for useful overviews of this literature).

From a psychobiographical perspective, a leader's paranoia is presumed to be a manifestation of underlying and pre-existing personality traits and dispositional tendencies. To explain a leader's vulnerability to conspiratorial cognition, for example, these accounts typically invoke various psychodynamic constructs of dubious explanatory value, and for which scant validating evidence can be convincingly marshaled. In this chapter, we attempt to take a different approach to conceptualizing the origins and dynamics of leader conspiracy theories. In particular, we argue that leader conspiracy theories can be viewed as complex social cognitions and cognitions that serve, from the perspective of the paranoid social perceiver, a number of useful functions. By viewing conspiracy theories as a form of social cognition, we propose, we can bring to bear a rather powerful and proven conceptual armamentarium from contemporary social cognitive theory and research on the problem of understanding the origins and dynamics of these rather peculiar cognitions.

To build a case for this general argument and approach, it is useful to begin first with the notion that conspiracy theories can be construed as complex social cognitions.

TRACING THE ORIGINS OF LEADER CONSPIRACY THEORIES: A BRIEF TOUR OF THE EXTANT LITERATURE

In order for social perceivers to develop and maintain a conspiracy theory, it is necessary for them to gather, interpret, and integrate a great deal of disparate, fragmentary, and often quite ambiguous bits of information in their social environment. In this respect, conspiracy theories can be construed as complex social cognitions that require, like other products of learning, acts of both information assimilation and accommodation (cf. March, 1995).

To make sense of these complex cognitions, it is useful to begin with a brief tour of some of the more prominent conceptions of distrust and suspicion encountered in the social cognition literature. Distrust has generally been conceptualized in the social sciences as an active cognitive state characterized by a specific constellation of negative expectations and beliefs regarding the lack of trustworthiness of other persons, groups, or institutions (Deutsch, 1958, 1973; Gambetta, 1988; Rotter, 1980). For example, Govier (1993) defined distrust in terms of the absence of "confidence in the other, a concern that the other may act so as to harm one, that he does not care about one's welfare or intends to act harmfully, or is hostile. When one distrusts, one is fearful and suspicious as to what the other might do" (p. 240). As Govier's definition suggests, suspicion constitutes one of the important components of distrust.

Fein (1996) defined such suspicion as a dynamic cognitive state in which a social perceiver "actively entertains multiple, plausibly rival, hypotheses about the motives or genuineness of a person's behavior" (p. 1165). As Fein and Hilton (1994) further noted, suspicion entails a "belief that the actor's behavior may reflect a motive that the actor wants hidden from the target of his or her behavior" (p. 169). Such beliefs have generally been viewed as largely history-dependent processes, insofar as they presumably derive from or reflect an individual's actual experiences with others (e.g., Deutsch, 1958; Lindskold, 1978, 1986; Pilisuk & Skolnick, 1968; Rotter, 1980). In other words, individuals learn to trust or distrust others in much the same way they learn other social beliefs (Hardin, 1992; Rotter, 1980). According to such models, individuals' distrust or suspicion of others "thickens" or "thins" as a function of their cumulative history of interaction with them.

In noting the formative role that actual experience plays in the emergence of distrust and suspicion, such models imply that individuals' judgments about another's trustworthiness or lack of it are anchored, at least in part, on their *a priori* expectations about the other's behavior and the extent to which subsequent experience affirms or discredits those expectations. Boyle and Bonacich's (1970) early and influential analysis of trust and distrust development in mixed-motive games is representative of such arguments. Individuals' expectations about trustworthy behavior, they proposed, tend to change "in the direction of experience and to a degree proportional to the difference between this experience and the initial expectations applied to it" (p. 130). Consistent with such arguments, numerous empirical studies have shown that interactions that reinforce individuals' expectations about other's trustworthiness increase trust, while interactions that violate those expectancies tend to undermine it (Lindskold, 1978; Pilisuk & Skolnick, 1968; Rotter, 1980).

In addition to implicating individuals' *a priori* expectations in judgments about a target's trustworthiness, other research has shown that the *a posteriori* attributions that individuals make about a target's behavior also influence such judgments (Kruglanski, 1970, 1987; Strickland, 1958).

Although recognizing that judgments about distrust and suspicion sometimes reflect this sort of careful and fairly rational attribution process, a number of researchers have noted that other variants of distrust and suspicion appear to be far less rational with respect to both their origins and their judgmental consequences (Barber, 1983; Deutsch, 1973; Luhmann, 1979). Deutsch (1973), for example, suggested it was useful to distinguish between pathological and nonpathological varieties of distrust. The essential feature of nonpathological or rational distrust, he proposed, "is that it is flexible and responsive to changing circumstances" (p. 170). Pathological forms of distrust are characterized, in contrast, by an "inflexible, rigid, unaltering tendency to act in a trusting or suspicious manner, irrespective of the situation or the consequences of so acting" (p. 171). The pathology of such irrational distrust, he went on to suggest, is reflected in "the indiscriminateness and incorrigibility of the behavioral tendency" it engenders (p. 171). These irrational forms of distrust and suspicion thus reflect exaggerated perceptual and attributional propensities, which can arise and may be sustained even in the absence of specific experiences that justify or warrant them.

Conspiracy theories can be regarded as perhaps the prototypic example of such extreme forms of irrational distrust and suspicion. As Robins and Post (1997) noted, among the hallmarks of such belief systems are suspicions "without sufficient basis, that others are exploiting, harming, or deceiving them, preoccupations with unjustified doubts about the loyalty, or trustworthiness, of friends or associates, and a reluctance to confide in others because of unwarranted fear that the information will be used maliciously against them" (p. 3). Along similar lines, Colby (1981) defined such perceptions in terms of "persecutory delusions and false beliefs whose propositional content clusters around ideas of being harassed, threatened, harmed, subjugated, persecuted, accused, mistreated, wronged, tormented, disparaged, vilified, and so on, by malevolent others, either specific individuals or groups" (p. 518).

As noted earlier, in their efforts to explain these rather peculiar, and in many respects quite striking belief systems, social scientists have turned most often to the clinical psychology literature, invoking psychodynamic constructs (Cameron, 1943; Colby, 1975; Siegel, 1994). Colby (1981), for example, posited that paranoid cognition was the end product of a "causal chain of strategies for dealing with distress induced by the affect of shame-humiliation" (p. 518). The strategy of blaming others for one's difficulties, he postulated, functions "to repudiate the belief that the self is to blame for an inadequacy" (p. 518). Such explanations presume that the primary causes of conspiracy perceptions are located "inside the head" of the social perceiver, rather than somehow connected to the social context within which such cognitions are embedded, and to which they might reflect some sort of attempted adaptation.

In sharp contrast to these clinical conceptions, recent social cognitive theory and research suggest a very different perspective on the nature of conspiracy theories—one, moreover, that affords considerably more attention to their social and situational origins (see Fenigstein & Vanable, 1992; Kramer, 1998; Zimbardo, Andersen, & Kabat, 1981). Research in this vein has taken two suggestive observations as starting points. The first observation is that, in milder forms, beliefs in conspiracy seem to be quite prevalent even among normal individuals. Findings from several recent survey studies provide support for such observations, suggesting that paranoid-like perceptions, including the perception that one has been the victim of a conspiracy involving a romance, friendship, school or work are far from uncommon (Goertzel, 1994). As Fenigstein and Vanable (1992) observed in this regard, it is not unusual for ordinary people "in their everyday behavior [to] manifest characteristics—such as self-centered thought, suspiciousness, assumptions of ill will or hostility, and even notions of conspiratorial intent—that are reminiscent of paranoia" (p. 130). There are many social occasions, they go on to note, where people may think they are "being talked about or feel as if everything is going against them, resulting in suspicion and mistrust of others, as though they were taking advantage of them or to blame for their difficulties" (p. 133).

Along similar lines, Siegel (1994) has pointed out that, "almost everyone has had a mild experience such as the vague suspicion that something is out there just waiting to get us. . . . Many people experience it when they are alone in the house at night or walk down an unfamiliar street. Others may have the vague feeling that their life paths are being jeopardized by jealous persons known and unknown" (p. 7).

The second observation pertains to the emergent and transient nature of these rather commonplace or "ordinary" variants of social paranoia. The results of numerous laboratory experiments and field studies have shown that paranoid cognitions arise from attempts by social perceivers to make sense of, and cope with, social situations they perceive as threatening. When those threats are adequately addressed or resolved, the paranoia diminishes. An important implication of such research is that these ordinary and more benign forms of paranoid cognition can be viewed as intendedly adaptive responses to disturbing situations rather than necessarily manifestations of disturbed individuals. They imply also that these social and organizational variants of paranoid cognition can be construed as forms of misperception and misjudgment characterized by *misplaced* or *exaggerated,* rather than necessarily false or delusional, distrust and suspicion of other actors in one's social or organizational environment. In this regard, conspiracy theories can be viewed, like many biases and illusions, as cognitive distortions that are nonetheless anchored or grounded to some degree in reality (i.e., have some correspondence to what is true). In this sense, they contain at least a kernel of veridicality. This insight suggests the usefulness of approaching the task of understanding conspiracy theories from the standpoint of a more general framework for thinking about how leaders make sense of, or test, reality—in much the same way that other social perceivers attempt to make sense of, and test the reality of, their understandings of the social world. In the next section, accordingly, we present a simple normative model of the leader as vigilant political auditor.

THE INTUITIVE POLITICAL AUDITOR MODEL: A STARTING POINT FOR THE FUNCTIONAL ANALYSIS OF LEADER PARANOIA

As noted in the introduction to this chapter, our analysis takes as a point of departure the presumption that conspiracy theories can be construed as complex forms of social cognition that are the end product of an intendedly adaptive sensemaking or coping process. They begin to form, much like the vortex of a tornado, when a confluence of conditions set into play a swirling pattern of cascading cognition. A better feel for this basic argument comes from consideration of a simple thought experiment. The experiment was inspired by Burt's (1992) provocative meditation regarding what he termed the "atavistic driver" experiment (p. 4). He asks us to imagine,

> You're on the freeway. There is a car ahead of you going 65. Pull up so your front wheels are parallel to his. Stay there. This won't take long. If he speeds up, speed up. If he slows down, slow down. You feel the tension, which you know is also building in the near car. He looks over. Is this a threat? . . . For a moment when you stood in common time and place, you were competitors. Break the parallelism and the competition is gone." (p. 4)

If we revise Burt's thought experiment slightly, we can see how readily paranoia can arise when events occur that threaten our security. Imagine that you are the innocent driver, alone very late at night on a darkened and isolated stretch of freeway, heading home. Your thoughts roam over the meeting you've just left in the city and the anticipation of a quiet evening reading with a glass of wine in hand. In your rear-view mirror, you spy the headlights from a single car far in the distance. You don't pay much attention to it, other than noting the apparent speed with which the headlights are catching up to you. The car rushes toward you, its headlights drawing nearer and nearer, and you expect any moment the car to change lanes and pass around you as it rushes on its way. However, as the car reaches your bumper, it hangs there—much too close for comfort. It's headlights flash at you to move over. Although irritated, you do so, expecting the car to rudely be on its way. But the car swerves over sharply to the lane you now occupy, so once again the car is directly behind you. You begin to get nervous, as a cascading chain of cognitions race through your head: Is someone following me? If so, why? Did I cut someone off at the last exit? Is this road rage? You move over yet again to the slowest lane, hoping it is just coincidence and that the other car will be on its way. To your relief, it does not pull into the lane behind you, but starts to pass—until it is side by side with you. And now it lingers, matching your speed perfectly. Your sense of fear increases again. You slow down, the other car slows down with you. You speed up and the other car does so. You try to look over at the other car, trying to be unobtrusive. The windows are dark. You see the vague outline of a face—is it turned toward you? You can't be sure. As this thought experiment makes evident, it is the perception of threat, coupled with uncertainty about its nature and severity, that animates the sensemaking predicament for the individual who feels in danger and in search of an effective response to it.

In a metaphorical sense, leaders in highly competitive and potentially perilous political environments continually find themselves "cheek and jowl" with others vying for their position—challenging their power, threatening their prestige, or challenging their credibility. Consequently, leaders often find themselves, figuratively speaking, looking over their shoulders at those they worry may be trying to challenge their power or take their place. In a threat perception game like this, there can be several possible outcomes (simplified here in terms of binary states of affairs). One can be too paranoid or not paranoid enough.

In response to such pressures, leaders can be viewed as vigilant social and political "auditors" who proactively and vigilantly monitor their environments for signs of emerging threat and opportunity. According to this auditor model, when threats occur that are perceived as threatening to their power or security as leaders, they are presumed to attend closely to those events and engage in attempts to pre-empt the threat or minimize its damage. They monitor the consequences of those actions. When perceived as successful, their attention may be claimed by other emergent concerns.

With this initial normative framework as a starting point, we elaborate now on how the cognitions of this intendedly rational and adaptive social perceiver might drift from vigilant and mindful appraisal of the political environment towards a paranoid misperception of it.

PERSISTENT THREATENING SCRUTINY AS A "TRIGGER" OF CONSPIRATORIAL HYPERVIGILANCE AND RUMINATION

All social, organizational, and political leaders think and act under the continual scrutiny of multiple audiences and constituencies to whom they feel accountable. As Pfeffer (1992) once observed, "To be in power is to be watched more closely, and this surveillance affords one the luxury of few mistakes" (p. 302).

Over the past several decades, an impressive body of theory and empirical evidence has accumulated regarding the effects of perceived accountability (Tetlock, 1992), surveillance (Strickland, 1958), social scrutiny (Fenigstein, 1984) and organizational scrutiny (Sutton & Galunic, 1996) on individual judgment and decision making. One conclusion emerging from this research is that intense and chronic scrutiny can prompt a dysphoric state of heightened self-consciousness (e.g., Fenigstein, 1984; Zimbardo et al., 1981). Such threatening scrutiny absorbs attention, interrupts pursuit of valued goals, and arouses strong negative emotions as decision makers find themselves forced to turn away from desired goals and address increasingly unpleasant and persistent identity-threatening predicaments.

In a thoughtful review of this evidence, Sutton and Galunic (1996) characterized such scrutiny as an "intensive and obtrusive form of attention from others" (p. 203). It encompasses, they go on to elaborate, "persistent attention to the leader or his or her organization, close and persistent performance monitoring and evaluation, frequent interruptions, and relentless questions about events that have occurred, are occurring, and will occur, along with requests that the reasons for such actions be explained" (p. 203).

In trying to understand how individuals respond to such scrutiny, our normative model predicts that leaders will begin to engage in vigilant appraisal of the situation and mindful reflection regarding its causes and possible remedies. Consistent with this image, a considerable body of empirical research on the coping and appraisal process has shown that when individuals encounter situations that are perceived as socially threatening or that evoke concerns about danger, they are likely to engage in proactive, energetic sensemaking (Clark, 1996; Janoff-Bulman, 1992; Lazarus & Folkman, 1984). For example, studies have shown that the perception of a social threat can induce vigilant appraisal of their actions, in an attempt to discern their presumably hidden intentions and motives. Experiments by Fein and his associates (Fein, 1996; Fein & Hilton, 1994; Hilton, Fein, & Miller, 1993) have shown, along these lines, that induced suspicion often triggers a fairly sophisticated analysis of others' intentions and motives—an analysis "characterized by active, careful consideration of the potential motives and causes that may influence [their] behaviors" (Fein, 1996, p. 1167).

When threats resist resolution and become chronic, however, individuals may begin to engage in a hypervigilant mode of social information processing (Janis, 1983, 1989; Janis & Mann, 1977). This hypervigilant appraisal leads to the over-interpretation or weighting of ambiguous information.

In addition to hypervigilant appraisal, a second form of dysfunctional cognition in response to chronic threats that can get leaders in trouble reflects the transition from constructive rumination regarding their troubles to a more destructive form of dysphoric rumination. From the standpoint of effective political cognition, rumination is a complex judgmental process. In the context of dealing effectively with day-to-day, difficult political predicaments, leaders' willingness to devote attentional resources to ruminating about events may greatly enhance the likelihood they will detect important causal linkages among the various elements in their predicament, hastening discovery of a solution. Thus, constructive or mindful thinking are hallmarks of the adaptive or mindful decision maker, and presumably contribute to the development of more cognitively complex views of a situation (Clark, 1996; Langer, 1989).

This sort of mindful and constructive deliberation can be contrasted with more superficial heuristic modes of information processing that are designed to economize on consumption of a decision makers' limited attentional resources and expedite sensemaking. In acute sensemaking predicaments, where the costs of misguided action may be catastrophic to a leader, more effortful and mindful modes of information processing may be enormously useful. Thus, precisely *because* leaders are so willing to allocate cognitive resources to sensemaking tasks, they might be more likely to detect early, and formulate response to, threats that others underestimate or overlook.

As with the line between adaptive vigilance and hypervigilance, there is a fine line between constructive, mindful reflection on one's difficulties and dysfunctional rumination about them. Along these lines, recent research on the cognitive consequences of rumination support several conclusions (see Janoff-Bulman, 1992; Kramer, Meyerson, & Davis, 1990; Lyubomirsky & Nolen-Hoeksema, 1993; Pyszczynski & Greenberg, 1987; Wilson & Kraft, 1993; Wyer, 1996). First, rumination following threatening or aversive events tends to increase negative thinking about those events and contributes to a pessimistic explanatory style. Second, rumination in contexts where trust concerns loom large can increase distrust and suspicion, even holding information about the target's behavior constant.

There is also evidence that rumination can increase individuals' confidence in their interpretation of events, even though those judgments might be in error (Wilson & Kraft, 1993). This finding might seem especially surprising because one could easily argue on *prima facie* grounds for just the opposite prediction (viz., that the more individuals ruminate about others' behavior, the more likely they would be to generate a large number of alternative interpretations of that behavior, leading to decreased confidence in any one interpretation). Greater mindfulness, according to this argument, should lead to better inferences. However, as Wilson and Kraft (1993) perceptively noted, "Because it is often difficult to get at the exact roots of [many] feelings, repeated introspections may not result in better access to the actual causes. Instead, people may *repeatedly focus on reasons that are plausible* and easy to verbalize" (p. 410, emphasis added). Such results suggest the operation of an interesting "cognitive effort heuristic" (i.e., "Since I've thought so much about this, it must be true"). This sort of misplaced confidence, of course, is intimately associated with paranoid modes of perception.

Hypervigilance and dysphoric rumination are theorized to contribute to several cognitive processes that facilitate the development of full-blown conspiracy theories. The first cognitive process is the *overly personalistic construal of others' actions,* which refers to decision makers' tendencies to overinterpret others' behavior in self-referential terms. This tendency is, of course, one of the hallmarks of the conspiratorial mindset. As Colby (1981) observed, "Around the central core of persecutory delusions [that preoccupy the paranoid perceiver] there exists a number of attendant properties such as suspiciousness, hypersensivity, hostility, fearfulness, and self-reference that lead such individuals to interpret events that have noth-ing to do with them as bearing on them personally" (p. 518).

In a series of clever experiments, Fenigstein (1984) provided some use-ful insights into the social and situational origins of this form of misper-ception. His basic hypothesis was that self-consciousness is a primary cause of the extent to which individuals construe others' behavior in self-referential terms (i.e., as intentionally focused on or directed towards them). In an initial study of this *overperception of self-as-target bias,* he investigated perceptions by undergraduate students that they were the "targets" of a professor's remarks. Prior to returning a set of blue book exams, the professor delivered carefully scripted remarks to two different classes about their midterm exams. In one class (the "bad exam" condi-tion), the professor derogated the exam performance of one unspecified student, suggesting it was one of the worst exams he had ever come across. In another condition (the "good exam" condition), he lavished praise on one of the exams, citing its erudition and brilliance. After providing this feedback, students in one condition (the self-as-target condition) were asked to indicate the probability (from 0% to 100%) that the exam to which the professor had alluded was theirs. Students in the second experimental condition (the other-as-target condition) were asked to indicate whether the exam belonged to the person seated to their left.

The results of this study were striking. Fenigstein found a main effect for the target manipulation, such that students were more likely to believe the exam belonged to them than to the classmate. Planned comparisons further revealed that the overperception of self-as-target bias was par-ticularly pronounced with respect to the bad exam condition. From the standpoint of the present chapter, this last result is particularly noteworthy because it suggests the especial salience of information that has negative evaluative implications for the self.

In a subsequent set of studies, Fenigstein and Vanable (1992) showed that individuals high in public self-consciousness were also more likely than individuals low in public self-consciousness to feel they were being observed in an experimental setting involving a two-way mirror. They fur-ther demonstrated that dispositional public self-consciousness was strongly correlated with responses to a newly developed instrument for measuring paranoid cognition, and that individuals who scored high on the paranoid cognition scale were more likely to feel they were being observed in the two-way mirror situation than those who scored low.

The results of these studies provide strong evidence that self-conscious-ness contributes to the overly personalistic construal of social interactions.

They also suggest that one of the consequences of such self-consciousness is that it activates "spontaneous" attributional search (Weiner, 1985). In other words, self-consciousness acts as a cue that stimulates sensemaking processes: when individuals become self-conscious, they look for reasons why they are self-conscious. If one is self-conscious, then someone must be watching. And if someone is watching, then something might be amiss.

A second cognitive process that can result from hypervigilant and ruminative social information processing is the biased punctuation of political interactions. The term *biased punctuation* refers to a tendency for individuals to construe the causal structure of events in which they are involved in idiosyncratic and often self-serving terms. For example, because of biased punctuation, a leader, *L*, is likely to construe the course of a conflictual interaction with a perceived adversary in his or her environment, *A*, as a sequence *A-L, A-L, A-L* in which the initial hostile or aggressive move was made by the adversary. However, the adversary is likely to punctuate the same history of interaction as *L-A, L-A, L-A*, in which the roles of aggressor and victim are reversed. At the heart of this bias, then, is a divergence between actors with respect to their basic causal construction of the same episode. Research suggests further that biased punctuation of interactions contribute to the development of what Deutsch (1986) characterized as "malignant spirals" of mutual distrust and suspicion, leading to escalating friction and annoyance (Deutsch, 1986; Kahn & Kramer, 1990; Lindskold, 1978; Mikolic, Parker, & Pruitt, 1997; Pruitt, 1987; Zimbardo et al., 1981).

This bias appears to be quite robust and has been attributed to several cognitive mechanisms. For example, research has shown that when individuals view ongoing social events, they typically do not perceive them as continuous events, as if there were a stream of consciousness. Instead, they tend to perceive social interactions in terms of discrete episodes or "punctuated" sequences comprised of discrete or discriminable "chunks" of causally interdependent activity (see, e.g., Forgas, 1982; Swann, Pelham, & Roberts, 1987; Watzlawick, Beavin, & Jackson, 1967). There is evidence that biased punctuation can be influenced by both cognitive and motivational processes that affect the differential availability of "on-line" cognitions and retrieval from memory (Gilovich, 1991; Kunda, 1987).

A third bias driven by hypervigilant and ruminative information processing is the *sinister attribution bias*. This term refers to the tendency for social perceivers to to be inappropriately suspicious of other's motives and intentions on the basis of ambiguous evidence and to overattribute lack of trustworthiness to them. In contrast to the sort of vigilant and careful consideration of the motives and causes influencing other people, the sinister attribution bias reflects a tendency to go beyond what the data warrant. Kramer (1994) has demonstrated that situational factors that increase uncertainty about others' behavior, coupled with higher self-consciousness and rumination, contribute to this tendency.

As noted earlier, conspiracy theories can be construed as complex social cognitions in the sense that a multitude of diverse fragments of evidence—often incomplete and ambiguous, and usually dispersed over time and across strategic actors and settings in one's political environment—are woven together into a tapestry of plausible—and from the perspective of the paranoid perceiver, *compelling*—doubt. It is when all of the individual cues that seem to legitimate the leader's growing distrust and suspicion begin to fall together into one coherent, seemingly well-organized cognitive structure that something resembling a full-blown "theory" emerges in the paranoid leader's mind.

Exaggerated perceptions of conspiracy thus entail the *overperception* of temporal and social linkages. In an insightful discussion of this process, Baumeister (1991) noted that the development of meaning is a "matter of associations—of connecting things up into broad patterns" (p. 304). He went on to observe,

> If the only broad pattern is happy and optimistic, then isolated contradictory events can be dismissed as minor problems and annoyances. Each problem seems minor and trivial in comparison with the totality of positive aspects. The crucial step occurs, however, when these contradictory events link together to form a larger pattern of negative, dissonant thought. (p. 304)

One of the more impressive features of conspiracy theories is their perceived explanatory power and their striking resilience to disconfirmation. Such theories have an impressive plasticity with respect to the accommodation of new information and assimilation of an impressive variety of bits of data and observational "odds and ends" that come the leader's way. Such theories explain everything, assimilating all evidence, no matter how seemingly discrepant from or at odds with the theory. In this respect, such theories enjoy both explanatory power and resilience to disconfirmation. From the possessor's standpoint, at least, such theories have high internal and external validity. As Shapiro (1965) perceptively noted along these lines, the heightened vigilance and rumination of the paranoid perceiver often produces a kind of social keenness that enables them to make "brilliantly perceptive mistakes" (p. 60)—brilliantly perceptive because they tie together so much evidence that others fail to discern; mistakes because they are nonetheless fundamentally wrong. It resembles social intelligence, but a form of social intelligence gone awry.

PROCESSES THAT SUSTAIN LEADER CONSPIRACY THEORIES: HOW THE KERNEL OF DOUBT GROWS

Up to this point, we have elaborated only on the cognitive engines driving the development of a conspiracy theory. We turn now to examining some of the processes that contribute to the resilience of leader conspiracy theories. The question of the mechanisms that support the maintenance of conspiracy theories merits attention because, all else equal, it might seem as if beliefs in conspiracy theories would be rather difficult for a leader to sustain. After all, there is a wealth of empirical evidence from behavioral decision theory and social learning theory that would lead one to conclude that decision makers update and correct their judgments in response to feedback that their judgments are in error. From the perspective of such research, even if we can understand the initial evidence or circumstances that give rise to a belief in conspiracy, we might expect such perceptual tendencies to be self-correcting over time. For example, as leaders acquire evidence that their fears and suspicions about other actors in their environment turn out to be exaggerated or groundless, those fears and suspicions should diminish over time. Yet, contrary to this expectation, one of the most compelling features of the belief in conspiracy is its striking tenacity and resilience. For the person who entertains such beliefs, conspiracy theories enjoy what Pruitt (1987) has aptly characterized as a "flinty persistence," enduring and thriving despite not only the absence of compelling evidence, but sometimes even in the presence of considerable countervailing evidence.

The resilience of such misperceptions invites consideration of some of the psychological, social, and organizational dynamics that help sustain them. How can we explain the flinty persistence of conspiracy perceptions within organizational or institutional contexts? In answer to this question, there are a number of cognitive, behavioral, and social dynamics that contribute to the resilience of a leader's conspiracy perceptions. These can be organized in terms of the difficulty the paranoid leader encounters when trying to generate useful learning opportunities and extracting useful inferences and lessons from those experiences.

As with other forms of learning, learning who can be trusted and who should be distrusted requires amassing relevant evidence about others' trustworthiness, and drawing sensible inferences from that accumulated evidence. For example, in order to learn how trustworthy others are, leaders must be willing to undertake risky experiments and then oberve the consequences of those experiments (see Hardin, 1992, for a particularly lucid and extended analysis of this issue). Leaders must engage in such experiments if they are to generate the sort of social feedback that produces diagnostic data necessary to learn who among them can be trusted and how much. Such experiments require that individuals expose themselves to both the prospect of misplaced trust and misplaced distrust on occasion. Any systematic bias in the generation of data samples, obviously, can dramatically influence the sort of inferences that result from these experiments, pushing individuals in wrong directions (toward inappropriately high trust or toward having too little trust).

As Hardin (1992) and Gambetta (1988) have perceptively noted, however, differences in one's level of presumptive trust or distrust can differentially impact the frequency with which individuals generate useful learning opportunities. In elaborating on this idea, Gambetta (1988) noted that distrust is very difficult to invalidate through experience, because it "prevents people from engaging in the appropriate kind of social experiment" (p. 234). Moreover, he argues, distrust "leads to behavior which bolsters the validity of distrust itself" (p. 234). As a consequence, presumptive distrust tends to become perpetual distrust.

Because of their heightened suspicion of others' motives and intentions, paranoid leaders tend to approach their interactions with an orientation of presumptive distrust. They are already prepared to expect the worst from their encounters. An instructive parallel can be drawn from research on the dynamics of hostile attribution among aggressive children (see Dodge, 1980, 1982, 1985). Such children, Dodge found, enter into their social interactions already "pre-offended" and prepared for aggression. They then elicit, through their own defensive and pre-emptive behaviors, the very outcomes they most dread from others (viz., hostility and rejection). He found, for example, that such children were likely to interpret an accidental bump in a cafeteria line as a deliberate shove. In much the same way, the paranoid leader in an organizational setting is prone to code even ambiguous encounters as further evidence of tainted trustworthiness. Just like the aggressive child's behavioral defenses, the paranoid perceiver's behavior, grounded as it is in presumptive wariness, ends up eliciting the very sort of uncomfortable, distant interactions that reinforce future mutual wariness, suspicion and discomfort. Thus, a dubious set of assumptions serves as a ground for justifying and prompting an equally questionable set of social strategies for dealing with others.

This argument receives experimental support from experimental and field studies on the sinister attribution error (Kramer, 1994) and, by analogy, from experiments by Kelley and Stahelski (1970a, 1970b, 1970c) that examined the differential difficulties that competitors and cooperators have when trying to learn about the cooperativeness and competitiveness of other people. Because competitors expect competition from others, they engage in defensively competitive behavior that, ironically, ends up eliciting the very behavior they expected. Even cooperatively oriented individuals become more competitive when interacting with competitive people. Thus, competitive people tend to overestimate the base rate of competitiveness in their population. In contrast, cooperative people, because of their willingness to initiate cooperative exchanges, have a more mixed experience, encountering some competition, but enjoying considerable cooperation as well. As a consequence, they more accurately discern that there are some people in their environment who will cooperate and some who will not.

Along similar lines, Gilovich (1991) has elaborated on how beliefs in ineffective influence strategies can develop and maintain themselves. Because a given strategy is initially thought to be effective, he notes, only that strategy is likely to be employed when individuals encounter similar-seeming situations. As a consequence, a person never learns what would have happened had a different approach to the situation been taken. Thus, the individual can not (or, more accurately, simply does not) assess the true effectiveness of their orientation or strategy. As Gilovich put it, "Because no single failure serves to disconfirm the strategy's effectiveness (after all, nothing works all the time), the only way it can be shown to be ineffective is by discovering that the rate of success is lower with this strategy than with others" (1991, p. 153). Given that the alternative strategies are not employed or systematically evaluated, however, the person never discovers that the strategy used is actually suboptimal, and that the theory behind it is simply wrong.

This pattern of dysfunctional social interaction can be aided and abetted, Gilovich goes on to note, by a self-fulfilling prophecy. Like someone who believes that the only way to get ahead is to be competitive or come on strong when dealing with other people, such a person will consistently push too aggressively for what he or she wants. The occasional success will "prove" the wisdom of the rule, and the individual never can learn, as a result, that an alternative strategy might have been even more effective and, importantly, also that the model of self, others, and the world on which the rule is predicated is in error. As Kelley and Schmidt (1989) noted in their analysis of their dynamics of overly aggressive boys, "with their apparent belief that persistence in coercion finally works, aggressive boys are likely to develop sustained exchanges of aggression" (p. 256).

An instructive parallel can be drawn, in this regard, with the experience of freeway drivers who drive much faster than other drivers in their environment. From the standpoint of these fast, time-urgent drivers, the everyday experience on a freeway is one of persistent annoyance and escalating hostility, as everyone else on the freeway seems always to be driving too slowly and to be in one's way. The world of the fast driver is a world populated by overly cautious, plodding people who constantly frustrate one in pursuit of reaching one's destination.

Note, however, that it is the simple fact that the fast driver remains "out of sync" with the rest of his or her social world that leads to self-generated and self-sustaining theories about others' basic stupidity, incompetence, and hostility. The theory can even be fairly complex about "why" other people are the way *they* are. Unfortunately, freeway driving also provides all too much time for isolated, dysphoric rumination about such people. To the extent people surround themselves (and drive with) people like themselves, there is the added confirmation of one's views from one's passengers.

Such individuals are probably even more oblivious to the possibility that their own fast, aggressive driving provokes slower, more careful behavior from other drivers around them. The common positive illusion that one is a better than average driver insulates one further from any suspicion that it is one's own location in a system of moving objects that generates the experience. It is easy in such situations for social actors to underestimate the extent to which their behaviors create opportunities or constraints on others' actions. Moreover, they may even generate with higher than chance levels the likelihood that others will be in their way—as others around them, seeing the rapidly approaching car in their rear view mirror, may defensively change lanes *just at the moment* that the fast driver has started to sweep around them on the assumption that they will continue to meander along in the fast lane when they should have obviously moved out of the way.

In addition to having problems generating diagnostic experiences, organizational leaders who operate from a stance of presumptive suspicion and wariness may also have trouble learning from the feedback that they do manage to generate about others. Because of their presumption that things around them may not be what they seem (i.e., can't be fully trusted), the perceived diagnostic value of any particular social cue is, from the paranoid leader's perspective, seriously tainted. As Weick (1979) noted in this regard, all social cues are corrupted and corrupted in a predictable direction. He cites, as an illustration of this inherent corruptibility of cues, an interesting historical example. The day before the Japanese attack on Pearl Harbor, an American naval attaché had informed Washington that he did not believe a surprise attack by the Japanese was imminent. To justify his prediction, he cited the "fact" that the Japanese fleet was still stationed at its home base. The clear and compelling evidence for this conclusion, he noted, was that large crowds of sailors could be observed casually strolling the streets of Tokyo. Without sailors, the fleet obviously could not sail. If sailors were in town, so was the fleet.

What the attaché did not know—and, more importantly, failed to even guess—was that these "sailors" were in actuality Japanese soldiers disguised as sailors. They had been ordered to pose as sailors and to happily and boisteriously stroll the streets in a carefree manner in order to conceal the fact that the Japanese fleet had, in fact, already sailed and was currently steaming towards Pearl Harbor. From the perspective of the Japanese, of course, this ploy was a brilliant example of strategic deception.

In elaborating on the implications of this incident, Weick noted that the very fact that the attaché had searched for a "foolproof" cue about Japanese intentions and actions made him, ironically, more vulnerable to manipulation about the nature of those intentions. Quoting a passage from Goffman (1969), Weick reasoned that

> the very fact that the observer finds himself looking to a particular bit of evidence as an incorruptible check on what is or might be corruptible, is the very reason he should be suspicious of this evidence; for the best evidence for him is also the best evidence for the [deceiver] to tamper with . . . when the situation seems to be exactly what it appears to be, the closest likely alternative is that the situation has been completely faked. (pp. 172–173)

From the perspective of the paranoid social perceiver, the attaché's experience dramatically illustrates what happens when individuals allow their social vigilance to become too lax. Naive innocence regarding others can be too readily assumed—and with deadly consequences. In a world presumed to be sinister, such cues are always corrupted and always in a predictably dangerous direction. Figuratively speaking, sailors are never just sailors and the fleet has always stealthily sailed away when one wasn't looking. Johnson provided an amusing instance of this when his teleprompter failed right before a major speech about Vietnam: "You better check the Teleprompters. They went wild on us last night," Johnson instructed aide George Reedy. When Reedy informed Johnson it was simply a short-circuit he replied, ". . . I thought that it was almost sabotage, George" (cited in Beschloss, 1997, p. 361).

Moreover, from the standpoint of the committed conspiracy theorist, even the nonexistence of evidence can become a powerful form of confirmatory evidence. Dawes (1988) has provided a nice illustration of this possibility in his discussion of the debate over the internment of Japanese Americans at the beginning of the Second World War. The question, of course, was the safety of American society given the presence of many hundreds of Japanese Americans in its midst in the middle of a war. Where would their loyalties lie? Could they be trusted?

When the late Supreme Court Chief Justice Earl Warren (then Governor of California) testified before a congressional hearing regarding this policy, one of his interrogators noted that absolutely no evidence of espionage or sabotage on the part of any Japanese Americans had been presented or was available to the committee. Thus, there was no objective evidence of danger at all. Warren's response as to how to construe this fact is revealing:

> I take the view that this lack [of evidence] is the most ominous sign in our whole situation. It convinces me more than perhaps any other factor that the sabotage we are to get, the Fifth Column activities we are to get, are timed just like Pearl Harbor was timed. . . . I believe we are just being lulled into a false sense of security (p. 251).

Recent research on trust suggests other cognitive "toeholds" for the development of paranoid social cognition. Numerous scholars have noted that it is easier to destroy trust than to create or sustain it (Barber, 1983; Janoff-Bulman, 1992; Slovic, 1993). To explain this "fragility" of trust, Slovic (1993) has argued that there are a variety of cognitive factors that contribute to asymmetries in the trust-building versus trust-destroying process. First, negative (trust-destroying) events are more visible and noticeable than positive (trust-building) events. Second, trust-destroying events carry more weight in judgment than trust-building events of comparable magnitude. As evidence for this *asymmetry principle,* Slovic evaluated the impact of hypothetical news events on people's trust judgments. Consistent with this argument, he found that negative events had more impact on trust judgments than positive ones. Slovic noted further that asymmetries between trust and distrust may be reinforced by the fact that sources of bad (trust-destroying) news tend to be perceived as more credible than sources of good news.

Along similar lines, other evidence suggest that violations of trust tend to "loom larger" than confirmations of trust. For example, studies of individuals' reactions to trust betrayals suggests that violations of trust are highly salient to victims, prompting intense ruminative activity, and evoking greater attributional search for the causes of the violation (Bies, Tripp, & Kramer, 1996; Janoff-Bulman, 1992). To the extent that violations of trust are coded as losses, they should loom larger than "mere" confirmations of trust of comparable magnitude. Thus, failure to keep a promise should have more impact on judgments about trustworthiness than "merely" keeping a promise. This general argument is supported as well by evidence that cognitive responses to positive and negative events are often highly asymmetrical (Peeters & Czapinski, 1990; Taylor, 1991). As Taylor (1991) noted, "negative events produce more causal attribution activity than positive events, controlling for expectedness" (p. 70).

In aggregate, such asymmetries imply that information supportive of one's distrust and suspicion should be weighted and evaluated differently than information of the same magnitude that is supportive of trust. For the paranoid social perceiver, it should be emphasized, such asymmetries are likely to be even more salient and pronounced because of the perceptual readiness to detect bad (trust-destroying) versus good (trust-affirming) evidence.

BETTER SAFE THAN SORRY: TOWARD A POSITIVE THEORY OF DOUBT: LEADER PARANOIA AS ADAPTIVE COGNITION

A primary aim of this chapter has been to further our understanding of the origins and dynamics of leader conspiracy theories. One of the central assumptions of the chapter is that we can view conspiracy beliefs, much like other forms of social cognitive error, as arising from ordinary social information processing strategies—intended as adaptive coping processes—that lead social perceivers astray. To advance this argument, the analysis per force emphasized the deleterious judgmental and behavioral consequences of leader paranoia. The paranoid perceiver has been portrayed largely as a social misperceiver who exaggerates others' hostility and who overreacts to others' behaviors. In certain respects, this emphasis is appropriate. After all, to the extent that paranoid cognitions contribute to misperception and self-defeating behavior in organizations, they are obviously maladaptive. However, it is important to put this construal in more balanced perspective, and to consider the possible adaptive roles such cognitions play in organizational life.

A few comments are in order first regarding some of the epistemological biases or stances taken toward the phenomena. Obviously, many of the labels employed in this chapter, such as "paranoid social cognition" and "overly personalistic construal," may be viewed by some readers as excessively perjorative and somewhat loaded. In effect, they seem to blame the victim insofar as they imply that there is something amiss inside the head of the social perceiver, rather than something flowing from the social circumstances in which they happen to find themselves. For example, characterizing the cognitive processes of leaders experiencing high levels of social scrutiny as simply "paranoid" might seem to minimize the legitimacy of their concerns, deflecting attention from the situational origins of their cognitive plight. Much like the clinical conceptions eschewed at the outset of this chapter, the label suggests a kind of conceptual "fundamental attribution error" by ignoring the role situational factors plays in eliciting and giving shape to such cognitions. This is far from the intent of the analysis, however. Rather, the spirit of this inquiry has been to suggest how one's structural "location" within an organization—especially the view from the top—can influence the focus, direction and intensity of social information processing. The research took as a point of departure the presumption that what is seen depends in no small measure on where one is standing in a social system. Thus, certain structural positions within any organization—and the informationally relevant properties correlated with them—may be likely to promote patterns of misconstrual and misattribution more readily than other locations in social systems.

Along similar lines, terms such as "sinister attribution error" and "exaggerated perception of conspiracy" might be regarded as casting unwarranted aspersions on the cognitive competence of the hapless social perceiver by implying a flawed process of judgment and inference. In defense of such labels, we would argue that, in so far as the results of the studies described here document that psychological processes such as heightened self-consciousness and dysphoric rumination lead to systematic distortions in the causal attribution process, terms such as error and *bias* seem quite appropriate. The usage of the term error or bias, in fact, is congruent with social psychological tradition with respect to other attributional errors, such as the fundamental attribution error and the ultimate attribution error (Hewstone, 1992; Pettigrew, 1979). A better understanding of the social and situational origins of such errors is a critical first step in developing better theory about how to avoid them.

In making this point, however, it is crucial not to misconstrue such cognitive errors, especially when made by leaders, as judgmental errors in a broader, more existential sense. As Fiske (1993) has noted, much of our social cognitive apparati are designed to help us make sense of ourselves and other people as we navigate through the various situations we encounter in life. Social cogitation is, in short, an intendedly adaptive and constructive process. As many of the situations described in this chapter illustrate, the potential costs associated with misplaced trust may be quite substantial and even, in some instances, outweigh the costs associated with misplaced distrust. For example, in highly competitive or political organizations, where an individual's ability to survive may require constant monitoring of their own and others' behavior, a propensity towards vigilance with respect to detecting others' lack of trustworthiness may be quite prudent and adaptive. In such environments, it may be far better to be safe than sorry.

Such arguments prompt consideration of other potentially adaptive functions that conspiracy beliefs may play in a leader's life. There are several ways in which the cognitive processes associated with a propensity to think in conspiratorial terms (e.g., heightened vigilance and rumination) may have adaptive consequences. As noted previously, distrust in others is not always irrational. Even though a leader's fears and suspicions may sometimes be exaggerated, this doesn't mean that such distrust and suspicion are necessarily without foundation or fundamentally misplaced. In highly political organizations, an individual may have quite legitimate cause for suspicion and concern. As Frank (1987) noted, "In their rise to power, leaders are almost certain to encounter superiors who wish to hold them back, rivals who seek to displace them, and subordinates seeking to curry favor" (p. 339). When viewed from this perspective, psychological states such as vigilance and rumination may be quite useful. For example, vigilant appraisal and mindfulness—which might be construed as the "normal range" variants of hypervigilance and rumination—are enormously important cognitive orientations that help individuals make sense of the social situations they are in and help them determine appropriate forms of behavior in those situations (Janis, 1989; Langer, 1989).

In a similar way, leaders' paranoia can function to help them maintain their motivation to detect emerging threats more quickly and to develop strategies for overcoming them, even if those dangers and obstacles seem—from the perspective of less vulnerable observers—to be exaggerated or false. Increased vigilance of others' behavior and the propensity to ruminate about their motives may be quite functional in such environments. As Goodwin (1988) noted, people in highly political and competitive environments often do have very real adversaries. Thus, the predisposition to view others "as a potential source of opposition or even danger" can help them remain "on the alert—observing and listening—to discern the hidden intentions of others, thus sharpening skills that can give them a remarkable intuitive undertanding of others—their concealed ambitions, weaknesses, greeds, and lusts" (p. 398).

In such environments, the cost of misplaced trust may be substantial. Thus, even though the fears and suspicions of paranoid individuals may seem exaggerated or inappropriate to others, this does not mean that their distrust is entirely misplaced or unwarranted.

When in doubt, it may be best to err on the side of caution, to be safe than sorry. As Intel President and CEO Andrew Grove frequently likes to say, "Only the paranoid survive" (p. 3). In elaborating on what he means by this maxim, Grove adds,

> The things I tend to be paranoid about vary. I worry about products getting screwed up, and I worry about products getting introduced prematurely. I worry about factories not performing well, and I worry about having too many factories. I worry about hiring the right people, and I worry about morale slacking off. And, of course, I worry about competitors. I worry about other people figuring out how to do what we do better or cheaper, and displacing us with our customers. (p. 3)

It is, in short, a healthy or adaptive paranoia he tries to maintain in himself and instill in his employees:

> When it comes to business, I believe in the value of paranoia. Business success contains the seeds of its own destruction. The more successful you are, the more people want a chunk of your business and then another chunk and then another until there is nothing left. I believe that the prime responsibility of a manager is to guard against other people's attacks and to inculcate this guardian attitude in the people under his or her management. (p. 3)

Thus, those in positions of power may intuit better than more trusting observers that prudence and caution are better than regret. Relatedly, the increased vigilance of others' behavior and the propensity to ruminate about their motives may be quite functional in such environments. As Goodwin (1988) noted in his discussion of Lyndon Johnson's paranoia, presidents have very real adversaries. Thus, the predisposition to view others "as a potential source of opposition or even danger" can help them remain "on the alert—observing and listening—to discern the hidden intentions of others, thus sharpening skills that can give them a remarkable intuitive undertanding of others—their concealed ambitions, weaknesses, greeds, and lusts" (p. 398).

In his rich and evocative study of the Sicilian Mafia, Gambetta (1993) documents in some degree the dilemmas of trust faced by actors within this world. In such a world, everything must be scrutinized—even luck, for "there is nothing as suspicious as luck" (p. 224).

In putting this functional analysis in perspective, we should note that there are some aspects of our argument that may seem at odds with other work on the effects of power on social information processing (notably, Keltner, Gruenfeld, & Anderson, in press). In their comprehensive review of the effects of power on individual affect, cognition, and behavior, Keltner et al. argue that high power is associated with automatic information processing and snap judgments, instead of the heightened vigilance, deliberative reasoning, and effortful rumination we posit in this chapter. Additionally, they observe that increased power leads to positive affect and attention to rewards, whereas it is reduced power that is associated with negative affect and attention to threat and punishment. This seeming contradiction with our framework can be reconciled by assuming that high perceived threat and enhanced accountability are moderators of the effects we posit (see Ginzel, Kramer, & Sutton, 1993; Kramer, 1995a, 1995b; Sutton & Galunic, 1996, for more detailed reviews of this evidence).

In terms of the efficacy of one's own influence attempts, there also may be a number of strategic advantages associated with cultivation and diffusion of the belief that one is a beleaguered victim engulfed and thwarted by a vast conspiracy. First, when viewed as an influence strategy, the reputation for being paranoid, coupled with a few carefully timed displays of paranoid behavior, may confer considerable bargaining leverage, especially when interacting with individuals whose taste for confrontation and willingness to bear the costs of conflict are low. Such individuals may decide, at the margin, to defer or avoid conflict (cf. Hersh, 1983). Thus, a carefully nurtured reputation for being an irrational, unpredictable, and explosive paranoid leader may serve a useful deterrent role. In this sense, strategic displays of paranoia may function much like strategic displays of anger and other forms of negative affect (cf. Smith's 1988 discussion of "porcupine power").

Along related lines, by strategically framing their problems in terms of powerful enemies, leaders may be able to recruit other individuals to come to their assistance. In this fashion, a leader may even deliberately foster a sense of collective paranoia in order to build cohesiveness within a group. By suggesting the existence of a common enemy against which a group can unite, the leader may be able to more effectively mobilize those around him or her. As Frank (1987) perceptively noted in this regard, "Perhaps the most common justification for the power drive today is the claimed necessity to defend against a powerful and evil enemy, thereby shifting responsibility for one's own aggressive actions to the opponent" (p. 340).

Relatedly, a leader can use such claims in order to force others to take sides and declare where their loyalties lie. Along these lines, Johnson frequently used the technique of sharing an intimate revelation about his suspicions of his enemies in order to assess the reaction of the person to whom he was speaking. By calibrating the level of enthusiasm they showed for Johnson's beliefs and/or their willingness to act on them, Johnson could more readily gauge their loyalty and commitment to him (see, e.g., Goodwin, 1988).

Leaders' convictions that they are (or even might be) the victims of powerful political conspiracies may also play an important role in the maintenance of their own motivation and persistence in difficult political situations. In much the same way that defensive pessimism enhances individuals' motivation to engage in effective pre-emptive failure-avoidant behavior (Norem & Cantor, 1986), so might paranoid cognitions help leaders maintain their motivation to overcome perceived dangers and obstacles, even in situations where those dangers and obstacles, from the perspective of a more neutral observer, seem grossly exaggerated. In fact, precisely *because* they are so willing to expend considerable cognitive resources, including the williness to maintain vigilance and to ruminate at length about others' intentions, motives, and plans, such individuals might actually be more likely to detect patterns of threat that others fail to see.

By maintaining a heightened, even if exaggerated, sensitivity to the interpersonal dangers that surround them, paranoid perceivers maintain their alertness and attentional focus. As Lewis and Weigert (1985) noted in this regard, distrust and suspicion help reduce complexity and uncertainty in social and organizational life by "dictating a course of action based on suspicion, monitoring, and activation of institutional safeguards" (p. 969). As Pruitt (1987) observed along these lines, conspiracy beliefs allow one to adopt not only an economy of thought about one's perceived enemies, but also an unequivocal attitude when dealing with them.

Leaders, perhaps even more than others, must maintain feelings of control, even if those feelings are partly—or even completely—illusory:

Conspiracy theory is a way to make sense of the randomness of the universe. It gives causes and motives to events that are more rationally seen as accidents. By attributing motives to chance happenings, believers gain control of the uncontrollable, bringing the disturbing vagaries of reality under their control, enough to make accurate predictions and maybe even alter reality: omnipotence, or at least omniscience. (Pipes, 1997, p. 181)

In this regard, conspiracy theories share a great deal with superstitious beliefs (cf. Vyse, 1997).

A functionalist account of conspiracy theorizing emphasizes, therefore, the role such cognitions play in a leader's attempt at making sense of the chaotic and often perilous environments in which their political actions are embedded. Under the best of circumstances, sensemaking in organizations is a problematic enterprise, fraught with ambiguity and risk (Weick, 1993a, 1993b). Leaders attempt to reduce this ambiguity and complexity using a variety of satisficing heuristics (George, 1980): conspiratorial theorizing—when viewed from the leader's perspective of remaining vigilant—provides one such heuristic. By maintaining a heightened, even if exaggerated, sensitivity to the interpersonal dangers that surround them, leaders maintain their alertness and focus their attention. As Lewis and Weigert (1985) have noted in this regard, distrust and suspicion help reduce complexity and uncertainty in organizational life by "dictating a course of action based on suspicion, monitoring, and activation of institutional safeguards" (p. 969).

Of course, at the very heart of the dilemma confronting all social perceivers in trust dilemmas of this sort is not simply *whether* to trust or distrust others, but rather *how much* trust and distrust are appropriate in a given situation. Knowing "how much is enough" in either direction poses a vexing judgmental dilemma (Kramer et al., 1990).

Ironically in this regard, Johnson's seemingly irrational suspicions that some conspiring must have taken place in turning his advisors against him turn out to have been not entirely misplaced. When Clark Clifford became Johnson's Secretary of Defense following Robert McNamara's dismissal, Clifford became convinced there was no way the war could be won under the current circumstances. He also recognized that a lone voice of dissent would, as had so many others, simply be dismissed by LBJ, who would view him as just another nervous Nellie or traitor. Accordingly, Clifford decided that if he wanted to successfully influence Johnson's thinking on Vietnam, he needed to turn to the so-called "wise men"—the very counselors who only months before had given their unanimous approval to the president's policy. As Clifford himself recounted,

Although it might sound somewhat conspiratorial, I thought it wise to contact a good many of [the "wise men"] first. So I did. I knew them all. . . . They all came back, went through the same process (reading cables, getting briefed). . . . I got a feeling from them. I made 4, 5, or 6 contacts. And found that in each instance, [the] Tet [offensive] had changed their mind. . . . They'd all turned around. The impact was profound—so profound [Johnson] thought something had gone wrong and he used the expression, "I think someone has poisoned the well." (Clifford, 1991, p. 203).

In a very real sense, of course, someone had poisoned the well and Lyndon Johnson, the ever-vigilant and ruminative sensemaker, had accurately intuited that something had gone wrong and that someone had put into play forces to thwart his ambitions and plans.

Similarly, Dawn Steel, the first woman to rise to the head of a major motion picture studio, described in humorous and often poignant detail how she came to believe that she was the victim of a conspiracy to undermine her power and influence in Hollywood. There were days, she noted, when:

I just knew my enemies were plotting against me. . . . I was beginning to have a vague sense of isolation. Things were happening without my knowledge. I was beginning to be excluded from meetings, meetings that I should have not only attended but led. I started to hear about deals being made that I knew nothing about, projects put into development that had never been discussed with me. . . . I felt surrounded by people plotting against me. . . ." (Steel, 1993, pp. 213–214)

It turned out that they were. Dawn Steel was displaced while she was away from the studio having her first baby. Thus, the old adage, "Just because you're paranoid doesn't mean they aren't out to get you" often contains more than a kernel of truth.

Such ironic realizations bring us, in a manner, full circle back to what seemed, at the outset of this chapter, to be a fairly sharp distinction between rational (prudent) and irrational forms of distrust and suspicion. When embedded in sensemaking conundrums of the sort that Johnson struggled with, untangling truth from error with respect to trust is an enterprise often fraught with peril. Although more self-assured social perceivers of such rantings may be bemused—and amused—by the ease with which their paranoid counterparts are lulled into a false sense of insecurity, just as easily they themselves may underestimate the concealed dangers lurking in their organizational environments. They press nonchalantly onward, much like the smug but unknowingly imperiled character in the Brecht play who "laughed because he thought that they could not hit him—he did not imagine they were practicing how to miss him." And it is this possibility, of course, that constitutes the other edge of the sword of suspicion. As Shapiro (1965) aptly observed, "suspicious thinking is unrealistic only in some ways . . . in others, it may be sharply perceptive. . . . Suspicious people are not simply people who are apprehensive and 'imagine things.' They are, in fact, extremely keen and often penetrating observers. They not only imagine, but also *search*" (pp. 55–58, emphasis added).

When it comes to successfully navigating through the murky and potentially dangerous political waters they routinely confront, the highly visible leader is continually poised on the edge of this judgmental razor: knowing who to trust, who is loyal, who will stand firm rather than run when the going gets tough. Moreover, the importance of these questions rises when leaders confront challenges or crises. Thus, prudent paranoia can be viewed as a kind of wisdom. As Weick (1993a) noted, "To be wise is not to know particular facts but *to know without excessive confidence or excessive cautiousness*" (p. 187, emphases added). Wisdom is "an attitude . . . a tendency to doubt [that widely held beliefs, values, knowledge, information, abilities, and skills] are necessarily true or valid and to doubt that they are an exhaustive set of those things that could be known" (p. 187). He goes on to elaborate, "In a fluid world, wise people know that they don't fully understand what is happening right now. . . . Extreme confidence and extreme caution both can destroy. . . . It is this sense in which wisdom, which avoids extremes, improves adaptibility" (p. 641). For the individual atop any highly competitive or political institution, wisdom when it comes to trust and distrust thus entails a delicate blend of vigilance, prudent wariness, and a sometime willingness to suspend doubt and act decisively.

ACKNOWLEDGMENTS

Preliminary versions of these ideas were presented at the Bellagio Conference on Distrust, University of Michigan ICOS seminar series, Harvard Negotiation Roundtable, John F. Kennedy School of Government seminar on public management, and the Jeffrey Rubin Memorial Conference held at Harvard Law School. Comments from participants at those seminars and conferences are gratefully acknowledged. We are also indebted to Keith Allred, Max Bazerman, David Gergen, Russell Hardin, Nancy Katz, Steve Kelman, and David Messick for their insightful comments and contributions to the early development of these ideas. Correspondence regarding this chapter should be addressed to either author, care of: Graduate School of Business, Stanford University, Stanford, CA 94305.

REFERENCES

Ambrose, S. (1991). *Nixon: Ruin and recovery, 1973–1990.* New York: Simon & Schuster.
American Psychological Association (1987). *Diagnostic and statistical manual of mental disorders.* Washington, DC: Author.
Barber, B. (1983). *The logic and limits of trust.* New Brunswick, NJ: Rutgers University Press.
Baumeister, R. F. (1991). *Meanings of life.* New York: Guilford Press.
Beschloss, M. R. (1997). *Taking charge: The Johnson White House Tapes, 1963–1964.* New York: Simon & Schuster.
Bies, R. J., Tripp, T. M., & Kramer, R. M. (1996). At the breaking point: Cognitive and social dynamics of revenge in organizations. In J. Greenberg & R. Giacalone (Eds.), *Antisocial behavior in organizations* (pp. 111–134). Thousand Oaks, CA: Sage.
Boyle, R., & Bonacich, P. (1970). The development of trust and mistrust in mixed-motives games. *Sociometry, 33,* 123–139.
Bullock, A. (1993). *Hitler and Stalin: Parallel lives.* New York: Vintage/Random House.
Burt, R. S. (1992). *Structural holes.* Cambridge, England: Cambridge University Press.
Cameron, N. (1943). The development of paranoic thinking. *Psychological Review, 50,* 219–233.
Clark, L. (1996). Restructuring and realigning our mental models: Rumination as guides to cognitive home repair. In R. Wyer (Ed.), *Ruminative thoughts* (pp. 79–82). Mahwah, NJ: Lawrence Erlbaum Associates.
Clifford, C. (1991). *Counsel to the president.* New York: Random House.
Colby, K. M. (1975). *Artificial paranoia: A computer simulation of paranoid processes.* New York: Pergamon Press.
Colby, K. M. (1981). Modeling a paranoid mind. *The Behavioral and Brain Sciences, 4,* 515–560.
Dawes, R. (1988). *Rational choice in an uncertain world.* New York: Harcourt Brace.
Deutsch, M. (1958). Trust and suspicion. *Journal of Conflict Resolution, 2,* 265–279.
Deutsch, M. (1973). *The resolution of conflict.* New Haven, CT: Yale University Press.
Deutsch, M. (1986). The malignant (spiral) process of hostile interaction. In R. K. White (Ed.), *Psychology and the prevention of nuclear war* (pp. 58–74). New York: New York University Press.
Dodge, K. A. (1980). Social cognition and children's aggressive behavior. *Child Development, 51,* 162–170.
Dodge, K. A. (1982). Social cognitive biases and deficits in aggressive boys. *Child Development, 53,* 620–635.
Dodge, K. A. (1985). Attributional bias in aggressive children. In P. C. Kendall (Ed.), *Advances in cognitive-behavioral research and therapy* (Vol. 4, pp. 161–194). New York: Academic Press.
Fein, S. (1996). Effects of suspicion on attributional thinking and the correspondence bias. *Journal of Personality and Social Psychology, 70,* 1164–1184.
Fein, S., & Hilton, J. L. (1994). Judging others in the shadow of suspicion. *Motivation and Emotion, 18,* 167–198.
Fenigstein, A. (1984). Self-consciousness and self as target. *Journal of Personality and Social Psychology, 47,* 860–870.
Fenigstein, A., & Vanable, P. A. (1992). Paranoia and self-consciousness. *Journal of Personality and Social Psychology, 62,* 129–138.

Fiske, S. T. (1993). Controlling other people: The impact of power on stereotypes. *American Psychologist, 48,* 621–628.

Forgas, J. P. (1982). Episode cognition: Internal representations of interaction routines. *Advances in Experimental Social Psychology, 15,* 59–101.

Frank, J. D. (1987). The drive for power and the nuclear arms race. *American Psychologist, 42,* 337–344.

Gambetta, D. (1988). Can we trust trust? In D. Gambetta (Ed.), *Trust: Making and breaking cooperative relationships.* Cambridge: Basil Blackwell.

Gambetta, D. (1993). *The Sicilian mafia: The business of private protection.* Cambridge, MA: Harvard University Press.

George, A. (1980). *Presidential decisionmaking in foreign policy: The effective use of information and advice.* Boulder, CO: Westview.

Gergen, D. (2000). *Eyewitness to power: The essence of leadership—Nixon to Clinton.* New York: Simon & Schuster.

Gilovich, T. (1991). *How we know what isn't so: The fallibility of human reason in everyday life.* New York: The Free Press.

Ginzel, L., Kramer, R. M., & Sutton, R. I. (1993). Organizational impression management as a reciprocal influence process: The neglected role of the organizational audience. In B. M. Staw & L. L. Cummings (Eds.), *Research in organizational behavior* (Vol. 15, pp. 227–266). Greenwich, CT: JAI Press.

Goertzel, G. (1994). Belief in conspiracy theories. *Political Psychology, 15,* 731–742.

Goffman, E. (1969). *Strategic interaction.* Philadelphia: University of Pennsylvania Press.

Goodwin, R. N. (1988). *Remembering America: A voice from the sixties.* New York: Harper & Row.

Govier, T. (1993). An epistemology of trust. *International Journal of Moral and Social Studies, 8,* 155–174.

Graumann, C. F. (1987). Conspiracy: History and social psychology. In C. F. Graumann & S. Moscovici (Eds.), *Changing conceptions of conspiracy* (pp. 245–251). New York: Springer-Verlag.

Grubin, D. (1991). *LBJ: A biography* [video]. Dallax, TX: North Texas Public Broadcasting.

Hardin, R. (1992). The street-level epistemology of trust. *Analyse & Kritik, 14,* 152–176.

Hersh, S. M. (1983). *The price of power: Kissinger in the Nixon White House.* New York: Summit Books.

Hewstone, M. (1992). The "ultimate attribution error"? A review of the literature on intergroup causal attribution. *European Journal of Social Psychology, 20,* 311–335.

Hilton, J. L., Fein, S., & Miller, D. T. (1993). Suspicion and dispositional inference. *Personality and Social Psychology Bulletin, 19,* 501–512.

Janis, I. L. (1983). *Groupthink* (2nd ed.). Boston: Mifflin.

Janis, I. L. (1989). *Crucial decisions.* New York: The Free Press.

Janis, I. L., & Mann, L. (1977). *Decision making.* New York: The Free Press.

Janoff-Bulman, R. (1992). *Shattered assumptions: Towards a new psychology of trauma.* New York: The Free Press.

Kahn, R. L., & Kramer, R. M. (1990). Untying the knot: De-escalatory processes in international conflict. In R. L. Kahn & M. N. Zald (Eds.), *Organizations and nation-states: New perspectives on conflict and cooperation* (pp. 341–362). San Francisco: Jossey-Bass.

Kelley, H. H., & Schmidt, A. (1989). The "aggressive male" syndrome: Its possible relevance for international conflict. In P. Stern, R. Axelrod, R. Jervis, & R. Radner (Eds.), *Perspectives on deterrence* (pp. 251–286). New York: Oxford University Press.

Kelley, H. H., & Stahelski, A. J. (1970a). Social interaction basis of cooperators' and competitors' beliefs about others. *Journal of Personality and Social Psychology, 16,* 66–91.

Kelley, H. H., & Stahelski, A. J. (1970b). Expectations of choice behavior held by cooperators, competitors, and individualists across four classes of experimental game. *Journal of Personality and Social Psychology, 34,* 69–81.

Kelley, H. H., & Stahelski, A. J. (1970c). The inference of intentions from moves in the Prisoner's Dilemma game. *Journal of Experimental Social Psychology, 6,* 401–419.

Keltner, D., Gruenfeld, D. H., & Anderson, C. P. (in press). Power, approach, and inhibition. *Psychological Review.*

Kramer, R. M. (1994). The sinister attribution error: Origins and consequences of collective paranoia. *Motivation and Emotion, 18,* 199–230.

Kramer, R. M. (1995a). In dubious battle: Heightened accountability, dysphoric cognition, and self-defeating bargaining behavior. In R. M. Kramer & D. M. Messick (Eds.), *Negotiation as a social process* (pp. 95–120). Thousand Oaks, CA: Sage.

Kramer, R. M. (1995b). The distorted view from the top: Power, paranoia, and distrust in organizations. In R. Bies, R. Lewicki, & B. Sheppard (Eds.), *Research on negotiations* (Vol. 5, pp. 119–154). Greenwich, CT: JAI Press.

Kramer, R. M. (1998). Paranoid cognition in social systems: Thinking and acting in the shadow of doubt. *Personality and Social Psychology Review, 2,* 251–275.

Kramer, R. M., Meyerson, D., & Davis, G. (1990). How much is enough? Psychological components of "guns versus butter" decisions in a security dilemma. *Journal of Personality and Social Psychology, 58,* 984–993.

Kruglanski, A. W. (1970). Attributing trustworthiness in supervisor-worker relations. *Journal of Experimental Social Psychology, 6,* 214–232.

Kruglanski, A. W. (1987). Blame-placing schemata and attributional research. In C. F. Graumann & S. Moscovici (Eds.), *Changing conceptions of conspiracy* (pp. 219–229). New York: Springer-Verlag.

Kunda, Z. (1987). Motivated inference: Self-serving generation and evaluation of causal theories. *Journal of Personality and Social Psychology, 53,* 636–647.

Kurtz, H. (1998). *Spin cycle: Inside the Clinton propaganda machine.* New York: The Free Press.

Langer, E. J. (1989). Minding matters: The consequences of mindlessnes-mindfulness. *Advances in Experimental Social Psychology, 22,* 137–173.

Lazarus, R. S., & Folkman, S. (1984). *Stress, appraisal, and coping.* New York: Springer.

Lewis, J. D., & Weigert, A. (1985). Trust as a social reality. *Social Forces, 63,* 967–985.

Lindskold, S. (1978). Trust development, the GRIT proposal, and the effects of conciliatory acts on conflict and cooperation. *Psychological Bulletin, 85,* 772–793.

Lindskold, S. (1986). GRIT: Reducing distrust through carefully introduced conciliation. In S. Worchel & W. G. Austin (Eds.), *Psychology of intergroup relations* (pp. 73–91). Chicago: Nelson Hall.

Luhmann, N. (1979). *Trust and power.* New York: Wiley.

Lyubomirksy, S., & Nolen-Hoeksema, S. (1993). Self-perpetuating properties of dysphoric rumination. *Journal of Personality and Social Psychology, 65,* 339–349.

March, J. G. (1995). *A primer on decision making.* New York: The Free Press.

Mikolic, J. M., Parker, J. C., & Pruitt, D. G. (1997). Escalation in response to persistent annoyance: Groups versus individuals and gender effects. *Journal of Personality and Social Psychology, 72,* 151–163.

National Archives and Records Administration. (2001). *Nixon Whitehouse Recordings: Selected Excerpts* (Vol. 3). Washington, DC: U.S. Government Printing Office.

Norem, J. K., & Cantor, N. (1986). Defensive pessimism: Harnessing anxiety as motivation. *Journal of Personality and Social Psychology, 51,* 1208–1217.

Peeters, G., & Czapinski, J. (1990). Positive–negative asymmetry in evaluations: The distinction between affective and informational negativity effects. *European Review of Social Psychology, 1,* 33–60.

Pettigrew, T. F. (1979). The ultimate attribution error: Extending Gordan Allport's cognitive analysis of prejudice. *Personality and Social Psychology Bulletin, 5*, 461–477.

Pfeffer, J. (1992). *Managing with power.* Cambridge, MA: Harvard Business School Press.

Pilisuk, M., & Skolnick, P. (1968). Inducing trust: A test of the Osgood Proposal. *Journal of Personality and Social Psychology, 8,* 121–133.

Pipes, D. (1997). *Conspiracy: How the paranoid style flourishes and where it comes from.* New York: The Free Press.

Pruitt, D. (1987). Conspiracy theory in conflict escalation. In S. Moscovici & C. F. Graumann (Eds.), *Changing conceptions of conspiracy* (pp. 73–92). New York: Springer-Verlag.

Pyszczynski, T., & Greenberg, J. (1987). Self-regulatory perseveration and the depressive self-focusing style: A self-awareness theory of reactive depression. *Psychological Bulletin, 102,* 122–138.

Robins, R. S., & Post, J. M. (1997). *Political paranoia: The psychopolitics of hatred.* New Haven, CT: Yale University Press.

Rotter, J. B. (1980). Interpersonal trust, trustworthiness, and gullibility. *American Psychologist, 35,* 1–7.

Shapiro, D. (1965). *Neurotic styles.* New York: Basic Books.

Siegel, R. K. (1994). *Whispers: The voices of paranoia.* New York: Crown.

Slovic, P. (1993). Perceived risk, trust, and democracy. *Risk Analysis, 13,* 675–682.

Smith, H. (1988). *The power game.* New York: Random House.

Steel, D. (1993). *They can kill you, but they can't eat you: Lessons from the front.* New York: Pocket Books.

Strickland, L. H. (1958). Surveillance and trust. *Journal of Personality, 26,* 200–215.

Sutton, R. I., & Galunic, D. C. (1996). Consequences of public scrutiny for leaders and their organizations. In B. M. Staw & L. L. Cummings (Eds.), *Research in organizational behavior* (Vol. 18, pp. 201–250). Greenwich, CT: JAI Press.

Swann, W. B., Pelham, B. W., & Roberts, D. C. (1987). Causal chunking: Memory and inference in ongoing interaction. *Journal of Personality and Social Psychology, 53,* 858–865.

Taylor, S. E. (1991). Asymmetrical effects of positive and negative events: The mobilization-minimization hypothesis. *Psychological Bulletin, 110,* 67–85.

Tetlock, P. E. (1992). The impact of accountability on judgment and choice: Toward a social contingency model. In L. Berkowitz (Ed.), *Advances in experimental social psychology* (Vol. 25, pp. 331–376). New York: Academic Press.

Vyse, S. A. (1997). *Believing in magic: The psychology of superstition.* Oxford, England: Oxford University Press.

Watzlawick, P., Beavin, J. H., & Jackson, D. D. (1967). *Pragmatics of human communication: A study of interactional patterns, pathologies, and paradoxes.* New York: Norton.

Weick, K. E. (1979). *The social psychology of organizing.* Reading, MA: Addison-Wesley.

Weick, K. E. (1993a). Sensemaking in organizations. In J. K. Murnighan (Ed.), *Social psychology in organizations: Advances in theory and practice* (pp. 101–139). Englewood Cliffs, NJ: Prentice-Hall.

Weick, K. E. (1993b). The collapse of sensemaking in organizations: The Mann Gulch Disaster. *Administrative Science Quarterly, 38,* 628–652.

Weiner, B. (1985). "Spontaneous" causal thinking. *Psychological Bulletin, 97,* 74–84.

Wilson, T. D., & Kraft, D. (1993). Why do I love thee? Effects of repeated introspections about a dating relationship on attitudes towards the relationship. *Personality and Social Psychology Bulletin, 19,* 409–418.

Wyer, R. (Ed.). (1996). *Ruminative thoughts.* Mahwah, NJ: Lawrence Erlbaum Associates.

Zimbardo, P. G., Andersen, S. M., & Kabat, L. G. (1981). Induced hearing deficit generates experimental paranoia. *Science, 212,* 1529–1531.

12

Leadership and the Psychology of Power

Joe C. Magee
Deborah H Gruenfeld
Stanford University

Dacher J. Keltner
University of California Berkeley

Adam D. Galinsky
Northwestern University

INTRODUCTION

Leaders wield power in many different ways. From the heroism of Martin Luther King, Jr., to the atrocities of Slobodan Milosevic — and the wide range of more mundane prosocial and antisocial behavior in between — many leaders' actions share something in common. They reflect a disregard for norms and a reduced concern for certain kinds of social consequences in the name of pursuing personal goals and objectives. In research on leadership, the willingness to take controversial stands and defy social convention is, like many other leadership qualities, most often attributed to personality characteristics, or to the fit between a leader's personality and the social context in which it is exhibited (for a review see Haslam, 2001).

In contrast, we suggest that leaders' responses to aspects of their own leadership status transform their behavior in ways that contribute to these phenomena. Our perspective suggests that leaders share a set of psychological processes that are not typically examined in leadership research. In this chapter, we offer some theory and data on the psychology of power that inform our understanding of how leaders think and how they behave.

We begin with a brief review of leadership research to illustrate how theories of power can inform future leadership studies. After discussing the connection between leadership and power, we present evidence of the psychological processes that explain counter-normative behavior—both prosocial and antisocial—in leaders who have power. Next, we describe important moderating conditions that help fine-tune the fit between our research and the study of leadership, and we conclude with some implications for the practice and study of leadership.

From Leadership to the Psychology of Leaders

Most studies of leadership have focused on four topics (for more complete reviews, see Bass, 1981; Goethals, chap. 5, this volume; Haslam, 2001; Hollander, 1985). First is the study of personal characteristics, such as charisma (Bass & Avolio, 1987, 1993; House & Shamir, 1993; Bligh & Meindl, chap. 2, this volume), and experiences (Gardner, 1995; Simonton, 1987) that breed effective leaders. A second interest of leadership researchers has been the concept of leadership style (e.g., directive, transactional, transformational), and studies have examined both the qualitative makeup (Bass & Avolio, 1993; House & Shamir, 1993) and effectiveness (Larson, Foster-Fishman, & Franz, 1998; Peterson, 1997) of the alternatives. A third class of research has investigated perceptions of leadership (Lord, 1977; Meindl, Ehrlich, & Dukerich, 1984; Peterson, 1999; Simonton, 1987). The fourth area is integrative, with researchers documenting dynamic processes between leaders and followers (Bass, 1990; Burns, 1978; Gardner, 1995; Hogg, Hains, & Mason, 1998; Messick, chap. 4, this volume).

These traditions treat many important aspects of the social psychology of *leadership*, yet most provide little insight into the psychological responses of *leaders*. That is, there is little research that can be used to predict what will happen inside a person's mind under leadership conditions. Once an individual occupies a leadership position, structural factors inherent in the leader–follower relationship—for example, power differences—can cause changes in the psychological functioning of that individual (e.g., Fiske, 1993; Galinsky, Gruenfeld, & Magee, 2000, 2003; Keltner, Gruenfeld, & Anderson, 2003; Kipnis, 1972). We believe that in becoming leaders, individuals may experience changes in how they think of their work, how they think of themselves, how they think of others, and, consequently, how they act. Thus, in contrast to the tenor of many writings of history, literature, journalism, and psychology, we believe that many of the more unusual behaviors displayed by those in leadership positions are attributable not just to personality or role requirements, but also to the experience of power and its psychological effects.

Power and Leadership

The concepts of power and leadership are historically and functionally linked (French & Snyder, 1959). Leadership is often defined as the *process* of guiding others' actions toward the achievement of group goals (Hollander, 1985). Power is generally defined as the *capacity* to guide others' actions toward whatever goals are meaningful to the power-holder (e.g., Blau, 1964; Dahl, 1957; Fiske, 1993; Gruenfeld, Keltner, & Anderson, 2003; Keltner et al., 2003; Thibault & Kelley, 1959; Weber, 1947). According to these definitions, power provides a means of accomplishing the work of leadership, and it can also be a by-product of having done so effectively. Thus, power and leadership often go hand-in-hand, yet the effectiveness of leaders and power-holders are judged using different criteria. Typically, great leadership is attributed to those who are perceived as having provided a vision that inspired others to cooperate for the benefit of the group (Cronshaw & Lord, 1987). Power, in contrast, is perceived in those who are able to influence others, using whatever means necessary, independent of the social value of the outcomes achieved. Good leadership is typically defined in terms of organization effectiveness; it is attributed to the individual who appears to have had the greatest *positive* impact on the behavior of many organization members. In contrast, a person's ability to wield power effectively is judged in terms of the power-holder's personal success and accomplishment. From this perspective, all effective leaders have power but not all power-holders are leaders.

Throughout this chapter, we refer to "leaders" as people who are categorically distinct from those who are "followers" and other non-leaders. We also refer to "the powerful" or "high-power" individuals, and, correspondingly, "the powerless" or "low-power" individuals as if these labels correspond with categorical positions, although we do not see power as a categorical variable. Rather, we view power as a relative condition, noting that in most social exchanges all parties possess power, even if some possess more than others (Gruenfeld & Kim, 2002). This is yet another way in which power and leadership differ, in theory, if not in practice.

THE PSYCHOLOGICAL EFFECTS
OF POWER ON LEADERS

In our review of the literatures on power and leadership, we have been struck by the evaluative assumptions underlying many of the approaches to understanding these phenomena. On the one hand, the "great man" approach to the study of leadership, which is still quite prominent in many disciplines, has involved attempting to identify the character attributes and specific behaviors that distinguish leaders, who are characterized as great, from mere mortals, who are not (e.g., Fleischman & Peters, 1962; Pears, 1992; Vroom & Yetton, 1973). On the other hand, there are some accounts of power and leadership that evoke Lord Acton's famous observation that "power corrupts, and absolute power corrupts absolutely."

In psychology, Kipnis (1972, 1976) was the first to empirically examine the notion that power can corrupt a person's disposition in predictable ways. In a role-playing exercise, managers who possessed power in addition to authority used more influence tactics, valued subordinate performance less, felt more control over subordinates' efforts, were more likely to perceive subordinates as "objects of manipulation," and expressed a greater desire for psychological distance from subordinates than managers who did not possess power (Kipnis, 1972). A study by Bargh, Raymond, Pryor, and Strack (1995) showed that power is associated with sex in the mind, and that males who are already prone to sexual harassment are even more prone to harass under conditions of power. Kipnis (1976) argued that, in general, power-holders exhibit egocentrism that breeds feelings of superiority, which contribute to corrupt behavior. Recent accounts of CEO hubris (Hayward & Hambrick, 1997; Zellner & Forest, 2001) are consistent with this perspective.

Thus, it appears that leaders and the powerful are often either revered or demonized by those who study them. Yet it almost goes without saying that the power leaders possess allows them to behave admirably as well as disgracefully. We believe that leaders with power are likely to be both more admirable and more disgraceful than those without power, and that these alternatives are likely to vary more within than across individuals. Consistent with this argument, there are many memorable examples of leaders whose public policies were inspirational while their personal lives were a public embarrassment. However, there have been relatively few attempts to account theoretically for both prosocial and antisocial leadership behaviors. Winter (1973, 1988, 1998) showed how the power motive can lead to both accomplishment and profligate behavior among U.S. presidents. Chen, Lee-Chai, and Bargh (2001) showed that the effects of power depend on a person's social relationship orientation: in a resource allocation task, participants with a communal orientation were more selfless, and participants with an exchange orientation were more selfish, under conditions of power. On average, participants' behavior corresponded to their internal standards rather than to any external standard, or norm, that they might have used to regulate their natural tendencies.

These findings are consistent with our earlier assertion that power affects leadership by facilitating the unfettered pursuit of personally meaningful goals. Power intensifies goal pursuit, we believe, via activation of the behavioral approach system. According to the approach theory of power (Keltner et al., 2003), the behavioral approach system induces positive affect, a focus on rewards rather than punishments, decisiveness and disinhibited social behavior among the powerful. In contrast, the behavioral inhibition system is activated in those without power. In this view, power frees those who possess it from inhibitions that might otherwise constrain their behavior. Thus, leaders can be transformed via the possession of power, becoming less deliberate and more action-oriented as their power increases (Galinsky et al., 2000; Gruenfeld & Kim, 2002). In the following sections we provide empirical evidence of how this can occur.

Power and Action-Orientation

Galinsky et al. (2000, 2003) have found direct support for the link between power and action-orientation in a series of experiments. Specifically, we have shown that participants in high-power conditions exhibited a greater intention to act, that they were more implemental than deliberative in their thinking about action, that they were more likely to act when it was unclear whether they were allowed to do so, and that they were more likely to act in both prosocial and antisocial ways than participants in low-power conditions.

In the first experiment (Galinsky et al., 2000), partners in a negotiation scenario were assigned to high-power or low-power conditions. High-power participants received role materials that explained they had an attractive alternative to a settlement with their partner (a strong "best alternative to negotiated agreement," or BATNA) whereas low-power participants' instructions did not suggest that there were any alternative opportunities available. Prior to negotiating, we measured participants' intentions, looking specifically at whether they spontaneously mentioned intending to make a first offer or not. Consistent with the notion that power increases an action-orientation, we found that subjects in the high-power condition were significantly more likely than those in the low-power condition to express an intention to make a first offer.

In the second experiment (Galinsky et al., 2000), half of the participants were asked to write about a time when they had power over someone else (high-power condition), and the other half were asked to write about a time when someone else had power over them (low-power condition). Participants were led to believe that this exercise was unrelated to subsequent tasks. Thus, this exercise served as a power-priming manipulation. Next, participants were asked to complete an unfinished fairy tale by writing three additional sentences. The partially completed fairy tale, taken from Gollwitzer, Heckhausen, and Steller (1990), describes a king who must go to war and seeks someone with whom he can entrust his daughter. Consistent with our expectations, participants in the high-power condition described an action-oriented king who was decisive and quick to act, whereas those in the low-power condition described a king who was more hesitant and prone to deliberate. In addition, content analysis revealed that high-power participants' fairy tales described the king as somebody who delegated tasks and asked for favors, and who faced significantly fewer obstacles than did low-power participants.

Thus, recollections of power and powerlessness seemed to activate different perceptions of the social environment. Whereas powerlessness led participants to project constraint onto the fairy tale protagonist, power led participants to project the absence of constraint onto the same protagonist. Moreover, those without power tended to view other people as barriers to the protagonist's goals, whereas people with power saw others as instrumental agents for their goals, as means to an end—a point to which we return later.

In a third experiment (Galinsky et al., 2003), participants completed either the high-power or the low-power priming task just described and were subsequently led to a room in which they were to complete the "real" experiment. On the desk in each room was a small fan, blowing at a moderately strong rate directly into the chair where they were supposed to sit and work. Consistent with our expectation, participants in the high-power condition were significantly more likely to either move the fan or turn it off than those in the low-power condition, who were more likely to complete the experiment with the fan blowing directly into their faces. Thus, participants with power were more likely to take action by removing an annoying stimulus in a situation where it was not clear whether or not they were allowed to do so.

These findings suggest that leaders with power have an action-orientation that leads to a narrowed focus on goals and a disregard for information that might hinder goal accomplishment. This bias should be functional when quick implementation is needed and there are many possible effective actions, but it should be dysfunctional when careful deliberation is required in order to determine the best alternative. Decision makers who consider alternatives carefully and weigh the trade-offs among them are often more accurate (Gruenfeld & Hollingshead, 1993; Tetlock & Kim, 1987), and they may stay in power longer than those who evaluate response options more single-mindedly (Suedfeld & Rank, 1976). Yet decisiveness and the ability to act quickly are considered key leadership strengths (Tetlock, Peterson, & Berry, 1993). This tension suggests that an action-orientation can have both positive and negative consequences for leaders.

Of course, the effectiveness of an action-orientation also depends on the consequences of the action chosen, not only for the actor, but also for those affected by his or her decisions. When actions are beneficial to the power-holder but not to dependents, the seeds of corruption are sown. To show that the association between power and action could lead to both functional and dysfunctional ends, Galinsky et al. (2003) compared the actions of participants with power and the actions of participants without power in two social dilemma games. In both games, we predicted that participants with power would be set on acting to solve a problem and, thus, would be more assertive than participants without power. Specifically, we expected high-power participants both to contribute more to a common resource in a Public Goods Dilemma (e.g., a public television station) and to take more from a finite common resource in a Commons Dilemma (e.g., electricity) than the low-power participants. As predicted, participants primed with power acted with greater intensity than participants primed with lack of power or control participants (who described a day in their life, rather than writing about power or powerlessness), regardless of whether the action was prosocial or antisocial. High-power participants gave more to the public good and took more from the commons than either the control participants or the low-power participants. Taking action was the consistent theme for those with power: the consequence of action, whether it was exhausting a resource or fostering a valuable fund, seemed less important than asserting oneself.

In sum, these considerations suggest that leaders with power tend toward an action-orientation: they are less prone to deliberate about their response options and to weigh the trade-offs associated with alternatives and are more prone to act decisively—perhaps impulsively—on the first action alternative that comes to mind. But what about when effective leadership requires *not* acting? We propose that the same psychological processes that help leaders strive toward the accomplishment of objectives make it extremely difficult for them to resist the temptation to act even when acting is inappropriate.

Power and Disinhibition

Leaders are typically held to high standards of discipline: they are expected to act decisively on behalf of the greater good but to control themselves when tempted to act for personal gain. Morally speaking, this seems like a reasonable set of expectations, but from the present psychological perspective, they appear less tenable. We have proposed that power activates an action-orientation, which should be functional when persistence is necessary. At the same time, an action-orientation is incompatible, we believe, with resistance.

Keltner et al. (2003) suggested that *disinhibition* occurs when behavioral approach, rather than inhibition, is activated for those in power, noting that the inhibitions that we experience in the presence of social constraint are simply not activated when social constraints are either absent, dismissed, or unobserved. In support of this argument, the authors document the effects of power on inhibitions related to eating and sexual behavior. In a study of eating and manners, Ward and Keltner (1998) showed that people who had power by virtue of their role as evaluator were more likely to consume (i.e., approach) food when it was a scarce resource (consistent with Galinsky et al., 2003), but also that they were less likely to exhibit table manners (i.e., inhibit) than people who were being evaluated. Evaluators, who had power, were more likely to take the remaining cookie from a plate, which left others without seconds. Furthermore, evaluators ate their cookies with greater abandon, chewing with their mouths open and spilling more crumbs on their faces and on the table than those without power.

Prior experimental research has shown a similar relationship between power and sexual activity. As noted earlier, Bargh et al. (1995) showed that power activates sexual thought and increases reports of attraction toward a female confederate for men who possess a chronic sexual approach goal (see Higgins, 1996, for a review of chronic goals). Also, both men and women who are in a position of high-power flirt more aggressively than their low-power counterparts (Gonzaga, Keltner, Londahl, & Smith, 2001).

These studies show how power can release inhibitions and affect the tendency to self-regulate. Self-regulation involves persistence toward accomplishing goals and resistance against temptations that distract from goal accomplishment (Carver & Scheier, 1990; Mischel, Cantor, & Feldman, 1996; Wegner & Bargh, 1998). Muraven, Baumeister, and colleagues (Baumeister, Bratslavsky, Muraven, & Tice, 1998; Muraven, Tice, & Baumeister, 1998; Muraven & Baumeister, 2000) have shown that people who are forced to either struggle through a difficult task or suppress desires early in an experiment are worse at self-regulation on later tasks. Rather than functioning like a skill that improves with practice, self-regulation appears to be like a resource that can run out, or like a muscle that tires after too much exercise (Muraven & Baumeister, 2000). We posit that power, by activating approach tendencies, can also lead to an overemphasis on persistence that ultimately weakens the ability to resist. Think of the self-regulation muscle as having a flexor and an extensor. The flexor, which is stronger, controls the work of approach, promotion, and persistence, effectively pulling goals closer. As a consequence, the extensor is less able to control avoidance, prevention, and resistance, and is ineffective in pushing temptation away. The dominance of the flexor over the extensor is a useful metaphor for understanding disinhibition in response to power. It explains how those with power can be both heroic and reprehensible.

In sum, these considerations suggest that leaders with power, while experiencing increased action-orientation, can also experience a decreased ability to control their responses to temptation. In this light, the examples of powerful leaders who disappoint their followers by revealing an unseemly personal life can be easily understood. Among the powerful, the ability to accomplish great work and the susceptibility to forces of depravity can be seen as two sides of the same coin.

Power and Objectification

The preceding discussion suggests that individuals with power pursue personal goals without concern for the social consequences of their actions, which can logically lead to social exploitation. The association between power and exploitation is widely held and passionately documented (e.g.,

Marx, 1970), although it is clear that the link between power and corruption is not absolute (Barber, 1972). However, it can be argued that individuals with power, because they are less dependent on others than vice versa, are less concerned with how others will judge their actions, and are less attentive to the internal experiences of others in general, than those without power. Perceivers who lack social control are motivated to understand the causal relations in their environment, which leads to systematic consideration of the factors that compel others to behave as they do, including dispositional and situational influences (Gilbert, 1998). In contrast, understanding how others feel and what they believe is less important for perceivers who possess power because these factors might appear less likely to have an impact on their own goal attainment (Miller, Norman, & Wright, 1978). Moreover, because their own goals are so salient and their concerns about others' evaluations are not, we believe that the powerful will often perceive others through a lens of self-interest, leading to what we call objectification.

Objectification is defined in this work as the process of viewing other people instrumentally, in terms of the qualities that make them useful to the perceiver as opposed to the qualities that allow them to be understood as unique human beings. Although we have only recently begun to investigate these ideas empirically, we believe that objectification involves, specifically, a lack of attention to others' internal experiences, or human qualities (e.g., feelings, beliefs, and preferences), the tendency to see others in terms of object qualities (e.g., physical attributes, and material possessions), and viewing others as tools for goal accomplishment (i.e., as means to an end). This perspective suggests that, contrary to the implications of some studies (e.g., Chance, 1967; Ellyson & Dovidio, 1985; Fiske, 1993), power does not necessarily reduce overall attentiveness to other people. Rather, we assert that power reduces attentiveness to others' interests, feelings, beliefs, expectations, and unique experiences, which are the qualities that define them as human beings.

To demonstrate the objectification phenomenon, we (Gruenfeld, Galinsky, & Magee, 2001) initially tested the hypothesis that power is associated with low levels of perspective-taking. After priming the experiences of power and powerlessness using the procedure described earlier, participants were asked to draw an "E" on their foreheads (Hass, 1984). Consistent with our expectations, subjects in the high-power condition displayed their disregard for others' perspectives by drawing the "E" so that it was illegible (i.e., backward) to any observer but legible (i.e., forward) to themselves. In contrast, subjects in the low-power condition were more likely to draw the "E" so that others could read it but it was illegible (i.e., backward) from their own perspective. Though participants in both conditions were more likely to draw an E oriented to an observer, high-power participants were almost three times as likely as low-power participants to draw an E oriented to the self (33% vs. 12%). These results suggest that power reduces one's ability to see the world through others' eyes, an effect that could logically contribute to social exploitation.[1] This finding adds to the literature on social inattentiveness among the powerful by demonstrating that power is associated with inattentiveness to targets' *experiences*.

Research by others demonstrates how power directs social attention to those aspects of others that are relevant to personal goals. In a study of the effects of power on stereotype use, Overbeck and Park (2001) showed that individuals with power who were asked to review possible job applicants were more likely to use stereotypes and less likely to use individuating information than those without power (see also Goodwin & Fiske, 1993) *unless* attention to individuating information was explicitly relevant to the organization's goals. These findings suggest that, consistent with our argument, those with power can be relatively inattentive to individuals' unique characteristics, except when those features of a target are relevant to personal goal attainment.

Research has also shown that the effects of power on social perception can bias their social judgments. For example, members of majority groups, who have power because they represent the status quo, are more likely to (inaccurately) characterize their minority-group counterparts as extremists than vice versa (Ebenbach & Keltner, 1998; Keltner & Robinson, 1996, 1997). In addition, power-holders have been shown to ascribe less-than-deserved credit to their subordinates. Kipnis (1972) found that experimental subjects with power attributed the performance of their subordinates to their own efforts and influence rather than to the subordinates themselves, and this effect increased with the degree of power. More recently, it was shown that after group tasks, low-power participants were more likely than high-power participants to acknowledge others' contributions

---

[1] Ironically, we have argued that power increases attentiveness to one's personal goals while simultaneously making one less self-aware. Yet we believe these are quite different, corresponding to Mead's (1934) "I" and "me," respectively. Self-attention corresponds to perception of one's needs and desires, whereas self-awareness is defined as consciousness of the self as an object of evaluation (Duval & Wicklund, 1972). The psychological profile associated with high self-attention and low self-awareness can logically be associated with all kinds of scandalous (and illegal) incidents that mar the reputations of high-profile leaders, including illegal forms of sexual misconduct and financial mismanagement, for example. These types of incidents are not only bad for the leader's reputation, but often they are exploitative of and destructive to others.

to collective outcomes (Fan & Gruenfeld, 1998; see also Pfeffer, Cialdini, Hanna, & Knopoff, 1998).

It is interesting to note that all of the misperceptions we have observed are associated with negative, rather than positive, evaluations of others. Consistent with this possibility, Kipnis (1972) found that high-power participants in his study were less interested in meeting with their subordinates socially, after the experiment, than subordinates were in meeting with them. Interestingly, we have found recently that subjects who completed our high-power prime subsequently described the experimenter—a high-power target—in more disrespectful terms than subjects who completed the low-power prime (Magee, Gruenfeld, & Galinsky, 2003). Thus, social perception by those under conditions of power can lead to negative evaluations of both high- and low-power co-workers.

These findings add to the previous literature on power and social perception by suggesting that the lens of self-interest, in addition to differences in cognitive load among individuals with power, probably contributes to biased social perceptions among the powerful. We believe that power deflects attention away from social cues, toward internal goals and psychological cues, affecting the *focus*, not just the *amount* of attention paid to others. Goodwin, Gubin, Fiske, and Yzerbyt (2000) have shown that power increases stereotyping both by increasing attention to stereotype-consistent information and by decreasing attention to stereotype-inconsistent information. We note that power can also lead to a lack of consideration of others' interests and emotions, to an increased focus on the characteristics of specific targets that are useful in attaining one's goals, and to a demonstrated disinterest in others who do not seem currently useful.

To accomplish organizational objectives and to satisfy their desires, power-holders can, and do, use the people around them. We have proposed that using others to accomplish personal goals often leads to their objectification. Objectification can be conscious, as when supervisors delegate "dirty work" that they themselves find distasteful or immoral (Kipnis, 1972); however, our perspective on this phenomenon highlights some of its non-conscious aspects. By focusing instrumentally on the aspects of others who are important for goal attainment, individuals with power often inadvertently ignore social information that is important to others. This would not matter if power-holders did not have morals, or if their power was absolute and invulnerable; however, many individuals with power come to regret their treatment of others in the past. In fact, Magee et al. (2003) found that among experimental participants who wrote about a time when they had power over others, their biggest regret was how they treated others. In contrast, those who wrote about a time when someone else had power over them regretted not having asserted their own interests.

To summarize, in this section we have described how power can lead to the objectification of social targets. It does not take much imagination to see how these processes can affect leadership effectiveness. As we noted earlier, objectification can lead to exploitation, which is likely to compromise leadership effectiveness in the long term, if not in the short term. Employees who feel they are treated without consideration of their interests contribute to turnover, malaise, and low organizational commitment. They are also responsible on occasion for expensive law suits and bad press for those who employ them. In light of current corporate debacles (Gladwell, 2002), it is important to note that people who are treated as though they are mindless vehicles for goal accomplishment can, through self-fulfilling prophecy, become mindless vehicles for goal accomplishment, behaving in ways they do not condone, while holding others (i.e., superiors) responsible for their own actions.

MODERATING FACTORS

The constellation of mechanisms described so far is expected to generalize across social systems to the extent that power differences exist. However, each of the mechanisms is susceptible to moderation by a number of other variables that can accompany power and leadership. Two of these variables are particularly relevant to leadership as it is discussed here. One is accountability: leaders are typically accountable for organization outcomes and generally are held personally responsible for the success and failure of the groups they lead (Meindl et al., 1984). Personal accountability is a form of social constraint that should counteract the disinhibiting effects of power, potentially increasing the extent to which leaders consider a wide range of possible consequences of their actions before choosing to act. Second, the stability of the social system in which a leader is embedded (i.e., the permanence of his/her position) could also affect the extent to which these processes occur. In this section, we discuss how accountability and social system instability might moderate the effects of power on leaders.

Accountability

One important variable that often accompanies structural power, particularly in organizational contexts, is personal accountability for one's actions. People who are able to control others' outcomes but know they will be held accountable for the means and consequences of their actions are more likely to consider social consequences and take others' interests into account than those who are not accountable (Lerner & Tetlock, 1999; Tetlock, 1992). This explains why U.S. presidents exhibit greater cognitive complexity after they are elected than prior to election (Tetlock, 1981). Although U.S. presidents possess greater power than presidential candidates, presidents are more accountable to a larger and more diverse set of constituents for the consequences of their policy actions than are presidential candidates. Presumably, accountability constrains the disinhibiting effects of power because leaders wish to avoid the social punishments that those with less power can potentially invoke, such as dislike, disapproval, disrespect, and ultimately the removal of power. Thus, leaders may attempt to control their behavior because they do not want to lose power and status.

System Stability

Conditions that affect the maintenance of power can also moderate its psychological effects. People become leaders through a number of different mechanisms and a variety of different systems, and these mechanisms can affect the conditions under which the leadership position is likely to change. A leadership position can be inherited due to circumstances of birth, acquired through hiring or promotion, won via an election, or stolen by attracting followers away from another, more "legitimate" leader. These are only a handful of leadership determinants, and each implies a different type of power base. The leaders of organizations and nations, for example, possess formal authority and control vast resources and, as we see in current world politics, both are a great source of power. The leaders of many kinds of grass-roots groups, in contrast, possess few material resources and little formal authority but are effective nonetheless based on their referent power (see French & Raven, 1959, for a discussion of reward, coercive, and referent power).

In a democracy or a meritocracy, leaders are vulnerable to having their power revoked or usurped. We assume that when power is negotiable, it is less likely to lead to disinhibition than when it is irrevocably bestowed. This suggests that leaders whose legitimacy is challenged should be less likely to disinhibit than those whose legitimacy is more secure. Consistent with this notion, studies of reasoning by Supreme Court justices show that the greater the challenge to the majority, the higher the complexity exhibited in majority opinions (Gruenfeld & Kim, 2002; Gruenfeld & Preston, 2000). It has also been shown that hate crimes against minority members peak when the power distance between majority and minority groups is the greatest, and that the incidence of hate crimes drops off as the proportion of minority members in a community grows (Green, Wong, & Strolovitch, 1996).

CONCLUSION

In this chapter, we reviewed the effects of power on those who possess it. We documented our central thesis—that power is disinhibiting—and explained the psychological mechanisms underlying this effect. We have argued that the experience of power increases a focus on goal implementation, changes self-regulation processes, and alters attention to the self and others, thereby restoring a direct link between goals and the acts that satisfy them. Furthermore, we explored the implications of these mechanisms for behavior in a number of specific social contexts, and we identified two important factors—accountability and stability of the system that supports the leader's position—that moderate the psychological effects of power.

The arguments presented here have important implications for leaders, who typically possess power over those whom they lead. It might be helpful for leaders to know that their power can incite them to act, not only when action is necessary and the correct response is obvious, but also when action is unnecessary, when the correct response is not clear, and when restraint is required. The knowledge that power can reduce perspective-taking and lead to objectification might also be useful for leaders who want to maintain positive relations with those who support them. That is, power may have opposing effects on two dimensions typically associated with being a leader: Power may attenuate feelings of responsibility for others, on the one hand, and accentuate the use of authority on the other. Surely, bringing responsibility to the forefront of consciousness must be required to maintain a leadership position, especially in an unstable social system. Leaders who recognize and learn to manage their own power are the most successful (Pfeffer, 1992).

The way in which a leader acts is often taken as a reflection of a dispositionally determined leadership style (Bass & Avolio, 1993; House & Shamir, 1993; Peterson, 1997; Simonton, 1988). However, a focus on leadership styles neglects the possibility that the leadership role is a strong situation, one that affects cognition and behavior in ways that are both consistent and inconsistent with effective leadership. Most leaders assume their positions with the noblest of intentions, but, as we have shown here, their power can get the best of them. Power is also crucial for effective leadership. Therefore, it would be a mistake to conclude from this discussion that leaders must somehow compromise their power. Our point in making these arguments is to suggest that to understand leadership behavior, it is important to consider the psychological effects of power on the leader.

ACKNOWLEDGMENTS

The authors would like to thank Alison Fragale and Maia Young for their helpful comments on an earlier draft of this chapter and Jesus Miguel Sanchez for help in preparing this chapter.

REFERENCES

Barber, J. D. (1972). *The presidential character: Predicting performance in the White House.* Englewood Cliffs, NJ: Prentice-Hall.

Bargh, J. A., Raymond, P., Pryor, J. B., & Strack, F. (1995). Attractiveness of the underling: An automatic power → sex association and its consequences for sexual harassment and aggression. *Journal of Personality and Social Psychology, 68,* 768–781.

Bass, B. M. (1981). *Stogdill's handbook of leadership.* New York: The Free Press.

Bass, B. M. (1990). From transactional to transformational leadership: Learning to share the vision. *Organizational Dynamics, 18,* 19–31.

Bass, B. M., & Avolio, B. J. (1987). Biography and the assessment of leadership at the world-class level. *Journal of Management, 13,* 7–19.

Bass, B. M., & Avolio, B. J. (1993). Transformational leadership: A response to critiques. In M. M. Chemers & R. Ayman (Eds.), *Leadership theory and research: Perspectives and directions* (pp. 49–80). San Diego: Academic Press.

Baumeister, R. F., Bratslavsky, E., Muraven, M., & Tice, D. M. (1998). Ego depletion: Is the active self a limited resource? *Journal of Personality and Social Psychology, 74,* 1252–1265.

Blau, P. M. (1964). *Exchange and power in social life.* New York: Wiley.

Burns, J. M. (1978). *Leadership.* New York: Harper & Row.

Carver, C. S., & Scheier, M. F. (1990). Principles of self-regulation. In E. T. Higgins & R. N. Sorrentino (Eds.), *Handbook of motivation and cognition* (Vol. 2, pp. 3–52). New York: Guilford.

Chance, M. (1967). Attention structure as the basis of primate rank orders. *Man, 2,* 503–518.

Chen, S., Lee-Chai, A. Y., & Bargh, J. A. (2001). Relationship orientation as a moderator of the effects of social power. *Journal of Personality and Social Psychology, 80,* 173–187.

Cronshaw, S. F., & Lord, R. G. (1987). Effects of categorization, attribution, and encoding processes on leadership perceptions. *Journal of Applied Psychology, 72,* 97–106.

Dahl, R. A. (1957). The concept of power. *Behavioural Science, 2,* 201–215.

Duval, S., & Wicklund, R. A. (1972). *A theory of objective self-awareness.* New York: Academic Press.

Ebenbach, D. H., & Keltner, D. (1998). Power, emotion and judgmental accuracy in social conflict: Motivating the cognitive miser. *Basic and Applied Social Psychology, 20,* 7–21.

Ellyson, S. L., & Dovidio, J. F. (1985). *Power, dominance, and nonverbal behavior.* New York: Springer-Verlag.

Fan, E. T., & Gruenfeld, D. H. (1998). When needs outweigh desires: The effects of resource interdependence and reward interdependence on group problem solving. *Basic and Applied Social Psychology, 20,* 45–56.

Fiske, S. T. (1993). Controlling other people: The impact of power on stereotyping. *American Psychologist, 48,* 621–628.

Fleischman, E. A., & Peters, D. A. (1962). Interpersonal values, leadership attitudes and managerial success. *Personnel Psychology, 15,* 43–56.

French, J. R. P., & Raven, B. (1959). The bases of social power. In D. Cartwright (Ed.), *Studies in social power* (pp. 150–167). Ann Arbor, MI: University of Michigan Press.

French, J. R. P., & Snyder, R. (1959). Leadership and interpersonal power. In D. Cartwright (Ed.), *Studies in social power* (pp. 118–149). Ann Arbor, MI: University of Michigan Press.

Galinsky, A. D., Gruenfeld, D. H, & Magee, J. C. (2000). Unpublished data, Kellogg Graduate School of Management, Northwestern University.

Galinsky, A. D., Gruenfeld, D. H, & Magee, J. C. (2003). From power to action. *Journal of Personality and Social Psychology, 85,* 453–466.

Gardner, H. (1995). *Leading minds: An anatomy of leadership.* New York: Basic Books.

Gilbert, D. T. (1998). Ordinary personology. In D. Gilbert, S. T. Fiske, & G. Lindzey (Eds.), *Handbook of social psychology* (4th ed., Vol. 2, pp. 89–150). New York: McGraw-Hill.

Gladwell, M. (2002). *The talent myth: Are smart people overrated?* Retrieved February 13, 2004, from http://www.gladwell.com/2002/2002_07_22_a_talent.htm

Gollwitzer, P. M., Heckhausen, H., & Steller, B. (1990). Deliberative and implemental mindsets: Cognitive tuning toward congruous thoughts and information. *Journal of Personality and Social Psychology, 59,* 1119–1127.

Gonzaga, G. C., Keltner, D., Londahl, E. A., & Smith, M. D. (2001). Love and the commitment problem in romantic relations and friendship. *Journal of Personality and Social Psychology, 81,* 247–262.

Goodwin, S. A., & Fiske, S. T. (1993). *Impression formation in asymmetrical power relationships: Does power corrupt absolutely?* Unpublished manuscript, University of Massachusetts at Amherst.

Goodwin, S. A., Gubin, A., Fiske, S. T., & Yzerbyt, V. Y. (2000). Power can bias impression processes: Stereotyping subordinates by default and by design. *Group Processes and Intergroup Relations, 3,* 227–256.

Green, D. P., Wong, J., & Strolovitch, D. (1996). *The effects of demographic change on hate crime.* Working paper no. 96-06. Institution for Social and Policy studies, Yale University.

Gruenfeld, D. H, Galinsky, A. D., & Magee, J. C. (2001). *Power and perspective-taking.* Unpublished raw data.

Gruenfeld, D. H, & Hollingshead, A. B. (1993). Sociocognition in work groups: The evolution of group integrative complexity and its relation to task performance. *Small Group Research, 24,* 383–405.

Gruenfeld, D. H, Keltner, D. J., & Anderson, C. (in press). The effects of power on those who possess it: How social structure can affect social cognition. In G. Bodenhausen & A. Lambert (Eds.), *Foundations of social cognition: A festschrift in honor of Robert S. Wyer, Jr.* Mahwah, NJ: Lawrence Erlbaum Associates.

Gruenfeld, D. H, & Kim, P. H. (2002). *Dissent and decision making on the U.S. Supreme Court: Conflict with a minority predicts cognitive complexity in the majority.* Working paper, Graduate School of Business, Stanford University.

Gruenfeld, D. H, & Preston, J. (2000). Upending the status quo: Cognitive complexity in Supreme Court justices who overturn legal precedent. *Personality and Social Psychology Bulletin, 26,* 1013–1022.

Haslam, S. A. (2001). *Psychology in organizations: The social identity approach.* London: Sage Publications.

Hass, R. G. (1984). Perspective taking and self-awareness: Drawing an E on your forehead. *Journal of Personality and Social Psychology, 46,* 788–798.

Hayward, M. L. A., & Hambrick, D. C. (1997). Explaining the premiums paid for large acquisitions: Evidence of CEO hubris. *Administrative Science Quarterly, 42,* 103–129.

Higgins, E. T. (1996). Knowledge activation: Accessibility, applicability, and salience. In E. T. Higgins & A. W. Kruglanski (Eds.), *Social psychology: Handbook of basic principles* (pp. 133–168). New York: Guilford Press.

Hogg, M. A., Hains, S. C., & Mason, I. (1998). Identification and leadership in small groups: Salience, frame of reference, and leader stereotypicality effects on leader evaluations. *Journal of Personality and Social Psychology, 75,* 1248–1263.

Hollander, E. P. (1985). Leadership and power. In G. Lindzey & E. Aronson (Eds.), *The handbook of social psychology* (2nd ed., Vol. 2, pp. 485–538). New York: Random House.

House, R. J., & Shamir, B. (1993). Toward the integration of transformational, charismatic, and visionary theories. In M. M. Chemers & R. Ayman (Eds.), *Leadership theory and research: Perspectives and directions* (pp. 81–107). San Diego: Academic Press.

Keltner, D., Gruenfeld, D. H, & Anderson, C. (2003). Power, approach, and inhibition. *Psychological Review, 110,* 265–284.

Keltner, D., & Robinson, R. J. (1996). Extremism, power, and the imagined basis of social conflict. *Current Directions in Psychological Science, 5,* 101–105.

Keltner, D., & Robinson, R. J. (1997). Defending the status quo: Power and bias in social conflict. *Personality and Social Psychology Bulletin, 23,* 1066–1077.

Kipnis, D. (1972). Does power corrupt? *Journal of Personality and Social Psychology, 24,* 33–41.

Kipnis, D. (1976). *The powerholders.* Chicago, IL: University of Chicago Press.

Larson, J. R., Foster-Fishman, P. G., & Franz, T. M. (1998). Leadership style and the discussion of shared and unshared information in decision-making groups. *Personality and Social Psychology Bulletin, 24,* 482–495.

Lerner, J. S., & Tetlock, P. E. (1999). Accounting for the effects of accountability. *Psychological Bulletin, 125,* 255–275.

Lord, R. G. (1977). Functional leadership behavior: Measurement and relations to social power and leadership perceptions. *Administrative Science Quarterly, 22,* 114–133.

Magee, J. C., Gruenfeld, D. H, & Galinksy, A. D. (2003, February). *Power and objectification: How powerholders perceive others in present and past.* Poster presented at the annual meeting of the Society for Personality and Social Psychology, Los Angeles, CA.

Marx, K. (1970). *The German ideology.* London: Lawrence & Wishart.

Mead, G. H. (1934). *Mind, self, and society.* Chicago, IL: University of Chicago Press.

Meindl, J. R., Ehrlich, S. B., & Dukerich, J. M. (1984). The romance of leadership. *Administrative Science Quarterly, 30,* 78–102.

Miller, D. T., Norman, S. A., & Wright, E. (1978). Distortion in person perception as a consequence of the need for effective control. *Journal of Personality and Social Psychology, 36,* 598–607.

Mischel, W., Cantor, N., & Feldman, S. (1996). Principles of self-regulation: The nature of willpower and self-control. In E. T. Higgins & A. W. Kruglanski (Eds.), *Social psychology: Handbook of basic principles* (pp. 329–360). New York: Guilford.

Muraven, M., & Baumeister, R. F. (2000). Self-regulation and depletion of limited resources: Does self-control resemble a muscle? *Psychological Bulletin, 126,* 247–259.

Muraven, M., Tice, D. M., & Baumeister, R. F. (1998). Self-control as a limited resource: Regulatory depletion patterns. *Journal of Personality and Social Psychology, 74,* 774–789.

Overbeck, J. R., & Park, B. (2001). When power does not corrupt: Superior individuation processes among powerful perceivers. *Journal of Personality and Social Psychology, 81,* 549–565.

Pears, I. (1992). The gentleman and the hero: Wellington and Napoleon in the nineteenth century. In R. Porter (Ed.), *Myths of the English* (pp. 216–236). Cambridge: Polity Press.

Peterson, R. S. (1997). Directive leadership style in group decision making can be both virtue and vice: Evidence from elite and experimental groups. *Journal of Personality and Social Psychology, 72,* 1107–1121.

Peterson, R. S. (1999). Can you have too much of a good thing? The limits of voice for improving satisfaction with leaders. *Personality and Social Psychology Bulletin, 25,* 313–324.

Pfeffer, J. (1992). *Managing with power.* Cambridge, MA: Harvard Business School Press.

Pfeffer, J., Cialdini, R., Hanna, B., & Knopoff, K. (1998). Faith in supervision and the self-enhancement bias: Two psychological reasons why managers don't empower workers. *Basic and Applied Psychology, 20,* 313–321.

Simonton, D. K. (1987). *Why presidents succeed: A political psychology of leadership.* New Haven, CT: Yale University Press.

Simonton, D. K. (1988). Presidential style: Personality, biography, and performance. *Journal of Personality and Social Psychology, 55,* 928–936.

Suedfeld, P., & Rank, A. D. (1976). Revolutionary leaders: Long-term success as a function of changes in conceptual complexity. *Journal of Personality and Social Psychology, 34,* 169–178.

Tetlock, P. E. (1981). Pre to postelection shifts in presidential rhetoric: Cognitive adjustment or impression management. *Journal of Personality and Social Psychology, 41,* 207–213.

Tetlock, P. E. (1992). The impact of accountability on judgment and choice: Toward a social contingency model. In M. P. Zanna (Ed.), *Advances in experimental social psychology* (Vol. 25, pp. 331–376). New York: Academic Press.

Tetlock, P. E., & Kim, J. I. (1987). Accountability and judgment processes in a personality prediction task. *Journal of Personality and Social Psychology, 52,* 700–709.

Tetlock, P. E., Peterson, R. S., & Berry, J. M. (1993). Flattering and unflattering personality portraits of integratively simple and complex managers. *Journal of Personality and Social Psychology, 64,* 500–511.

Thibaut, J. W., & Kelley, H. H. (1959). *The social psychology of groups.* New York: Wiley.

Vroom, V. H., & Yetton, P. W. (1973). *Leadership and decision making.* Pittsburgh: University of Pittsburgh Press.

Ward, G., & Keltner, D. (1998). *Power and the consumption of resources.* Unpublished manuscript.

Weber, M. (1947). *The theory of social and economic organization.* New York: The Free Press.

Wegner, D. M., & Bargh, J. A. (1998). Control and automaticity in social life. In D. Gilbert, S. T. Fiske, & G. Lindzey (Eds.), *Handbook of social psychology* (4th ed., Vol. 2, pp. 446–496). New York: McGraw-Hill.

Winter, D. G. (1973). *The power motive.* New York: The Free Press.

Winter, D. G. (1988). Using motive scores in the psychobiographical study of an individual: The case of Richard Nixon. *Journal of Personality, 56,* 75–103.

Winter, D. G. (1998). A motivational analysis of the Clinton first term and the 1996 presidential campaign. *Leadership Quarterly, 9,* 367–376.

Zellner, W., & Forest, S. A. (2001). *The fall of Enron: How ex-CEO Jeff Skilling's strategy grew so complex that even his boss couldn't get a handle on it.* Retrieved February 13, 2004, from http://www.businessweek.com/magazine/content/01_51/b3762001.htm

13

The Demise of Leadership: Death Positivity Biases in Posthumous Impressions of Leaders

Scott T. Allison
Dafna Eylon
University of Richmond

> *'Tis after death that we measure men.*
> —James Barron Hope (1895)

On November 7, 2000, voters in the state of Missouri elected Governor Melvin Carnahan to the U.S. Senate. Ordinarily, the act of electing a senator is not a newsworthy event; what made Carnahan's victory extraordinary was that voters had cast their ballots knowing that he had died in a plane crash three weeks prior to the election. It is important to note that Carnahan's posthumous victory did not simply reflect voters' sustained admiration of him. Indeed, opinion polls taken just prior to his death showed that he trailed his opponent by several percentage points. Only after his death did polls show Carnahan gaining on, and ultimately surpassing, his opponent. How is it that Carnahan's popularity could climb so dramatically after his demise?

The purpose of this chapter is to explore the psychological impact that a leader's death has on those who perceive him or her. We first review past philosophical and psychological perspectives on death and on evaluations of leadership. We then review the results of several studies we have conducted suggesting that our ways of forming impressions of dead leaders are strikingly different from our ways of forming impressions of living leaders. In reviewing these findings, we provide an overview of several posthumous impression phenomena, one of which nicely explains Mel Carnahan's posthumous rise in popularity. We conclude our chapter by highlighting the ways that posthumous impression phenomena can contribute to the practice of effective leadership and by exploring some potential areas for future research.

PAST PERSPECTIVES
ON POSTHUMOUS EVALUATIONS

Not surprisingly, the notion of death has long been the subject of great philosophical attention. From our review of the literature, at least two recurring themes emerge from philosophers' musings on the specific topic of how people form judgments about the dead. The first theme, which we do not explore in much detail, focuses on the tendency of people's impressions of the dead to be less malleable than their impressions of the living. "One does not know more facts about a man because his is dead," observed British author John Berger (1967), "but what one already knows, hardens, and becomes more definite." In other words, once people die our posthumous impressions of them become "frozen in time."

The second philosophical theme, which is at the core of our analysis, focuses on the tendency of people to view the dead more favorably than the living. Philosophers, authors, and poets have long been keenly aware of this evaluational bias. For example, Sophocles warned his audiences "not to insult the dead." The great Greek historian Thucydides echoed this sentiment in his observation that "all men are wont to praise him who is no more." Athenian statesman and legislator Solon implored citizens to "speak no ill of the dead." Centuries later, Francis Bacon noted that "death openeth the gate to good fame, and extinguisheth envy." In modern times, American poet John Whittier (1890) writes that "death softens all resentments, and the consciousness of a common inheritance of frailty and weakness modifies the severity of judgment."

Consistent with these ideas are the myriad examples of physical and behavioral manifestations of human beings' reverence for the dead. The

ancient Egyptians constructed huge pyramids to honor their dead pha-
raohs. Similarly, the Taj Mahal was built by the Hindus to preserve and
honor their deceased kings. The ancient Chinese participated in ancestor
worship, a practice that citizens of many Asian societies continue to this
day. Ancient Greeks and Romans venerated their dead heroes by crafting
epic tales of sacrifice and conquest, illustrated most vividly in Homer's
Iliad and *Odyssey,* and Vergil's *Aeneid.* To this day, Catholics revere their
saints, and different groups in countries across the world create and revere
their martyrs. Terrorist organizations routinely martyrize their suicide
bombers, and ironically organizations targeted by those terrorists martyrize their victims of terrorist attacks.

In both ancient and modern times, people have constructed monuments
and statuary to honor their dead heroes. More contemporary ways of exalting the dead have included the practice of posthumously naming universities, buildings, endowed chairs, and awards after departed heroes. Lav-
ish testimonials to the dead, moreover, are not limited to society's most
famous and accomplished individuals. Eulogies at the funerals of even
the most ordinary citizens overflow with praise and sweet remembrances
(Schaefer, 2000). Elaborate headstones with moving epitaphs adorn our
cemeteries, and moments of silence are commonly observed to honor the
dead at social gatherings.

From these examples, it is clear that people throughout history and
across cultures have elevated the status of the dead and engaged in rituals
aimed at honoring them. Indeed, we suggest that the practice of exalting
the dead satisfies a natural and fundamental human need. Scientific evidence supports this assertion. For example, anthropologists' examination
of early hominid settlements reveals that ritualistic practices of burial and
ceremony surrounding death are—along with language—a unique and
hallmark feature of being human (Metcalf, 1991). In addition, sociologists and psychologists have found that an important and natural part of
the bereavement process includes a period of "idealization" of the dead,
during which people form idealized images of the deceased person by
focusing almost exclusively on the person's positive qualities (Benton,
1978).

RESEARCH ON POSTHUMOUS
IMPRESSIONS OF LEADERS

To our surprise, there has been no prior empirical research on the manner
in which people evaluate dead leaders, nor has there been any previous

work at all on the question of how opinions and judgments are formed of the dead in general. A voluminous literature in social psychology speaks to the process of how we come to understand others (e.g., Fiske & Taylor, 1991; Gilbert, 1998, Hamilton & Sherman, 1996), and yet the entire focus of this work has been on impressions of living persons. There also exists a sizeable body of work in the area of organizational culture that examines the role of corporate leaders as heroes, myths, and legends (Schein, 1983). Although this literature acknowledges the importance of strong leaders who have passed away, it does not speak specifically to the impact of a leader's death in affecting judgments of the leader, nor does it focus on the more general topic of posthumous impression formation.

One possible explanation for the absence of research exploring perceptions of the dead may be an implicit assumption that our ways of knowing the dead are entirely the same as our ways of knowing the living. Yet, as we have already shown, it seems clear that our impressions and evaluations of people do change considerably once we learn they are dead.

To shed light on posthumous impressions of leaders, we have recently initiated a program of research aimed at investigating how people form judgments of dead leaders, and how these judgments differ from those formed of living leaders (Allison & Eylon, 2000; Allison, Eylon, Bachelder, & Beggan, 2003). Our methodological approach is typical of experimental social psychologists, featuring laboratory experiments designed to illuminate lay-perceptions of hypothetical individuals described as business leaders. The participants in all the studies we describe next were college undergraduates who were provided with descriptions of leaders and were then asked to form judgments about those leaders on a variety of trait dimensions.

The Death Positivity Bias

In our first study, our participants were told about a man named Erik Sullivan, who established a company in 1937 and turned it into a highly profitable organization. The vignette contained details of Sullivan's life and his role in promoting the company's growth to the time of his retirement in 1980. Participants were randomly assigned to one of two conditions. At the conclusion of the vignette, half the participants read that Sullivan was still living, whereas the other half read that Sullivan died in 1985. After reading the vignette, participants answered a number of questions intended to assess their impression of Sullivan. Participants were asked how much they respected him, how favorably they rated him as a leader and businessman, how proud they would be to work for him, how proud they believed his employees were to work for him, how much they believed he sacrificed for the company, how inspired they were by him, and how inspired they believed his employees were to work for him. Participants responded to each of these questions by circling a number on a numerical bipolar scale anchored at the low end (1) by "not at all" and at the high end (14) by "extremely."

Our results showed that, overall, participants formed significantly more favorable impressions of Sullivan when they believed he was dead than when they believed he was alive. This difference in impressions was obtained despite the fact that Sullivan's life history was described identically in both conditions. As compared to the living Sullivan, the dead Sullivan was judged as a significantly better leader, as a better businessman, as more inspirational, as having sacrificed more, and as engendering more pride and motivation from his employees.

We call this phenomenon the *death positivity bias,* which we define as the tendency of people to assign more positive traits to dead individuals than to equivalent living individuals. In a number of follow-up studies, we have demonstrated the robustness of the death positivity bias (see Allison et al., 2003). The bias emerges in judgments of nonleaders as well as leaders; in impressions of males as well as females; in judgments of those who die young as well as old; and for many different causes of death, such as murder, accident, and disease.

Our next studies were aimed at exploring the limits of the death positivity bias. At this point in our research, we had only asked participants to generate impressions of a fairly successful and competent leader, and we had found that the leader's death appeared to raise their already favorable views of him. But would our participants be equally magnanimous in their posthumous ratings of an ineffective leader?

Our second series of studies was designed to test between two competing hypotheses. The first hypothesis is that the death positivity bias is so robust that it transcends the leader's ability level: Just as people will form a more positive impression of a dead competent leader than a living competent leader, they may be similarly inclined to rate a dead incompetent leader more favorably than a living incompetent leader. The second, competing, hypothesis is that death does not inflate impressions but rather amplifies them. From this perspective, posthumous judgments are simply polarized versions of judgments made of living leaders. Thus, although a dead competent leader will be viewed more favorably than an equally competent living leader, a dead incompetent leader may be viewed *less* favorably than an equally incompetent living leader.

To test these ideas, we described our leader, Sullivan, in one condition as having made visionary investment decisions, hired good employees, and developed innovative products. In another condition, Sullivan was described as having made shortsighted investment decisions, hired bad employees, and developed useless products. These behaviors were pretested to ensure that they were perceived as either competent or incompetent by our participants. Once again some participants learned that Sullivan was still living while others learned that he was dead. The results showed clear support for the robustness of the death positivity bias. Regardless of whether Sullivan was effective or ineffective as a leader, he was viewed more favorably when participants believed he was dead than when they believed he was alive. The results of two additional follow-up studies later replicated this finding, and we display the aggregate means from all three studies in Fig. 13.1.

We also obtained one additional finding from these studies which is most noteworthy and has potentially important implications for organizations and leadership. Not only did we give our participants behavioral information about Sullivan, we also gave them a profile of the financial health of Sullivan's company. The profile gave a mixed picture of the organization, with both good and bad financial data included so that participants in both the competent and incompetent leader conditions would find the information believable. The profile read as follows:

At the end of the 1999 fiscal year, Sullivan's posted a profit of $46 million, an increase of 10% from 1998 but still 20% below the industry average.

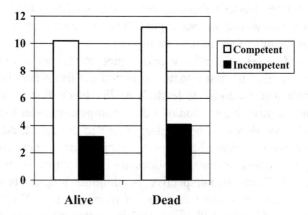

FIG. 13.1. Impressions of living and dead leaders who were described as competent or incompetent. The higher the rating, the more favorable the impression.

Sullivan's stock yielded a return of 13% in 1999, again bettering 1998's return but slightly below average in the industry. Sullivan's employs over 12,000 people worldwide and appears 264th in the Wall Street Journal's list of the 500 best companies to work for in America.

After making their ratings of Sullivan, participants were asked to rate the financial health and success of the company, as well as its future prospects. Our analysis of participants' responses to these items revealed that the death positivity bias extended to their perceptions of the company. Participants judged the company to be significantly more successful and more healthy financially when they believed that Sullivan was dead than when they believed he was alive. Moreover, they believed the company had a brighter future when Sullivan was dead than when he was alive. These findings held true for both the competent-Sullivan and the incompetent-Sullivan conditions. We discuss the potential implications of these interesting findings later in this chapter.

Death Positivity Versus Death Polarization

In our third series of studies, we again sought to identify the delimiting conditions of the death positivity bias. Our previous studies showed that people are disposed toward forming more favorable impressions of dead leaders and their organizations than of living leaders, independent of the leaders' standing on the dimension of competence. But how might people form judgments about leaders whose actions vary on the dimension of morality?

There are at least two reasons to believe that people may show less posthumous forgiveness of immorality than they would of incompetence. First, people may be less likely to show the death positivity bias for the dimension of morality because they may view moral and immoral actions as reflecting volitional choice. Individuals cannot control their level of intelligence but they can freely choose whether to behave morally (see Allison, Messick, & Goethals, 1989; Van Lange & Sedikides, 1998). To the extent that leaders have control over performing negative actions, perceivers may be unwilling to form more favorable posthumous evaluations of them.

A second reason why the death positivity bias may be weaker for the dimension of morality than for competence is based on past research findings in support of terror management theory (Greenberg, Solomon, & Pyszczynski, 1997). In one terror management study, participants served as judges who were asked either to levy monetary fines to others who had behaved immorally or to allocate rewards to others who had behaved morally. Some participants, in the mortality salience condition, had earlier answered questions about their own deaths. According to terror management theory, death anxiety intensifies allegiance to moral codes of conduct, and thus participants in the mortality salience condition should impose more severe fines to moral transgressors and give higher rewards to moral upholders. The results of this study, as well as the others, support this hypothesis (Rosenblatt, Greenberg, Solomon, Pyszczynski, & Lyon, 1989).

From these considerations, we hypothesized that the death positivity bias should emerge only for the dimension of competence, and that a death *polarization* bias should characterize participants' judgments for the dimension of morality. Participants in our next studies were informed about a leader who was either competent, incompetent, moral, or immoral. Once again, some participants were told that the leader had passed away while others learned that he was still living. Our examples of the leader's moral and immoral actions were pre-tested and included such actions as the legal (or illegal) disposing of toxic waste, the generous (or stingy) treatment of employees, and the giving (or not giving) of money to local charities.

The results of our studies revealed a very clear pattern, shown in Fig. 13.2. First, replicating our prior findings, participants once again showed the death positivity bias for the dimension of competence. Dead leaders were judged more favorably than living leaders, even when their leadership was inept. However, for the dimension of morality, we found strong

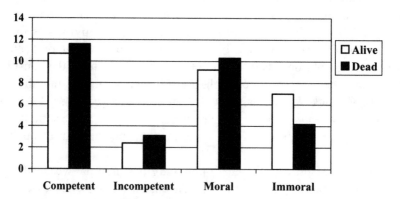

FIG. 13.2. Impressions of living and dead leaders who were described as competent, incompetent, moral, or immoral. The higher the rating, the more favorable the impression.

evidence of a death polarization bias. Dead moral leaders were judged significantly more favorably than living moral leaders, whereas—with one notable exception—dead immoral leaders were rated significantly *less* favorably than living immoral leaders. Compared to living immoral leaders, dead immoral leaders were viewed as weaker leaders, as less inspirational, as less motivational, and as engendering less respect and pride from others in the organization.

Interestingly, the one exception to this extremitization pattern occurred in ratings of the leader's business savvy. An immoral leader, whether dead or alive, was judged as being a better businessman than was a moral leader. Apparently, our participants believed that it was good business acumen to save the company money by withholding employee benefits and by cheaply disposing of toxic waste. However, they rated a leader who took these moral shortcuts as a less effective and less inspiring leader overall, and they were especially critical of the overall leadership abilities of immoral leaders who were dead.

We also found once again that our participants' judgments about the financial health and future of the company mirrored their judgments about the leader. The dead leader's company was judged to be more successful than the living leader's company, independent of the leader's competence level. However, death polarization characterized judgments of a company whose leader behaved morally or immorally. Specifically, whereas a dead moral leader's company was rated more favorably than a living moral leader's company, a dead immoral leader's company was judged as less successful than a living immoral leader's company. Again, we will discuss some possible implications of this finding shortly.

The St. Augustine Effect

Our next set of studies of posthumous impressions have explored the manner in which people interpret changes in a leader's behavior over time. Prior social psychological work has investigated people's intuitive notions of dispositional change in others (Heider, 1958; Mackie & Allison, 1987; Silka, 1984), and there has been an abundance of research examining primacy and recency biases in people's sensitivity to changes in information about others (Asch, 1946; Jones & Goethals, 1987). To the best of our knowledge, however, no one has explored how people form impressions of leaders who undergo a significant change in behavior during their careers, nor has anyone addressed this topic from the perspective of posthumous impression formation.

To study this question, we gave participants behavioral information about a leader, described as either living or dead, who underwent a change in competence or morality during his career. Participants were randomly assigned to one of four conditions. Some were informed that the leader performed competent actions during the first half of his career but performed incompetent actions during the latter half of his career. Other participants were informed of a leader who experienced the reverse change in competency, a shift from incompetent to competent. Still other participants were given information about a leader who performed moral actions early in his career but immoral ones later in his career. The final group of subjects was presented with a leader who was immoral at first and then moral later.

Our hypotheses regarding participants' impressions of the leader differed markedly as a function of whether the leader's change in behavior occurred on the competency dimension or the morality dimension. For the competency conditions, we predicted that participants would generate more favorable ratings of a leader whose competencies increased over time than of a leader whose competencies decreased. Moreover, we expected to replicate our earlier finding that regardless of the direction of change in the leader's competency, participants would form more positive impressions of a dead leader than of a living leader.

For the morality change conditions, we predicted that our North American cultural emphasis on Judeo-Christian beliefs would prompt participants to form the most favorable impressions of an immoral leader who transformed into a moral leader over time. That is, we expected participants to love sinners who became saints, a tendency we call the *St. Augustine effect,* named after the fifth century philosopher and priest who underwent such a transformation (Wills, 1999). We also expected participants to loathe saints who became sinners, a phenomenon we call the *fallen angel effect.* Because our earlier studies showed a death polarization pattern for the morality dimension, we expected both the St. Augustine and fallen angel effects to be stronger when participants formed impressions of a dead leader as compared to a living leader.

The results of this study were supportive of some of our hypotheses but also surprising in some respects. We display the relevant means in Fig. 13.3, where one can see support for our predictions in the competency change conditions. Our participants made more favorable judgments of the leader whose competencies increased over time than of the leader whose competencies declined. This finding is consistent with Aronson and Linder's (1965) gain-loss model of attraction, as well as research on contrast effects (Kenrick & Gutierres, 1980), adaptation levels (Helson,

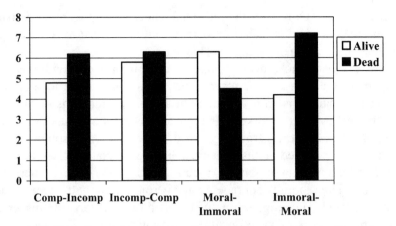

FIG. 13.3.   Impressions of living and dead leaders whose behavior changed during their careers from competent to incompetent, from incompetent to competent, from moral to immoral, or from immoral to moral. The higher the rating, the more favorable the impression.

1964), and framing (Kahneman & Tversky, 1979). More importantly, and consistent with our previous studies, our results showed that participants rated the dead leader more favorably than the living leader regardless of the direction of the leader's change in competency. These data were consistent with our expectations and again showed that people are posthumously forgiving of incompetence.

However, the morality change conditions produced some surprising results. As Fig. 13.3 shows, our participants' impressions of a leader who underwent a moral transformation were sensitive to the time period during the leader's life when he performed his moral or immoral actions. Specifically, participants' impressions of the living leader tended to be influenced by the leader's behavior performed early in his career, whereas their impressions of the dead leader tended to be influenced by the leader's behavior performed later in his career. Thus, the St. Augustine effect and the fallen angel effect emerged only in impressions of dead leaders but not of living leaders.

Why should judgments of the dead, rather than the living, be based more on moral or immoral behaviors performed late in life? One possible answer to this question can be found by considering participants' responses to our debriefing questions at the conclusion of our study. Participants were asked to explain why they provided favorable or unfavorable ratings of the leader. We discovered that our participants were hesitant to bestow saintly status to a living reformed sinner because "the jury was still out on that person." Only after the reformed sinner's death were participants willing to concede that a change toward saintliness must have reflected a genuine and permanent change in character.

The terrorist attacks of September 11, 2001, provide vivid anecdotal support for the idea that we reserve our greatest reverence for individuals whose final act is an act of supreme morality. Hundreds of firefighters, emergency rescue workers, and law enforcement personnel sacrificed their lives to save others from the World Trade Center. Although roughly 3,000 people perished in this tragedy, a disproportionate amount of media attention, and national mourning, focused on the loss of these emergency personnel. Their morally courageous and heroic actions at the time of their deaths "sealed" our impressions of them forever. Clearly, living emergency rescue workers have our great admiration, but as our data on the St. Augustine effect suggest, our greatest veneration is reserved for individuals whose deaths occur in the performance of their altruistic emergency services.

Why Do People Show a Death Positivity Bias?

The underlying cause of the death positivity bias is not the central focus of this chapter, and so we will not devote much space here to this issue. We will, however, briefly review two possible mechanisms that may contribute to the death positivity bias. First, we speculate that the bias may reflect the use of a strong social norm prescribing respect for the dead. The norm, we believe, is so powerful that its activation requires little thought at all, suggesting that it serves as a judgment heuristic that people use to make quick, efficient social inferences about the dead. We also propose that people are most likely to rely on this simple heuristic when forming impressions of dead individuals with whom they shared no significant affective or cognitive relationship. We suspect that the participants in our studies relied on this heuristic process to generate posthumously favorable judgments about the leaders that we presented to them.

However, what happens when one has enjoyed a close affective or cognitive connection to a person who has just died? We suggest that under these conditions the death positivity bias does not reflect the use of a simple heuristic but rather stems from deeper processing about the deceased person specifically, and about life and death in general. This deeper processing can assume many forms, such as a thoughtful deliberation of one's relationship with the deceased, of spiritual or religious issues, or of the more cosmic significance of human existence. Becker (1973) posits that the death of a loved one leads people to a heightened focus on the miraculous uniqueness of the individual, which he calls "the ache of cosmic specialness" (p. 64).

If the idea of death is associated with heightened appraisals of others, then it is very possible that this association can be triggered even by near-death experiences. For example, Ronald Reagan's popularity soared after he was nearly assassinated in 1981, suggesting that he benefited from some sort of near-death positivity bias. Again, the mechanisms underlying a near-death positivity bias are supported by current theoretical models of social inference processes. According to Gilbert (1998), people automatically assign traits to others but then fail to adequately correct those judgments when presented with information suggesting that their trait assignments may be erroneous. Adapting from Gilbert's (1998) model, we can speculate that social perceivers first observe a life-threatening behavior (e.g., "Ronald Reagan was shot"), then they make tentative death positivity judgments about the person ("Reagan is a good person"), but then later fail to adequately correct for information indicating that death did not occur ("He survived but he's still a pretty good person"). In the aftermath of the shooting, Reagan's grace under pressure and one-line quips to the press may have endeared him to the public, thus reinforcing their near-death positivity bias judgments. Clearly, future research is needed to determine whether, and how, near-death positivity biases occur.

In sum, we speculate that the death positivity bias can emerge from two completely different processes, one focusing on the fast application of a simple heuristic requiring only superficial thought, and the other involving an extremely thoughtful analysis of more spiritual, cosmic, or existential issues. It is interesting to note that the death positivity bias is consistent with the tenets of commodity theory (Lynn, 1991), which posits that any commodity's value increases to the extent that it is no longer available. Consistent with our analysis, scarcity's effects on value formation have been shown to derive from both heuristic processes (Cialdini, 1993) and more elaborative processing (Brannon & Brock, 2001). More details about the precise mechanisms underlying the death positivity bias can be found in Allison et al. (2003).

Summary of Findings

To summarize the findings from our research, we have discovered that people tend to generate more positive trait judgments of dead leaders than of identically described living leaders, a phenomenon we call the death positivity bias. We have ample evidence that this bias transcends the leader's age, gender, station in life, level of competence, and cause of death. In addition, we have found that people do not display the bias when perceiving dead leaders whose lives were characterized by obvious moral turpitude. In fact, judgments of leaders who vary on the morality dimension show an extremitization bias, with people forming more favorable judgments of dead moral leaders than of living ones but less favorable judgments of dead immoral leaders than of living ones.

It is very significant that people's judgments of the current and future financial condition of a leader's organization tend to parallel their judgments of the leader. Thus, a dead leader's organization is generally viewed more favorably than a living leader's organization, except when the dead leader was known to have performed immoral actions. In this latter case, the organization receives the same extremitized negative trait ratings that the dead immoral leader receives. Finally, we discovered that although living leaders are judged by the moral actions they performed early in their careers, dead leaders are judged more by their moral actions performed late in their careers, near the time of their death.

POSTHUMOUS IMPRESSIONS AND EFFECTIVE LEADERSHIP

What role do these posthumous impression phenomena play in the practice of effective leadership? We propose that there are at least three ways that our findings can promote better and more responsible leadership. First, posthumous impression phenomena clearly underscore the importance of proactive moral leadership. Our findings suggest that a leader's moral conduct may be a more central determinant of leadership effectiveness than other, more traditional, criteria for evaluating leadership (see Meindl & Ehrlich, 1987). Second, these phenomena have implications for influencing employee attitudes and behavior in the workplace. Leadership has long been known to shape the values and performance of those who follow (Gardner, 1995), and our data speak to the role of moral leadership in influencing followers. Finally, posthumous phenomena suggest strategies for leaders to craft constructive posthumous legacies for themselves and for their organizations. Although firms and individuals work hard at building reputations, it is clear that the focus needs to be on the long term (including issues related to social concern), rather than on short-term profitability or pizzazz (Fombrun & Shanley, 1990). We explore each of these three ideas in turn next.

The Importance of Proactive Moral Leadership

One conclusion that can be drawn from our research is that a leader's immoral actions are likely to posthumously stain both the leader's reputation and the organization's image. This idea may appear trite and obvious, but what is less obvious is that the damage done by a leader's moral improprieties may be far worse than people realize. Death intensifies the affective reactions people have in response to a leader's moral or immoral behavior, and this affective intensification influences impressions of both the leader and the organization. The good news for organizations is that they stand to reap extremitized benefits from their departed leaders' beneficent actions, but at the same time their image may also incur extremitized damage from their departed leaders' corrupt actions.

For this reason, it is imperative that organizations ensure that their leaders engage in numerous well-publicized moral actions and, more importantly, avoid any moral breaches. Leaders, we argue, have both a moral and a fiscal responsibility to their companies to be visibly and proactively ethical at all times. Our argument builds on the wealth of literature that supports this view, among them Etzioni's (1988) work, that supports that most human decisions and actions are motivated not only by economic reasons, but also by moral concerns. The vast literature on stakeholder theory also provides a convincing case for why executives should act morally (e.g., Freeman, 1984), and why they should do so when there is no clear economic payoff (Swanson, 1995). In addition, due to the increased scrutiny by the media, organizational leaders are becoming more aware that they can no longer afford to assume that their actions, even personal ones, will escape public notice. Overall, we now know that the media can influence the reputation of the organization, thereby influencing executives to act more morally than they may have otherwise (Trevino & Nelson, 1999).

Leaders' Impact on Employee and Organizations' Moral Behavior

Currently there is strong consensus that leaders have significant impact on organizational culture, often long after they have passed away (e.g., organizations such as Disney, University of Virginia, Hewlett Packard, etc.).

In addition, numerous studies suggest that a critical role of the organizational leader involves guiding the ethical behavior of the employees (e.g., Trevino, Butterfield, & McCabe, 1998). Our findings extend this work by suggesting that the leader's influence goes well beyond the sphere of the culture of the organization, or of the individual actions of any particular employee. Rather, leaders' overt ethical behavior may markedly enhance their company's stature and well-being long after they are gone, whereas failing to behave ethically can have magnified negative posthumous consequences for themselves, for the decisions future employees make, and for the overall future success of the organization.

The most surprising finding of our research was that the moral (or immoral) actions of a living leader had their strongest impact when the actions were performed early in the leader's career, whereas these same actions performed by a dead leader wielded the greatest influence when they appeared late in the leader's career. Two possible lessons for business leaders may be gleaned from this result. First, leaders may benefit their own reputations and perceived effectiveness by ensuring that their early career moral actions are widely known. Second, our findings suggest that the ideal time for leaders to increase their level of philanthropic activity, or at least the visibility of such activity, is toward the end of their careers. In this way, a leader's positive legacy will be cemented long after he or she is gone. We next address legacy management more specifically.

Leaders' Legacy Management

Although many leaders aspire to exert a positive and enduring impact on an organization long after they are gone, they often find it challenging to craft this legacy effectively. In the political arena, Richard Nixon and Bill Clinton both left the office of U.S. President with their reputations morally stained, although for very different reasons and to a very different degree. After leaving office, Nixon made numerous efforts to repair his criminal image by serving as an elder statesman, writer, consultant, and informal ambassador to subsequent administrations. Upon his death, criticism of his presidency and of his personal character were softened out of respect for the dead, but his post-presidential activities did not feature the type of moral emphasis needed to overcome his past ethical indiscretions. Although he was eulogized as a skillful and insightful statesman, he was never quite able to shed his image as a morally corrupt individual, and in fact many historians are convinced that he is doomed to be eternally associated with his immoral transgressions as president (Hoff, 1994). Indeed, in comparison to other past presidents, Nixon continues to receive low public opinion poll ratings.

Other presidents have more complex legacies. Clinton's legacy, for example, is still unclear because his behavior as a philanderer while in office tended to be castigated by conservatives but condoned by liberals. Moreover, his lying under oath was problematic for members of both parties. To improve impressions, Clinton would be wise in his remaining years to emulate the post-presidential life of Jimmy Carter, whose widespread philanthropic activity has endeared him the the public and may have succeeded in silencing some of the critics of his presidency.

The legacy of John F. Kennedy is a fascinating example, inasmuch as the public's fixation with Kennedy's administration as the perfect Camelot was no doubt due to a heightened death positivity bias resulting from his premature death. Admired as a president, Kennedy and his reputation have withstood posthumous revelations of his own numerous marital infidelities and self-calculating behaviors (Lasky, 1963). Had JFK lived to fulfill a second term, the realities of his lechery and dealings with the Mafia would have most likely gravely damaged the presidency, debilitated his administration, and disillusioned his supporters (Reeves, 1991).

Similarly to JFK, Thomas Jefferson's image has remained intact despite recent DNA confirmations that he fathered several children with his slave, Sally Hemings. Why are Kennedy's and Jefferson's positive reputations so seemingly bullet-proof, despite new information emerging that calls into question their moral conduct while serving as president?

We believe that there are several reasons why Kennedy and Jefferson have retained their positive legacies despite highly publicized evidence of their moral misdeeds. As noted earlier in this chapter, philosophers have long suspected that impressions of the dead are more resistant to change than are impressions of the living. We have collected some preliminary data supporting this tendency of posthumous impressions to first become more favorable (the death positivity bias) and then become "frozen in time." We suspect that this frozen-in-time effect is derived from several factors. First, the dead are obviously not available to perform new behaviors from which to modify one's existing impression. Second, as in the case of Kennedy and Jefferson, people recognize the inherent unfairness of slinging mud at those who are no longer around to defend themselves. Third, there is often a suspicion that posthumous mudslingers have some political, economic, or personal agenda. Finally, for many people, there are certain categories of behavior—sexual promiscuity among them— that are simply not relevant dimensions on which to evaluate a political leader's contributions. This last point, focusing on the relevant dimensions of morality, is a rich area for future research in the context of the topic of posthumous leader assessment.

In the business world, legacy management is also pervasive and can be informed by the findings from our research on posthumous impression formation. The "robber barons" of the late 19th century keenly left a remarkable philanthropic legacy in the arts and education. Steel magnate Andrew Carnegie built libraries and museums, and he helped establish the Carnegie Endowment for International Peace. As he aged he donated larger amounts of his fortune, in sum totaling $350 million by the time he died in 1919, a sum that would be worth over $3 billion in today's dollars. As a result he became known as St. Andrew (Strouse, 1999). Rockefeller gave away $540 million before his death in 1937, which would amount to roughly $7 billion today (Strouse, 1999). Additional examples include Henry Clay Frick and J. Paul Getty, who funded the creation of numerous art galleries, and railroad tycoon Leland Stanford, who founded a university that is unique in its co-educational, nondenominational, and practical emphasis. The pejorative term "robber baron," and the accompanying resentment of many to the vast wealth of these industrial tycoons, no doubt played a role in the decisions to establish these generous philanthropic legacies.

The modern analog to these examples is Bill Gates and his recent $2.4 billion gift to MIT, Columbia University, the Global Fund for Children's Vaccines, and other charities. Currently, the Bill and Melinda Gates Foundation is the largest in the world. Americans have great admiration for those who achieve vast wealth, but it is also clear that with this great admiration comes great expectations for extreme generosity. Gates' large gift, and others sure to follow, should seal his extremitized, positive, posthumous legacy. Other modern, instantly-wealthy millionaires of the technology-driven boom of the 1990s are also making it a priority to bestow large philanthropic gifts to various foundations and charities. These individuals include Steve Case of America Online, Henry Samueli of Broadcom, and Steve Kirsh of Propel Software and Infoseek. We are not implying that a leader's legacy will be based solely on the moral dimension; however, our data suggest that when making posthumous evaluations of leaders, we seem to use different criteria when evaluating leadership effectiveness based on the leader's standing on the competence versus morality dimensions.

Another intriguing example of highly effective legacy management can be seen in the life and death of Walt Disney. An examination of his career reveals a man who went to great lengths to project the cleanest and most wholesome of images to the public (Eliot, 1993; Thomas, 1976). We believe that there are at least two strategies that Disney used to successfully create a remarkable and enduring posthumous legacy. First, he painstakingly ensured that his body of work, in the form of dozens of cartoon motion pictures and theme parks, reflected positive family values and a love for children. Second, he employed many public relations individuals whose primary job was to ensure that all of America, and eventually the world, would associate Disney's name with morality, innocence, kindness, and family fun. Disney's efforts were eminently successful, and to this day the many dark sides to his personality and behavior remain largely unknown to the public (Eliot, 1993).

CONCLUSIONS AND FUTURE DIRECTIONS

From our research findings presented here, it appears that a principal factor that people consider when evaluating a leader's effectiveness is the leader's status as living or deceased. We suspect that people are largely unaware of their use of this factor, and that they would ardently deny that it has any bearing at all on their assessment of a leader. But our data clearly show that people exalt dead leaders, judging them to be more effective and inspirational than equivalent living leaders. Interestingly, it seems that not only do we exalt the dead, but there is some generalized effect so that the leader's organizational association gains from this posthumous adulation as well. However, on issues of morality, we have found a pattern of extremitization: the good are exalted and the bad are viewed very negatively, far more so than if they were still alive. Again, these evaluations also influence how the leader's organization is perceived.

Thus, we propose that a leader's legacy of morality is just as important, if not more so, than a legacy of competence. Because our research also suggests that a leader's legacy and the organization's reputation appear to be intertwined, a leader's actions, especially on the morality dimension, may be far more significant than either the leader or his or her followers realize. The implications of these findings for leaders and their organizations include constant vigilance directed toward the moral implications of their actions. In other words, even if actions lead to enhanced competence, we now know that the moral judgment of such actions may exceed material gain, although the shift in evaluation may occur only after the leader's death.

Clearly, our work is at the beginning stages and there is significant room for further exploration of the topic. In addition to identifying what dimensions of leader morality are the most significant to the organization's identity and reputation, there are several more venues that we believe are important in clarifying our understanding of posthumous impressions of leaders. One promising area for future work is to establish further evidence for the "frozen in time" effect, which we defined earlier as the tendency of judgments about the dead to be less malleable than judgments about the living. At the time that this chapter is going to press, our pilot data are highly suggestive that judgments of the dead are indeed highly resistant to change. When our pilot subjects received new information (either good or bad) that surfaced about a dead leader, their impressions of the leader changed less than when they received the identical information about a living leader. To the extent that posthumous revelations of good deeds appear to be largely ignored, leaders may need to take special care to ensure that those good deeds are known by the organization and by the public while they are still alive.

We also believe that a rich area of future investigation is the manner in which people process information differently about the dead than they do about the living. Our data suggest that death jolts people out of their ordinary ways of thinking and may therefore disrupt the automatic routine of everyday social perception. For example, current social cognition research suggests that people engage in "on-line" processing of living individuals, forming spontaneous trait inferences about them as information in encoded (Hamilton & Sherman, 1996). We suggest the possibility that information processing about dead individuals proceeds in a more "memory-based" fashion, with social perceivers withholding judgment about the dead until all available information about them is known. As a result of these processing differences, we suspect that people are slower to make trait judgments about the dead than about the living, and that judgments about the dead are more likely to show a recency effect rather than the standard primacy effect found in judgments about the living. As more is known about the cognitive processes underlying posthumous judgment phenomena, more applications to the promotion of leadership effectiveness will become illuminated.

Finally, from a methodological standpoint, our work needs to evolve beyond the laboratory setting that measures only college undergraduates' perceptions of fictitious leaders. Obviously, the advantage of the methodology we have chosen to employ to date is the high level of control of competing variables. However, much will be gained by exploring perceptions of real-world leaders and verifying that our findings generalize to lay-judgments of actual leadership. Overall, we believe that the contributions of this work have the potential of making an impact not only on the academic literature, but also in raising our awareness in how we evaluate organizations and their leaders. Recognizing that leaders' moral choices may posthumously magnify employees' beliefs and values far into the future may help elevate the recognition that leaders carry an important responsibility as organizational moral role models.

ACKNOWLEDGMENTS

The authors thank Teri Schrettenbrunner, Elizabeth Haines, Jennifer Bachelder, Emily Breiner, and Sarah Myers for their contributions to the research described in this chapter.

REFERENCES

Allison, S. T., & Eylon, D. (2000, October). *Principles of posthumous impression formation.* Paper presented at the annual meeting of the Person Memory Interest Group, Helen, GA.

Allison, S. T., Eylon, D., Bachelder, J., & Beggan, J. K. (2004). *Death becomes her: The death positivity bias in posthumous impression formation.* Unpublished manuscript, University of Richmond.

Allison, S. T., Messick, D. M., & Goethals, G. R. (1989). On being better but not smarter than others: The Muhammad Ali effect. *Social Cognition, 7,* 275–296.

Aronson, E., & Linder, D. (1965). Gain and loss of esteem as determinants of interpersonal attractiveness. *Journal of Experimental Social Psychology, 1,* 156–172.

Asch, S. (1946). Forming impressions of personality. *Journal of Abnormal and Social Psychology, 41,* 258–290.

Becker, E. (1973). *The denial of death.* New York: The Free Press.

Benton, R. G. (1978). *Death and dying.* New York: Van Nostrand Reinhold Company.

Berger, J. (1967). *A fortunate man: The story of a country doctor.* New York: Centennial Books.

Brannon, L. A., & Brock, T. C. (2001). Scarcity claims elicit extreme responding to persuasive messages: Role of cognitive elaboration. *Personality and Social Psychology Bulletin, 27,* 365–375.

Cialdini, R. B. (1993). *Influence: Science and practice.* New York: HarperCollins.

Eliot, M. (1993). *Walt Disney: Hollywood's dark prince.* Secaucus, NJ: Carol Publishing Group.

Etzioni, A. (1988). *The moral dimension: Toward a new economics.* New York: The Free Press.

Fiske, S. T., & Taylor, S. E. (1991). *Social cognition.* New York: McGraw-Hill.

Fombrun, C.m & Shanley, M. (1990). What's in a name? Reputation building and corporate strategy. *Academy of Management Journal, 33*(2), 233–258.

Freeman, E. (1984). *Strategic management: A stakeholder approach.* Boston: Pitman/Ballinger.

Gardner, J. W. (1995). Leaders and followers. In J. T. Wren (Ed.), *The leader's companion*. New York: The Free Press.

Gilbert, D. T. (1998). Ordinary personology. In D. Gilbert, S. Fiske, & G. Lindzey (Eds.), *The handbook of social psychology* (pp. 89–150). New York: McGraw-Hill.

Greenberg, J., Solomon, S., & Pyszczynski, T. (1997). Terror management theory of self-esteem and cultural worldviews: Empirical assessments and conceptual refinements. In M. Zanna (Ed.), *Advances in experimental social psychology* (Vol. 29, pp. 61–139). San Diego: Academic Press.

Hamilton, D. L., & Sherman, S. J. (1996). Perceiving persons and groups. *Psychological Review, 103*, 336–355.

Heider, F. (1958). *The psychology of interpersonal relations*. New York: Wiley.

Helson, H. (1964). *Adaptation-level theory: An experimental and systematic approach to behavior*. New York: Harper & Row.

Hoff, J. (1994). *Nixon reconsidered*. New York: Harper Collins Publishers.

Hope, J. B. (1895). Our heroic dead. In J. H. Marr (Ed.), *A wreath of Virginia bay leaves* (p. 71). Richmond, VA: West, Johnston & Co.

Jones, E. E., & Goethals, G. R. (1987). Order effects in impression formation: Attribution context and the nature of the entity. In E. E. Jones & D. E. Kanouse (Eds.), *Attribution: Perceiving the causes of behavior* (pp. 27–46). Hillsdale, NJ: Lawrence Erlbaum Associates.

Kahneman, D., & Tversky, A. (1979). Prospect theory: An analysis of decision under risk. *Econometrica, 47*, 263–291.

Kenrick, D. T., & Gutierres, S. E. (1980). Contrast effects and judgments of physical attractiveness: When beauty becomes a social problem. *Journal of Personality and Social Psychology, 38*, 131–140.

Lasky, F. (1963). *The man or the myth*. New York: The Free Press.

Lynn, M. (1991). Scarcity effects on desirability: A quantitative review of the commodity theory literature. *Psychology and Marketing, 8*, 43–57.

Mackie, D. M., & Allison, S. T. (1987). Group attribution errors and the illusion of group attitude change. *Journal of Experimental Social Psychology, 23*, 460–480.

Metcalf, P. (1991). *Celebrations of death: The anthropology of mortuary ritual*. New York: Cambridge University Press.

Meindl, J. R., & Ehrlich, S. B. (1987). The romance of leadership and the evaluation of organizational performance. *Academy of Management Journal, 30*, 91–109.

Reeves, T. C. (1991). *A question of character: The life of John F. Kennedy* New York: The Free Press.

Rosenblatt, A., Greenberg, J., Solomon, S., Pyszczynski, T., & Lyon, D. (1989). Evidence for terror management theory I: The effects of mortality salience on reactions to those who violate or uphold cultural values. *Journal of Personality and Social Psychology, 57*, 681–690.

Schaefer, G. (2000). *A labor of love: How to write a eulogy*. New York: Genesis Press.

Schein, E. H. (1983). The role of the founder in creating organizational culture. *Organizational Dynamics, 18*, 13–28.

Silka, L. (1984). Intuitive perceptions of change: An overlooked phenomenon in person perception. *Personality and Social Psychology Bulletin, 10*, 180–190.

Strouse, J. (1999). *How to give away $21.8 billion*. New York: Random House.

Swanson, D. (1995). Addressing a theoretical problem by reorienting the corporate social performance model. *Academy of Management Review, 20*, 43–64.

Thomas, B. (1976). *Walt Disney: An American original*. New York: Simon and Schuster.

Trevino, L., Butterfield, K., & McCabe, D. (1998). The ethical context in organizations: Influences on employee attitudes and behaviors *Business Ethics Quarterly, 8*, 447–476.

Trevino, L. K., & Nelson, K. A. (1999). *Managing business ethics* (2nd ed.). New York: John Wiley.

Van Lange, P. A. M., & Sedikides, C. (1998). Being more honest but not necessarily more intelligent than others: Generality and explanations for the Muhammad Ali effect. *European Journal of Social Psychology, 28,* 675–680.

Whittier, J. G. (1890). *Ichabod.* Retrieved March 29, 2004, from http://www.assumption.edu/ahc/WhittierIchabod.html

Wills, G. (1999). *Saint Augustine.* New York: Viking.

IV

Commentary

14

When Leadership Matters and When It Does Not: A Commentary

Suzanne Chan
Arthur P. Brief
A. B. Freeman School of Business
Tulane University

Neither of the authors of this chapter are, nor desire to be, leadership scholars. Indeed, our level of ignorance is such that we find the "leadership" construct a bit scary. However, our intuition, not to mention all the results yielded from numerous leadership studies, have led us to be concerned that our own programs of research are missing an essential element that we are neither equipped nor, truthfully, interested in dealing with (i.e., leadership). Given our fears, we approached the chapters in this volume with a specific agenda.

First, we wanted to discover what the chapters tell us about when it is safe to avoid the study of leadership. Second, given that one cannot always avoid it, what do the chapters teach us about leadership that is relevant to our own research interests? Thus, this commentary is highly personalized and focused. It does not supply an analysis of how the chapters may serve to push the leadership literature forward in this or that direction. Again, our aims are more selfish, and we, as leadership novices, are not qualified to assess how the chapters affect the "big picture" of leadership research. We suspect, however, that our approach to reading the chapters is not unlike that of most other readers. Our understanding is that the volume is not intended to be for or by leadership researchers. Rather, we think the editors intended to bring folks like us into the leadership fold. Let's see if they have succeeded.

In each of the following three sections, a question consistent with our agenda is posed, and, the answers, if any, we found to it in the chapters are presented. The commentary concludes with a few general observations about the collection and the importance of the "leadership" construct.

WHEN CAN LEADERSHIP BE IGNORED?

We, and we suspect many other organizational scientists, have relied implicitly upon Kerr and Jermier's (1978) ideas about substitutes for leadership to justify turning a blind eye toward the "leadership" construct. Essentially, Kerr and Jermier argued that when substitutes are present, such as when subordinates have a high need for independence, when tasks are unambiguous and highly standardized, and when formal written work rules and procedures are in place, leaders' actions become less relevant in shaping organizational outcomes. Regrettably, Podsakoff, MacKenzie, and Bommer (1996) demonstrated, based on an exhaustive review of the literature, that the "substitutes" idea really does not hold water. So, we remain in search of those circumstances under which leadership can be ignored.

Three of the chapters in this volume provided us, at least implicitly, with some degree of comfort that leadership does not matter all of the time; the others seemed to assume that leaders always matter. Examining leadership through a strategic management lens, Ganz (chap. 10, this volume) provided a delightful metaphor of how David, with fewer resources, effectively used his creative strategic capacity to triumph over the resource-rich giant, Goliath. He claimed that leaders, by devising creative strategies to make the best and most efficient use of available resources, play a vital role in shaping organizational outcomes. Drawing upon Amabile's (1996) creativity model, Ganz asserted that in order to generate creative strategies to ensure organizations' success, leaders must be motivated, possess the necessary skills related to the problems at hand, and be able to recontextualize and make use of similar situations experienced in the past to produce new, imaginative solutions to the problems currently encountered. For instance, to beat Goliath, David simply used "his five smooth stones, his skill with a sling," elements of his shepherding repertoire, not previously used for man-to-man combat.

In his chapter, Ganz focused on how David, using creative strategic leadership, triumphed over Goliath and tended to ignore the role of strategic leadership in the case of Goliath. In other words, he implicitly assumed that in "David-like" organizations, the roles of leaders and their formulation of creative strategies to make the best use of available scarce resources matter more to organizations' success than in "Goliath-like" organizations. After all, in the case of Goliaths, their chances of beating Davids are essentially greater because of their initial advantages, such as in size and strength. Thus, leadership simply does not matter as much in shaping the successes or failures of organizational outcomes in "Goliath-like" organizations. In this sense, Ganz has teased out conditions under which leadership matters (i.e., in resource-poor, or "David-like" organizations) and when it may not matter so much (i.e., in resource-rich, or "Goliath-like" organizations).

Hackman's (chap. 6, this volume) position, at least initially, appears to be consistent with that of Ganz. Based on an analysis of team leadership in the Orpheus Chamber Orchestra and Wageman's (2001) program of research on team effectiveness, he argued that the extent to which leadership matters depends on the context in which a group functions. Hackman defined a favorable context as entailing three enabling conditions. First is the existence of "real teams." "Real teams" develop over time with "actions . . . taken to establish and affirm the team's boundaries, to define . . . task[s] for which members are collectively responsible, and to give the team ample authority to manage both . . . [its] own team processes and . . . [its] relations with external entities" (p. 124). Second is the presence of unambiguous, challenging, and meaningful overall directions or goals for the group. Third is the existence of a work design that encourages competent teamwork by providing ready access to the resources that members need to perform tasks collectively. Hackman asserted that such an enabling work design may be marked by small group size, clear team membership criteria, and well-defined tasks. He also claimed that a favorable context (so defined) provides the opportunity for a leader who does the "right things" (e.g., who minimizes process losses) to have a positive effect. Hackman sees "the rich getting richer" (p. 133).

In recognizing that the world is not so simple, Hackman further argued that even if a group is embedded in a favorable context, leadership might not matter when the leader fails to do the right things. That is, when leaders do not facilitate interdependent work among team members, do not minimize process losses, or when they dictate the one best way to conduct collective work, their influence on group outcomes is minimal in an already favorable context. However, in an unfavorable context, these same actions might irritate an already bad situation. Conversely, leaders doing the right things in an unfavorable context likely are futile. This is so because an unfavorable context produces so many dysfunctions, the leaders' hands, in essence, are tied; "the poor get poorer." To summarize, it appears that leadership matters to a lesser extent under two conditions: namely, when there is a combination of favorable context and a failed leader, and when an unfavorable context is matched with an effectual leader.

Peterson and Jackson (chap. 7, this volume) tackled our question of when leadership can be ignored by offering an explanation of why leadership matters in uncertain environments and why it may not matter so much in stable environments. Drawing upon control theory (Carver & Scheier, 1982), they claimed that when a business environment is uncertain, the leader's role as "group regulator" is vital to organizational performance. As group regulators, leaders, for example, set clear goals and standards for the group as well as motivate group members to improve performance so as to reduce any discrepancies that exist between groups' goals and actual group performance. One way for leaders to be effective group regulators is to utilize and to learn from past chronic mistakes to avoid future failures. Such learning, according to the authors, constitutes leadership vision at the group level because it entails persuading the group to change its course of action after recurring failures. As such, in an uncertain environment, where goals and performance may need to be continuously reevaluated and altered as a result of external demands, leaders function as "corrective tools."

For our purposes, however, the good news is that this story does not hold in a stable environment. According to Peterson and Jackson, in a stable environment, where goals do not have to be adjusted or be clarified due to limited external pressures and where the amount of available resources to achieve goals does not fluctuate, leaders no longer matter so much, for organizations would have established self-regulatory systems that keep routines on target. Leaders no longer are needed to play the role of "corrective tools" because, in essence, the organization maintains itself in a stable environment.

So, what does the collection tell us about when leadership does not matter? The first and last chapters we reviewed provided a rather straightforward answer. Favorable situations, entailing plentiful resources, and stable environments, lessen the need to consider leadership as either an asset or a liability. But Hackman's intriguing notions that the "rich get richer" and the "poor get poorer" complicated matters by not being wholly consistent with the ideas advanced by Ganz and by Peterson and Jackson. So who is right? Under what conditions can we safely ignore the "leadership" construct? While the chapters reviewed do not supply a consistent answer, they do give us confidence that the import of leadership can and will become more clearly bounded. Of course, our optimism is contingent upon others tackling the ideas advanced by Ganz, Peterson and Jackson, and Hackman as a puzzle in need of a solution.

WHEN DON'T FOLLOWERS FOLLOW?

Our interest in this question stems from attempts to understand the problem of followers heeding the wishes of their leaders to engage in various forms of organizational wrongdoing, such as "cooking the books" and acts of discrimination (e.g., Brief, Dietz, Cohen, Pugh, & Vaslow, 2000; Brief, Dukerich, & Doran, 1991; Smith-Crowe, Umphress, Brief, Chan, & Tenbrunsel, 2003). Obviously, one solution to the problem is for followers not to follow; that is to engage in what could be called *functional disobedience* (Brief, Buttram, & Dukerich, 2001; Darley, 1995). Another way of construing the problem is in terms of Barnard's (1938) "zone of indifference," beyond which employees will refuse to comply. Thus, we approached the chapters with an eye toward seeking to better understand when followers do not follow the wishes of their leaders. Four essays supplied answers.

Goethals' (chap. 5, this volume) analysis of Freud's treatment of leadership provided an understanding of "thirst for obedience" (originally discussed by LeBon, 1969), an instinctive need of followers to comply with the wishes of leaders. According to Goethals' reporting of Freud, this "thirst" is the result of qualities leaders possess in the eyes of their followers (e.g., prestige, forcefulness, persuasiveness) and the result of followers' identification with and idealization of their leaders' qualities and actions. He went on to explain how followers can have "the illusion that the leader loved each of them equally" (p. 100) and how followers love the leader in return. This illusion is yet another mechanism through which leaders gain followers' compliance because it binds followers together under a common ideal (i.e., being loved by the leader) and it erases the competition among followers, as leaders are believed to love all followers equally.

Goethals' analysis implied two conditions under which followers may not heed the wishes of their leaders. First, followers are more likely to be disobedient when they fail to identify with and exalt their leaders. This occurs, according to Goethals, for instance, when leaders are perceived as weak and unconvincing. Second, disobedience may occur when leaders do not act as if they love each and every follower equally. Freud's concern with unequal love leads us to the chapter by Tyler concerned with fairness.

Tyler (chap. 8, this volume) posited that followers give up their autonomy and comply with requests of *legitimate* authorities because they assume that such authorities only make "moral" demands. He also asserted that this behavior, which he called "rule-following," is intensified when there is high procedural fairness (Thibaut & Walker, 1975) and high interactional justice (Bies, 1987). This is so because followers feel that it is their "personal responsibility" to obey the leader, since they have been treated fairly by him or her. Conversely, if leaders make decisions based on unjust processes and treat followers without respect, one can assume that followers would be more likely to disobey. Tyler, therefore, highlighted the possible dysfunctional effects of high procedural and interactional justice, in that there might be a decreased likelihood of functional disobedience on the part of the followers.

Messick's chapter (chap. 4, this volume) is similar in flavor to that of Tyler's. It focused on leader–follower psychological exchanges and, in particular, the importance of those characterized as quid pro quo in nature. Messick asserted, for example, that if leaders provided security to their followers, the followers would repay leaders with gratitude and loyalty. The essay implies that followers' "zones of indifference" are breached when leaders violate their "give and take" relationships with followers. Hence, followers would return the harsh or merely indifferent treatment of leaders with disobedience.

Hackman's chapter (chap. 6, this volume), once again, was a real eye-opener. He asserted that a focus on influence as flowing from leaders to followers was misplaced. Alternatively, Hackman argued that attention should be placed on "team leadership," where leaders "lead from above," and followers and peers "lead from below and laterally." He also conceived that individuals outside a team could exercise team leadership. For example, while airline pilots and flight attendants form on-board teams/crews, they are often "led" by individuals from air traffic control, ground operations, or the airline's dispatching department.

Hackman's chapter led us to speculate that employees subjected to team leadership are more likely to question and disobey the wishes of leaders for two reasons. First, because leadership is shared, authority is diffused. Such dispersion, as Brief and his colleagues (2001) have suggested, "opens the door for lower level participants to question directives received from one party by giving them the opportunity to appeal to the other" (p. 492). Second, because individuals who exercise team leadership may not hold formal leadership positions, followers might be more likely to question their orders. Taken together, if our intuition is correct, "shared leadership" sets the stage for followers to question the wishes of their leaders. Unfortunately, we suspect that shared leadership, as described by Hackman, is a low base rate phenomenon.

In sum, what have we learned about disobedience (or when followers don't follow)? From Freud, via Goethals, we learned that failure to identify with a leader likely is associated with disobedience. According to Hogg (chap. 3, this volume), identification with a leader is a product of how group prototypical he or she is perceived to be. So, it would seem the less prototypical, the less obedience. We know of no research directly addressing such a conclusion.

Though based on somewhat different reasoning, a lesson evident in several chapters was that leaders who treat their followers in unjust ways are repaid with disobedience. The converse of this none-too-surprising conclusion is more intriguing. Fairness on the part of leaders toward their followers should be associated with compliance, even when the leader's wishes entail followers engaging in unsavory acts.

Finally, Hackman's chapter suggested to us that shared leadership may protect against blind obedience. In total, we should expect to observe more functional disobedience when leaders are less prototypical, more unfair, and when leadership is diffused. Are these expectations on target, and what do they imply for other outcomes—for example, for organizational efficiency? Again, only future data hold the answers.

WHY DO LEADERS GO MORALLY ASTRAY?

Our previous question concerned how followers respond to a leader's request to do wrong. Now, we take a step back to examine the collection of chapters to learn what they have to say about the causes of such immoral requests or, more generally, of corrupt leadership.

Abraham Lincoln (1809–1865) stated that "nearly all men can stand adversity, but if you want to test a man's character, give him power" (QuoteDB, n.d.). He was suggesting that power can be a corruptive force;

and Kipnis and his colleagues' research (e.g., Kipnis, 1972; Kipnis, Schmidt, Price, & Stitt, 1981) has shown this to be the case. The power vested in formal leadership positions, therefore, to us is a key to understanding how leaders become morally corrupt.

To explain the role that power plays, Magee and his colleagues (chap. 12, this volume) integrated the research on its metamorphic effects in terms of how leaders psychologically function and, consequently, behave. They found that when leaders exercised power, they were more likely to view others as instrumental agents to their personal goals, to deliberate less in making decisions, and to resist less the temptations to act for personal gains. Moreover, according to Magee et al., the action-orientation of leaders depletes their abilities to self-regulate, and, thus, to control their responses to temptations to do wrong, thereby exacerbating the effects of power. In addition, leaders, in their action-oriented mode, show less empathy and instead focus on only those aspects of others that are relevant to their personal goals. Based on Peterson and Jackson (chap. 7, this volume), we suspect that for some types of individuals the metamorphic effects of power are stronger, more corrupting. More specifically, they noted that as people exhibit more of the personality trait "conscientiousness" (e.g., John & Srivastava, 1999), they are better at goal persistence, gratification delay, impulse control, and thus, self-regulation. Leaders low in the trait, therefore, would be expected to succumb more readily to the moral temptations of power.

Magee and his colleagues went on to explain that these ugly outcomes are not inevitable. They asserted that power is a weaker corruptive force when leaders are held personally accountable for means as well as ends. This is so because such accountability heightens leaders' motivation to consider others' interests as opposed to only self-interests. In order to avoid being disliked and disrespected by those they lead, Magee et al. also argued that power might not corrupt when there is a chance that the leader may lose his or her position. Leaders whose positions are in question strive to maintain power by gaining support from followers, and, thus, are less likely to devalue followers and to act for self-interests alone.

Hogg (chap. 3, this volume) provided another appealing account of how power corrupts leaders. He reasoned that highly group-prototypical leaders define norms that followers internalize because of an "empathic bond" with the leaders based on common ingroup identity. Under such conditions, leaders coercing followers would be akin to directing coercion at themselves. Essentially, it is an "all for one and one for all" situation.

Over time, however, Hogg argued, highly prototypical leaders almost inevitably become less so, for the role they perform (including the influence they exercise) differentiates them from other group members. They are treated as high status deviants, thereby breaking their empathic bonds with followers. A common identity no longer yields compliance; and, leaders turn to coercion to produce obedience; and, it is such exercise of power, we surmise, that is associated with moral corruption.

Kramer and Gavrieli's chapter (chap. 11, this volume) takes us down a different path to understanding moral corruption than did Magee et al.'s and Hogg's. Their fascinating analysis centers on the development and consequences of leader paranoia. Kramer and Gavrieli told a story about President Lyndon Johnson to help demonstrate the negative consequences of paranoia. In the 1960s, President Johnson was convinced that opposition to the Vietnam War was a result of a conspiracy, in part, led by his domestic political enemies. He became obsessed with crushing these so-called "enemies." His paranoia also caused him to force his followers to take sides and to judge their loyalty by how fiercely they aligned themselves with him. Kramer and Gavrieli's story about Johnson shows us the relationship between a leader's conspiracy theory and the exercise of power driven by *irrational* distrust and suspicions. One can readily imagine that leader behaviors so driven can transform virtue into corruption. This is so even though Kramer and Gavrieli's focus of attention was on leader paranoia as adaptive cognition.

Hackman (chap. 6, this volume) provided a twist to his story previously discussed, of how favorable conditions may lead to better organizational outcomes. He asserted that when a team's directions are "clear, specific, and of great consequence" (p. 127), those exercising team leadership are more likely to focus on the consequence rather than the means of achieving these directions. This led him to observe that leaders often can go awry morally even when functioning in organizations with seemingly positive attributes, like clear and specific goals. More generally, it seems that organizational watchers, including members of the business press (e.g., Eichenwald, 2002; Fisher, 1992), attribute organizational wrongdoing to the presence of specific, difficult performance goals. While we suspect they are correct, we would love to see data addressing the relationship.

Goethals (chap. 5, this volume) reported a disheartening tale told by Freud. Freud (1920) described powerful male leaders of primitive societies as totally narcissistic and as the only person in the primal horde whose sexual desires were satisfied without delay. These leaders were jealous and intolerant of other men's sexuality. (Recall Kramer and Gavrieli's ideas about leader paranoia.) Freud noted that this jealousy and intolerance were dangerous to other male group members. Jealousy and intolerance are not, at least in contemporary terms, the "stuff" of moral leadership. They are, however, the qualities possessed by a powerful male acting as the despotic ruler of the primal horde (Freud, 1920). Freud further argued that while social dynamics have evolved, people have retained "an archaic heritage," describing strong leaders as "the dreaded primal father." In this way, Freud warns us, by way of Goethals, to question the morality of all dominant leaders.

From the chapters reviewed herein, we do not want to conclude that all leaders inevitably will stray from the morally correct path. But, it is tempting to do so, for as Kramer and Gavrieli stated, "being a bit paranoid, it might be argued, simply comes with the territory" (p. 242). More conservatively interpreted, the lessons taught by Magee et al., Hogg, Kramer and Gavrieli, Hackman, and Goethals are that leaders are morally at risk, that all of us, when placed in such positions of influence, could be seduced to stray. Power, nonprototypicality, insecurity, paranoia, consequential outcome goals, and sex represent some of the underlying causes evoked by the authors for this sad state of affairs. Whatever the causal mechanisms, it is clear that the organizational problem that has captured our interests (i.e., wrongdoing) will not be fading away soon.

CLOSING OBSERVATIONS

In the end, neither of us have become leadership mavens. *But,* we surely have been convinced that we no longer can turn a blind eye toward the leadership phenomenon. Indeed, we now recognize that, most of all, the first question we posed, "When can leadership be ignored?" was a reflection of our ignorance. That is, we learned that David Kipnis was too often right about the metamorphic effects of power and that students of organizational wrongdoing, like ourselves, must more seriously address why seemingly otherwise very "good" people, in positions of authority, often lead their followers morally astray. Our previous exclusive focus on followers clearly was inadequate. The relationship between leaders and followers simply cannot be ignored in attempts to understand better organizational wrongdoing. In approaching these relationships, we, theoretically, were most turned on by Goethals' treatment of Freud. This probably was the case because psychodynamic theories, prior to Goethals' chapter, represented to us a foreign territory that our friends and relatives, inaccurately, had told us was not worth a visit.

As we wrote these final words, our dominant emotion was that of guilt. The commentary provided, quite clearly, was rooted in our self-interests. This led us not to attend adequately to the breadth of what this very rich collection has to offer. For instance, the Bligh and Meindl chapter (chap. 2, this volume) did not fit into our agenda. Consequently, we did not note how intrigued we were with their clever analysis of popular leadership books used to illustrate how our society defines and interprets the "leadership" construct. In reference to the chapters we did mention, each of these was slighted too. We loved, for example, Ganz's (chap. 10, this volume) assertion that "strategy is how we turn what we have into what we need to get what we want" (p. 214) and Kramer and Gavrieli's (chap. 11, this volume) convincing tale about why being paranoid "ain't" all bad.

We started reading this volume as organizational scholars who were decidedly not interested in conducting leadership research. Now, we no longer are so firm in our convictions. The collection worked. We would not be surprised to find ourselves pursuing one or more of the questions raised by this provocative collection. We suspect other readers will find themselves in the same situation.

REFERENCES

Amabile, T. M. (1996). *Creativity in context: Update to the "The social psychology of creativity."* Boulder, CO: Westview Press.

Barnard, C. I. (1938). *The functions of an executive.* Cambridge, MA: Harvard University Press.

Bies, R. J. (1987). The predicament of injustice: The management of moral outrage. In L. L. Cummings & B. M. Staw (Eds.), *Research in organizational behavior* (Vol. 9, pp. 289–319). Greenwich, CT: JAI.

Brief, A. P., Buttram, R. T., & Dukerich, J. M. (2001). Collective corruption in the corporate world: Toward a process model. In M. E. Turner (Ed.), *Groups at work: Advances in theory and research* (pp. 471–499). Hillsdale, NJ: Lawrence Erlbaum Associates.

Brief, A. P., Dietz, J., Cohen, R. R., Pugh, S. D., & Vaslow, J. B. (2000). Just doing business: Modern racism and obedience to authority as explanations for employment discrimination. *Organizational Behavior and Human Decision Processes, 81,* 72–97.

Brief, A. P., Dukerich, J. M., & Doran, L. I. (1991). Resolving ethical dilemmas in management: Experimental investigations of values, accountability and choice. *Journal of Applied Social Psychology, 21,* 380–396.

Carver, C., & Scheier, M. (1982). Control theory: A useful conceptual framework for personality—Social, clinical, and health psychology. *Psychological Bulletin, 92,* 111–135.

Darley, J. M. (1995). Constructive and destructive obedience: A taxonomy of principal–agent relationships. *Journal of Social Issues, 51,* 125–154.

Eichenwald, K. (2002, March 1). Paid huge bonuses in '01; Experts see a motive for cheating. *The New York Times,* p. A1.

Fisher, L. M. (1992, June 22). Sears auto centers halt commissions after flap. *The New York Times*, p. D1.

Freud, S. (1920). Group psychology and the analysis of the ego. In J. Strachey (Ed.), *The standard edition of the complete works of Sigmund Freud: Vol. 28. Beyond the pleasure principle, group psychology and other works* (pp. 65–143). London: Hogarth Press.

John, O. P., & Srivastava, S. (1999). The "Big Five" trait taxonomy: History, measurement, and theoretical perspectives. In L. Pervin & O. P. John (Eds.), *Handbook of personality: Theory and research* (2nd ed, pp. 102–138). New York: Guilford.

Kerr, S., & Jermier, J. M. (1978). Substitutes for leadership: Their meaning and measurement. *Organizational Behavior and Human Performance, 22,* 375–403.

Kipnis, D. (1972). Does power corrupt? *Journal of Personality and Social Psychology, 24*(1), 33–41.

Kipnis, D., Schmidt, S., Price, K., & Stitt, C. (1981). Why do I like thee: Is it your performance or my orders? *Journal of Applied Psychology, 66*(1), 324–328.

LeBon, G. (1969). *The crowd.* New York: Ballantine. (Original work published 1895)

Podsakoff, P. M., MacKenzie, S. B., & Bommer, W. H. (1996). Meta-analysis of the relationships between Kerr and Jermier's substitutes for leadership and employee job attitudes, role perceptions, and performance. *Journal of Applied Psychology, 81*(4), 380–399.

QuoteDB. (n.d.). Retrieved September 12, 2003, from http://quotedb.com/quotes

Smith-Crowe, K., Umphress, E., Brief, A. P., Chan, S., & Tenbrunsel, A. (2004). *Corporate wrong-doing: A person by situation explanation.* Manuscript in preparation, Tulane University, New Orleans, LA.

Thibaut, J. T., & Walker, L. (1975). *Procedural justice: A psychological perspective.* Hillsdale, NJ: Lawrence Erlbaum Associates.

Wageman, R. (2001). How leaders foster self-managing team effectiveness: Design choices versus hands-on coaching. *Organization Science, 12,* 559–577.

Author Index

Note: Page numbers in *italic* indicate pages on which full bibliographical references appear.

Subject Index